Israel's Guaranteed Future Glory

Kit R. Olsen

World Bible Society
Costa Mesa, California

Israel's Guaranteed Future Glory

Copyright 2016, 2017 © by Kit R. Olsen

Published by the World Bible Society

First Printing June 3, 2016
Updated Printing - October of 2017

Printed in the United States of America

ISBN 13: 9781940241111
ISBN: 1940241111

Scripture quotations are from the Holy Bible New King James Version copyright ©1982 Thomas Nelson, Inc., the Holy Bible Authorized King James version, copyright ©1987 by Thomas Nelson, and the New American Standard Bible © 1995 Holman Bible Publishers, the American Standard Bible, copyright 1901 by Thomas Nelson & Sons.

Emboldened Scripture is added by the author for emphasis.

Interior Design: Kit R. Olsen

All of Kit R. Olsen's books are Scripture-based and published by the World Bible Society.

This heartfelt book is dedicated by Friends of Yeshua Ministries to sharing the prophetic Word of God with both Jews and Gentiles; strongly supporting Israel's right to exist as a nation in her God-given land. We seek no notoriety and the author of this work does not wish to get caught-up in any type of personal self-promotions. We work to glorify the Lord, not ourselves. We simply want to share this book and do the work of evangelists (2 Timothy 4:5).

God Blesses Those Who Love Israel

"I will make you [Israel] a great nation; I will bless you and make your name great; and you shall be a blessing. I will bless those who bless you, and I will curse him who curses you; and in you all the families of the earth shall be blessed" (Genesis 12:2-3).

Contents

🌿 Dedication 🌿

In memory of my dear beloved brother, Rick, who recently graduated from this life's journey and has been relieved of his earthly duties—so unexpectedly. Rick led me to the Lord when I was barely 19. I can still remember the look of wonder and enthusiasm on his face when he shared the gospel with me so long ago. We had the Lord as our very special bond, our adventures traveling the world together and so many other wonderful shared memories.

All the frequent talks we had about our future glory in heaven are now his to see and live. He is missed beyond what I can express in words. But I can rest peacefully knowing he is safe with the Lord, and no longer has to toil in this fledgling broken-world. Rick fought the good fight and finished the race. He kept his faith at all times; through the good and the bad. He is now enjoying his victory in his true and forever home with our blessed Lord and Savior.

Rick had an outstanding knowledge of the Scriptures and often spoke of the growing apostasy. He also frequently mentioned that in these last days false teachers would arise in the Church, pointing out how the prophetic warnings in Galatians 5:7-12; 2 Peter 2:1-3; 2 Timothy 2:3-4 were being fulfilled. He shared how these false "teachers" are particularly dangerous because they appear to be genuine; that these teachers certainly do not represent themselves as those who make a false profession of faith. They rise up as those who are one with us in Christ. As Jesus warned, they come as "wolves in sheep's clothing" (Matthew 7:15). They carry out their ministry in Jesus' name.

Rick's encouraging words to keep reaching others with the gospel and biblical truth remain strong in my heart. I will always be grateful that the Lord gave us each other to share and explore this life—for the time we had together here on earth. I look forward to the day we are reunited and share eternal life with the King of kings and Lord of lords—our faithful Messiah. "For now we see in a mirror dimly, but then face to face; now I know in part, but then I will know fully just as I also have been fully known" (1 Corinthians 13:12).

Israel's Faithful Messiah

From God's Covenant with David
1 Chronicles 17:22-24

"And who *is* like Your people Israel, the one nation on the earth whom God went to redeem for Himself *as* a people—to make for Yourself a name by great and awesome deeds, by driving out nations from before Your people whom You redeemed from Egypt?

For You have made Your people Israel Your very own people forever; and You, LORD, have become their God.

And now, O LORD, the word which You have spoken concerning Your servant and concerning his house, *let it* be established forever, and do as You have said.

So let it be established, that Your name may be magnified forever, saying, 'The LORD of hosts, the God of Israel, *is* Israel's God.' And let the house of Your servant David be established before You."

✡✡✡✡✡

God's Protective Angels

Israel is the center of the earth where God's covenant people live and belong. I would not be surprised if right now at this very moment—the LORD God of Israel has His heavenly host holding flaming swords, securely guarding and protecting every inch of Israel's borders in the spiritual realm.

Almighty God's Allegiance to Israel

"This is what the Lord says, 'He who appoints the sun to shine by day, Who decrees the moon and stars to shine by night, Who stirs up the sea so that its waves roar -- the Lord Almighty is His Name; only if these ordinances vanish from My sight,' declares the Lord, 'will the descendants of Israel ever cease to be a nation before Me.'"

—Jeremiah 31:35-36

✡✡✡✡✡

✑ Foreword ✑

I have the utmost respect for Kit R. Olsen. Her dedication to sharing the gospel and her unwillingness to get caught-up in the media sensationalism of the Christian celebrity, media "personality" circuit and self-glorifying promotions, is a strong testimony of her love for the Lord, and her sincere, genuine heart motives. Her precise application of God's Word is evident in her writing. Last year when she told me she was writing a book primarily on Israel, I was very pleased.

In her new compelling and thought-provoking book, *Israel's Guaranteed Future Glory,* it is evident that Kit understands the important dynamics surrounding God's chosen Land of Israel. Her scholarly, yet straight-forward easy to understand writing style, gives the reader a renewed understanding of Israel's tremendous importance in His plan of redemption for mankind. Each chapter gives foundational truths very much needed in the Body of Christ—and the world in general. We are living at a time when many have altered God's Holy Word to suit their own agendas. Kit clearly spells out that the Word of God in relation to Israel is of paramount importance, and intrinsic to the divine nature of God. I consider her to be very perceptive and exceptionally discerning; she has a brilliant mind. I can see it is her tremendous heart for the Lord, her love for Israel and biblical truth that motivate her.

Kit causes the reader to think through and carefully analyze prophetic Scriptures and correctly assess their meanings. The section on "Understanding Bible Interpretation" should be carefully studied by all Christians. It is imperative for believers to carefully study God's Word by using the Golden Rule of interpretation—otherwise the analysis will be flawed. By reading this book you will better understand some important prophetic dynamics relating to Israel and the entire world. You will better understand why Israel will ultimately prevail and how history has moved us to where we are today—prophetically, and what is yet ahead for God's chosen nation.

In my seventy-plus years as pastor, Bible teacher and founder of the World Bible Society, I've never met anyone who can grasp the truths of Scripture as quickly and thoroughly as Kit. We have worked together for many years; it is always inspiring to me to discuss the Scriptures with her. Kit's writing gives important insights surpassing many authors who grind out one book after book—often with redundant, sensationalized padded contents just to keep their names in the public venues. Kit has become an outstanding Bible expositor and author.

Israel's Guaranteed Future Glory will give the reader a renewed passion for Israel as God's revered nation, as well as a yearning for the glorious future that every true believer will partake in when the Messiah of Israel intervenes in world history; a very important book for all those who seek to have a better understanding of the Scriptures—especially in relation to Israel and for those who love God Almighty, and long to be with Him in His coming millennial kingdom.

Dr. F. Kenton Beshore
(D.D., Litt.D., D. Sac. Th., Ph.D., Th.D.)
President and Executive Director, World Bible Society

∾ **Introduction** ∾

I am exceedingly blessed to have wonderful Christian friends who love the Lord and understand the prophetic significance of the nation of Israel. The Lord God of Israel intends to make Jerusalem His headquarters during His 1000-year millennial reign. Time is short, as the final days of world history (as we know them) are coming to a close. Reaching others for Messiah Jesus is every believer's calling. Israel is truly God's heartbeat for these last days.

This book is primarily a brief overview of some of Israel's past, present and future; including various geopolitical matters relating to Bible prophecy; careful exposition of prophetic Scripture. Day by day events in the Middle East and all over the world are moving and changing so quickly; it is nearly impossible to keep up with all the current events that may relate to Bible prophecy. It is my heart's desire to share the love of the Savior with all those who do not know Him. The Lord cannot be separated from Israel, especially when it comes to prophecy and the future destiny of mankind. God makes it perfectly clear that He will bless those who love Israel and curse those who don't. Israel is the "apple of God's eye."

Today, anti-Israel sentiments are running wild and one prophetic declaration after another given to us by the Lord in Scripture is coming to fruition. Tragically, Israel is yet destined to suffer terribly for her rebellion and rejection of Him, but He promises to never forsake His covenant people. Israel as a nation will be redeemed, and will then receive all the blessings promised to her in the Abrahamic Covenant.

Vast numbers of people do not understand that the entire Bible is a Jewish book and that Christianity has Jewish roots. God used all Jewish men to pen the Bible from beginning to end, both Old and New Testaments. The first Christians were all Jews. Jews brought the gospel to the Gentiles. We should be thankful for that; the entire Bible is a Jewish book. And contrary to popular thinking, no one is born a Christian. The true meaning of what or who a Christian is has been often sorely distorted, and misrepresented by various religious groups and cults. Scripture teaches that each person must decide to accept or reject the truths of Christ. God has given us free will to choose and He holds each one of us personally accountable for our acceptance or rejection of Him.

Many historical and current portrayals of Christianity have nothing to do with an authentic born-again personal relationship with Jesus the Christ—which constitutes genuine Christianity as intended in the true biblical sense. For example, historically, the Crusades were sanctioned by the Catholic Church in the Middle Ages, and have been called the "Christian Crusades." In a broad sense the Crusades were an expression of a militant "Christianity" and European expansionism. They combined religious interests with secular and military enterprises. Overall, the men involved in the Crusades had little or nothing to do with Christ—the Spirit of the indwelt Savior or His teachings.

If you don't know the Savior or if you have been led astray by those who do not know how to interpret God's prophetic messages causing them to speak against Israel, it is my prayer and hope that this book will help take you to the Scriptures that will reveal God's everlasting devotion and love for Israel. We must never rely on the teachings of men but solely on the teachings of Almighty God, found in His infallible God-breathed Word—the Holy Bible.

If you are a professing believer who thinks Israel is no longer significant to God and the future or that the Christian church has replaced Israel, search the Scriptures for yourself where the truth is easily found. The massive numbers of Scriptures that spell out Israel is God's chosen nation cannot be denied.

Everywhere we turn on any given day we hear the term "occupied territory" in relation to Israel. We hear it repeatedly, "Israel is living in occupied territory." This tall tale is perpetuated by all the major news agencies in every corner of the world. Ignorance has surely found many friends. Without question it is apparent that we have an inordinate number of misinformed critics throughout the world who boisterously condemn Israel, yet have never fully studied the true histories affecting the current status of the so-called Palestinians, the Persians (Iranians) or the Jewish people.

Biased anti-Israel critics even make the absurd statement that if Israel can have nuclear weapons that Iran, a known state sponsor of terrorism should be able to as well. Today that issue is becoming a huge controversy and only because of ignorance or worse—the evil intentions of those who want to divide and destroy God's chosen nation. Apparently these biased critics fail to recognize that Israel is the *only* true democratic nation in the Middle East where women are treated with equality and dignity, where all religions are accepted and can freely worship; where minorities *including* Arabs are given full civil rights.

In July of 2015, the U.S. administration and the P5+1 powers incomprehensibly made a deal with a ruthless barbaric unrepentant enemy—the terrorist state of Iran. As a result the anti-Israel, anti-Christian, anti-America, anti-betterment of America, pro-Islamic former Obama administration assisted the Iranians in furthering their nuclear ambitions. They placed $150 billion ("sanctions relief" money) into the war chests of this rogue regime even as they chant "Death to America" and "Death to Israel." (Although the actual dollar amount keeps changing on any given day depending on the news source.) Last year I wrote that I would not be surprised if Obama gives Iran more U.S. taxpayer money as time goes by. (He did just that as you will read in the following updated introductory pages). This interchange was nothing less than a diabolically engineered plot to undermine the United States and Israel. Yes, "change" came to America and it was "fundamentally" being transformed. Western civilization has been under methodical assault from within by Obama, and countless merciless godless violent degenerates in every corner of the world.

Dan Bongino, former Secret Service Agent (Secret Service's Presidential Division) actually resigned from his prestigious position because he could no longer tolerate the out-of-control immoral behavior he witnessed in the highest ranks of government. He has stated, "We are living in a government-created liberal dystopia where right is wrong, wrong is covered up, enemies are coddled and heroes are hunted down."

I will add, "Woe unto them that call evil good, and good evil; that put darkness for light, and light for darkness; that put bitter for sweet, and sweet for bitter!" (Isaiah 5:20). And, "This is the judgment, that the Light has come into the world, and men loved the darkness rather than the Light, for their deeds were evil. For everyone who does evil hates the Light, and does not come to the Light for fear that his deeds will be exposed. But he who practices the truth comes to the Light, so that his deeds may be manifested as having been wrought in God" (John 3:19-21).

The February 13, 2016 the sudden and suspicious death of the great U.S. Supreme Court Justice Antonin Scalia seems a bit too convenient. Especially considering he stood up against tyranny, and voted to put Obama's Clean Power Plan regulation on hold. He was also expected to soon vote against the legality of this multi-trillion dollar so-called Clean Power Plan (Obama's gift to his globalist banker henchmen which would take away countless jobs from hard working Americans, tax and regulate us into oblivion). Another nail in the coffin of America. Many other crucial issues were to be voted on soon by Justice Scalia, all relating to our personal constitutional freedoms.

If the 2016 presidential election had been won by Hillary Clinton, Antonin Scalia's vacancy would have been replaced with one of her extreme leftist globalist accomplices. Very convenient for the godless globalists who are determined to take the United States apart. The Bible warns of a one world government, a "New World Order" as proclaimed by George H. Bush in 1990 when he was president. The ramifications of the tragic loss of Justice Scalia could have been a serious potential blow to our freedoms, and cannot be overlooked. No autopsy was performed on such an important powerful government figure as Antonin Scalia? But all illegal aliens found dead in the same Texas county are given mandatory autopsies? His cause of death was diagnosed and declared without a medical exam or physical presence of a physician or coroner; but instead without seeing him, over the phone by a local judge in a notoriously corrupt Texas county (Presidio). The loss of this great Supreme Court Justice would have been another step toward a globalist takeover if the Democratic Party had won the election.

All throughout the world the parasitic oligarchs are seizing control and moving ahead with their coercion, working to collapse the nation states.

Israel is often chastised by these same global tyrants. Out of the ashes of an orchestrated collapse these globalists intend to institute a new corporate worldwide government endorsed by religious leaders; borderless with multi-nationals above the law, tax-exempt with diplomatic immunity. Evil corruption is worse than we can possibly imagine. May God Almighty protect us in these perilous last days. We must hold on to our faith like never before.

Simultaneously the world's elite and all the devil's representatives are huffing and puffing trying to blow the house (Israel) down. But all their efforts and manipulations will ultimately cause the great God of Israel, the Mighty One—the Creator of heaven and earth—to personally rescue His chosen people and His beloved Land of Israel. The day is soon coming when the Almighty King, the King of kings and Lord of lords will once and for all end the reign of wicked rulers on this earth, forever. But before that, get ready!

Jesus the Messiah is going to remove His Church to the safety of heaven—that is, all true born-again believers. Place your faith and trust in the Jewish Messiah, not in Man. He will save you from the coming wrath that will shock this godless world when the prophesied seven-year Tribulation erupts. Be sure you belong to Christ so you will be included in the Pre-Tribulation Rapture. This world is on a fast track to destruction, but be of good cheer—our redemption draweth nigh (Luke 21:28).

God promises to rapture (snatch away) all true believers to heaven: "Behold, I tell you a mystery: We all shall not sleep, but we shall all be changed, in a moment, in the twinkling of an eye, at the last trump: for the trumpet shall sound, and the dead shall be raised incorruptible, and we shall be changed. For this corruptible must put on incorruption, and this mortal must put on immortality. But when this corruptible shall have put on incorruption, and this mortal shall have put on immortality, then shall come to pass the saying that is written, 'Death is swallowed up in victory.'

"For the Lord himself shall descend from heaven, with a shout, with the voice of the archangel, and with the trump of God: and the dead in Christ shall rise first; then we that are alive, that are left, shall together with them be caught up in the clouds, to meet the Lord in the air: and so shall we ever be with the Lord. Wherefore comfort one another with these words" (1 Corinthians 15:51-53; 1 Thessalonians 4:16-18).

Kit R. Olsen
May 10, 2016

Updated 2017 Presidential Inaugural Introductory Commentary

The Pro-America Pro-Israel Trump Era Begins

President Donald J. Trump's inaugural address on January 20, 2017 strategically hit upon points that the Judeo-Christian population of the United States and the world have been yearning to hear. His no holds barred message was like no other inaugural speech given by a U.S. president. Unlike his failed predecessor, Barack Hussein Obama, President Trump immediately called out Islamic terrorism for what it is: "Radical Islamic terrorism." In another highlight of his speech he pointed out this very important fact:

> For too long, a small group in our nation's Capital has reaped the rewards of government while the people have borne the cost. Washington flourished—but the people did not share in its wealth. Politicians prospered—but the jobs left, and the factories closed. The establishment protected itself, but not the citizens of our country. Their victories have not been your victories; their triumphs have not been your triumphs; and while they celebrated in our nation's capital, there was little to celebrate for struggling families all across our land.

President Trump also brought Almighty God into his inaugural address. He stated that the United States "will be most importantly protected by God." He finished his speech with these words: "Thank you, God bless you, and God bless America. Thank you. God bless you. And God bless America." At long last we have a president who is believably *for the people and by the people*; a president who places America's well being, prosperity and safety first. A president who has publicly brought the true God of Abraham, Isaac and Jacob back into the American dialogue.

This country is clearly divided; one group is comprised of low-information gullible people who believe the obnoxious leftist lies—foolishly giving their loyalty to those who undermine freedom and prosperity under the false narrative of "human rights." And another group that holds to the principles of the U.S. Constitution's law-abiding principles laid out by the Founding Fathers. Human rights should be respected on both sides; that does not mean anything goes for those who are not legally part of America or for those who viciously work to undermine the American way of life. The hatred generated by the intolerant left while they are having temper tantrums claiming they are "protesting" (rioting) for "tolerance" reveals their unhinged and psychotic temperaments.

I understand firsthand the immigration process. I came here as an immigrant from Austria when I was a young child—legally. I had a green card for many years. My parents went through complicated red-tape bureaucracy to get here. We never once received handouts of any type, and certainly not from the U.S. government. My parents brought with them their professionalism and education. They became Americans by greatly contributing their knowledge and talents to America. Our family eagerly learned English and did not expect or demand special rights. We spoke our European languages only at home, never out in public. When we became American citizens each member of our family had to take oral and written tests in English. We worked hard for our privilege to become Americans. I applaud President Trump for immediately implementing an English only White House website. It's time people of all nations respected our culture and our English language. Unlike Obama and his misfits, we need not apologize for being Americans and for holding to common sense values.

The globalists whom I addressed in the first introductory chapter of this book are scurrying and scheming to see how they can destroy our new patriotic president and resume the intended destruction of this great nation. The coming years will continue to be a battle between globalism and patriotism/sovereignty; a battle between good and evil. The battle in the spiritual realm will peak to a very high crescendo; the battle on the tangible physical level will also greatly escalate, as the globalists desperately work to push their despotic will upon those who have rejected their dangerous tyrannical agendas. This is not a time to think that the enemies of God and freedom are going to retreat and stop working to implement their sinister plans.

The media all around the world are part of the new world order cabal. I expect we will see continued outrageous lies and more "fake news" (invented news) dominate the press. President Trump will continue to be relentlessly attacked by these enemies of God and country. Every believer and every patriotic American must be vigilant and not take our U.S. Constitutional freedoms for granted. This is the time to pray like never before for God's continued protection for our country and for our president. Far too many people living in America (and around the world) have fallen for the globalist lies of bringing peace and harmony to the world by agreeing to break down borders and internationalizing all the nations. We know the Bible teaches there will be an overt one-world government. But we don't have to step aside and help it manifest. It is especially important at this time to share the gospel and Bible prophecy.

On President Trump's first Monday in office he quashed U.S. participation in the (anti-U.S. sovereignty) Trans-Pacific Partnership (TPP) and placed a freeze on hiring federal workers, except for the military and necessary public safety and public health staff. He reinstituted an intermittent policy that prevents federal family-planning money from being sent to international organizations that discuss or perform abortion services.

President Trump also signed an executive order stating that the administration's official policy is "to seek the prompt repeal" of the Affordable Care Act (Obamacare), which has proven to be anything but affordable. It has been a terrible hardship on Americans. Of course that was the intention of the plan all along; it was designed to fail and usher in an even more draconian single-payer socialist "health" care system that would enable government control over every man, woman and child. Obama deliberately lied to the American people when he said, "If you like your doctor you can keep your doctor." Of course he did this to further his desired one world government Marxist agenda.

Each day we will see President Trump swiftly implement policies that will benefit the American people. He is very savvy, exceptionally experienced and successful when it comes to taking on and completing complex projects. In just one short week in office he has done more for America than any other sitting president in American history (within that amount of time). He is obviously working intensely to keep his promises to the American people. I don't see that he will slow down as he fully focuses his attention on taking our great country back from the globalist criminals. I see a very courageous man of great resolve and determination.

President's Trump's pro-America, pro-Israel policies will continue to drive the leftist media and the pompous globalists berserk. These anti-American, anti-Israel puppet masters and their puppets are working relentlessly to make it appear as if the majority of the people are against President Trump, trying to viciously discredit him at every turn. Their propaganda is deeply entrenched in every form of media including social media, even creating fake people with fake anti-Trump narratives by using computer generated messages impersonating humans—to deliberately create an atmosphere of overwhelming anti-Trump opinions—all outright lies and deception.

Just hours before leaving office on Friday January 20, former President Barack Hussein Obama quietly released $220 million to the Palestinian Authority; this is American taxpayer money that the Republican members of Congress have been blocking because of the tyrannical record of the Palestinians. Obama just had to get in one last jab against Israel and the American people. But glory to God, the payment itself, Obama's love gift to the enemies of Israel, has been frozen by the State Department under President Donald J. Trump.

Unfortunately, during the presidential primaries in August of 2016, the former Obama Administration was unable to be stopped from sending stacked pallets piled high holding $400 million in foreign cash that Obama arranged to shuttle from Geneva to Tehran as ransom (or as Obama preferred to say, "leverage" for the release of American hostages)—via an unmarked cargo plane belonging to Iran Air, a terrorist arm of the mullahs' terrorist coordinator, the Islamic Revolutionary Guards Corps. It is very likely that the Trump Administration will investigate and uncover hidden details of many of Obama's deceptive and dangerous deals with Iran, other Anti-American enemies, and orders he gave that undermined and placed in harm's way—the work of government/ military officials, and in turn the American people. Without a doubt Obama has been the most corrupt lawless president in American history.

We can now breathe a huge sigh of relief that the divisive racially-biased lawless open-borders new world order president is no longer in the White House. But no doubt he will be working as a radical community organizer to undermine the Trump Administration and our constitutional freedoms. We have already seen Obama rearing his determined radical interventionist Marxist head only about ten days after our new pro-America president was sworn into office. Obama's public praise of paid "protestors" and their hysterical meltdowns, regardless of whatever they are supposedly "protesting" is all part of his Marxist Saul Alinsky agitation tactics to dismantle our freedom-loving country. The hysterical left is already saying they want to make this country ungovernable. The hatred of the institutionalized left is deep seeded, far-reaching and incorrigible. The Democratic Party as a whole has become the party of hate. They cannot be reasoned with; freedom of speech only applies to them and to those who go along with their subversive agendas.

We can count on the obstructionists, the well-organized well-funded leftists to continue their bullying regardless of what President Trump says or does. Their mission is to cause constant opposition and disorder. The trained cult-like "protestors" are programmed to cause pandemonium and react to anything that opposes the Marxist agenda of the globalists. This is all a carefully designed plan supported and bankrolled by the enemies of this country. While in office, Obama never missed an opportunity to praise chaos and disorder—he even encouraged it under the pretense of "human rights."

During his tenure Obama was involved in training thousands of dedicated leftist organizers who in turn recruit and train tens of thousands of impressionable youth (Obama's brown shirts). These low-information misled individuals serve as stooges for the cause of destroying America. Organizing For Action (OFA) is a subversive propaganda group in which Obama is deeply involved, and even promotes on his new personal website. This radically charged organization (Obama's army) was created for the purpose of taking down America—to "fundamentally transform" it. After looking over Obama's website, a naïve uniformed person would think Obama's call to action to become a part of the OFA group—is for the betterment of humanity. But it is an anti-America "progressive" (Marxist) group of agitators trained to work against the constitutional freedoms of all Americans. In 2015 Obama told his supporters, "I may hold this office for another 14 months, but I'm not going anywhere." Also while in office, Obama stated that he wanted to "Rub raw the sores of discontent," a well-known slogan taught by Saul Alinsky. Obama's seditious Marxist tentacles are deeply entwined and wide-reaching.

I thank God that we have a new pro-America, pro-Israel president. President Trump is not going to put up with the race-baiting, the victimization mantras, the political bigotry, the incessant fear and scaremongering tactics used by the Democrats. He is not going to put up with the globalist rhetoric by sold-out establishment Republicans or any other new world order lackeys. Our new president is not going to be intimidated by the incessant lies aided and abetted by the abusively biased and corrupt media. The corrupt establishment Republicans who are not much different than the corrupt Democrats, may prove to be some of President Trump's most aggressive and problematic enemies who will attempt to stop implementation of his pro-America "for the people" agenda.

President Trump is already proving that he will fight for America's sovereignty as well as Israel's. A stronger America is a stronger Israel. I expect he will soon greet Prime Minister Benjamin Netanyahu with open arms at the White House and treat him with tremendous respect. We can also breathe a great sigh of relief regarding the future appointment of Supreme Court judges by President Trump. He has already essentially stated that it will be someone whose ideology is to abide by the rule of law and the Constitution of the United States. Now the vacancy left by Supreme Court Justice Antonin Scalia will not be replaced by a liberal activist, which would have been devastating for our country. God has shown us His mercy. Nevertheless we must be wise as serpents and gentle as doves (Matthew 10:16), and be aware daily of the escalating deception and malfeasance—the wickedness in high places:

> "For we wrestle not against flesh and blood, but against principalities, against powers, against the rulers of the darkness of this world, against spiritual wickedness in high places" (Ephesians 6:12).

In an exclusive interview with The Brody File on Friday, January 7, President Donald Trump said that persecuted Christians will be given priority when it comes to applying for refugee status in the United States "We are going to help them," President Trump tells CBN News. "They've been horribly treated. Do you know if you were a Christian in Syria it was impossible, at least very tough to get into the United States? If you were a Muslim you could come in, but if you were a Christian, it was almost impossible and the reason that was so unfair, everybody was persecuted in all fairness, but they were chopping off the heads of everybody but more so the Christians. And I thought it was very, very unfair."

As I've documented later in this book, the former Obama Administration repeatedly denied Christian refugees from Syria and other nations from entering the United States. He showed no sympathy for persecuted Christians whatsoever. Now we have a president who will place them first in line. With our newly elected president we can see the dawn of a new era in America (and the world) for which so many faithful Christians and Jews have prayed.

"God shed His grace on thee," the famous words from the classic song "America the Beautiful"—ring true today. God *has* shed His grace on America. How Bible prophecy in relation to Israel will specifically unfold now that we have a pro-Israel, pro-America president will be fascinating to watch. A point to keep in mind is this: When the one-world government of Daniel 7:23 comes to power it will become obvious that the Roman type of government never died. At some point it will break into ten divisions and join the Antichrist in ruling the world (Daniel 7:24). Later, in the middle of the Tribulation the Antichrist will take total control.

Three of the ten kings (nations) who hinder the Antichrist during the first half of the Tribulation will succeed in putting the Antichrist to death, but his "death" is not permanent. The entire world will be shocked when through Satan's power, the Antichrist is resuscitated back to life. It is then that he will go into the temple of God in Jerusalem and in no uncertain terms declare himself to be God (as prophesied in 2 Thessalonians 2:4-5).

Many commentators have speculated that the United States has no place in Bible prophecy. I say, think again. It is possible, and conceivable that one of the three kings (nations) that reject and *do not* go along with the one world order (government) and ultimately the Antichrist—is the United States of America. We can see glimpses of that already with the new direction President Trump is taking our country. According to Daniel 7, the civil governments of three of the kings (nations) will be destroyed by the Antichrist after he is resuscitated by Satan's power. (But all true believers will have been taken up to heaven in the Rapture by then.)

> "And as for the ten horns, out of this kingdom shall ten kings arise: and another shall arise after them; and he shall be diverse from the former, and he shall put down three kings." (Daniel 7:24)

Be sure your seatbelts are fastened. It is going to be a wild and tumultuous ride to fend off the elitist powerbrokers who are hell-bent on destroying the United States and Israel. But be of good cheer, Jesus *has* overcome the world (John 16:33). I am including a list on the following pages detailing some specifics that will help make "America great again."

Kit R. Olsen
January 27, 2017

Making America Great Again

The following list presents just *some* of the President Donald J. Trump's plans for America which he intends to initiate as soon as possible:

Immigration
Stop all federal funding to sanctuary cities - places where local officials don't arrest or detain immigrants living in the country illegally for federal authorities.

Begin deporting what Trump estimates to be more than 2 million criminal persons illegally living in the country.

Cancel visas for citizens of foreign countries that won't take those criminals illegal immigrants back.

Immediately terminate former President Barack Obama's two illegal executive amnesties. That presumably includes DACA, which protects people who were brought into the country illegally as children.

Begin working on an impenetrable physical wall along the southern border.

Ask Congress to pass "Kate's Law," which would increase penalties on people who unlawfully re-enter the United States after being removed.

Security and Defense
Immediately suspend the Syrian refugee program.

Convene his generals and inform them that they have 30 days to submit a new plan for defeating the Islamic State group.

Suspend immigration from terror-prone regions where he says vetting is too difficult.

Implement new extreme immigration vetting techniques.

Trade
Announce his intention to renegotiate or withdraw from the North American Free Trade Agreement with Canada and Mexico.

Formally withdraw from the 12-nation Trans-Pacific Partnership.

Direct his treasury secretary to label China a currency manipulator.

Draining the Swamp and Government Reform
Propose a Constitutional amendment to impose term limits on all members of Congress.

Ban White House and congressional officials from becoming lobbyists for five years after they leave the government.

Ban former White House officials from lobbying on behalf of foreign governments for the rest of their lives.

Ban foreign lobbyists from raising money for U.S. elections.

Impose a hiring freeze on federal employees, excluding military, public safety, and public health staff.

Impose a requirement that for every new federal regulation imposed, two existing regulations be eliminated

Energy and the Environment

Remove any Obama-era roadblocks to energy projects such as the Keystone XL pipeline.

Lift restrictions on mining coal and drilling for oil and natural gas.

Cancel payments to the U.N.'s climate change programs and use the money to fix America's water and environmental infrastructure.

Healthcare, Gun Control and Other Issues

Cancel every unconstitutional executive action, memorandum and order issued by President Obama.

Ask Congress to send him a bill to repeal and replace Obama's signature health care law.

Begin the process of selecting a new Supreme Court justice.

Eliminate gun-free zones in schools and on military bases.

Move the U.S. Embassy in Israel to Jerusalem.

Cut taxes and implement regulation reforms that are choking American businesses.

Education

President Trump's proposal calls for using $20 billion in federal funds to incentivize the states to start (or expand their existing) school choice programs. From there, "if the states collectively contribute $110 billion of their own education budgets toward school choice," said Trump, "on top of the

$20 billion in federal dollars, that could provide $12,000 in school choice funds to every K-12 student who today lives in poverty."

"The money will follow the student," he said. "That means the student will be able to attend the public, private, charter, or magnet school of their choice – and each state will develop its own system that works for them." President Trump reportedly has added homeschooling to the proposal.

✡✡✡✡✡

President Trump's Full Inaugural Address

President Trump's full inaugural speech is included here out of respect for the fact that he is one hundred percent behind Israel, unlike the previous "president" who went out of his way to place Israel (and our country) in grave danger. May God bless our new president and keep him safe and healthy every minute of his life. The prophet Isaiah wisely wrote these words in regard to Israel:

> "Behold, all those who were incensed against you shall be ashamed and disgraced; they shall be as nothing, and those who strive with you shall perish. You shall seek them and not find them—those who contended with you. Those who war against you shall be as nothing, as a nonexistent thing" (Isaiah 41:11-12).

President Trump Delivers His Inaugural Speech

Chief Justice Roberts, President Carter, President Clinton, President Bush, President Obama, fellow Americans and people of the world, thank you.

We, the citizens of America, are now joined in a great national effort to rebuild our country and restore its promise for all of our people.

Together, we will determine the course of America and the world for many, many years to come. We will face challenges. We will confront hardships. But we will get the job done.

Every four years we gather on these steps to carry out the orderly and peaceful transfer of power.

And we are grateful to President Obama and first lady Michelle Obama for their gracious aid throughout this transition.

They have been magnificent.

Thank you.

Today's ceremony, however, has a very special meaning because today we are not merely transferring power from one administration to another or from one party to another, but we are transferring power from Washington, D.C., and giving it back to you, the people.

For too long, a small group in our nation's capital has reaped the rewards of government while the people have bore the cost. Washington flourished, but the people did not share in its wealth. Politicians prospered but the jobs left and the factories closed.

The establishment protected itself, but not the citizens of our country. Their victories have not been your victories. Their triumphs have not been your triumphs. And while they celebrated in our nation's capital, there was little to celebrate for struggling families all across our land.

That all changes starting right here and right now, because this moment is your moment.

It belongs to you.

It belongs to everyone gathered here today and everyone watching all across America.

This is your day.

This is your celebration.

And this, the United States of America, is your country.

What truly matters is not which party controls our government, but whether our government is controlled by the people.

January 20th, 2017, will be remembered as the day the people became the rulers of this nation again.

The forgotten men and women of our country will be forgotten no longer. Everyone is listening to you now. You came by the tens of millions to become part of a historic movement, the likes of which the world has never seen before.

At the center of this movement is a crucial conviction that a nation exists to serve its citizens. Americans want great schools for their children, safe neighborhoods for their families and good jobs for themselves.

These are just and reasonable demands of righteous people and a righteous public.

But for too many of our citizens, a different reality exists.

Mothers and children trapped in poverty in our inner cities, rusted out factories scattered like tombstones across the landscape of our nation.

An education system flush with cash but which leaves our young and beautiful students deprived of all knowledge.

And the crime and the gangs and the drugs that have stolen too many lives and robbed our country of so much unrealized potential. This American carnage stops right here and stops right now.

We are one nation, and their pain is our pain.

Their dreams are our dreams, and their success will be our success. We share one heart, one home and one glorious destiny.

The oath of office I take today is an oath of allegiance to all Americans.

For many decades we've enriched foreign industry at the expense of American industry, subsidized the armies of other countries while allowing for the very sad depletion of our military.

We've defended other nations' borders while refusing to defend our own. And we've spent trillions and trillions of dollars overseas while America's infrastructure has fallen into disrepair and decay.

We've made other countries rich while the wealth, strength and confidence of our country has dissipated over the horizon.

One by one, the factories shuttered and left our shores with not even a thought about the millions and millions of American workers that were left behind.

The wealth of our middle class has been ripped from their homes and then redistributed all across the world. But that is the past, and now we are looking only to the future.

But that is the past and now we are looking only to the future.

We assembled here today are issuing a new decree to be heard in every city, in every foreign capital and in every hall of power. From this day forward, a new vision will govern our land. From this day forward, it's going to be only America first — America first.

Every decision on trade, on taxes, on immigration, on foreign affairs will be made to benefit American workers and American families. We must protect our borders from the ravages of other countries making our products, stealing our companies and destroying our jobs.

Protection will lead to great prosperity and strength. I will fight for you with every breath in my body. And I will never, ever let you down.

America will start winning again, winning like never before.

We will bring back our jobs. We will bring back our borders. We will bring back our wealth, and we will bring back our dreams. We will build new roads and highways and bridges and airports and tunnels and railways all across our wonderful nation. We will get our people off of welfare and back to work rebuilding our country with American hands and American labor. We will follow two simple rules — buy American and hire American.

We will seek friendship and goodwill with the nations of the world.

But we do so with the understanding that it is the right of all nations to put their own interests first. We do not seek to impose our way of life on anyone but rather to let it shine as an example. We will shine for everyone to follow.

We will reinforce old alliances and form new ones. And unite the civilized world against radical Islamic terrorism, which we will eradicate completely from the face of the earth.

At the bedrock of our politics will be a total allegiance to the United States of America and through our loyalty to our country, we will rediscover our loyalty to each other. When you open your heart to patriotism, there is no room for prejudice.

The Bible tells us how good and pleasant it is when God's people live together in unity. We must speak our minds openly, debate our disagreement honestly but always pursue solidarity. When America is united, America is totally unstoppable.

There should be no fear. We are protected, and we will always be protected. We will be protected by the great men and women of our military and law enforcement. And most importantly, we will be protected by God.

Finally, we must think big and dream even bigger. In America, we understand that a nation is only living as long as it is striving. We will no longer accept politicians who are all talk and no action, constantly complaining but never doing anything about it.

The time for empty talk is over. Now arrives the hour of action.

Do not allow anyone to tell you that it cannot be done. No challenge can match the heart and fight and spirit of America. We will not fail. Our country will thrive and prosper again. We stand at the birth of a new millennium, ready to unlock the mysteries of space, to free the earth from the miseries of disease and to harness the energies, industries and technologies of tomorrow.

A new national pride will stir ourselves, lift our sights and heal our divisions. It's time to remember that old wisdom our soldiers will never forget — that whether we are black or brown or white, we all bleed the same red blood of patriots.

We all enjoy the same glorious freedoms, and we all salute the same great American flag.

And whether a child is born in the urban sprawl of Detroit or the windswept plains of Nebraska, they look up at the same night sky, they fill their heart with the same dreams and they are infused with the breath of life by the same Almighty Creator.

So to all Americans in every city near and far, small and large, from mountain to mountain, from ocean to ocean, hear these words — you will never be ignored again.

Your voice, your hopes and your dreams will define our American destiny. And your courage and goodness and love will forever guide us along the way. Together, we will make America strong again. We will make America wealthy again. We will make America proud again. We will make America safe again. And yes, together, we will make America great again. Thank you, God bless you, and God bless America. Thank you. God bless you. And God bless America.

☆☆☆☆☆☆

The Lord God of Israel Is
Our Refuge and Fortress

"For our citizenship is in heaven, from which also we eagerly wait for a Savior, the Lord Jesus Christ; who will transform the body of our humble state into conformity with the body of His glory, by the exertion of the power that He has even to subject all things to Himself" (Philippians 3:20-21).

Anyone who understands basic Bible prophecy and has a true heart for the Lord would be amongst those longing to go home. Never in my lifetime have I seen and heard such bombastic, constant in-your-face propaganda and nonsensical stupidity being dished out so relentlessly—one heaping sensationalized lie after another. The blatant hate-filled dishonesty is outrageous. Outright intentional disinformation has become the everyday operating weapon of the enemies of God and of righteousness.

Not only do these enemies of God and righteousness want to discredit and destroy President Trump, they want to ruin the lives of all those who are unwilling to accept the globalist agenda (a one world ruling elitist hierarchy; a borderless world of chaos and oppression). In other words, a total end to national sovereignty and personal freedoms; a one world government with a tyrannical stronghold over the masses. The irony is that all those who ignorantly surrender their individual sovereignty to the globalists *will* suffer greatly. That time is coming when the prophesied seven-year Tribulation becomes a reality—after the Lord raptures His Church to the safety of heaven.

The ongoing fake refugee crisis has been deliberately created to cause chaos, to impair the nation-states; to flood the Western nations with millions from crowded impoverished countries seeking to freeload off taxpayers, and enjoy the fruits of advanced Western society. Efforts to end the freedoms we have known and cherished in this great country are greatly accelerating. Only God knows how much President Trump can do to stop the fleecing of America. How intense it will get before the Tribulation begins remains to be seen. Along with the United States, the nation of Israel is also standing in the way of those who are working to bring about a new world order of totalitarianism—despotism. The media worldwide are radically unhinged and egregious; very useful puppets of the criminal new world order puppeteers. So much so that it is tough to comprehend how complicit and willing they are to lie, slander and destroy. Decency and professionalism do not exist amongst this unscrupulous gang of deceivers.

In lockstep with the deranged media is the Democratic Party, especially their members in Congress. The fear-mongering is rampant. Their only agenda now is to resist, resist, resist—resist anything that would improve the lives of the American people—to the point of acting like a whiney group of pathetic worthless imbeciles; fools to the nth degree. And I might add that includes some of the sell-out Republicans who are a disgrace to their constituents. Judeo-Christian values have had a strong foundational role in our great country and are aggressively threatened. Demonically led hordes are obsessively determined to take this nation down and turn it into a godless immoral sewer—a bankrupt third world ghetto. The radical left's jihad against our duly-elected new president is ferocious and lethal.

Never before has a previous "president" set up such an aggressive, well-orchestrated plan to create constant chaos and discord in order to undermine the following administration, and to destroy our great nation. Clearly, the plan to "fundamentally change America" is still front and center for citizen Obama and his degenerate radical left entourage. Obama looms large in the shadows as a useful seditious underling of the ruling globalist elites, obediently pushing for collectivism, working to bring about an overt dictatorial one-world government. After all, individual rights are passé—not in step with the demands of the rent-a-mob social justice warriors and their totalitarian criminal bosses. What all these vicious leftists don't understand is that they are essentially in a war against God Himself. And God is on *our* side.

Some of the most frustrating aspects of the subversive tactics, the assaults used by the extreme radicalized left—is recognizing how approximately half this country is asleep and clueless; oblivious as to what is really going on around them. It is equally astounding to see how large numbers of dumbed-down low-information, willfully ignorant individuals are being used by anarchist revolutionaries. These radicalized subversive lackeys are foolishly working for their own disempowerment, their own demise by siding with the enemies of freedom. These pitiful folks are essentially tying a noose around their own stiff necks. They are caught-up in a death spiral and don't even know it. Left wing extremism is becoming a way of life for millions. For most of these psychotically delusional patsies, the noose will be pulled tight during the prophesied seven-year Tribulation, and much sooner for some.

The good news is that our great Lord and Savior is wide-awake and working behind the scenes, moving history along to the very moment when He calls His Church home in the Pre-Tribulation Rapture. The Blessed Hope is a promise every true born-again believer can count on (1 Corinthians 15:51-52; 1 Thessalonians 4: 15-17; 5:9); Revelation 3:10, Titus 2:13). President Trump is constantly being attacked day in and day out; he is a very strong man but surely only by the grace of God can he withstand the fiery darts constantly directed at him. We must fervently pray for him and not tolerate moves to censor our First Amendment rights to speak up.

The godless left only recognize the First Amendment for themselves; they holler and screech at anyone who does not agree with their activist warped ideologies and oppressive views. As the well-known saying goes, "All that is necessary for evil to triumph is to do nothing." Enraged, weak-minded, spiritually bankrupt individuals—radical leftists at the top abuse their authority, and take advantage of others. Destruction and chaos are their end-goals; the suppression of individual rights and wholesale tyranny are at the top of their To-Do lists. Their sinister methodologies abound, working to ensnare the masses.

The strong-minded work to help others to bring about harmony. They don't need to quash others to elevate themselves. This is true in all walks of life. When weeding a garden, it is no surprise to see new weeds quickly pop up; an annoying dilemma. Our new patriotic president is navigating his way around poisonous weeds that must be eradicated from so many aspects of government. President Trump makes some progress, and then another batch of misfits rear their greedy godless heads. The enemy within is all pervasive, bold, cunning and determined. We can see that the corrupt and contentious overreaching government bureaucrats—these globalist nanny state advocates are not going to leave quietly. They are deeply embedded in government bureaucracy. The hostile arrogance of these cornered rats is mind-boggling. They are fighting like mad to keep the American people from regaining what belongs to them. They dismiss anything that refutes their toxic narratives by twisting and turning reality into distorted fanatical behavior accompanied by their senseless drivel.

The corruption is so deep and widespread that only God can silence the disruptive elements, and bring back some sense of order to our way of life (if that is His plan, but we can't be sure at this point in time). We may be so far along prophetically that the chaos will continue to dramatically increase. Almighty God has President Donald J. Trump at the helm of our nation; he is courageously navigating his way through treacherous territory with spiritual landmines erupting every day, manifesting in the physical world through what appears to be demonic strongholds in all aspects of government, media, education, business, you name it—the devil is in the details most everywhere.

Are the fraudulent "news" commentators and members of the press so dumbed-down that they cannot differentiate between a bold-faced lie and reality? Is it sheer a stupidity? Is it self-righteous arrogance? Or are these parasitic media leeches willing and evil accomplices working to bring about the destruction of the greatest country on earth? Without a doubt, these saboteurs are incessantly and deliberately lying and creating fake news; no holds barred at any cost in order to further their radical agendas in their outrageous attempts to delegitimize our new pro-American, pro-Israel anti-globalist president.

> Recently, six "top" traditional "news" sites excluded President Trump from their Gorsuch headlines after the judge was confirmed for a seat on the Supreme Court (April 7, 2017)—despite the incessant over-the-top hysterical opposition of the Democrats. ABC, CBS, NBC, CNN, *Washington Post* and *New York Times* censored any headline mention of Trump's greatest victory since taking office, and treated it as an insignificant non-event. Politico did the same. It took the *Jerusalem Post* to make the journalistic point honestly with this headline: "In Big Win for Trump, Senate Approves Conservative Court Pick Neil Gorsuch." This is a tremendous achievement for President Trump—for liberty and freedom. Our country came very close to possible judicial tyranny on the Supreme Court of the United States with the vacancy left by the sudden and mysterious death of Justice Antonin Scalia.

We have all heard the term, "Liberalism is a mental disorder." I would say liberalism is a serious spiritual disorder which results in a mental disorder; a mental disorder which seems to be untreatable unless a person is awakened to the true God of Abraham, Isaac and Jacob, and surrenders to Him through an authentic spiritual rebirth (John 3:3). That is where the Great Commission comes in. It is not fashionable to preach the gospel. No, not at all. Preach "social justice" or which bathroom is okay to use, and you are a hero. Make a scene about the "rights" of any number of irrational liberal causes and you are—in. The tragedy is that those who are oblivious as to how they are being used by the globalist misfits will one day have to face the Lord. A tragic day for them unless they snap out of their spiritual atrophy and realize the error of their ways.

The power of prayer is a huge topic in the Bible. As believers, prayer is the most powerful weapon against the enemy. The devil uses people to do his bidding. Can we give up a good chunk of our own free time to pray for those who hate us and want to harm us? Remember what Jesus said on the cross: "Father, forgive them for they know not know not what they do." That statement from the Lord is a tough one for us in our limited human condition to accept. I have to swallow hard to even type out our precious Lord's statement when relating it to the massive injustices taking place every day around us all over the world. Whatever happened to accountability? It seems that the more unhinged and evil the situation, the greater and more positive the spin—the spin generated by the press to cover-up dastardly deeds and criminal activities. But it is true; most of the lost rabble-rousing useful idiots really have no idea what they are doing.

Millions of wayward souls are being used by the devil in destructive ways. We know his mission is to destroy people. Our mission should be to intercede through prayer and help break down dark spiritual strong-holds, and share the gospel at every opportunity. Saul of Tarsus, better known as the apostle Paul (after his conversion), is a prime example of what would appear to be a hopelessly lost and evil man; a man who was dedicated to the intense persecution of Christians. But God in His infinite mercy and grace brought Saul to his knees. Paul became an extraordinary spokesperson and advocate for the Lord Jesus. He was given a special anointing and wrote down God's messages in some of the greatest books of the Bible.

We are living in very perilous times (2 Timothy 3:1)—all part of God's plan to save those who can be reached, and bring judgment upon those who are hopelessly unrepentant. Now is the time like never before to methodi-cally persevere and "press toward the mark for the prize of the high calling of God in Christ Jesus" (Philippians 3:4). Scripture teaches that during the Tribulation multitudes of people will come to faith. We can plant those faith seeds now while there is still time. May God have mercy on those who are frantically stumbling along on the broad road to hell (Matthew 7:13-14). May He open their hearts and minds to His everlasting truths.

> "But evil men and impostors shall wax worse and worse, deceiving and being deceived. And because lawlessness will abound, the love of many will grow cold" (2 Timothy 3:13; Matthew 24:12).

Kit. R. Olsen
April 30, 2017

President Trump's Historic
America-First Promise Gains Momentum

For decades, and especially during the past eight years of the Marxist-leaning Obama Administration immigration laws have been virtually ignored, placing every American in danger. This lawlessness encouraged by Barack Hussein Obama essentially invited anyone, good or bad, to illegally cross the southwestern border of the United States and take advantage of our country on multiple levels—all to the detriment of hard working patriotic Americans.

In his first address to Congress, President Trump announced that due to the high numbers of crimes committed throughout the USA by illegal aliens, he would be creating a new government office with the very specific purpose of serving American victims of crimes committed by persons who are living in the U.S. illegally. The name of the new government office is appropriately called VOICE—Victims Of Immigration Crime Engagement. On April 26, 2017 Homeland Security Secretary John Kelly announced the launch of this new department. Every American is at risk from illegal alien criminal gangs and individuals. Although liberals, "progressive" Democrats and the media seem to think and act as if they are immune to any possibility of becoming victims of these criminal invaders.

A more secure and stronger America, makes for a more secure and stronger Israel, and world overall. Border security was one of the primary reasons President Trump won the election. Israel understands all too well why border security is vital to a nation's safety and economic prosperity. We now have a president who places America first, and is on excellent terms with our greatest ally in the Middle East—God's chosen nation, Israel. We won't see President Trump bowing down to Saudi royalty like his predecessor or taking a world tour to apologize for America.

The Democratic Party foolishly and smugly underestimated a great number of the American people when they thought that they could hoodwink us into another four to eight years of godless dangerous failed anti-American, anti-Israel "progressive" policies. The word *progressive* is covertly used by some in the Democratic Party as a substitute for communism. Progressivism is actually the opposite of true progress; it is a code word for Marxist principles of totalitarian collectivism; a system whereby the individual is essentially deemed irrelevant. Marxism, socialism, progressivism are all falsely peddled as social "equality."

Already after just a few short months since our new president was sworn into office, he is implementing new strategies to benefit the American people—despite the constant roadblocks placed before him by his enemies. On April 4, 2017 the *Washington Times* reported that illegal migration across the southwest border is down *more* than 60 percent so far. Some sources (border residents) report that the decrease is as high as 90 percent. Illegal entry into the U.S. has plummeted under President Trump. He expressed his enthusiasm for the record reductions in illegal crossers, saying he is already saving Americans' jobs by preventing them from having to compete with unauthorized workers (illegal aliens that do not belong in this country). And I would add that President Trump is saving lives by curtailing the entry of dangerous criminals into our great nation.

Nevertheless, our country has already been infiltrated by very dangerous individuals who wish to harm us. It is a serious problem that must continue to be dealt with by the United States Justice Department, led by the very competent law and order man, our new Attorney General, a true American patriot—Jeff Sessions. He has directly called out the former Obama Administration for the lack of border security and lack law enforcement—which has enabled the heinous MS13 gang and militant Islam to infiltrate and establish their crime networks in the United States. Local, state and federal law enforcement have reported that MS13 and Islamic terror groups have joined together working in drug trafficking, human trafficking and other violent crimes of death and destruction. Under the previous lawlessness Obama Administration these purveyors of death and terror were allowed to enter into the United States, to take root and expand.

The attempted destruction of this country is clearly by design. What the criminal globalists fail to understand is this: They are battling the Almighty Creator of heaven and earth, and in the end they will be silenced forever as prophesied in the book of Revelation. When the Tribulation takes hold, the globalists will think they have won and succeeded with their sinister plans, but their time of global ruling will be short-lived. The Antichrist will spare no one who opposes him, and in due time all the champions of tyranny and their subordinates will be dealt with by God Himself. Their permanent home will be in the lake of fire for all eternity with no hope of escape or pardon.

We have seen President Trump quickly gain respect on the international stage by meeting with a number of prominent world leaders, resulting in strengthened relations. Our president and his aides worked for several weeks with Egyptian President Abdel Fatah al-Sissi to secure the freedom of Aya Hijazi, 30, a U.S. citizen, as well as her husband, Mohamed Hassanein, who is an Egyptian citizen. President Trump personally engaged in the successful release of the Egyptian American charity worker and her husband along with four other humanitarian workers. They were imprisoned in Cairo for three years under false charges of child abuse, when in fact they were working with the Belady Foundation to protect children. Hijazi and her husband established the Belady Foundation as a haven and rehabilitation center for street children in Cairo.

The former Obama Administration unsuccessfully petitioned Sissi's government for the release of Aya Hijazi and Mohamed Hassanein. It was not until President Trump moved to reset U.S. relations with Egypt by embracing President Sissi at the White House on April 3, and offered the U.S. government's "strong backing"—that Egypt's posture changed. On April 16, 2017 a court in Cairo dropped all charges against Hijazi and the others.

The dropping of charges set in motion the release of Hijazi and Hassanein from custody and their journey to the United States, which was personally overseen by President Trump. This type of successful international diplomacy has been sorely lacking for a very long time. Now we have a president who knows how to negotiate, can think on his feet and does not need a teleprompter to tell him what to say. What Obama failed to do, President Trump succeeded by using the art of the deal.

Earlier, in January of this year soon after President Trump was inaugurated, the Charisma News website reported that ten companies had already promised to add jobs in the United States. We can expect this list to grow and for jobs to increase for Americans. Since then the list has grown and continue to grow.

1. Kroger says that it intends to fill 10,000 permanent positions in the United States this year.

2. IBM has announced that it will be hiring an additional 25,000 workers in the United States over the next four years.

3. Foxconn is considering setting up a $7 billion plant in the United States that would create between 30,000 and 50,000 jobs.

4. Amazon.com has pledged to add 100,000 full-time jobs in the United States by mid-2018.

5. Wal-Mart has announced it plans to add approximately 10,000 retail jobs in the United States in 2017.

6. Sprint has announced that 5,000 jobs will be brought back to the United States instead of overseas.

7. After meeting with Trump, the CEO of SoftBank stated his intention to create 50,000 new jobs in the United States.

8. After a phone call from Trump, industrial manufacturing giant Carrier promised to keep hundreds of jobs in the United States instead of moving them out of the country.

9. Hyundai has promised to spend $3.1 billion supporting their current factories in Georgia and Alabama and has said it is now considering adding an additional factory in the United States as well.

10. GM has pledged to invest $1 billion in U.S. factories and to add or keep 7,000 jobs in the United States

Trump's First 100 Days Have Been Better Than You Think
Mike Walsh, *New York Post*, April 15, 2017

As the end of Donald Trump's first 100 days in office approaches, now's a good a time to cut through the fog of misinformation, disinformation, media propaganda, ideological bias and outright hostility that has greeted his arrival in Washington and take a clear-eyed look at how he's really doing. Answer: Much better than you think.

Let's take the area that was supposed to be his Achilles' heel—foreign policy. After flirting publicly with the likes of John Bolton, Rudy Giuliani and David Petraeus, Trump settled on dark horse Rex Tillerson, the former chief of ExxonMobil, to be his secretary of state. Like his boss, Tillerson had no prior experience in government—which has turned out so far to be an excellent thing.

Unencumbered by the can't-do conventional wisdom of the Foggy Bottom establishment and its parrots in the Washington press corps, Tillerson has played the carrot to Trump's stick, soothing Chinese feathers ruffled during the campaign with a March visit to Beijing and setting up the successful meeting earlier this month between The Donald and the Chinese president at Mar-a-Largo that—purely coincidentally, coincided with the cruise-missile salvo fired at Syria's Bashar al-Assad.

Since then, the Chinese have openly cautioned the troublesome regime of Kim Jong un in North Korea not to antagonize the U.S. with further nuclear saber-rattling in the region; "Trump is a man who honors his promises," warned the *People's Daily*, the ruling party's official newspaper. Among those promises: a better trade deal for China and an ominous presidential tweet to the North Koreans that they're "looking for trouble," and signed "USA." Even now, U.S. warships are steaming Kim's way.

Regarding Russia, Rex Tillerson rocked the former Soviets with a "frank discussion" in Moscow on Wednesday—diplo-speak for "contentious." Meanwhile, at the UN, ambassador Nikki Haley has already proven her mettle, taking a hard line toward the Russians for their tactical alliance with Assad while making clear the U.S. commitment to Israel.

Domestically, a first attempt at repealing and replacing Obamacare flopped when Speaker Paul Ryan's needlessly complex "better way" couldn't muster enough GOP votes to make it to the House floor. But the fault was the ambitious Ryan's. Now the way's clear for a cleaner repeal. And, yes, tax reform's on its way, too.

True, the president's two executive orders regarding visitors from several Muslim countries have been stayed by federal judges refusing to acknowledge the plain letter of both the Constitution and the U.S. Code 1182, which give the president plenary power regarding immigration. But the recent confirmation of Neil Gorsuch as an associate justice will very quickly clear up that misunderstanding when the cases land in the Supreme Court. Further, the Republicans' use of the "nuclear option" to eliminate the filibuster for high court nominees means Trump's next pick is guaranteed a speedy confirmation.

Over at the National Security Council, H.R. McMaster has brought order out of the chaos that followed the abortive tenure of Mike Flynn, shuffling some staffers but retaining the services of crucial personnel. And at the Pentagon and Homeland Security, former Marine generals James Mattis and John Kelly can be counted on to faithfully execute presidential policy. Worries that they're too soft on radical Islam are unfounded.

Less remarked but equally important has been the administration's speedy action on downsizing the federal government, proposing real spending cuts and reorganizing the bloated bureaucracy, which has drawn bleats of protest from the DC swamp creatures watching their sinecures circling the drain. Trump's also lifted the hiring freeze, in order to flesh out a still-undermanned executive staff and replace Obama holdovers.

Buy American, Hire American

On April 18, 2017 major news outlets reported that President Trump signed an executive order that would tighten rules that award visas to skilled foreign workers and directs the federal government to enforce rules that bar foreign contractors from bidding on federal projects. The order is a first strong effort to promote a "Buy American, Hire American" agenda, a decisive promise President Trump made during the campaign.

Speaking at the headquarters of Wisconsin-based toolmaker Snap-on, President Trump said that the executive order "declares that the policy of our government is to aggressively promote and use American-made goods and to ensure that American labor is hired to do the job." He also stated, "We're going to do everything in our power to make sure more products are stamped with those wonderful words 'Made in the USA.' For too long we've watched as our factories have been closed and our jobs have been sent to faraway lands."

With the signing of this executive order, senior administration officials said during a briefing with reporters that the White House is moving forward with an agenda that cuts across party lines. Labor unions, which typically lean Democratic, have long complained about free-trade pacts that they say leave American workers behind, and the "Buy American, Hire American" slogan is one that both parties are eager to support. "Those are two very specific policy positions that have long been advocated by many groups that represent workers in our country in particular by many labor unions and labor groups in our country," one senior administration official said.

The executive order directs federal agencies to crack down on fraud and abuse in the H-1B visa program, which is heavily used by technology companies. It also directs the federal government to fully enforce federal guidelines prioritizing the use of American firms and goods in federal projects. Both changes are aimed at discouraging the use of foreign labor, which displaces American workers and reduces wages. It also aims to give a boost to U.S. steel mills and steelworkers.

It is heartening to see a president working hard for the American people instead of trying to undermine them. Despite the constant fake news and the never-ending badgering by the deluded mind-numbed robotic liberal left, President Trump is well on his way to a victorious presidency. May Almighty

God continue to protect and guide him. God honors those who honor Him. We must honor the Lord with our prayers and our faithfulness. "The effectual fervent prayer of a righteous man availeth much" (James 5:16b).

President Trump's Cabinet Members Praying and Studying The Bible Together
April 24, 2017 CBN News

Members of President Donald Trump's cabinet are gathering for prayer weekly. Vice President Mike Pence and eight cabinet secretaries sponsor the sessions, which occur weekly in Washington. It's led by the founder of Capitol Ministries, Ralph Drollinger, who started working on arranging the Bible study during the Trump team's transition to the White House.

Sponsors include Vice President Pence; Secretaries Betsy DeVos, Ben Carson, Sonny Perdue, Rick Perry, Tom Price and Jeff Sessions; EPA Administrator Scott Pruitt and CIA Director Mike Pompeo. These are some of the most influential people in the U.S. government gathering weekly to grow themselves spiritually. "In terms of a country's health and direction, when its leaders are seeking God, the nation is in a position to be blessed by God in ways that are 'far more abundantly beyond all that we ask or think,'" said Drollinger referring to Ephesians 3:20.

Capitol Ministries also hosts weekly Bible studies in the House and Senate. The ministry has started Bible studies in a number of state capitols and is currently working on expanding into international capitols. "This has been a wonderful time of prayer and fellowship as I am presently teaching through the Sermon on the Mount, as well as handing out my weekly written Bible study as a homework assignment on a particular topic," Drollinger continued. Leaders of the Bible study say President Donald Trump is always welcome to join them. Prayer has been an evident part of this administration with pastors often praying over Trump throughout the campaign.

President Trump Is Cleaning Up
The Mess He Inherited

The challenges President Trump faces are far reaching, extending to all aspects of governing this great nation—issues that touch our lives in one way or another. They consist of deconstructing radical job killing regulations; repatriating multinational corporations; reforming the complex tax system; repealing the abomination of Obamacare; improving our domestic infrastructure by lifting restrictions on the production of $50 trillion dollars worth of job-producing American energy reserves like shale, oil, coal, and natural gas; lifting the Obama-Clinton roadblocks and completing energy infrastructure projects such as the Keystone Pipeline.

Rebuilding our military is high on President Trump's list of making America great again (which includes taking care of and honoring our great veterans). He is also working to undo the damage done by the former Obama Administration's crusade to undermine the police. Additionally, the following issues are also being addressed: crushing militant Islamic terrorism; arresting and deporting illegal alien criminals; securing our borders (which includes building the wall across the southern border), eliminating lawless sanctuary cities, scaling down government overreach imposed by the so-called environmental laws and regulations; strengthening our economy by identifying and ending all foreign trading abuses that unfairly impact American workers; dealing with numerous domestic and foreign policies, and restoring America's leadership in the world. These are just some of issues our new president is addressing.

President Trump is encountering intense opposition from many members in Congress when it comes to actually moving forward with various aspects of his pro-America agenda. Many members of Congress are controlled by people who have been never voted into office, primarily unelected bureaucrats (the "swamp"). These special interest groups and lobbyists have a strong hold on Democrats and far too many Republicans. It is too early in Trump's presidency to see how this simmering battle between him and the official "Washington insiders" will play out. Nonetheless, progress is being made; overall our country is already in much better shape than it was before President Trump took office.

In 2016 the *Huffington Post*, known for its anti-Israel bias predicted that Hillary Clinton had a 98.1% chance of winning the presidency, which would have meant a mere 1.6% chance for Donald Trump to be victorious. The incessant attempts to demoralize the population and stop votes for candidate Trump fizzled—despite the media's all-out blitzkrieg against him. They failed then and as we can see, they are failing today. Despite the brazen ongoing circulation of fake news, overwhelming numbers of patriotic Americans are not buying into the media's hysterical anti-Trump propaganda.

Previous liberal administrations, especially the deceptive lawless Obama Administration have greatly harmed and betrayed our nation—creating so many serious problems that they seem insurmountable. With the stroke of a pen on his way out the door at the end of his term, Obama seized land from Utah and Nevada to add to his total land grab of over 553 million land and sea acreage, making it all unavailable to the American people—declaring it all government property. He also smugly declared that the action he took cannot be undone; that it is irreversible. Obama was allowed to simply snatch land from under the feet of the American people because of the Antiquities Act of 1906. The Act was initially intended to set aside *small* portions of land for monuments and national parks, but has since been abused by lawmakers to control large quantities of property.

President Trump is already taking steps to stop this excessive land-grab and find a way to reverse this abuse of government power. He has ordered the Interior Department to review national monument designations dating back twenty years for millions of acres of land, pointing out that former presidents have abused the system. He has vowed to return such authority to citizens and state lawmakers. At issue is the 1906 Antiquities Act, which gives presidents authority to "protect" land. President Trump said the law also gives the federal government "unlimited power to lock up millions of acres of land and water" and that it has been used on hundreds of millions of acres. He has vowed to "end these abuses." Government land grabs hinder economic growth by denying the exploration and use of our natural resources—which would ultimately result in energy independence. This government overreach of land confiscation also prohibits human settlement in those specific areas, wasting good land which could be used to build new homes and create thriving communities and businesses.

Government abuses against the American people seem unending. But God still intervenes in our lives and we have a new president who loves and respects this country. He is a great advocate for liberty, individual freedoms and prosperity—the basic tenants upon which this nation was founded—as documented in the Constitution of the United States. Rogue government officials in every state throughout the U.S.A. are working to undermine the constitutional rights of the American people. Activist liberal judges use their power to abrogate our constitutional system; they wrap their judicial tyranny around the lives of the American people.

Judges are not appointed to conduct foreign policy undermining federal laws and the constitutional powers of the president of the United States. But Obama appointees are doing exactly that (for the time being until they can be stopped by the United States Supreme Court). We can see a concentrated effort by corrupt leftist activist judges trying to stop President Trump from enforcing existing laws and succeeding as president. A pattern has been established over the years by liberal Democratic presidents appointing biased leftist judges to actively work against the rule of law, which in turn helps facilitate the implementation of lawless global tyranny. When liberals lose at the ballot box they turn to judicial activists to get their way.

The tentacles of the globalist criminals are strategically woven into all aspects of government, education, business, you name it—their evil presence can be found nearly everywhere. The Scriptures encourage Christians to be aware of what is going on around them, to watch for signs leading to the end of the Church Age and Jesus' return. By being aware of what is going on politically and globally we can better discern the times in which we live, and better reinforce to others the many reasons why the need to accept Jesus' free gift of salvation is so necessary.

"But of the times and the seasons, brethren, ye have no need that I write unto you. For yourselves know perfectly that the day of the Lord so cometh as a thief in the night. For when they shall say, Peace and safety; then sudden destruction cometh upon them, as travail upon a woman with child; and they shall not escape. **But ye, brethren, are not in darkness, that that day should overtake you as a thief**. Ye are all the children of light, and the children of the day: we are not of the night, nor of darkness. **Therefore let us not sleep, as do others; but let us watch and be sober** " (1 Thessalonians 5:1-6).

President Trump is obviously for the American people, and our new pro-life president does not shy away from acknowledging Almighty God. He is taking deliberate steps to undo the damage done by the enemies of American sovereignty. President Trump is working to strengthen our God-given rights for the pursuit of life, liberty and happiness.

On April 18, 2017, the same day President Trump signed his "Buy American, Hire American" executive order, Adam Credo reported in the *Washington Free Beacon* that federal authorities have opened investigations into radical Islamic terrorists in all 50 states, according to the Department of Homeland Security. The DHS warned that the threat of terrorism in the United States has reached an all time high with radicalized individuals in the country plotting to strike "each and every single day." This effort to make our country safer, identify and weed out dangerous people would have never happened under Obama's watch.

We can thank the previous Obama Administration, former presidents George W. Bush and Bill Clinton for keeping our borders wide open for decades. Many enemies of this country have already invaded our country. The

Trump Administration has been able to dramatically slow down the flow of illegal aliens entering our nation, but it will take more time and effort to firmly secure the borders, and to find ways to carefully vet those who seek to enter the USA. We can also credit former president, Bill Clinton for enabling North Korea to have nuclear weapons; a very delicate and dangerous situation threatening the world at this very moment.

"The North Korean deal of 1994 is the prototype for why open societies should not negotiate arms control agreements with rogue regimes," said Robert Kaufman, professor of public policy at Pepperdine University. "The North Koreans duped Jimmy Carter—an emissary of Clinton, and the Clinton Administration to subsidize the North Korean nuclear program in exchange for the counterfeit promise that North Korea would limit itself to civilian nuclear power." Obama made the same terrible mistake with his Iran deal. He made a deal with the number one terrorist state, essentially enabling it to eventually create nuclear weapons. Whenever Obama tried to undermine Israel during his tenure as president, his anti-Semitic bias and hatred of God's chosen nation was loud and clear. The disastrous deal he made with Iran is most dangerous for Israel. These reckless liberal presidents need to be held accountable for the damage they have done to the security of our nation and others.

President Trump's call for "extreme vetting" is greatly needed and methods to investigate those who are already here illegally or legally must be a priority—in order to identify and stop those who intend to cause us harm. We can be sure those who comprise the fascist left—the irrational hate-filled hostile Democrats, the leftist lapdog media along with some turncoat Republicans, rogue Washington insiders, liberal lawless activist judges and the paid loony activist protestors (agitators) will continue to oppose President Trump's administration as they work to stop the efforts of the globalists—the godless tyrants who are trying to takeover our sovereign nation. With God's help, positive inroads will be made by President Trump to investigate and bring to justice those who pose a threat to our country.

We know one of the methods of the fascist left is to target good people and try to take them down. When it comes to President Trump, they have outdone themselves and yet he remains standing. His pro-America agenda *is* moving forward. He has made a lot of progress in a very short time. An example of how deranged and brainwashed some people have become can be seen in this "news" headline recently posted on a number of websites: "Cry Baby Students Say Truth Is a Tool of White Supremacists." I am unable to come up with any words to adequately comment on such a ridiculous statement and belief. But it makes perfect sense when analyzing the ongoing demise of any kind of common sense to be found amongst the dumbed-down, brainwashed population.

The politically correct days of not investigating mosques and other possible terrorist hideouts may be over, thanks to the Trump Administration's new policies of stopping terrorism full-force, and not appeasing the enemy. According to DHS Secretary John Kelly there have been at least 37 "ISIS-linked plots to attack our country" since 2013, a number that shows no signs of diminishing. Even with the recent slow-down of illegal aliens entering our country, our borders still need to be effectively secured. Secretary Kelly, in his first wide-ranging public address on the threat of terrorism in America since taking office, warned that there is evidence terror-linked individuals continue to exploit our national security weaknesses and are entering the United States. All of these security weaknesses can be attributed to the previous presidents who took a weak stance on enforcing immigration laws.

I will never forget when George W. Bush made this gushing doe-eyed statement, "Family values don't stop at the Rio Grande River." He was (is) all for illegal aliens getting into and staying in our country under the guise of "charitable" amnesty. I knew then for sure that he is a sell-out open borders globalist just like Obama and the Clintons. To add fuel to the fire of Islamic terrorism, in May of 2011, the former administration of Barack Hussein Obama eliminated the National Security Entry-Exit Registration System (NSEERS) program requiring non-citizens from high risk countries to register in a federal database—primarily Arab and Muslim men from many high risk countries. How *progressive* of Obama to make it easy for Muslim terrorists to penetrate our borders and place the lives of Americans at risk.

"We don't know their intentions," John Kelly said during an address at George Washington University. "We don't know why they're here or why they're coming. We are completely blind to what they're capable of." The United States, he continued, is "under attack" from a wide variety of bad actors, including "failed states, cyber-terrorists, vicious smugglers, and sadistic radicals." President Trump said those very same things again and again during his presidential campaign, warning Americans that the flood of illegal aliens into the U.S. must stop; that many dangerous people with bad intentions are living amongst us with many more trying to get in. He also stressed that many individuals come into our country legally through various visa programs posing as students or any number of legally accepted identities; but their true intentions to cause Americans harm could be masked.

"These threats just scrape the surface of the danger posed to America by terrorists inside and outside of the country," Kelly said. "This is all bad news, but it gets much worse," he explained. "Experts estimate that perhaps 10,000 citizens of Europe have joined the caliphate in Syria and Iraq. Thousands more are from nations in Asia, Africa and the Western Hemisphere. They have learned how to make IEDs, employ drones to drop ordnance, and acquired experience on the battlefield that by all reports they are bringing back home."

These highly trained terrorist fighters are likely to return to their countries of origin and "wreak murderous havoc" across Europe, Asia, and the United States, among other countries. America lacks the ability to properly vet these individuals when they attempt to enter the country, according to Kelly, who warned that scores of radicalized individuals are trying each day to enter America. "Many are citizens of countries in our Visa Waiver Program; they can more easily travel to the United States which makes us a prime target for their exported violence," he said. The threat to America "has metastasized and decentralized, and the risk is as threatening today as it was that September morning almost 16 years ago," Kelly warned. "We are under attack from terrorists both within and outside of our borders," he said. "They are without conscience, and they operate without rules. They despise the United States, because we are a nation of rights, laws, and freedoms. They have a single mission, and that is our destruction."

This type of assessment from the current Department of Homeland Security should cause every American to support stronger immigration policies, and at the very least—support the strict enforcement of immigration laws that already exist. Yet we continue to find willfully ignorant people in every aspect of government, media and in all walks of life—dismissing the truth of terrorist threats and other serious problems that work against the safety and wellbeing of the American people. President Trump has tried to awaken people to the dangers around us but as the saying goes, "The patients are running the asylum." The arrogant cynics refuse to listen. Instead they relentlessly mock our president and anyone who holds to conservative principles and a virtuous way of life. When a major terrorist attack hits the U.S. the same psychotic people who have ignored the president's warnings will blame him.

I see all these issues as a strong indication of the end-times; so many people are self-absorbed, deceived and so full of hate that they have no common sense. A demonic rage is seething from so many people that we can be sure that the "father of lies" (John 8:44) is working overtime in the spiritual realm to keep his useful stooges actively participating in anything dark and sinister. When the Tribulation begins, these same people will line up to support the Antichrist and the False Prophet. I don't see that the spiritual apathy of the majority of these gullible naysayers and opponents of God and individual liberty dissipating. They are far too self-righteous and fully committed to bringing down our Judeo-Christian way of life.

President Trump has said many times over that he has inherited "A mess." The "mess" is enormous. It is evident that he has a huge number of issues to deal with, far beyond what any of us can fully know. Most believers understand that we are living in a spiritual war zone. We can see that the battles fought in the spiritual realm are manifesting in the physical world through the hostile irrational behavior of individuals and groups. Evil is well represented and its advocates are increasing in number. The hatred for President Trump is very similar to the hatred toward Israel. Both Donald Trump and Israel are treated with great disdain by much of the world. The ongoing efforts to delegitimize Trump's presidency and deny Israel's right to exist are very telling of growing satanic strongholds.

Every day we can see evidence and signs of thousands, if not millions of demonically oppressed people behaving in ways that can only be explained in spiritual terms. We see it in the crazed anti-Trump brigades. We see it in the anti-Semitic, anti-Israel mantras and threats; and of course in many other aspects of this life. Some of these lost souls serve phantom gods that don't exist; some proudly profess atheism. The only "safe zone" is with Jesus. We must trust Him completely and keep His words close to our hearts, and share the gospel with those willing to listen. The broad road to eternal destruction is getting very crowded (Matthew 7:13).

"Let not your heart be troubled: believe in God, believe also in me. In my Father's house are many mansions; if it were not so, I would have told you; for I go to prepare a place for you. And if I go and prepare a place for you, I come again, and will receive you unto myself; that where I am, *there* ye may be also" (John 14:2-4).

✡ ✡ ✡ ✡ ✡

Part One
Israel Is God's Chosen Nation

Why Is Israel the Holy Land?

The Lord Chose to Establish His Name in the Land of Israel

"I will gather them [the Jews] and will bring them to the place where I have chosen as a dwelling for My name" (Nehemiah 1:9b).

"Also your people shall all be righteous; they shall inherit the land forever, the branch of My planting, the work of My hands, that I might be glorified" (Isaiah 60:21).

✡✡✡✡✡

Chapter One

Satan's Jihad Against God and Israel

God's Chosen People—Israel

"For you are a holy people to the Lord your God; the Lord your God has chosen you to be a people for Himself, a special treasure above all the peoples on the face of the earth" (Deuteronomy 7:6).

Lucifer (Satan) rebelled against God—trying to usurp Him. This caused the Lord God Almighty to cast him out of heaven along with his demonic entourage (fallen angels). Since that time Satan has been a maligning foe wreaking havoc anywhere and everywhere, and the conflict between God and Satan has been going full force. Jesus Christ chose Israel as his earthly birth and dwelling place. His identity while on earth came through Jewish lineage, which places Israel at the center of this conflict. The majority of Jews have rejected Jesus, their Messiah, for thousands of years.

"He was in the world, and the world was made by Him, and the world knew Him not. He came to His own, and those who were His own [the Jews] did not receive Him" (John 1:10-11).

Israel generally does not recognize Jesus the Christ for who He is. Nevertheless, Satan is working day and night to destroy the Jews. Evil, vicious, satanic forces are behind the ongoing attacks against Israel. In Matthew 24:21 Jesus forewarned that a time is coming upon this earth when there will be great tribulation. Close to the very end of that horrific unprecedented time, Israel as a nation *will* repent. Israel must (and will) recognize and acknowledge Jesus Christ as her true Messiah before He will return.

The Lord tells us through Scripture that Israel must repent and urgently cry out to Him. That is what God says must be done before there can be a Second Coming.

God's archenemy, the father of lies—the devil—is obsessed with eradicating the Jews. If the Jews can be eliminated, they will not be able to send that pleading, prophesied, necessary and urgent call to the Lord begging for His return. Satan would then have complete control of this planet. He knows Scripture states Messiah Jesus will not come back until Israel recognizes and accepts the identity of her true Messiah, and repents. So it is Satan's ongoing mission to destroy the Jews (and Israel). No Jews, no Messiah. That is Satan's goal. But the devil cannot circumvent Messiah's plan of redemption for Israel and the world. Satan uses godless men to carry out his dirty deeds. God intends to put an end to the overwhelming influence the devil has over the day-to-day operations of this fallen world.

The hate campaign, the verbal and physical assaults engineered by Satan that threaten to totally demolish Israel will ultimately bring on Armageddon. Tragically, the prophet Zechariah forewarned that two-thirds of the Jewish population would be already wiped out before that final battle at Armageddon (Zechariah 13:8-9). It is at that final battle that all the nations led by the Antichrist will be gathered to challenge and physically assault Jesus Christ—when He returns at the very end of the seven-year Tribulation at the Second Coming. And make no mistake about it, the Lord Himself will draw His enemies and the enemies of Israel to that last climactic battle. It might look like Satan and his yes-men are in control but ultimately it will be the Messiah of Israel who will gather together these enemy nations to their final place of expulsion as cited in Joel 3:2:

> "I will gather all the nations and bring them down to the valley of Jehoshaphat. Then I will enter into judgment with them there on behalf of My people and My inheritance, Israel, whom they have scattered among the nations; and they have divided up My land."

4

Jesus Christ, the sovereign Messiah of Israel and the world, will prevail and win this intense and complex spiritual war between good and evil with His breath alone:

> "He shall strike the earth with the rod of His mouth, and with the breath of His lips He shall slay the wicked" (Isaiah 11:4b).

After a short seventy-five day interval (Daniel 12:11-12), the long awaited literal 1,000-year millennial reign of King Jesus on the newly rejuvenated earth will begin.

Israel Is Forever God's Holy Land

Israel's enemies are ready to pounce on her when the moment is right. The world's nations as a whole continue to berate the "apple of God's eye," seemingly oblivious to the consequences which will ultimately lead to that final campaign (battle at Armageddon). A two-nation state dividing Israel into an even smaller land mass is an ongoing discussion by ungodly elitists, politicians and radical religious zealots. This anti-Israel, anti-Semitic rhetoric is intensely gaining ground all over the world.

God has forever chosen Israel as His Holy Land. He intends to come back and set things right. Instead of the nation being totally destroyed by her enemies and quashed into a mass of nothingness, Israel will ultimately greatly expand in both territory and stature. This is guaranteed to Israel will not gain territories incrementally expanding into a larger empire before the millennial kingdom. She is having enough trouble holding on to the land that she has now. The only reliable place in Scripture where Israel expands her borders in a great and glorious way is *after* the Second Coming of Christ, during the millennial kingdom when *all* the land promised to Israel by God—in the Abrahamic Covenant—is given to her by Jesus Himself.

happen as promised by the Lord Himself. But first, Jesus the Messiah *must* return. It is *then* that He will fulfill His everlasting Covenant giving Israel all the land from the Nile to the Euphrates; that is what Scripture teaches.

> "On that day the Lord made a covenant with Abram, saying, 'To your descendants I have given this land, from the river of Egypt as far as the great river, the river Euphrates: the Kenite and the Kenizzite and the Kadmonite and the Hittite and the Perizzite and the Rephaim and the Amorite and the Canaanite and the Girgashite and the Jebusite'" (Genesis 15:18-21).

As believers, it is imperative that we understand the tremendous significance the nation of Israel has in today's world and the coming millennial kingdom. When Christ returns, rejuvenates the earth, takes His rightful place on the throne of David and lifts the curse from the earth, He will make converted Israel the head of all the nations. Her land will greatly expand during His millennial reign, but not before.

> "And the LORD will make you the head and not the tail; you shall be above only and not be beneath, if you heed the commandments of the LORD your God, which I command you today, and are careful to observe *them*" (Deuteronomy 28:13).

Understanding Israel's Glorious Beginning

In Isaiah 46, God illustrates Israel as "stouthearted" and far from righteousness, but says He will place salvation in Zion for Israel "my glory." What is this salvation that He speaks of? It is His righteousness—in the Person of the Messiah—the Lord Jesus Christ, His Righteous One.

> "Listen to Me, you stubborn-hearted, who *are* far from righteousness: I bring My righteousness near, it shall not be far off; My

salvation shall not linger. And I will place salvation in Zion, for Israel My glory" (Israel 46:12-13).

God chose Abram (Abraham) and made a covenant with him:

"You alone *are* the LORD; You have made heaven, the heaven of heavens, with all their host, the earth and everything on it, the seas and all that is in them, and You preserve them all. The host of heaven worships You. You *are* the LORD God, who chose Abram, and brought him out of Ur [Iraq] of the Chaldeans, and gave him the name Abraham; you found his heart faithful before You, and made a covenant with him, to give the land of the Canaanites, the Hittites, the Amorites, the Perizzites, the Jebusites, and the Girgashites—to give it to his descendants. You have performed Your words, for You *are* righteous" (Nehemiah 9:6-8).

Now the LORD had said to Abram: 'Get out of your country, from your family and from your father's house, to a land that I will show you. I will make you a great nation; I will bless you and make your name great; and you shall be a blessing. I will bless those who bless you, and I will curse him who curses you; and in you all the families of the earth shall be blessed'" (Genesis 12:1-3).

Qualifications for High Priesthood

God called Abraham from the land of Ur (Iraq) to go to Canaan to meet Melchizedek—a priest king:

"For every high priest taken from among men is appointed for men in things *pertaining* to God, that he may offer both gifts and sacrifices for sins. He can have compassion on those who

7

are ignorant and going astray, since he himself is also subject to weakness. Because of this he is required as for the people, so also for himself, to offer *sacrifices* for sins. And no man takes this honor to himself, but he who is called by God, just as Aaron *was*" (Hebrews 5:1-4).

The Messiah Jesus—High Priest Forever

"So also Christ did not glorify Himself to become High Priest, but *it was* He who said to Him: "You are My Son, today I have begotten You. As *He* also *says* in another *place*:

'You *are* a priest forever according to the order of Melchizedek;' who, in the days of His flesh, when He had offered up prayers and supplications, with vehement cries and tears to Him who was able to save Him from death, and was heard because of His godly fear, though He was a Son, *yet* He learned obedience by the things which He suffered.

And having been perfected, He [Jesus] became the author of eternal salvation to all who obey Him, called by God as High Priest 'according to the order of Melchizedek,' of whom we have much to say, and hard to explain, since you have become dull of hearing" (Hebrews 5:5-11).

Abraham left Ur (Iraq) by faith being led by God. God spoke directly to Abraham and he built an altar to God.

"Then the LORD appeared to Abram and said, 'To your descendants I will give this land.' And there he built an altar to the LORD, who had appeared to him. And he moved from there to the mountain east

8

of Bethel, and he pitched his tent *with* Bethel on the west and Ai on the east; there he built an altar to the LORD and called on the name of the LORD" (Genesis 12:7-8).

Abraham went to Egypt through the circumstances in Genesis 12:10-13:1. He became a wealthy man. The promise again was given to Abraham of the land in Genesis 13:14-18, Abraham built another altar to God.

Genesis 13:14-18

"And the LORD said to Abram, after Lot had separated from him: 'Lift your eyes now and look from the place where you are— northward, southward, eastward, and westward; for **all the land which you see I give to you and your descendants forever.**

And I will make your descendants as the dust of the earth; so that if a man could number the dust of the earth, *then* your descendants also could be numbered. Arise, walk in the land through its length and its width, for I give it to you.'

Then Abram moved *his* tent, and went and dwelt by the terebinth trees of Mamre, which *are* in Hebron, and built an altar there to the LORD."

In Genesis 14 Abraham meets with Melchizedek. They share bread and wine as in the Lord's Supper.

"Then Melchizedek king of Salem brought out bread and wine; he *was* the priest of God Most High. And he blessed him and said: 'Blessed be Abram of God Most High, Possessor of heaven and earth; and blessed be God Most High, who has delivered your enemies into your hand.' And he gave him a tithe of all" (Genesis 14:18-20).

Abraham was saved by faith. In Genesis 22, in the story of the offering of Isaac, Abraham took Isaac off the altar and put a ram in his place, instead of his son.

> "And Abraham called the name of the place, The-LORD-Will-Provide; as it is said *to* this day, 'In the Mount of the LORD it shall be provided'" (Genesis 22:14 NKJ).

Here is the same verse in the King James translation:

> "And Abraham called the name of that place Jehovah-jireh: as it is said to this day, in the mount of the LORD it shall be seen."

When the Old Testament was translated into Greek in 250 B.C., called the Septuagint (by 70 scholars in 70 days) they used the Greek word "ANTI" meaning: in place of. Later, in the New Testament the same word is used in Matthew 20:28 – that Jesus gave "his life as a ransom" (in the place of) the Greek word "ANTI" – the substituting atonement.

God's Great Promise to Israel

The promise of the Seed:

> "That in blessing I will bless thee, and in multiplying I will multiply thy seed as the stars of the heaven and as the sand which is upon the sea shore; and thy seed shall possess the gate of his enemies" (Genesis 22:17).

> "And in thy seed shall all the nations of the earth be blessed; because thou hast obeyed my voice" (Genesis 22:18).

In the New Testament Paul reasserted and defined God's promise to Abraham. The promise of the land and the promise of salvation in Christ the Messiah:

"Now to Abraham and his Seed were the promises made. He does not say, 'And to seeds,' as of many, but as of one, 'And to your Seed,' who is Christ" (Galatians 3:16).

Abraham through Isaac and Jacob became the father of the Jewish race. Abraham had seen the gospel. John wrote:

"Your father Abraham rejoiced to see My day, and he saw it and was glad" (John 8:56).

The Glorious Call God Gave Israel

Through Israel all the families of the earth are to be blessed:

"Now the LORD had said to Abram: Get out of your country, from your family and from your father's house, to a land that I will show you. I will make you a great nation; I will bless you and make your name great; and you shall be a blessing. I will bless those who bless you, and I will curse him who curses you; and in you all the families of the earth shall be blessed" (Genesis 12:1-3).

God gave Israel the glorious call to give the gospel to the world:

"This people I have formed for Myself; they shall declare My praise."

In Isaiah 48:11, God declared: "For My own sake, for My own sake, I will do *it*; for how should *My name* be profaned? And I will not give My glory to another."

In turn, Israel gave God's Glory (Jesus the Messiah) to the world in the Person of our Lord and Savior—a Jew. Here, we find the fulfillment of Isaiah 61:1-3:

> "The Spirit of the Lord GOD *is* upon Me, because the LORD has anointed Me to preach good tidings to the poor; He has sent Me to heal the brokenhearted, to proclaim liberty to the captives, and the opening of the prison to *those who are* bound; to proclaim the acceptable year of the LORD, and the day of vengeance of our God; to comfort all who mourn, to console those who mourn in Zion, to give them beauty for ashes, the oil of joy for mourning, the garment of praise for the spirit of heaviness; that they may be called trees of righteousness, the planting of the LORD, that He may be glorified."

The early Church grew when all Jewish believers took the gospel to the world. In Acts 8 we are given an insight as to how the gospel was preached throughout the entire world. Phillip ministered to and led the Ethiopian to the Lord:

> "Now when they came up out of the water, the Spirit of the Lord caught Philip away, so that the eunuch saw him no more; and he went on his way rejoicing" (Acts 8:29).

Based on the previous Scripture it is very likely that the Lord carried the early apostles and disciples miraculously all over the world.

> "Now to Him who is able to establish you according to my gospel and the preaching of Jesus Christ, according to the revelation of the mystery which has been kept secret for long ages past, but now is manifested, and by the Scriptures of the prophets, according to the

commandment of the eternal God, **has been made known to all the nations**, *leading* to obedience of faith" (Romans 16:25-26).

"We give thanks to the God and Father of our Lord Jesus Christ, praying always for you, since we heard of your faith in Christ Jesus and of your love for all the saints; because of the hope which is laid up for you in heaven, of which you heard before in the word of the truth of the gospel, which has come to you, as *it has* also in all the world, and is bringing forth fruit, as *it is* also among you since the day you heard and knew the grace of God in truth" (Colossians 1:3-6).

Israel, Always the Scapegoat for the World

Today Israel is loudly and ignorantly condemned, even by those who have never studied the true history of the so-called Palestinians, the Persians (Iranians), or the Jews. But this is all in keeping with biblical prophecy, which will culminate at the final battle, the battle at Armageddon:

"I will also gather all nations, and bring them down to the Valley of Jehoshaphat; and I will enter into judgment with them there. On account of My people, my heritage Israel, Whom they have scattered among the nations; they have also divided up My land" (Joel 3:2).

"And they gathered them together to the place called in Hebrew, Armageddon" (Revelation 16:16).

"And it shall come to pass in that day, that I will make Jerusalem a burdensome stone for all the peoples; all that burden themselves with it shall be sore wounded; and all the nations of the earth shall be gathered together against it" (Zechariah 12:3).

The Christian Church Has Not Replaced Israel

A popular movement within the Christian church is Dominion Theology. It is a false doctrine misleading many Christians. This ideology has created a clamor of controversy amongst believers for many years. I am going to discuss this especially for anyone who is new to faith in Christ so you will recognize this puzzling, false teaching.

Another term for Dominion Theology is "Kingdom Now Theology." It is a corrupt teaching asserting that God has entrusted mankind to bring the entire world under the dominion of Christianity. This belief system can sound appealing because of the many social maladies in society. Dominion exponents refuse to accept and acknowledge the obvious fact that until the Lord returns, the conditions of this world will continue to deteriorate. No man will ever be able to bring this world into harmony and unity.

According to the dominion theorists, Christ will not return until the Christian church gains an upper hand and has control of government and social establishments. However, Scripture simply does not say that. Mankind will never bring peace to this tainted world—that is precisely why the Lord has to come back—to once and for all put a final finish to this age of never-ending escalating chaos, and discord. When the Lord returns it will be at the height of hell on earth. He will come as a warrior, to destroy those who have irreverently taken control of the world.

Preterism and Replacement Theology are also two false belief systems that fall within the sphere of Dominion Theology. Preterists teach that "last days" Bible prophecy has already been fulfilled. That claim is preposterous, especially to those who understand biblical Scripture relating to the topic. Preterists deny the Rapture teachings, and convolute all the Bible passages that clearly define the Lord's promised Rapture event (1 Corinthians 15:51-52; 1 Thessalonians 4:16-18).

Replacement Theology promotes the lie that Israel has no further place or standing in God's prophetic plans, and that when Israel underwent judgment for rejecting Messiah Jesus, they were cut-off for eternity. Because of Israel's disobedience, these Bible twisting theorists have come to believe that all the promises that God made to Israel, now belong to the Christian church. These dominionists teach that the Christian church has *replaced* Israel.

They consider themselves to be "spiritual Israel." They believe that they and the entire Christian church collectively to be present-day Israel. Their teachings allegorize the literal truths of God's living holy Word, and confound it by saying Israel was cast off forever in 70 A.D. when Jerusalem was captured and the temple was destroyed. And from that point forward all references and prophecies of Scripture regarding Israel allude to what they believe to be spiritual Israel (the Christian church), not the true literal nation of Israel. Nothing could be further from the truth.

This kind of heretical thinking and teaching is dangerously treading on sacrilegious ground and infiltrating many Christian churches. Many of these professing evangelicals are blatantly aligned *against* Israel. This is a tragic-trend gaining momentum in the Christian "church" today. Those involved do not understand the Bible or are not true Christians, and have their own agendas contrary to the God of the Bible.

God's love for Israel has never changed. His blessing for Israel has never been removed. Israel has been under godly discipline, but the Lord has never turned His back on His chosen people. God has never, and will never discard, or abandon His covenant with Israel.

"For you are a holy people to the LORD your God; the LORD your God has chosen you to be a people for Himself, a special treasure above all the peoples on the face of the earth" (Deuteronomy 7:6).

"And yet for all that, when they be in the land of their enemies, I will not cast them [the Jews] *away*, neither will I abhor them, to destroy them utterly, and to break my covenant with them: for I *am* the LORD their God. But I will for their sakes remember the covenant of their ancestors, whom I brought forth out of the land of Egypt in the sight of the heathen, that I might be their God: I *am* the LORD" (Leviticus 26:44-45).

"If his children forsake my law, and walk not in my judgments; if they break my statutes, and keep not my commandments; then I will visit their transgression with the rod, and their iniquity with stripes. Nevertheless my lovingkindness will I not utterly take from him, nor suffer my faithfulness to fail.

My covenant will I not break, nor alter the thing that is gone out of my lips. Once I have sworn by my holiness that I will not lie unto David. His seed shall endure forever, and his throne as the sun before me. **It shall be established forever** as the moon, and *as* a faithful witness in heaven. Selah" (Psalm 89:30-37).

A thorough study of the entire chapter of Romans 11, *without spiritualizing* and allegorizing the nation of Israel and its people, will quickly dissolve the false notions purported by those who mistakenly believe themselves to be the remaining remnant of Israel. The following key Scriptures help unravel such false teachings.

To profess that God has cut-off Israel because of her past disobedience entirely misses the point of God's grace. How often does the Christian church fail today? The Lord put aside Israel for the purpose of evangelism *only*. God has not stopped working in Israel, with the Jews. But He has stopped using Israel in proclaiming the doctrine of Christ.

"I say then, has God cast away His people? Certainly not! For I also am an Israelite, of the seed of Abraham, of the tribe of Benjamin. God has not cast away His people whom He foreknew. I say then, have they [Israel] stumbled that they should fall? Certainly not! But through their fall, to provoke them to jealousy, salvation *has come* to the Gentiles" (Romans 11:1-2a, 11).

"For I do not desire, brethren, that you should be ignorant of this mystery, lest you should be wise in your own opinion, that blindness in part has happened to Israel until the fullness of the Gentiles has come in. And so all Israel will be saved, as it is written: 'The Deliverer will come out of Zion, and He will turn away ungodliness from Jacob; for this is My covenant with them; when I take away their sins'" (Romans 11:25-27).

The majority of the early Church fathers did not believe in Replacement Theology and taught that there would be a literal millennial kingdom; Clement of Rome, Barnabas, Hermas, Polycarp, Ignatius, Papias, Pothinus, Justin Martyr, Melito, Hegisippus, Tatian, Irenaeus, Tertullian, Hippolytus, Apollinaris, Cyprian, Commodian, Nepos, Coracion, Victorinus, Methodius and Lactantius. (Chafer, Lewis Sperry, *Systematic Theology*, Vol. 4, p. 271-274) At the Nicene Council, "318 bishops from all parts of the earth placed themselves on record" in believing in a literal millennial kingdom. (Ibid., p. 275)

The opposite is true of the Roman Catholic Church and it cannot be excluded from the long list of Replacement Theology advocates. The Roman Catholic Church amongst its many other corrupt false teachings considers itself to be "The New Israel." This is what a Catholic website titled *Catholic Bible 101* states; notice how they destroy and convolute what Jesus taught; recorded in the book of Matthew:

The Church = The New Israel. So to sum up, the Catholic Church is the Kingdom of God on earth, the new Israel (Jesus said in Matthew 21:43 that he was taking the Kingdom away from Israel, and giving it to a nation that will produce the fruits of it - namely, the Catholic Church), and is modeled after David's Kingdom, with a huge temple (the Vatican), a prime minister (our Pope), a sacred tabernacle containing the Ark of the Covenant (our tabernacle containing the Eucharist), officers who take care of the kingdom (our Cardinals and bishops), high priests (our priests), a Passover Meal (our Eucharist), and a Queen Mother (The Blessed Virgin Mary).

Official proponents of Replacement Theology include the Roman Catholic Church, the United Methodist Church, the Evangelical Lutheran Church of America (ECLA), the Presbyterian Church, the Lutheran Church (Missouri Synod), the Episcopal (and Anglican) Church, the Greek Orthodox Church, the United Church of Christ, the Mormons, the Jehovah's Witnesses, and Islam which also claims that it has "replaced" Israel as God's chosen people on earth.

Yes, the apostasy that Jesus forewarned in the Scriptures is well underway. The Roman Catholic Church is one of many false religions leading millions astray ushering them to the gates of hell. Professing Christians and any persons or groups that do not support Israel's right to exist in their God-given land—those who support *dividing* the Land of Israel are doing nothing less than fueling anti-Semitism. These biblically illiterate practitioners of the many false religious teachings would do well to repent as quickly as possible and spend serious time learning all the Scriptures that clearly give Israel God's blessing.

For the benefit of those who do not understand that Israel is God's chosen nation I will repeat God's warning cited in the early pages of this book; God blesses those who love Israel: "I will make you [Israel] a great nation; I will bless you and make your name great; and you shall be a blessing. I will bless those who bless you, and I will curse him who curses you; and in you all the families of the earth shall be blessed" (Genesis 12:2-3).

The early Christian church was totally comprised of Jewish believers. Salvation in Christ has come to us through the Jewish people (Israel). Through the Jews, mankind was given the Word of God. It is essential to study the Hebraic roots of Christianity to understand that without Israel, without the Jews, there would not be a Christian church. Matthew 1:18-25 and Luke 3:23-38 show that Jesus was brought up by Jewish parents who were both from the lineage of King David and from the tribe of Judah making Him a legitimate successor to the throne of King David; His reign will be *forever without end.*

> "He will be great, and will be called the Son of the Most High; and the Lord God will give Him the throne of His father David; and **He will reign over the house of Jacob forever; and His kingdom will have no end**" (Luke 1:32-33).

Jesus was born in Bethlehem, the town King David was from. In the Tanakh, the prophet Micah, prophesied that the Messiah would come from Bethlehem and be the future ruler (beginning in the Millennium).

> "But you, Bethlehem Ephrathah, *though* you are little among the thousands of Judah, y*et* out of you shall come forth to Me the One to be Ruler in Israel, whose goings forth *are* from of old, from everlasting" (Micah 5:2).

Jesus was born during the time frame when the prophet Daniel said the Messiah must be present and be killed (cut off). He described a time when the Anointed One—the Messiah would be killed as a ransom for many. The atoning death of Jesus was a prerequisite to bring future, lasting peace to the world. We are still waiting for that peace to come. It is a future event that will begin when Jesus returns. Messiah rose from the dead and is destined to return, to take the throne of David to rule and reign.

"And He [Jesus] began to teach them that the Son of Man [Jesus] must suffer many things, and be rejected by the elders and chief priests and scribes, and must be killed, and after three days rise again" (Mark 8:31).

Isaiah the prophet recorded that Messiah would suffer and die to atone for the sins of His people, the nation of Israel—spoken of in Isaiah 53. This had to happen before the Messiah could return and bring true peace to the world. If Messiah was destined to die, and if *peace* is still a future prophecy yet to be fulfilled, then Jesus—the Messiah of Israel—had to come back from the dead, just as we are told in Scripture: "after three days rise again."

Jesus' eternal fate is to take the throne of David, to rule and reign over this earth bringing in true, everlasting peace—fulfilling prophecy. There is an undeniable connection between the promises of David and Abraham, the land of Israel, and the role of Jesus Christ in the promised future redemption of the world. The prophets of the Bible are consistent in their support for this view.

God's Love for Israel Is Forever

We are to love Israel as God does. We must stand with Israel and support her as the entire world rages against her. When we support Israel we are in right standing with the Lord.

> "From the standpoint of the gospel they are enemies for your sake, but from the standpoint of God's choice, they are beloved for the sake of the fathers; for the gifts and the calling of God are irrevocable. For just as you once were disobedient to God, but now have been shown mercy because of their disobedience, so these also now have been disobedient, in order that because of the mercy shown to you they also may now be shown mercy. For God has shut up all disobedience that He might show mercy to all" (Romans 11 28-32).

> "Because your God has loved Israel, to establish them forever, therefore He made you king over them, to do justice and righteousness."
> —Queen Sheba's statement to Solomon
> (2 Chronicles 9:8b)

Chapter Two

A Brief History of Israel
From Abraham to 1948

Ezekiel 16 gives us a heartwarming illustration of God finding Israel as a little baby girl—still in her birthing fluids—unwashed and her umbilical cord not cut. God takes her in, treats her as a royal princess and ultimately takes her as His wife.

Israel's Rebellion

But Israel ungratefully acts like an unbridled harlot. God gives her a special dowry but she uses it to bring forth idols.

Ezekiel 16:16-22

"'You took some of your garments and adorned multicolored high places for yourself, and played the harlot on them. *Such* things should not happen, nor be.

You have also taken your beautiful jewelry from My gold and My silver, which I had given you, and made for yourself male images and played the harlot with them.

You took your embroidered garments and covered them, and you set My oil and My incense before them.

Also My food which I gave you—the pastry of fine flour, oil, and honey *which* I fed you—you set it before them as sweet incense; and *so* it was,' says the Lord GOD.

'Moreover you took your sons and your daughters, whom you bore to Me, and these you sacrificed to them to be devoured.

Were your *acts* of harlotry a small matter, that you have slain My children and offered them up to them by causing them to pass through *the fire?*

And in all your abominations and acts of harlotry you did not remember the days of your youth, when you were naked and bare, struggling in your blood.'"

God also gives Israel the picturesque Mediterranean coast seafront area, which she gives to other countries to be her lovers (metaphorically speaking).

"Behold, therefore, I stretched out My hand against you, diminished your allotment, and gave you up to the will of those who hate you, the daughters of the Philistines, who were ashamed of your lewd behavior.

You also played the harlot with the Assyrians, because you were insatiable; indeed you played the harlot with them and still were not satisfied. Moreover you multiplied your acts of harlotry as far as the land of the trader, Chaldea; and even then you were not satisfied" (Ezekiel 16:27-29).

Israel's Idolatry Cut-Off

Zechariah 13:1-7

"In that day a fountain shall be opened for the house of David and for the inhabitants of Jerusalem, for sin and for uncleanness.

It shall be in that day, says the LORD of hosts, *That* I will cut off the names of the idols from the land, and they shall no longer be remembered. I will also cause the prophets and the unclean spirit to depart from the land.

It shall come to pass *that* if anyone still prophesies, then his father and mother who begot him will say to him, 'You shall not live, because you have spoken lies in the name of the LORD.' And his father and mother who begot him shall thrust him through when he prophesies.

And it shall be in that day *that* every prophet will be ashamed of his vision when he prophesies; they will not wear a robe of coarse hair to deceive. But he will say, 'I *am* no prophet, I *am* a farmer; for a man taught me to keep cattle from my youth.' And *one* will say to him, 'What are these wounds between your arms?' Then he will answer, '*Those* with which I was wounded in the house of my friends.'"

God Ultimately Sees Israel as Worse than Sodom

"'As I live,' says the Lord God, 'Neither your sister Sodom nor her daughters have done as you and your daughters have done. Look, this was the iniquity of your sister Sodom: She and her daughter had pride, fullness of food, and abundance of idleness; neither did she strengthen the hand of the poor and needy. And they were haughty and committed abomination before Me; therefore I took them away as I saw fit.

Samaria did not commit half of your sins; but you have multiplied your abominations more than they, and have justified your sisters by all the abominations which you have done You who judged your sisters, bear your own shame also, because the sins which you committed were more abominable than theirs; they are more righteous than you. Yes, be disgraced also, and bear your own shame, because you justified your sisters'" (Ezekiel 16:48-52).

God Warns of His Judgments

"'And I will judge you as women who break wedlock or shed blood are judged; I will bring blood upon you in fury and jealousy. I will also give you into their hand, and they shall throw down your shrines and break down your high places. They shall also strip you of your clothes, take your beautiful jewelry, and leave you naked and bare.

They shall also bring up an assembly against you, and they shall stone you with stones and thrust you through with their swords. They shall burn your houses with fire, and execute judgments on you in the sight of many women; and I will make you cease playing the harlot, and you shall no longer hire lovers.

So I will lay to rest My fury toward you, and My jealousy shall depart from you. I will be quiet, and be angry no more. Because you did not remember the days of your youth, but agitated Me with all these *things,* surely I will also recompense your deeds on *your own* head,' says the Lord GOD. 'And you shall not commit lewdness in addition to all your abominations'" (Ezekiel 16:38-43).

God Is Finally So Frustrated with Israel That He Gives Her a "Bill of Divorcement"

"Then I saw that for all the causes for which backsliding Israel had committed adultery, I had put her away and given her a certificate of

26

divorce; yet her treacherous sister Judah did not fear, but went and played the harlot also" (Jeremiah 3:8).

But in Isaiah God takes back Israel as His wife through the promised prophesied Messiah. In the Old Testament Israel is the "wife of Jehovah." In the New Testament, the Church is the "bride of Christ."

The Servant—Israel's Hope

"Thus says the LORD: 'Where *is* the certificate of your mother's divorce, whom I have put away? Or which of My creditors *is it* to whom I have sold you? For your iniquities you have sold yourselves, and for your transgressions your mother has been put away'" (Isaiah 50:1).

"The Lord GOD has given Me the tongue of the learned, that I should know how to speak a word in season to *him who is* weary. He awakens Me morning by morning, He awakens My ear to hear as the learned.

The Lord GOD has opened My ear; and I was not rebellious, nor did I turn away. I gave My back to those who struck *Me,* and My cheeks to those who plucked out the beard; I did not hide My face from shame and spitting.

For the Lord GOD will help Me; therefore I will not be disgraced; therefore I have set My face like a flint, and I know that I will not be ashamed" (Isaiah 50:4-7).

God Judicially Blinds Israel

Because of all we have learned about Israel's wickedness, God judicially blinds her:

27

"What then? Israel has not obtained what it seeks; but the elect have obtained it, and the rest were blinded. Just as it is written: God has given them a spirit of stupor, eyes that they should not see and ears that they should not hear, to this very day" (Romans 11:7-8).

"Yet the LORD has not given you a heart to perceive and eyes to see and ears to hear, to this *very* day" (Deuteronomy 29:4).

"For the LORD has poured out on you the spirit of deep sleep, and has closed your eyes, namely, the prophets; and He has covered your heads, *namely,* the seers" (Isaiah 29:10).

Why Does God Call Israel His Chosen People?

Considering all the blatant rebellion and wickedness shown by Israel why are they called God's chosen people? Because: God *chose them*, it was His desire and His call. In the book of Deuteronomy God gave Israel a warning about disobedience:

"So it shall be, when the LORD your God brings you into the land of which He swore to your fathers, to Abraham, Isaac, and Jacob, to give you large and beautiful cities which you did not build, houses full of all good things, which you did not fill, hewn-out wells which you did not dig, vineyards and olive trees which you did not plant—when you have eaten and are full—*then* beware, lest you forget the LORD who brought you out of the land of Egypt, from the house of bondage.

You shall fear the LORD your God and serve Him, and shall take oaths in His name. You shall not go after other gods, the gods of the peoples who *are* all around you (for the LORD your God *is* a jealous God among you), lest the anger of the LORD your God be aroused against you and destroy you from the face of the earth" (Deuteronomy 6:10-15).

It is important to remember Ezekiel 16:18:

"'When I passed by you again and looked upon you, indeed your time *was* the time of love; so I spread My wing over you and covered your nakedness. **Yes, I swore an oath to you and entered into a covenant with you, and you became Mine,' says the Lord GOD."**

Israel was chosen to set forth God's praise (Isaiah 43:20-21; 44:12) but because she rejected God's "call" and "choosing" He let the events of 70 A.D. come upon her. Israel was once the greatest nation on earth in the days of David and Solomon. Jesus prophesied the events of 70 A.D. in Matthew 22 in the parable of the Wedding Feast:

Matthew 22:1-7

"And Jesus answered and spoke to them again by parables and said: 'The kingdom of heaven is like a certain king who arranged a marriage for his son, and sent out his servants to call those who were invited to the wedding; and they were not willing to come.'

Again, he sent out other servants, saying, 'Tell those who are invited, See, I have prepared my dinner; my oxen and fatted cattle *are* killed, and all things *are* ready. Come to the wedding.'

But they made light of it and went their ways, one to his own farm, another to his business. And the rest seized his servants, treated *them* spitefully, and killed *them*.

But when the king heard *about it,* he was furious. And he sent out his armies, destroyed those murderers, and burned up their city."

Then Israel is put aside during the Christian Dispensation. Following the Rapture and during the Tribulation, Israel will come back in God's plan as highlighted by the prophesied 144,000 Jewish witnesses of Revelation 7—who will take the gospel all throughout the world. In Ezekiel 37, the Valley of Dry Bones from 70 A.D., Israel is pictured as bones scattered and Israel in graves.

"Can these bones live?" Ezekiel prophesies that the bones come together. World War I, with the Balfour Declaration prepared the land for the Jew. World War II, when Hitler killed half the Jews in the world also prepared the Jew for the land. Israel then became a nation again on May 14, 1948 with "an exceedingly great army" (Ezekiel 37:10).

> "Therefore say to the house of Israel, Thus says the Lord GOD: 'I do not do *this* for your sake, O house of Israel, but for My holy name's sake, which you have profaned among the nations wherever you went'" (Ezekiel 36:22).

Israel's Future Redemption

> "For I do not desire, brethren, that you should be ignorant of this mystery, lest you should be wise in your own opinion, that blindness in part has happened to Israel until the fullness of the Gentiles has come in. And so all Israel will be saved, as it is written:

> 'The Deliverer will come out of Zion, And He will turn away ungodliness from Jacob; for this *is* My covenant with them, when I take away their sins'" (Romans 11:26-27).

> "For the gifts and the calling of God are irrevocable" (Romans 11:29).

Israel's Faithful Messiah

From God's Covenant with David

1 Chronicles 17:22-24

"And who *is* like Your people Israel, the one nation on the earth whom God went to redeem for Himself *as* a people—to make for Yourself a name by great and awesome deeds, by driving out nations from before Your people whom You redeemed from Egypt?

For You have made Your people Israel Your very own people forever; and You, LORD, have become their God.

And now, O LORD, the word which You have spoken concerning Your servant and concerning his house, *let it* be established forever, and do as You have said.

So let it be established, that Your name may be magnified forever, saying, 'The LORD of hosts, the God of Israel, *is* Israel's God.' And let the house of Your servant David be established before You."

Jeremiah 24:6-8

"For I will set My eyes on them for good, and will bring them back to this land; I will build them and not pull *them* down, and I will plant them and not pluck *them* up.

Then I will give them a heart to know Me, that I *am* the LORD; and they shall be My people, and I will be their God, for they shall return to Me with their whole heart."

Israel Is Reborn

God's Promise to "This Generation"

Recognition of modern-day Israel in 1948 began the prophetic countdown to Armageddon and the final years of history, as we know them. The rebirth of Israel is a major fulfilled prophetic sign showing that we are living very close to Christ's promised return.

> "Now learn the parable of the fig tree [Israel]: when its branch has already become tender, and puts forth its leaves, you know that summer is near; even so you too, when you see all these things, recognize that He is near, right at the door. Truly I say to you, this generation will not pass away until all these things take place" (Matthew 24:32-34).

Jesus said: "This generation will not pass away until all these things take place." *This generation* is in reference to those who will witness the things Jesus described relating to the end of the age in Matthew 24, including the restoration of the nation of Israel in *one* day (May 14, 1948).

An Awesome Fulfillment of Prophecy

> "Before she travailed, she brought forth; before her pain came, she gave birth to a boy. Who has heard of such a thing? Who has seen such things? Can a land be born in one day? Can a nation be brought forth all at once?" (Isaiah 66:7-8a)

The previous Scripture shows that the prophet Isaiah foretold the rebirth of Israel, which came about in one day (on May 14, 1948). We are living in the generation pictured by the Jewish boy in Isaiah 66:7-8a. The Jewish boy portrays how Israel will grow-up as a nation, and by the time he is eighty (2028), the Millennium could very well begin. I think this is a possibility but no one can say for sure. This is not a prediction.

If we use Psalm 90 as a lifespan gauge (70-80 years), the Scripture is not exactly precise on where within or around those lifespan years that the Rapture/Tribulation could take place. And we cannot say decisively if Psalm 90 is even to be used in relation to the Rapture and Second Coming. The Lord's return may happen sooner or even some time well past the eighty-year mark. None of us know. Although, if we watch for the foreshadowing signs we can have a general idea when critical prophetic events will come to fulfillment. The important thing is to stay vigilant and share the gospel at every opportunity while there is still time.

Matthew 24:32-34 is in relation to when Jesus said: "This generation will not pass away until all these things take place." *This generation* is in reference to those who will witness the things Jesus described relating to the end of the age in Matthew 24, including the restoration of the nation of Israel in *one* day (May 14, 1948).

In 1917, the Balfour Declaration was created. The purpose of this mandate was to confirm support from the British government for the establishment of a Homeland for the Jewish people. The Balfour Declaration (dated November 2, 1917) was a letter from the United Kingdom's Foreign Secretary Arthur James Balfour to Baron Rothschild (Walter Rothschild, 2nd Baron Rothschild), a leader of the British Jewish community, for transmission to the Zionist Federation of Great Britain and Ireland.

His Majesty's government view with favour the establishment in Palestine of a national home for the Jewish people, and will use their best endeavours to facilitate the achievement of this object, it being clearly understood that nothing shall be done which may prejudice the civil and religious rights of existing non-Jewish communities in

Palestine, or the rights and political status enjoyed by Jews in any other country.

The text of the letter was published in the press one week later, on November 9, 1917. The "Balfour Declaration" was later incorporated into the Sèvres peace treaty with the Ottoman Empire and the Mandate for Palestine. The original document is kept at the British Library.

One major reason the Balfour Declaration came to be is due to England's Prime Minister David Lloyd George's extreme gratitude to a young man who ultimately helped change the course of World War I. England was having a rough time, and a brilliant young Jewish scientist, Dr. Chaim Weitzmann, was commissioned by the prime minister to assist the Brits by developing acetone in very large quantities to be used in making cordite, a smokeless gun powder. Acetone is required for the production of cordite, a powerful propellant explosive needed to fire ammunition without generating tell-tale smoke. Germany had cornered supplies of calcium acetate, a major source of acetone.

Other pre-war processes in Britain were inadequate to meet the increased demand in World War I, and a shortage of cordite would have severely hampered Britain's war effort. Lloyd George, then minister for munitions, was grateful to Weizmann and so supported his Zionist aspirations. In his *War Memoirs*, Lloyd-George wrote of meeting Weizmann in 1916 that Weizmann:

> ...explained his aspirations as to the repatriation of the Jews to the sacred land they had made famous. That was the fount and origin of the famous declaration about the National Home for the Jews in Palestine...As soon as I became Prime Minister I talked the whole matter over with Mr. Balfour, who was then Foreign Secretary.

This may, however, have been only a part of a longer series of discussions about Britain and Zionism held between Weizmann and Balfour which had begun at least a decade earlier. In late 1905 Balfour had requested of Charles Dreyfus, his Jewish constituency representative, that he arrange a meeting with Weizmann, during which Weizmann asked for official British support for Zionism; they were to meet again on this issue in 1914. Dr. Weitzman found a way to synthesize acetone at extremely low production costs. The prime minister was so grateful he offered anything at all as payment to the young scientist. Weitzman asked nothing for himself but he did express his great desire for his fellow Jews to have a Homeland. This action fits right into Ezekiel's prophecy:

> "Then He said to me, 'Son of man, these bones are the whole house of Israel. They indeed say, 'Our bones are dry, our hope is lost, and we ourselves are cut off!' Therefore prophesy and say to them, 'Thus says the Lord God: 'Behold, O My people, I will open your graves and cause you to come up from your graves, and bring you into the land of Israel.
>
> Then you shall know that I *am* the LORD, when I have opened your graves, O My people, and brought you up from your graves. I will put My Spirit in you, and you shall live, and I will place you in your own land. Then you shall know that I, the LORD, have spoken *it* and performed *it*,' says the LORD" (Ezekiel 37:11-14).

On May 14, 1948, the Jewish people proclaimed the independence of Israel and the end of their worldwide captivity as prophesied by the prophet Ezekiel. On this very day a united Israel took its place as a sovereign, independent state among the nations. Prophecies in the Bible are found in a number of passages pointing to the rebirth of the nation of Israel but the main one is in Ezekiel 37. God told Ezekiel that the nation of Israel would be scattered among the nations, but brought back by Him to the Land of Israel (Ezekiel chapters 12-14).

Immediately in the next two chapters of Ezekiel, the prophecy for the battle of Ezekiel 38 and 39 (Gog-Magog war) is given.

The people of Gog and Magog, led by the leader, Rosh, will attack Israel with a co-alition of nations – Persia (Iran), Ethiopia, Put, Gomer, Beth-togarmah and many other peoples (38:1-6). See Appendix A for more on the participating nations.

This coalition of nations will be destroyed by God Almighty Himself. He will stop them by launching His spectacular divine intervention upon these enemies of Israel. (Ezekiel 38:22). The defeat of this coalition will be so unbelievable that the nation of Israel will get a serious wake-up call that God is alive, and many will come to understand that YAHWEH is their God (Ezekiel 38:23; 39:7, 22, 28). The defeat of the coalition of nations that vastly outnumbers Israel also causes the people of the world to see that their destruction was a divine act.

The Arabs Revolt Against Jewish Immigration To Palestine (Israel)

Around the start of the 20th century Jews began to immigrate to Israel, which was called Palestine. They lived in peace with the so-called Palestinians and the neighboring Arabs until 1936 when the Arabs revolted against British control of the land. They revolted because the British refused to stop Jewish immigration. During that revolt thousands of Palestinians died while a few hundred Jews were killed.

According to official British figures, the army and police killed more than 2,000 Arabs in combat and they hung 108[1] and 961 died because of gang and terrorist activities.[2] In an analysis of the British statistics, Palestinian historian, Walid Khalidi, disputes those figures claiming 19,792 total casualties for the Arabs – 5,032 dead (3,832 killed by the British and 1,200 dead because of terrorism) and 14,760 wounded.[2] Over ten percent of the adult male Palestinian Arab population between 20 and 60 were killed, wounded, imprisoned or exiled.[3] Estimates of the number of Palestinian Jews killed are estimated to be several hundred.[4]

The Haganah was founded in 1920 in response to the Arab riots of that year. The Irgun was founded in 1931 and its acts of violence against the British and Palestinians magnified the struggle for the Holy Land. When the revolt was put down in 1939 there was no peace. The Haganah and Irgun were joined by the *Lohamei Herut Israel – Lehi* (Fighters for the Freedom of Israel) in 1940. It was commonly referred to in English as the Stern Gang. The continued conflict in the Holy Land continued until the War of 1948 broke out when the Arab nations attacked the newly created nation of Israel.

Egypt gained partial independence in 1922, but Britain continued to exert a strong influence on the country until Anglo-Egyptian Treaty of 1936, which limited Britain presence to a garrison of troops on the Suez Canal. The British were finally forced out in 1945. Lebanon became an independent state in 1943, but French troops did not withdraw until 1946 the same year that Syria won its independence from France. Transjordan, under Abdullah I, gained independence from Britain in 1946 and was called Jordan in 1949. It still remained under strong British influence.

In 1945 the British enticed Egypt, Iraq, Lebanon, Saudi Arabia, Syria, Transjordan, and Yemen to form the Arab League to coordinate policy between the Arab states. Iraq and Transjordan coordinated policies closely, signing a mutual defense treaty. Egypt, Syria, and Saudi Arabia feared that Transjordan would annex Palestine and use it as a steppingstone to attack or undermine Syria, Lebanon, and the Hijaz, a strip of land in the western section of Saudi Arabia where Medina and Mecca are located.[5]

On November 29, 1947, the United Nations General Assembly adopted Resolution 181 recommending the adoption and implementation of a plan to partition Palestine into two states, one Arab and one Jewish. It also partitioned Jerusalem.

Israel included the fertile eastern Galilee and coastal plain, where most of the Jewish population lived, as well as most of the Negev desert, which was more than half of the total area. The Arab state was to have the central Galilee, the mountains area later known as the West Bank, part of the southern coastal area, extending into the Negev, where 5% of their population lived.

The Jews, who made up 33% of the population and owned about 7% of the land, were to get 55% of the land while the Arabs (66% of the population), who owned about 47% of the land, would be allotted 43% of the land. The population of Israel would consist of 498,000 Jews and about 409,000 Arabs. The Arab state would consist of 735,000 Arabs with just 10,000 Jews.[6]

The Jewish leadership accepted the partition plan as "the indispensable minimum." Menachem Begin, the leader of the Irgun, rejected the portioning of the land. He believed nothing was more sacred than the integrity of the whole territory of "Eretz Israel."[7] The Arab leadership also rejected the portioning opening the door for war.

Between November 30, 1947 and April 7, 1948, fighting broke out between the Arabs and the Jewish freedom fighters led by the Irgun, Stern Gang and Haganah. During this time 959 Arab civilians died with 1,941 being wounded. Jewish civilian deaths were 840 with 1,785 wounded.[7]

Abd al-Qadir al-Husayni led the Army of the Holy War from Egypt with several hundred men. He recruited a few thousand volunteers and organized the blockade of the 100,000 Jewish residents of Jerusalem.[8] The Israelis tried to supply the city with convoys of up to one hundred armored vehicles, but it failed. By March almost all of Haganah's armored vehicles had been destroyed, the blockade was working and hundreds of Haganah members who had tried to bring supplies into the city had been killed. The Jews in Jerusalem were on the verge of starvation. The situation for those who dwelt in the Jewish settlements in the highly isolated Negev and North of Galilee was even more critical.

The Israelis held their ground in the face of defeat at all costs.[9] Many Arabs panicked and up to 100,000 fled from Haifa, Jaffa and Jerusalem. By the end of March, 2,000 had been killed and 4,000 injured.[10]

The fighting prompted the United States to withdraw their support for the Partition plan, which encouraged the Arab League to believe they could put an end to the plan for partition. The British sided with the Arabs and on February 7, 1948, supported the annexation of the Arab part of Palestine by Transjordan.

David Ben-Gurion reorganized Haganah and made conscription obligatory. Every Jewish man and woman in the country had to receive military training. With the funds that Golda Meir raised from sympathizers in America and Joseph Stalin's decision to support the Zionist cause, Jewish representatives were able to sign armament contracts with Czechoslovakia, which also sold arms to Syria.

Other Haganah agents scrounged stockpiles of weapons from abroad left over from the Second World War. The first shipment of significant numbers of light arms and ammunition arrived in Tel Aviv in early April of 1948. Ben-Gurion ordered Yigael Yadin to plan a defense of the birthing nation from the imminent attack by the surrounding Arab states. He developed Plan Dalet, which was immediately put in place. The adoption of Plan Dalet marked the second stage of the civil war, in which Haganah switched from a defensive mode to an offensive one.

The first stage of Plan D was to end the blockade of Jerusalem.[11] During the early stage of the new offensive Abd al-Qadir al-Husayni was killed in combat. Irregular troops from Irgun and Stern Gang attacked Arab villages resulting in the deaths of hundreds of Arabs.[12-13] The death of nearly all the residents of the small village of Deir Yassin, which was harshly criticized by the principal Jewish authorities, had a devastating impact on the morale of the Arabs contributing to the exodus of much of the Arab population. The first large-scale operation by the Arab Liberation Army ended in a "debacle" with total defeat at Mishmar HaEmek,[14] followed with the loss of their Druze allies through defection. [15]

By late April, the U.S. State Department, concerned to avoid a foreseeable conflagration after the British withdrawal, proposed a truce. The State Department convinced the Arab states that wished to avoid war to accept informally proposals by Ben-Gurion that they had previously rejected, including a Jewish immigration rate of 48,000 each year. They promised the Jews assistance if the Arab nations were to invade subsequent to the truce. Aware that arm shipments from both Czechoslovakia and France were flowing in, and that local Palestinian forces were demoralized, the Jewish authorities turned down the proposal.[16] Several Arab leaders, including King Ibn Sagud and Azzam Pasha, secretly requested the British to remain on for another year in order to avert catastrophe.[17]

The Haganah, Palmach and Irgun continued their campaign of securing the boundaries of Israel taking the cities of Tiberias, Haifa, Safed, Beisan, Jaffa and Acre resulting in the flight of 250,000 more Arabs.[18]

The British had withdrawn most of their troops. The situation pushed the leaders of the neighboring Arab states to intervene, but their preparation was not finalized, and they did not assemble sufficient forces to turn the tide of the war. The majority of Palestinian Arab hopes lay with the Arab Legion of Transjordan's monarch, King Abdullah I, but he had no intention of creating a Palestinian Arab-run state, since he hoped to annex as much of the territory of the British Mandate for Palestine as he could. He was playing a double game, being in contact with the Jewish authorities as with the Arab League.

In preparation for the Arab states invasion, Haganah successfully launched Operations Yiftah[19] and Ben-'Ami[20] to secure the Jewish settlements of Galilee, and Operation Kilshon, which created a united front around Jerusalem. The inconclusive meeting between Golda Meir and Abdullah I, followed by the Kfar Etzion massacre on May 13, by the Arab Legion, led to predictions that the battle for Jerusalem would be merciless.

On May 14, 1948, David Ben-Gurion, the Executive Head of the World Zionist Organization and president of the Jewish Agency for Palestine, declared, "The establishment of a Jewish State in Eretz Israel, to be known as the State of Israel." The war entered its second phase with the intervention of the Arab state armies. The first Israeli-Arab War was fought from May 15, 1948 to March 10, 1949.

The Arab/Muslim nations that attacked Israel were: Egypt, Syria, Jordan, Iraq and Lebanon. These four and one-half nations were defeated by the civilian forces of Israel – Haganah, Palmach, Irgun and Lehi (Stern Gang). Once the conflict became an official war on May 15, 1948, the Jewish paramilitary forces became the Israeli Defense Forces.

Israel retained all of the land given to her by the United Nations partition and she took control of almost sixty percent of the area allocated to the proposed Arab state, including the West Bank.[21] Transjordan took control of the remainder of the West Bank and East-Jerusalem, and Egypt took control of the Gaza Strip. No Arab Palestinian state was created.

During the war about 700,000 Palestinians fled or were expelled from the area that became Israel and they became Palestinian refugees. The war and the reestablishment of the nation of Israel also triggered the Jewish exodus from Arab lands. In the three years following the war, about 700,000 Jews immigrated to Israel.

This war was followed by three more, leaving Israel with the West Bank, the Golan Heights and the Gaza Strip. In 2007 Israel gave the Gaza Strip to Hamas. This was a fulfillment of the Zephaniah 2:4 prophecy:

"For Gaza shall be forsaken, and Ashkelon desolate; they shall drive out Ashdod at noonday. And Ekron shall be uprooted."

The rebirth of Israel is a major fulfilled prophetic sign showing that we are living very close to Christ's promised return. Does it make a bit of sense that this tiny nation is continuously being badgered by the much larger countries surrounding her? Trying to force Israel to surrender pieces of land in order to appease her enemies for an unattainable "peace" is essentially picking a fight with God.

What other nation on earth is hounded like this? Israel is the center of spiritual warfare because it is God's Holy Land. He has entrusted it to the Jewish people. It is not up for sale (or theft). It is God who ultimately holds the title deed. Jesus Christ took on a Jewish identity when He came to die for all of humanity, to be the sacrificial "Lamb" for all our sins. Israel was His earthly home, and it is still "the apple of His eye."

"For thus says the LORD of hosts; He sent Me after glory, to the nations which plunder you; for he who touches you touches the apple of His eye" (Zechariah 2:8).

"For you are a holy people to the Lord your God; the Lord your God has chosen you to be a people for Himself, a special treasure above all the peoples on the face of the earth" (Deuteronomy 7:6).

If you reread the previous Scripture, notice: "In you [Israel] all the families of the earth shall be blessed." In other words, the blessings for all nations and people, "the families of the earth," are contingent on how Israel is treated. This includes, of course, the United States. Never before has Israel—the only democracy in the Middle East—received as much pressure and derogatory interference from the "Washington elite" as she did under the previous Obama Administration. No one has the right to tell the people of Israel to give up land, stop building homes, or stop breathing air in their God-given land.

It is foolhardy to conspire against Israel. Israeli Prime Minister, Benjamin Netanyahu made the following statements in his speech before members of the American Israel Public Affairs Committee (AIPAC) on March 23, 2010 in Washington D.C.:

The connection between the Jewish people and the Land of Israel cannot be denied. The connection between the Jewish people and Jerusalem cannot be denied. The Jewish people were building Jerusalem three thousand years ago, and the Jewish people are building Jerusalem today. Jerusalem is not a settlement. It is our capital!

The Western nations seem to be utterly blind to the life-and-death cultural differences between Islamic nations and the West. In his book, *Planet Earth—2000 A.D: Will Mankind Survive*, Hal Lindsey discusses a principle called "takiya":

[Takiya is] the right within Islam to fake peace when you're weak, so you can wait for better timing to conquer your enemy. There is a famous Arab saying: "When your enemy is strong, kiss his hand and pray that it will be broken one day." Hudayblya is a small oasis between Mecca and Medina where Muhammad fought a battle in the early years of Islam.

When he saw he was losing the struggle, Muhammad signed a ten-year peace agreement with the people of Mecca. Two years later, when his forces were stronger and the Meccans were living securely and off their guard, Muhammad marched into the city and captured it (pp. 256-257, reference is made to Isaac Cohen: Chicago Tribune, September 23, 1993).

Moreover there is yet another Muslim technique called: Tawriya ("Creative Lying") advocated by Muslims. A doctrine that allows lying in just about any circumstance:

The authoritative *Hans Wehr Arabic-English Dictionary* defines *tawriya as,* "hiding, concealment; dissemblance, dissimulation, hypocrisy; equivocation, ambiguity, double-entendre, allusion." Conjugates of the trilateral root of the word, *w-r-y,* appear in the Quran in the context of hiding or concealing something (e.g., 5:31, 7:26). As Sheikh al-Munajid puts it: "Tawriya is permissible if it is necessary or serves a Sharia interest."

Consider the countless "sharia interests" that can run directly counter to Western law and civilization -- from empowering Islam, to subjugating infidels. To realize these Sharia interests, Muslims, through tawriya, are given a blank check to lie, which undoubtedly comes in handy—whether at high-level diplomatic meetings or the signing of peace-treaties.

Land for Peace?

Previous American administrations, especially the former Obama Administration have strongly suggested sovereign Israel should forsake her land with the naïve notion that the result would be "peace." The "peace process" cannot succeed because it is based on an unreasonable and totally fraudulent proposal, incomprehensively suggesting that by giving away land, there will be an assurance of peace. In 2005, Israel relinquished Gaza to the Palestinians. Soon after, the terrorist group, Hamas was actually voted in by the same Palestinians who reside there. So they can blame no one but themselves for their continued demise.

It has been nothing but hell for the Palestinians who live there, and the Israelis have been constantly under attack from the terrorists in that region ever since. Where is the peace? And now Israel is required to hand over more land because some foreign political thugs say so? The Palestinians have Gaza, and Israel surrendered it for nothing but misery and heartache. But I can tell you this tragic situation, was specifically prophesied long ago by the Old Testament prophet, Zephaniah as cited earlier:

> "For Gaza shall be forsaken, and Ashkelon desolate; they shall drive out Ashdod at noonday. And Ekron shall be uprooted" (Zephaniah 2:4).

According to God's Word, trying to force Israel to give up land is definitely bad "policy." Much documentation has been recorded regarding bazaar weather patterns whenever U.S. officials have tried to force Israel to surrender some of her land. In recent years California experienced a drought like never before, which is no coincidence considering God controls the weather (Psalm 135:7; 148:8), and this went on during the time former U.S. Secretary of State John Kerry made at least a dozen trips to Israel during his tenure trying to force her to divide her God-given land.

"For the day of the LORD upon all the nations *is* near; As you have done, it shall be done to you; your reprisal shall return upon your own head" (Obadiah 1:15).

Israel has said it is more like "Land for blood" than "Land for peace." For example, the myth has grown over the years that the West Bank was once part of a country called Palestine and Israel stole it. (The Israelis regained the West bank in 1967 Six-Day War, fair and square.) In response to the kidnapping and killing of three Jewish teens from the West Bank by Hamas militants in June of 2014, a couple of months later Israel announced her intention to build around Gush Etzion in the West Bank near Bethlehem. The West Bank is also known as the historical heartland of the Jewish people known as Judea and Samaria. The world press went crazy accusing Israel of building on "occupied territory" and stolen land.

Anytime Israel tries to build on her own land she is threatened and accused of using stolen land by heavily funded Palestinian media sources, and a hostile, ignorant world that continues to fuel the "Palestinian land" myth. Israel has come under intense international criticism and is vilified over its building activities, which most countries insanely regard as illegal under international law, and consider to be a major obstacle to the creation of a viable "Palestinian state" in any future "peace" deal.

Former U.S. President Barack Hussein Obama has been at odds with Prime Minister Netanyahu over building on Israeli land ever since taking office in 2009, and he always pushed back against the Israelis right to build on their own land. It was an ongoing point of contention between him and Israel. Israel has had no shortage of enemies, whom I must say, without a doubt—will reap God's wrath as they continue to work to divide God's Holy Land—the Land of Israel.

God's Command: Israel Undivided

"And the LORD spoke to Moses on Mount Sinai saying, 'Speak to the children of Israel, and say to them: When you come into the land which I gave you, then the land shall keep a Sabbath to the LORD.

The land shall not be sold permanently, for the land is Mine; for you are strangers and Sojourners with Me.

And I will enter into judgment with them there on account of My people, My heritage Israel, whom they have scattered among the nations; they have also divided up My land.'"

—Leviticus 25:1, 23; Joel 3:2b

✡✡✡✡✡

Chapter Three

The Significance of the Six-Day War

On June 7, 1967, IDF paratroopers advanced through the Old City toward the Temple Mount and the Western Wall, bringing Jerusalem's holiest site under Jewish control for the first time in 2000 years, truly a significant and monumental feat. Glory to God!

The Six-Day War (היממ ששת הימים מלחמת, *Milhemet Sheshet Ha Yamim*), was the third Arab-Israeli War. It was fought between June 5 and 10, 1967, by Israel and the neighboring states of Egypt, Jordan, and Syria. A period of high tension had preceded the war. In response to sabotage acts aimed at Israeli targets,[1-3] Israel launched a raid into the Jordanian-controlled West Bank.[4-5] She also sent sorties into Syrian airspace engaging Syrian fighters.[6] Syria responded with artillery attacks against Israeli civilian settlements in the border area which was countered by Israeli assaults against Syrian positions in the Golan Heights.[7]

Egypt entered the conflict by blocking the Straits of Tiran.[8] deploying its troops near Israel's border and ordering the evacuation of the U.N. force from the Sinai Peninsula.[9-10] Within six days, Israel had won a decisive land war. Israeli forces had taken control of the Gaza Strip and the Sinai Peninsula from Egypt, the West Bank and East Jerusalem from Jordan, and the Golan Heights from Syria.

Jordan

In response to Palestine Liberation Organization (PLO) guerrilla activity,[11-12] including a mine attack that killed three Israeli soldiers,[13] the Israeli Defense Force (IDF) attacked the village of as-Samu in the Jordanian-occupied West Bank.[14] The casualties were 18 killed, 130 wounded, 125 houses destroyed along with the school and the clinic.[15] The retaliation by Israel brought swift condemnation by the United Nation Security Council which declared that military reprisals would not be tolerated.[16]

The Samu raid shattered the fragile trust between Israel and Jordan,[17] causing the Jordanian leadership to believe Israel's strategic goal was to occupy the West Bank. Some believe this fear is what prompted King Hussein to sign a joint defense pact with Egypt[7] while others believe Hussein signed the pact to placate domestic pressures and preserve his throne.[18]

Syria

Israel also had problems with Syria to the north. She was using water from the Sea of Galilee to irrigate the Negev and using a large amount of water from the Jordan River for irrigation. This caused great friction between the two nations.

The Syrians, in cooperation with the Arab League, started the Headwater Diversion Plan in 1964 to divert two of the three sources of the Jordan River preventing them from flowing into the Sea of Galilee. Israel prevented the project's development by conducting airstrikes in Syrian territory in April of 1967.

Starting in 1966, Syria backed Palestinian terrorists and was rebuked by UN Secretary General U Thant. Israel responded by staging numerous provocations along the Israeli-Syrian border area.[19] Israeli armored tractors guarded by police would start to plow in a disputed area of the DMZ. From its high ground positions, Syria would fire at tractors. The police would return fire so Syria responded by firing on civilian settlements in the Hula Valley. The IDF would in turn assault Syrian positions with soldiers and air strikes.[20-21]

UN officials blamed both Israel and Syria for destabilizing the borders.[21] The escalation led the Syrians and the Soviets to believe Israel was planning to overthrow the Syrian government using military force.[19] On April 7, 1967, a serious incident broke out between Israel and Syria, after Israel's Cabinet gave approval for farmers to cultivate more westerly tracts in the Ha'on sector of the demilitarized zone a few days earlier.[22-23]

Both sides employed artillery, tanks, and mortars.[24] During the clash Israeli airstrikes bombed border villages and military targets. After several hours the United Nations managed to arrange a cease-fire. Following this incident in which numerous Syrian fighters were shot down Arab governments pledged their support to Syria. They also criticized King Hussein for not sending his fighters up to help Syrian fighters that were shot down over Jordanian airspace.[25]

Egypt

After the 1956 Suez Crisis, Egypt agreed to the stationing of U.N. peacekeepers (United Nations Emergency Force – UNEF) in the Sinai to ensure all parties would comply with the 1949 Armistice Agreements.[26-28]

In May of 1967, Nasser received false intelligence reports from the Soviet Union that an Israeli attack on Syria was imminent. [29-33] These false reports followed Israeli officials threatening military action against Syria if the Syrian authorities did not stop Palestinian guerrillas from crossing the border into Israel.[34] Egyptian intelligence later confirmed that the Soviet reports of Israeli force concentrations were in fact groundless,[35-37] but Nasser had by then already started his buildup and he feared that since a large portion of his army was already in the Sinai, a sudden callback of those forces would result in humiliation at a time when Nasser could ill afford being humiliated.[38]

On May 19, U Thant called statements attributed to Israeli leaders by Arab leaders "so threatening as to be particularly inflammatory in the sense that they could only heighten emotions and thereby increase tensions on the other side of the lines."[39] Nasser then misled the Egyptian people by perpetuating the falsehood claiming in an address on the anniversary of the Egyptian revolution, that the IDF was concentrating forces "on Syria's doorstep."[40] Israel's threats to invade Syria appeared serious to Arab leaders,[41-43] and foreign observers suspected that an Israeli strike on Syria was imminent.[44]

According to Michael Oren, Nasser disregarded the counsel of his own intelligence[44] and began massing his troops in the Sinai Peninsula on Israel's border on May 16, expelled the UNEF force from Gaza and Sinai on May 19 and took up UNEF positions at Sharm el-Sheikh, overlooking the Straits of Tiran.[45-46] According to Moshe Shemesh, as Egypt and Syria shared a mutual defense pact, Nasser responded to the Israeli threats by beginning to concentrate his troops in the Sinai Peninsula according to the "Qahir" (Conqueror) defense plan. He also decided to prepare the feda'iyyun for carrying out the "Fahd 2 (Leopard) Plan" which called for murderous attacks inside Israel.[47]

The Straits of Tiran was regarded by the Western powers and Israel as an international waterway[48] but its legal status was the subject of international controversy.[51] The Arabs believed that they had the right to regulate passage of ships while Israel, with the support of other major world powers, argued the Arab were legally not valid.[52] In 1967 Israel reiterated declarations made in 1957 that any closure of the Straits would be considered an act of war, or a justification for war.[53-54] On May 22, Nasser declared the Straits closed to Israeli shipping.[48, 55] Nasser stated he was open to referring the closure to the International Court of Justice to determine its legality, but this option was rejected by Israel.[56-57]

Egyptian propaganda attacked Israel,[58] and on May 27, Nasser stated "Our basic objective will be the destruction of Israel. The Arab people want to fight."[59]

On May 30, Jordan and Egypt signed a defense pact. The following day, at Jordan's invitation, the Iraqi army began deploying troops and armored units in Jordan.[60] They were later reinforced by an Egyptian contingent. On June 1, Israel formed a National Unity Government by widening its cabinet, and on June 4 the decision was made to go to war. Israel's defense forces were confident of victory in any conflict with the Arab states, and military leaders provided Prime Minister Levi Eshkol with alarmist information to persuade him to support an attack.[61] The next morning, Israel launched Operation Focus, a large-scale surprise air strike that was the opening of the Six-Day War.

Preemptive Strike vs. Unjustified Attack

Initially, both Egypt and Israel announced that they had been attacked by the other country. Gideon Rafael, the Israeli Ambassador to the UN, received a message from the Israeli foreign office: "Inform immediately the President of the Sec. Co. that Israel is now engaged in repelling Egyptian land and air forces." At 3:10 am, Rafael woke Ambassador Hans Tabor, the Danish President of the Security Council for June, with the news that Egyptian forces had "moved against Israel"[62] and that Israel was responding to a "cowardly and treacherous" attack from Egypt..."[63] At the Security Council meeting of June 5, both Israel and Egypt claimed to be repelling an invasion by the other,[62] and "Israeli officials – Eban and Evron – swore that Egypt had fired first."[64]

On June 5, Egypt supported by the USSR, charged Israel with aggression. Israel claimed that Egypt had struck first, telling the council that "in the early hours of this morning Egyptian armored columns moved in an offensive thrust against Israel's borders. At the same time Egyptian planes took off from airfields in Sinai and struck out towards Israel. Israeli artillery in the Gaza strip shelled the Israel villages of Kissufim, Nahal-Oz and Ein Hashelosha..." In fact, this was not the case.[65] The U.S. Office of Current Intelligence "...soon concluded that the Israelis – contrary to their claims – had fired first"[66] and it is known the war started by a surprise Israeli attack against Egypt's air forces that left its ground troops vulnerable to further Israeli air strikes.

Though Israel had struck first, Israel initially claimed that it was attacked first. Later it claimed that its attack was a pre-emptive strike in the face of a planned invasion of Israel by the Arab countries.[67] As anti-Israeli propaganda goes, Israel, facing economic strangulation and the imminence of war on three fronts, felt she had little choice but to initiate preemptive action.[68] According to Israeli historian and previous Israeli ambassador to the United States, Michael Oren, the Arabs, "had planned the conquest of Israel and the expulsion or murder of much of it Jewish inhabitants in 1967.

Many of the very controversial and biased revisionist historians today are claiming that the Arabs never had aggressive intentions toward the Jewish State and that Israel precipitated the Six-Day War in order to expand territorially. The documentary evidence refutes this claim unequivocally."[69-70]He further asserted that with hundreds of thousands of Arab soldiers gathered on its borders, Israel could not respond to even a minor Palestinian guerilla attack without precipitating a general Arab assault and that pre-emption was Israel's only option.[70] Israel's attack is often cited as an example of a pre-emptive attack and according to a journal published by the U.S. State Department it is "perhaps the most cited example."[71-72]

One scholar referred to Israel's actions as an act of "interceptive self-defense." According to this view, though no single Egyptian step may have qualified as an armed attack, Egypt's collective actions that included the closure of the Straits of Tiran, the expulsion of UN peacekeepers, the massive armed deployment along Israel's borders and her constant saber rattling, made clear that Egypt was bent on armed attack against Israel.[73] In 2002 radio broadcast NPR correspondent Mike Shuster stated that although Israel struck first, the prevailing view among historians is that the Israeli strike was defensive in nature.[74]

The Arabs attempted again to annihilate Israel in 1967, and were denigrated in only six days, in which they lost the lands that they had previously stolen and usurped in 1948. Those lands included Judea and Samaria, which comprise the biblical and ancestral Jewish heartland, tracing its history back some 4,000 years.

After studying the chart on the outline of Military Strength and Casualties later in this chapter, it is obvious that Israel was greatly out-numbered. Many stories have been told about how various members of the IDF felt the presence and hand of God during this landmark war. The Arab armies were miraculously defeated by a tiny handful of Jewish defenders.

On June 7, 1967, IDF paratroopers advanced through the Old City toward the Temple Mount and the Western Wall, bringing Jerusalem's holiest site under Jewish control for the first time in 2000 years, truly a significant and monumental feat. Glory to God! And the success of the Six-Day War opened the door to the future fulfillment of the rebuilt Tribulation temple cited in Isaiah 66:1-6.

IDF Commander Motta Gur

The recorded words of Commander Motta Gur to his brigade upon their recapture of Jerusalem's Old City and Holy Sites:

For some two thousand years the Temple Mount was forbidden to the Jews. Until you came — you, the paratroopers, and returned it to the bosom of the nation. The Western Wall, for which every heart beats, is ours once again. Many Jews have taken their lives into their hands throughout our long history, in order to reach Jerusalem and live here.

Endless words of longing have expressed the deep yearning for Jerusalem that beats within the Jewish heart. You have been given the great privilege of completing the circle, of returning to the nation its capital and its holy center...Jerusalem is yours forever.

General Shlomo Goren, Chaplain of the Israeli Defense Forces

I am speaking to you from the plaza of the Western Wall, the remnant of our Holy Temple. "Comfort my people, comfort them, says the Lord your God." This is the day we have hoped for, let us rejoice and be glad in His salvation. The vision of all generations is being realized before our eyes: The city of God, the site of the Temple, the Temple Mount and the Western Wall, the symbol of the nation's redemption, have been redeemed today by you, heroes of the Israel Defense Forces.

By doing so you have fulfilled the oath of generations, "If I forget thee, O Jerusalem, may my right hand forget its cunning." Indeed, we have not forgotten you, Jerusalem, our holy city, our glory. In the name of the entire Jewish people in Israel and the Diaspora, I hereby recite with supreme joy: Blessed art Thou, O Lord our God, King of the universe, who has kept us in life, who has preserved us, and enabled us to reach this day. This year in Jerusalem – rebuilt!

Defense Minister Dayan speaks after Israel liberates the Western Wall:

On June 7, 1967, the Israel Defense Forces liberated the Old City of Jerusalem and nineteen years of Jordanian rule came to an end. The Defense Minister, accompanied by the Chief of Staff and senior officers, arrived at the Western Wall at noon on that day. The Minister made the following statement:

This morning, the Israel Defense Forces liberated Jerusalem. We have united Jerusalem, the divided capital of Israel. We have returned to the holiest of our Holy Places, never to part from it again.

To our Arab neighbors we extend, also at this hour - and with added emphasis at this hour - our hand in peace. And to our Christian and Muslim fellow citizens, we solemnly promise full religious freedom and rights. We did not come to Jerusalem for the sake of other peoples' Holy Places, and not to interfere with the adherents of other faiths, but in order to safeguard its entirety, and to live there together with others, in unity.

Israeli Prime Minister Eshkol

Prime Minister Eshkol's Address to the spiritual leaders of all communities in Jerusalem, June 7, 1967:

Before proceeding to the Western Wall, the Prime Minister invited the Chief Rabbis and spiritual leaders of other communities to his office and read the following declaration:

Honorable Chief Rabbis, Honorable Community Leaders:

I have taken the liberty to call you to this meeting in order to enable you to share with me the news of the events taking place these last few days in Jerusalem, the Holy and Eternal City.

On the Monday of this week, after the Egyptian aggression against Israel began, I announced in a radio broadcast that Israel would take no military action against any State that did not attack it. Despite this statement, the government of Jordan, under Egyptian command - declared war upon the State of Israel and its forces and embarked upon hostile action by land and in the air.

Our forces were compelled to take the necessary military steps in order to put an end to this aggression and to protect human lives. By its actions, the Government of Jordan, with the agreement of Egypt and following upon pressure from Cairo, violated international law, the United Nations Charter, and the neighborly relations between our two countries. In its aggression Jordan made no distinction between civilians and soldiers.

Crime was piled upon crime by Jordan when it carried war into Jerusalem, thus desecrating the eternal peace of this city, which has always been a source of hallowed inspiration to mankind. As a result of Jordanian aggression, dozens of people were killed and many hundreds were wounded. Blood was shed in the streets of Jerusalem and hundreds, perhaps thousands, of dwellings were hit. There was shelling specifically directed at hospitals, synagogues, Yeshivoth, the president's residence, the Hebrew University, the Israel Museum and Government buildings.

Likewise a large number of schools in the city were hit. The shelling continued uninterruptedly from Monday until today, Wednesday. Out of consideration for the sanctity of the city, and in accordance with our policy of avoiding casualties among the civilian population, we have abstained from any answering action inside the city, despite the casualties incurred by our soldiers and citizens.

The criminal actions of Jordan's government shall stand before the court of international opinion and before the judgment of history.

Peace has now returned with our forces in control of all the city and its environs. You may rest assured that no harm whatsoever shall come to the places sacred to all religions. I have requested the Minister of Religious Affairs to get in touch with the religious leaders in the Old City in order to ensure regular contact between them and our forces, so as to make certain that the former may continue their spiritual activities unhindered.

Following upon my request, the Minister of Religious Affairs has issued the following instructions:

a) Arrangements in connection with the Western Wall shall be determined by the Chief Rabbis of Israel.

b) Arrangements in connection with the Moslem Holy Places shall be made by a council of Moslem clerics.

c) Arrangements connected with the Christian Holy Places shall be made by a council of Christian clergy.

With the aid of the Rock and Salvation of Israel, from Jerusalem—a symbol of peace for countless generations, from this Holy City now returned to its peace, I would like to have you join me in this call for peace among all the people of this area and of the whole world.

Before the Tribulation begins there will be great devastation in Egypt. Considering what we currently hear and read in the daily news headlines, this prophecy (possibly tied in with the battle of Ezekiel 38 and 39) is nearing its time of fulfillment. Egypt is plagued with problems, protests and extreme political upheaval.

"The word of Jehovah came again unto me, saying, 'Son of man, prophesy,' and say, thus saith the Lord Jehovah: Wail ye, Alas for the day! For the day is near, even the day of Jehovah [the Tribulation] is near; it shall be a day of clouds, a time of nations, and a sword shall come upon Egypt, and anguish shall be in Ethiopia, when the slain shall fall in Egypt; and they shall take away her multitude, and her foundations shall be broken down, Ethiopia, and Put [Libya], and Lud and all the mingled people, and Cub, and the children of the land that is in league, shall fall with them by the sword. Thus saith Jehovah: They also that uphold Egypt shall fall; and the pride of her power shall come down" (Ezekiel 30:1-8).

Military Strength and Casualties

Strength

Israel	Egypt: 240,000 troops
50,000 troops	**Syria, Jordan, and Iraq**: 307,000 troops
214,000 reserves	
300 combat aircraft	957 combat aircraft
800 tanks	2,504 tanks
Total troops: 264,000	**Total troops: 547,000**
100,000 deployed	240,000 deployed

Casualties and losses

Israel	Egypt
776https://en.wikipedia.org/wiki/Six-Day_War - cite_note-Israel_Ministry_of_Foreign_Affairs-4–983 killed	10,000–15,000 killed or missing
	4,338 captured
4,517 wounded	**Jordan**
15 captured	6,000 killed or missing
46 aircraft destroyed	533 captured
	Syria
	2,500 killed
	591 captured
	Iraq
	10 killed
	30 wounded
	Totals
	18,510-23,510 killed or missing
	5,562 captured hundreds of tanks destroyed 452+ aircraft destroyed

Facts and Illusions Relating to the Six-Day War

Illusion: Israel's occupation of the West Bank (Judea and Samaria) and the Gaza Strip during the Six-Day War caused Palestinian terrorism.

Fact: Arab terrorism not only pre-dates Israeli control of the disputed territories, but also the creation of Israel itself.

The car and truck bombs of Islamic extremists in today's Middle East and beyond are nothing new; a triple-truck bombing at Jerusalem's Zion Square on Feb. 22, 1948 murdered 54 Jews and wounded many others. It was organized by Abdul Khader al-Husseini at the behest of the Palestinian leader, Haj Amin al-Husseini, the Grand Mufti of Jerusalem. This was almost three months before Israel's independence, more than 19 years before Israel gained the West Bank and Gaza Strip.

Terrorism Deaths in Israel: 1920-1966	
1920-1929	164
1930-1939	181
1940-1949	756
1950-1959	347
1960-1966	65
Total	1513

As early as 1920, deadly anti-Jewish riots erupted in British Mandatory Palestine. On May 1, Arab rioters in Jaffa, joined by Arab police, murdered 27 Jews and wounded 104. In August, 1929, in apparently pre-planned rioting across western Palestine, Arabs killed 133 Jews and wounded 339. Inspired by Mussolini's conquest of Ethiopia over British objection, Hitler's rise to power and oppression of the Jews in Germany, and opposed to continuing Jewish immigration, the Arab Revolt of 1936 - 1939 targeted both British authorities and Palestinian Jewry. Terrorist murders of individual Jews and lethal anti-Jewish riots were widespread from October 1937 to the end of 1938.

Contemporary Palestinian Arab terror began in the 1950s, with fedayeen (Palestinian militants) backed by Arab governments, including Egypt, in-filtrating Israel and attacking non-combatants. In 1959, Yasser Arafat and several associates formed al-Fatah — Fatah being a reverse Arabic acronym for Movement for the Liberation of Palestine.

That is, a movement dedicated to the use of "armed struggle" to "liberate" Israel from the Jews. In 1964, Fatah became the largest component of the newly-organized Palestine Liberation Organization, an umbrella grouping of at least eight terrorist organizations. The PLO, initiated by Egypt but with constituents backed by other Arab governments, relied on terrorism as both tactic and strategy in the war against Israel.

This was three years prior to Israel's conquest of the Jordanian-occupied West Bank and the Egyptian-occupied Gaza Strip. According to the Israeli Ministry of Foreign Affairs, from 1920 to 1966, Arab terrorists murdered 1,513 Jewish residents of British Mandatory Palestine (1920-1948) and citizens of Israel (1948-1966) and wounded thousands more before the Six-Day War and Israeli control of the territories.

Illusion: Solving the Israeli-Palestinian conflict, particularly by ending Israel's so-called occupation of the West Bank and Gaza Strip, is the key to Middle East stability.

Fact: Reality repeatedly contradicts this naive notion.

Nevertheless, people who ought to know better periodically endorse it. For example, former United Nations Secretary-General Kofi Annan declared that "as long as the Palestinians live under occupation, so long will passions everywhere be inflamed." British Prime Minister Tony Blair alleged that an Israeli-Palestinian settlement was "the core" of efforts to resolve other Middle East problems and to defeat "global extremism." And U.S. Secretary of State Condoleezza Rice claimed that Israeli-Palestinian difficulties were "at the core of a lot of problems in the region" ("Rice Cautions Israel on Syria; 'No Substitute' for peace with Palestinians, Secretary" say, *Washington Post*, May 30, 2007).

Rice had reversed her more accurate analysis from six months earlier: "I think we have to be careful not to say, well, if there is an Israeli/Palestinian breakthrough that will help in Iraq. Iraq is involved in its own struggles." (*Agence France Presse*, November 15, 2006.) In fact, when the Iraq Study Group recommended late in 2006 that the Bush Administration refocus on obtaining an Israeli-Palestinian settlement to defuse widespread anti-Americanism in the Arab-Islamic world and improve U.S. prospects in Iraq, a study group staffer said, "Does anyone think that if we solve the [Israeli-Palestinian] conflict the insurgent in Fallujah will say, 'Great, now I can put back my AK-47 and go home.'" (*The Forward*, January 30, 2007)

In fact, as Egyptian President Hosni Mubarak once observed, "Osama bin Laden made his explosions [the Sept. 11, 2001 attacks on the World Trade Center in New York City and the Pentagon in Washington, D.C.] and then started talking about the Palestinians. He never talked about them before." If "ending Israel's occupation" of the West Bank (Judea and Samaria) and the Gaza Strip is the key to deflating anti-Americanism and achieving peace in the Middle East and adjacent regions, what did the Israeli-Palestinian conflict and Israeli occupation post-1967 have to do with the following?

- Seizure of the Grand Mosque in Mecca in 1979 by Islamic radicals violently opposed to what they termed the impious, corrupt rule of the Saud dynasty.

- Ayatollah Khomeini's Islamic revolution in Iran after the 1979 ouster of the Shah, that helped fuel Islamic extremism world-wide.
- The 1980 - 1988 Iraq-Iran war, with its estimated one million-plus dead.
- Syrian dictator Hafez al-Assad's 1982 suppression of the anti-regime Muslim Brotherhood in the city of Hama, leveling entire neighborhoods and causing a reported 10,000 to 20,000 fatalities, most of them civilians.
- Syria's relentless attempts since the eruption of Lebanon's civil wars in 1975 to dominate that country, including repeated assassinations of Lebanese politicians, journalists and others sometimes as anti-Israel as Syria's Lebanese proxies.
- The atrocity-filled war starting in 1992 between the Algerian government and military and Islamic extremists that resulted in an estimated 150,000 killed in the 1990s, most of them non-combatants. This bloodshed still continues.
- Genocide in the Darfur region of the Sudan by government-supported Arab Muslim Sudanese against black Muslim Sudanese, which has resulted in 200,000 reported dead, two million displaced.
- Iraq's 1990 invasion of Kuwait.
- Libyan dictator Muamar Qaddafi's chronic interventions in Chad, which contributed to the deaths of thousands, mostly civilians.
- Taliban depredation in Afghanistan.
- Somalia's status as a failed state.
- Chechen terrorism in Moscow, Beslan and elsewhere that has murdered hundreds of civilians.
- The long and bloody conflict between India and Pakistan over Kashmir.
- Shi'ite Iran's drive for nuclear weaponry and regional, if not international, hegemony, including over its Sunni Arab neighbors.
- Intra-Palestinian violence, like that in the Gaza Strip between Hamas (the Islamic Resistance Movement) and Fatah (Movement for the Liberation of Palestine) after complete Israeli withdrawal in 2005.

The roots of these and many other regional and international problems, including the Western struggle against jihadist imperialism sometimes called the war on terror, predate Israeli control of the West Bank and Gaza Strip. However desirable on its own, resolving the Israeli-Palestinian conflict itself (more a symptom of Middle East turmoil than its cause), would have little or no effect on these larger difficulties.

Despite its oil wealth, the Arab Middle East is, as the U.N.'s 2002 and 2003 Arab Human Development Reports noted, a region with grave "deficits" of education, political freedom, religious tolerance, cultural pluralism, technological and literary advances, women and minority rights, and so on.

None of those basic ills stem from Israel's control of the West Bank and Gaza Strip and none would be transformed by the absence of such control. The Arab-Islamic Middle East is, as the above examples suggest, a region still strongly gripped by a culture in which intimidation and violence frequently are primary means of conflict resolution. In this region, America would be the "Great Satan" even without Israel, and Israel would be the "little Satan" even without the West Bank and Gaza Strip.

Illusion: Israel's attack was unprovoked.

Fact: In speeches for at least the previous two years, Egyptian President Gamal Abdel Nasser had been threatening war.

Terrorists supported by Syria and Egypt dramatically increased their attacks, from 41 raids in 1966 to 37 in the first four months of 1967. Syria used the Golan Heights as a platform to continue the shelling Israeli villages near the Jordan River and Lake Kinneret (Sea of Galilee). On April 7, 1967 Israeli retaliated, shooting down six Russian-built Syrian MiG fighters. Early in

May, Moscow falsely told Syria that Israel was mobilizing forces for a massive attack. Syria then invoked its joint defense treaty with Egypt.

On May 15, Israeli Independence Day, Egypt began moving troops into the Sinai Peninsula toward Israel's borders. The following day, it requested that the United Nations Emergency Force—installed to help keep peace after the 1956 Sinai Campaign—evacuate, which UNEF did. By May 18, Syrian troops were ready for battle along "northern frontier." The same day the Voice of the Arabs radio declared that, "We shall not complain any more to the U.N. about Israel. The sole method we shall apply against Israel is total war, which will result in the extermination of Zionist existence."

On May 22, Egypt closed the Straits of Tiran to Israeli shipping and all foreign ships bound for Israel's Red Sea port of Eilat, an act of war that cut the route from Israel's main oil supplier, Iran. Nasser continued to threaten Israel, asserting on May 27 that coexistence was out of the question and that "the war with Israel is in existence since 1948.

Jordan signed a defense pact with Egypt on May 30. Other Arab countries sent forces to Egypt and Jordan to assist, and by June 4, approximately 250,000 enemy troops with more than 2,000 tanks and 700 aircraft surrounded Israel. By then on a socially and economically unsustainable alert for three weeks, Israel's best option was to pre-empt Arab attack, which it did on June 5, first knocking out the Egyptian air force.

Years later, Salah al-Hadidi, the Egyptian judge presiding over trials of army officers held accountable for his country's defeat, admitted Egypt's responsibility for causing the war: "I can state that Egypt's political leadership called Israel to war. It clearly provoked Israel and forced it into a confrontation" (Michael Oren, *Six Days of War*, pp. 310-11).

Illusion: Israel attacked Syria and Jordan first during the Six-Day War.

Fact: A continual state of war existed with Syria in the months and years leading up to June 5, 1967.

Artillery exchanges and hundreds of attempted infiltrations occurred between February 1966 and May 1967. At noon on June 5, Syrian aircraft attacked Israeli villages in the North of the country. Israel struck back almost immediately and destroyed much of Syria's air force.

That same day, Syrians artillery attacked Israel from positions in the Golan Heights. On June 6, Syria opened the morning with an intense artillery bombardment followed by an attack on the Israeli communities of Tel Dan, Kibbutz Shaar Yashuv and Ashmura. The attack was repelled by Israeli forces. Israel attacked Syrian forces on the Golan Heights on June 9, and concluded the operation on June 10.

Despite Israel's entreaties to King Hussein to stay out of the war, Jordan shelled Jerusalem and Tel Aviv on June 5th and then occupied the United Nations headquarters in Jerusalem. Israeli forces responded and drove the Jordanian forces out of Jerusalem and the West Bank by June 7th.

Notice the next category below; Israel in no way had the desire to conquer new lands or expand her borders. This attitude still stands today.

Illusion: Israel sought war in 1967 to conquer territory.

Fact: This is a false narrative.

While a pre-emptive strike was seen as one way to avoid being wiped out, Israeli Prime Minster Levy Eshkol looked for a diplomatic resolution to the crisis, and insisted on delaying all military action as long as possible so as to allow for diplomacy to run its course, even while military officials warned that delays would work to the Egyptian's advantage by allowing them to build their forces.

The fact that Israel had not considered a war for conquest became clear almost as soon as the fighting ended on June 10, 1967.

In what they perceived as the existential crisis leading to the Six-Day War, no Israeli political leader argued in favor of conflict on the basis that it would enable the nation to conquer new lands. The debate was over how to avoid what appeared to be impending destruction, not how to expand territory.

The national unity government appeared to be looking for a way to shed most of the newly-acquired territory. (The Sinai Peninsula, Golan Heights, West Bank [Judea and Samaria] and Gaza Strip more than tripled the area under Israel's control.)

In Defense Minister Moshe Dayan's phrase, Israel was "waiting for a telephone call" from Arab leaders, expecting to hear that now they were ready to negotiate peace.

Some Israeli leaders asserted that the country would never return to the vulnerable, pre-war armistices lines of 1949 and 1950 or permit the newly-reunified Jerusalem to be divided again; nevertheless, Foreign Minister Abba Eban said the Jewish state would be "unbelievably generous in working out peace terms." In direct talks with Arab countries, "everything is negotiable," he said.

But Arab leaders rejected negotiations, rejected recognition, and rejected peace. Even so, rather than annex the West Bank or Gaza Strip, for example, Israel instituted a military administration and maintained their status under international law as disputed territories, subject to eventual negotiations.

This suggested that the country did not intend to absorb these areas, or the bulk of them, into Israel proper.

Further, Israel eventually negotiated the return of the Sinai-site of Israeli-developed oil fields, Israeli-built air bases, and the newly-constructed Jewish town of Yamit with its surrounding agricultural settlements - to Egypt as part of the 1979 peace treaty. The 1993 Oslo accords with the Palestine Liberation Organization and their provisions for final status talks by 1998 on the West Bank and Gaza Strip, much of which were to be administered by the new Palestinian Authority, likewise confirmed that the Six-Day War *had not been launched* for territorial conquest.

Illusion: The United States aided Israel Against the Arabs.

Fact: In May of 1967, the United States tried unsuccessfully to defuse rising Arab-Israeli tension through negotiations.

The administration of President Lyndon B. Johnson, while not unsympathetic to Israel's danger, warned it not to strike first. The administration recognized the Egyptian blockade of Eilat as illegal but when war broke out, the State Department announced that America was "neutral in thought, word and deed."

While the Arabs falsely accused the United States of airlifting supplies to Israel, Washington actually imposed an arms embargo on both Israel and the Arabs. On the other hand, the Soviet Union did supply massive amounts of weaponry to the Arab countries. After their swift and virtually total defeat by the Jewish State, Nasser and other Arab leaders tried to save face by claiming that American and even British involvement was largely to blame.

Illusion: United Nations Security Council Resolution 242 requires Israel to withdraw from all of the territories it occupied during the Six-Day War.

Fact: Resolution 242 does not call for Israel to cede all the land.

In fact, the drafters of the resolution intentionally referred to an Israeli withdrawal "from territories" rather than "from the territories" or "from all the territories" so that Israel would not be compelled to return to its precarious pre-1967 lines.

Illusion: The eastern portion of Jerusalem, which came under Israeli control during the Six-Day War, is the Arab section of the city.

Fact: While there is certainly an Arab tradition in the eastern portion of the city, the Jewish tradition is equally (if not more) worthy of mention.

There has been a Jewish presence in eastern Jerusalem for thousands of years. The City of David, the ancient Jewish Quarter, the 2,000 year old Jewish cemetery on the Mt. of Olives, and institutions such as Hadassah Hospital and Hebrew University are all in eastern Jerusalem, as are the Temple Mount and Western Wall, Judaism's most sacred religious sites.

Today, eastern Jerusalem is ethnically and religiously mixed: Jews make up slightly less than half—forty-three percent—of the area's residents. Moreover, this portion of the city has had a long tradition of Jewish plurality. Reforms that came with Egyptian rule over Jerusalem in 1831, and continued with the Ottoman re-conquest in 1840, improved the status of non-Muslims and allowed the Jews to become the largest religious group in Jerusalem.

In 1838 there were 6,000 Jews in Jerusalem, compared to 5,000 Muslims and 3,000 Christians (Martin Gilbert, *Jerusalem: Rebirth of a City*). *Encyclopedia Britannica* of 1853 "assessed the Jewish population of Jerusalem in 1844 at 7,120, making them the biggest single religious group in the city" (Terence Prittie, *Whose Jerusalem*). (These numbers do not refer to the western portion of the city, since until about 1860 Jerusalem residents lived almost exclusively within the walls of the Old City, in eastern Jerusalem.)

It was only during the 19 years of illegal Jordanian occupation from 1948, when Jews were expelled, through 1967—that Jews were prevented access to their holy city. In an effort to erase evidence of centuries of Jewish presence, all 58 synagogues in the Jordanian controlled sector were destroyed.

The Yom Kippur War

The Yom Kippur War was fought from October 6 to October 26, 1973. It was an attack against Israel by a coalition of Arab states led by Egypt and Syria against Israel as a way of trying to recapture part of the territories which were regained by the Israelis in the Six-Day War. The Yom Kippur War of 1973 began on October 6 when Egypt and Syria launched a surprise attack on Israeli positions in Israeli territories on Yom Kippur, the holiest day in Judaism. That year Yom Kippur fell during the Muslim holy month of Ramadan. Egypt attacked Sinai Peninsula while Syrian forces attack the Golan Heights. Both territories had been captured by Israel in the 1967 Six-Day War.

The United States quickly initiated massive resupply effort for Israel and the Soviet Union did the same for Egypt and Syria. The two nuclear powers came very close to confrontation during the crisis. President Nixon put all armed forces on "alert" and the Soviet Union followed suit. The world was on the verge of nuclear holocaust just as it had been eleven years earlier during the Cuban Missile Crisis.

The war began with a successful Egyptian crossing of the Suez Canal with its forces advancing unopposed into the Sinai Peninsula. After three days Israel halted the Egyptian offensive creating a stalemate. Even though the Syrian army drove deep into the Golan Heights they were pushed back to the 1967 border after just three days. Israel then launched a four-day counter-offensive deep into Syria.

Within a week, Israeli artillery began to shell the outskirts of Damascus. Seeing the catastrophe in Syria, Egyptian president Anwar Sadat believed that capturing two strategic passes located deeper in the Sinai would make his position stronger during the inevitable peace negotiations. He ordered his troops to go back on the offensive, but the IDF held them in check. Israel then counter-attacked and crossed the Suez Canal into Egypt. They advanced southward and westward towards Cairo in over a week of heavy fighting that inflicted heavy casualties on both sides.

On October 22, a United Nations-brokered ceasefire fell apart with each side blaming the other. Two days later the Israelis had improved their positions considerably and completed their encirclement of Egypt's Third Army and the city of Suez. This development led to tensions between the United States and the Soviet Union. As a result, a second ceasefire was imposed on October 25 to end the war.

The war had far-reaching implications. The Arab World, which had been humiliated by the lopsided rout of the Egyptian–Syrian–Jordanian alliance in the Six-Day War, felt psychologically vindicated by early successes in the conflict. In Israel, despite impressive operational and tactical achievements on the battlefield, the war led to recognition that there was no guarantee it would always dominate the Arab states militarily. These changes paved the way for the subsequent peace process. The 1978 Camp David Accords that followed led to the return of the Sinai to Egypt and normalized relations – the first peaceful recognition of Israel by an Arab country. Egypt continued its drift away from the Soviet Union and eventually left the Soviet sphere of influence entirely.

The Yom Kippur War was the war to end all wars between the Arab nations and Israel. But of course it did not. Since then all other conflicts have been to stop Hamas and Hezabollah terrorists from firing rockets into Israel. The next major biblically prophesied war will be the Gog-Magog war as described in Ezekiel chapters 38 and 39. That war will most likely take place at least three and one-half years prior to the start of the Tribulation.

The Arab nations initiated four wars against Israel: 1948 War of Independence, 1956 Sinai War, 1967 Six-Day War, 1973 Yom Kippur War. Israel defended herself each time and won. After each war the Israeli army withdrew from most of the areas it captured. This is unprecedented

Never once has Israel shown herself to be a nation seeking to devour other nations and greatly expand her territory. Jews learn in the Torah that all the covenant land will be given to her by Messiah Himself and not by military expansionism.

in world history and shows Israel's willingness to reach peace even at the risk of fighting for its very existence each time she is faced with war and aggression from her neighbors.

Israel's Only Savior

Isaiah 43:1-2

"But now, thus says the LORD, who created you, O Jacob, and He who formed you, O Israel: Fear not, for I have redeemed you; I have called *you* by your name; you *are* Mine. When you pass through the waters, I *will be* with you; And through the rivers, they shall not overflow you. When you walk through the fire, you shall not be burned, nor shall the flame scorch you."

Chapter Four

Israel's Rejection Is Not Final

In this chapter the concentration is on how precisely Scripture reveals God's relationship with Israel. Later, we will go into even more detail on some of the things touched upon here. According to *Bible Statistics and History*, the word *Israel* is mentioned in the Bible approximately 2,575 times. The word *Jerusalem* is cited over 800 times.

God's Message to Israel

"I say then, have they stumbled that they should fall? Certainly not! But through their fall, to provoke them to jealousy, salvation has come to the Gentiles. Now if their fall is riches for the world, and their failure riches for the Gentiles, how much more their fullness!

For I speak to you Gentiles; inasmuch as I am an apostle to the Gentiles, I magnify my ministry, if by any means I may provoke to jealousy those who are my flesh and save some of them.

For if their being cast away *is* the reconciling of the world, what *will* their acceptance *be* but life from the dead? For if the firstfruit *is* holy, the lump *is* also *holy*; and if the root *is* holy, so *are* the branches" (Romans 11:11-16).

But Israel and all the Jews who remain on earth after the Rapture have some very tough days ahead. Scripture tells us that the Antichrist, diabolically driven by Satan, will go to great lengths to kill two-thirds of the Jews during the Tribulation. This slaughter will be far worse than the torturous real-life nightmare of the Holocaust.

"'And it shall come to pass in all the land,' Says the LORD, '*That* two-thirds in it shall be cut off *and* die, but *one*–third shall be left in it'" (Zechariah 13:8).

When Will the Nation of Israel Be Redeemed?

A major purpose of the Tribulation is to break the stubborn stoutheartedness of the nation of Israel. God will do this through His judgment as warned in Ezekiel 20:33-38, resulting in national regeneration.

> "'As I live,' declares the Lord GOD, 'Surely with a mighty hand and with an outstretched arm and with wrath poured out, I shall be king over you. I will bring you out from the peoples and gather you from the lands where you are scattered, with a mighty hand and with an outstretched arm and with wrath poured out; and I will bring you into the wilderness of the peoples, and there I will enter into judgment with you face to face.

> As I entered into judgment with your fathers in the wilderness of the land of Egypt, so I will enter into judgment with you,' declares the Lord GOD. 'I will make you pass under the rod, and I will bring you into the bond of the covenant; and I will purge from you the rebels and those who transgress against Me; I will bring them out of the land where they sojourn, but they will not enter the land of Israel. Thus you will know that I am the LORD.'"

The overriding sentiment for thousands of years among the Jews has been one of unbelief. Few Jews in Israel and few Jews throughout the world long for their Messiah. One of the purposes of the Tribulation will be to bring Israel to repentance and accept her Messiah. The Tribulation will not be a persecution of the Church, but a time of upheaval and judgment for the Christ-rejecting world and to break the stubborn rebellion of the Jewish nation.

As I have already touched upon in Chapter One, Israel as a whole has totally rejected Christ. Israel generally does not recognize Him for who He is. But Israel as a nation will ultimately repent. The Lord tells us in Scripture that Israel must repent and cry out to Him. That is what God says must be done before there can be a Second Coming. One of the major purposes of the Tribulation period is to open the eyes and hearts of the spiritually blinded Jewish nation and bring about national regeneration.

> "'And it shall come to pass in all the land,' says the LORD, '*That* two-thirds in it shall be cut off *and* die, but *one*–third shall be left in it: I will bring the *one*–third through the fire, will refine them as silver is refined, and test them as gold is tested. They will call on My name, and I will answer them. I will say, This *is* My people; and each one will say, The LORD *is* my God'" (Zechariah 13:8-9).

In the following verses we read that Israel *will* seek her Savior, Yeshua Ha Mashiach, wholeheartedly repent and finally accept Him as her Messiah:

> "I will go away and return to My place until they acknowledge their guilt and seek My face; in their affliction they will earnestly seek me" (Hosea 5:15).

> [Jesus said,] "For I say to you, from now on you shall not see Me until you say, 'BLESSED IS HE WHO COMES IN THE NAME OF THE LORD'" (Matthew 23:39).

For two days at the very end of the Tribulation the Jews will be praying and pleading for the Lord's return, then on the third day He will come and save repentant Israel.

"Come and let us return to the LORD; For He has torn, but He will heal us; He has stricken, but He will bind us up. After two days He will revive us; on the third day He will rise us up, that we may live in His sight. Let us know, let us pursue the knowledge of the LORD. His going forth is established as the morning; He will come to us like the rain, like the latter and former rain to the earth" (Hosea 6:1-3).

"And I will pour out on the house of David and on the inhabitants of Jerusalem, the Spirit of grace and of supplication; so that they will look unto Me whom they have pierced; and they will mourn for Him, as one mourns for an only son, and they will weep bitterly over Him, like the bitter weeping over a first-born" (Zechariah 12:10).

Israel Turns to Her Messiah at Long Last

The Jews who hold onto their rebellion will be destroyed (purged) by God's judgment but Israel will—at long last, finally turn to the Lord the last three days of the Tribulation:

"Come, and let us return to the LORD; for He has torn, but He will heal us; He has stricken, but He will bind us up. After two days He will revive us; **on the third day He will raise us up, that we may live in His sight**" (Hosea 6:1).

Finally, after Israel's long history of rejecting her Messiah, she will cry out to Him for forgiveness and beg Him to rescue her from the horrors of the Tribulation. Israel will recognize and confess the sins of her forefathers who rejected Yeshua, Jesus, and will ask for deliverance. Israel's plea to the Lord will last two days, then on the third day He will answer their cries as previously cited in (Hosea 6:1-3).

Scripture tells us the Lord laments over Jerusalem and will not return until Israel recognizes her Messiah—repents, and with tremendous grief, asks Him to return to rescue her, to restore her covenant land and nation mercilessly ravaged by war. In reference to this, Jesus said: "For I say to you, from now on you shall not see Me until you say, 'BLESSED IS HE WHO COMES IN THE NAME OF THE LORD'" (Matthew 23:39).

God Almighty Again Chooses Jerusalem and Blesses Israel

Zechariah 2:9-12

"'For surely I will shake My hand against them, and they shall become spoil for their servants. Then you will know that the Lord of hosts has sent Me.

Sing and rejoice, O daughter of Zion! For behold, I am coming and I will dwell in your midst,' says the Lord. 'Many nations shall be joined to the Lord in that day, and they shall become My people. And I will dwell in your midst. Then you will know that the LORD of hosts has sent Me to you.

And the LORD will take possession of Judah as His inheritance in the Holy Land, and will again choose Jerusalem. Then you will know that the Lord of hosts has sent Me to you. And the Lord will take possession of Judah as His inheritance in the Holy Land, and will again choose Jerusalem.'"

But first, as already noted, Israel will suffer greatly and then Messiah Jesus will return at the end of the Tribulation when she cries out in repentance. He will make converted Israel a glory among the nations throughout the Millennium.

The Shepherd Savior—Jesus the Messiah
Returns to Rescue Israel and to Judge the Nations

Zechariah 13:7-9

"'Awake, O sword, against My Shepherd, against the Man who is My Companion,' says the LORD of hosts. 'Strike the Shepherd, and the sheep will be scattered; then I will turn My hand against the little ones. And it shall come to pass in all the land,' says the LORD, '*That* two-thirds in it shall be cut off *and* die, but *one*–third shall be left in it:

I will bring the *one*–third through the fire, will refine them as silver is refined, and test them as gold is tested. They will call on My name, and I will answer them. I will say, This *is* My people; and each one will say, The LORD *is* my God.'"

The Coming Day of the Lord

Zechariah 14:1-5

"Behold, the day of the LORD is coming, and your spoil will be divided in your midst. For I will gather all the nations to battle against Jerusalem; the city shall be taken, the houses rifled, and the women ravished. Half of the city shall go into captivity, but the remnant of the people shall not be cut off from the city.

Then the LORD will go forth and fight against those nations, As He fights in the day of battle. And in that day His feet will stand on the Mount of Olives, which faces Jerusalem on the east. And the Mount of Olives shall be split in two, from east to west, *making* a very large valley; half of the mountain shall move toward the north and half of it toward the south.

Then you shall flee *through* My mountain valley, for the mountain valley shall reach to Azal. Yes, you shall flee as you fled from the earthquake in the days of Uzziah king of Judah. Thus the LORD my God will come, *and* all the saints with You."

God's Future Judgment of the Nations

Ezekiel 16 which has already taken place is also an illustration of what is yet to come. This is where God finds Israel as a little newborn baby girl and in her birthing fluids takes her, washes her and raises her to a beautiful lady. He loves her and marries her giving her a great dowry. The dowry is described in Ezekiel 16:17, the beautiful land of Israel with breathtaking shores on the Mediterranean, which she gives away. So God's judgment falls on Israel because she gave her land away and divides it.

Scripture warns that Israel is facing a time of division and the nations that come against her will be judged by the Lord Himself at Armageddon, as described in Joel 3:1-3:

"For behold, in those days and at that time, when I bring back the captives of Judah and Jerusalem, I will also gather all nations, and bring them down to the Valley of Jehoshaphat; and I will enter into judgment with them there on account of My people, My heritage Israel, whom they have scattered among the nations; they have also divided up My land. They have cast lots for My people, have given a boy as payment for a harlot, and sold a girl for wine, that they may drink."

God's plagues will fall upon those who fight against Israel in the Tribulation:

Zechariah 14:12-15

"And this shall be the plague with which the LORD will strike all the people who fought against Jerusalem: Their flesh shall dissolve while they stand on their feet. Their eyes shall dissolve in their sockets, and their tongues shall dissolve in their mouths.

It shall come to pass in that day *that* a great panic from the LORD will be among them. Everyone will seize the hand of his neighbor, and raise his hand against his neighbor's hand; Judah also will fight at Jerusalem.

And the wealth of all the surrounding nations shall be gathered together: Gold, silver, and apparel in great abundance. Such also shall be the plague on the horse *and* the mule, on the camel and the donkey, and on all the cattle that will be in those camps. So *shall* this plague *be*."

Psalm 121

The LORD the Keeper of Israel

A Song of Ascent

"I will lift up my eyes to the mountains;
From where shall my help come?
My help *comes* from the LORD,
Who made heaven and earth.
He will not allow your foot to slip;
He who keeps you will not slumber.
Behold, He who keeps Israel
Will neither slumber nor sleep.
The LORD is your keeper;
The LORD is your shade on your right hand.
The sun will not smite you by day,
Nor the moon by night.
The LORD will protect you from all evil;
He will keep your soul.
The LORD will guard your going out and your coming in
From this time forth and forever."

✡ ✡ ✡ ✡ ✡

Pray for the Peace of Jerusalem

According to Psalm 122:6, Israel is the key to our blessing and prosperity. When we pray for the peace of Jerusalem we are in essence praying for the Messiah's return because there will not be peace until He returns and all the prophecies that have been foretold, come to pass:

"Pray for the peace of Jerusalem: 'May they prosper who love you. Peace be within your walls, prosperity within your palaces. For the sake of my brethren and companions, I will now say, Peace *be* within you'" (Psalm 122:6-8).

Chapter Five

Jerusalem Is the Physical And Spiritual Center of the World

Scripture tells us that God's Name, His eyes and His heart are forever tied to Jerusalem—His chosen city.

> "Thus says the Lord GOD: This is Jerusalem; I have set her in the midst of the nations and the countries all around her" (Ezekiel 5:5).

> "Yet I [God] have chosen Jerusalem, that My name might be there...For now I have chosen and sanctified this house [the Temple], that My name may be there forever; and My eyes and My heart will be there perpetually...In this house of God and in Jerusalem, which I have chosen out of all the tribes of Israel, I will put My name forever" (2 Chronicles 6:6, 7:16, 33:7b). Scripture sequencing (partially) taken from: *A Cup of Trembling: Jerusalem and Bible Prophecy* by the late Dave Hunt.

> "The burden of the word of the LORD concerning Israel, thus declares the LORD who stretches out the heavens, lays the foundation of the earth, and forms the spirit of man within him, 'Behold I am going to make Jerusalem a cup that causes reeling to all the peoples around; and the siege is against Jerusalem, it will be against Judah. And it will come about in that day that I will make Jerusalem a heavy stone for all the peoples; all who lift it will be severely injured. And all the nations of the earth will be gathered against it'" (Zechariah 12:1-3).

The previous passages explicitly state that Jerusalem is God's beloved favored, Holy City. Jerusalem is the pivotal point in these last days. Anyone who comes against Jerusalem or tries to take it from the Jewish people is guaranteed to experience the Lord's fury. Jerusalem belongs to the God of the Bible—to Israel. Attempts to internationalize this sacred city will result in total mayhem: The final battle of Armageddon.

Jerusalem (God's Heart)

Tremendous history revolves around God's city, the "City of the great King" as cited in Matthew 5:35. Yeshua Ha Mashiach (Jesus the Christ) has a special love for Jerusalem and spent much time there when he was here on earth.

"When they had finished the days, as they returned, the Boy Jesus lingered behind in Jerusalem. And Joseph and His mother did not know *it*" (Luke 2:43).

"Now when He was in Jerusalem at the Passover, during the feast, many believed in His name when they saw the signs which He did" (John 2:23).

"From that time Jesus began to show to His disciples that He must go to Jerusalem, and suffer many things from the elders and chief priests and scribes, and be killed, and be raised the third day" (Matthew 16:21).

Jesus Wept for Jerusalem

"When He [Jesus] approached *Jerusalem*, He saw the city and wept over it" (Luke 19:41).

Jesus placed His eternal mark in Jerusalem. It was in very close proximity to this blessed city where He suffered on the Cross for all mankind so we could be redeemed and reconciled unto Him. It is just outside the walls of ancient Jerusalem that the Lord Jesus paved the way to eternal glory through His blood sacrifice at Golgotha—where He was brutally crucified, buried, resurrected and then ascended into heaven. The Christian church was established in Jerusalem (Acts 1:4; 12; 2:1-40). We wait for Him to return and take His rightful place on the throne of King David. According to Scripture, God started the creation of His universe in Jerusalem (the Foundation Stone as cited in Isaiah)

"Therefore thus saith the Lord GOD, Behold, I lay in Zion for a foundation a stone, a tried stone, a precious corner stone, a sure foundation: he that believeth shall not make haste" (Isaiah 28:16).

Jerusalem is the most recorded name of a city in the Bible. The Pentateuch (first five books of the Bible) refers to Moriah as the location of the binding of Isaac, and 2 Chronicles 3:1 connects this to the Temple Mount in Jerusalem.

"Jerusalem is surrounded by mountains as God surrounds his people forever" (Psalm 125:3).

"The builder of Jerusalem is God, the outcast of Israel he will gather in...Praise God O Jerusalem, laud your God O Zion" (Psalm 147:2-12).

As recorded in the New Testament, Jerusalem is the city to which Jesus was brought as a child to be presented at the Temple (Luke 2:22) and to attend festivals (Luke 2:41). According to the Canonical gospels (the first four books of the New Testament), Jesus preached and healed in Jerusalem, especially in the Temple Courts. Jerusalem historian, Dan Mazar reported in a series of articles in the *Jerusalem Christian Review* on the archaeological discoveries made at this location by his grandfather, Professor Benjamin Mazar, which included the 1st century stairs of ascent, where Jesus and his disciples preached, as well as the "mikvaot" (or baptismals) used by both Jewish and Christian pilgrims. The events of Pentecost, which are recorded in the New Testament in the book of Acts, also took place at this location. There is also an account of Jesus' cleansing of the Temple at the Temple Court, chasing various traders out of the sacred precincts.

"And Jesus went into Jerusalem and into the temple. So when He had looked around at all things, as the hour was already late, He went out to Bethany with the twelve" (Mark 11:11).

"So they came to Jerusalem. Then Jesus went into the temple and began to drive out those who bought and sold in the temple, and overturned the tables of the money changers and the seats of those who sold doves" (Mark 11:15).

Much of this area was also uncovered by the excavations conducted by the elder Mazar. At the end of each of the gospels, there are accounts of Jesus' Last Supper in an Upper Room in Jerusalem, His arrest in Gethsemane, His trial, His crucifixion at Golgotha, His burial nearby and His resurrection and ascension and prophecy to return. Tradition holds that the place of the *Last Supper* is the Cenacle, on the second floor of a building onhttp://en.wikipedia.org/wiki/Mount_Zion Mount Zion where David's Tombhttp://en.wikipedia.org/wiki/David%27s_Tomb is on the first floor.

It is documented that archaeologist Bargil Piner found three walls of the original structure that still exist today. The place of Jesus' anguished prayer and betrayal, Gethsemane, is probably somewhere near the Church of All Nations on the Mount of Olives. Jesus' trial before Pontius Pilatehttp://en.wikipedia.org/wiki/Pontius_Pilate may have taken place at the Antonia Fortress, to the north of the Temple area. Popularly, the exterior pavement where the trial was conducted is beneath the Covent of the Sisters of Zion; some Christians believe that Pilate tried Jesus at Herod's palace on Mount Zion.

The location of Jesus' crucifixion is often contemplated. A rock cliff west of Herod's Gate and just beyond the Old City of Jerusalem's northern wall, overlooking the garden tomb is the likely location of Golgotha. Jesus' garden tomb is located outside the city walls of Jerusalem and close to the Damascus Gate. Many believe more accurately that this location, and not the traditional site of the burial thought to be in the Catholic Church's,

Church of the Holy Sepulcher, is the place where Jesus' body was buried after he died on the cross.

In 1842 A.D. a man by the name of Otto Thenius proposed that the actual place of where Jesus was crucified, called Calvary (Golgotha) in Scripture, is the same as the place called the "Place of the Skull." In 1867 A.D., the discovery of the garden tomb (shown in the picture on the next page) occurred near the "skull place" thought to be where Jesus died.

"And when they had come to a place called Golgotha, that is to say, Place of a Skull, they gave Him sour wine mingled with gall to drink. But when He had tasted it, He would not drink. Then they crucified Him, and divided His garments, casting lots, that it might be fulfilled which was spoken by the prophet: 'They divided My garments among them, and for My clothing they cast lots'" (Matthew 27:33-35).

The Garden Tomb of Jesus

Jesus' burial location (The Empty Tomb)

89

Jerusalem Belongs to Israel

For over 3,300 years, Jerusalem has been the Jewish capital. Jerusalem has never been the capital of any Arab or Muslim nation. Even when the Jordanians occupied Jerusalem from 1948 to 1967, they did not show any interest in claiming it as their capital, and Arab leaders and dignitaries never came to visit.

In the Old Testament, Jerusalem is mentioned over 669 times and Zion (which usually means Jerusalem, sometimes the Land of Israel) 154 times, or a total of 823 times. Jerusalem is not mentioned once in the Koran. Jerusalem is also not mentioned in the Palestinian Covenant.

The history of Jerusalem and the site of the Jewish Holy Temple, constructed in 956 B.C.E. by King Solomon, son of King David according to God's specific instructions (is fully described in detail in the Old Testament). King David established the city of Jerusalem as the capital of the whole Land of Israel. Mohammed never came to Jerusalem. Jerusalem remained under Turkish Ottoman Empire rule from 1517 to 1917, and under British rule from 1917 to 1948.

The Temple Mount in Jerusalem

The Temple Mount in Jerusalem is the holiest site for Jews. It was the site of the Temple built by King Solomon (950 BCE), which was destroyed by Nebuchadnezzar (587 BCE), rebuilt in 541 BCE, and then destroyed again by the Roman army in 70 CE leading to the exile of Jews from Israel for, 1,878 years. However, for all that time there *was* a Jewish presence and those dispersed across the globe prayed daily: "Next Year in Jerusalem!"

The City and the Temple have always been central to Jewish thought and identity. (Note: Despite Arafat's claim that there was no Jewish Temple, the Romans memorialized their capture of the Jews and their Temple in 70 C.E. by carving it in stone.)

The streets of Jerusalem and the Holy Jewish Temple were walked upon by Jewish kings and prophets long before the 7th century C.E. when a man named Mohammed had a vision that he was the last chosen prophet of God, the god they called Allah. Mohammed was driven out of Mecca by the Arab community and fled to Medina which had three Jewish tribes. Mohammed offered himself to the Jews as God's (Allah) final Prophet.

Mohammed used the trick of a temporary truce (permitted in Islam) to make a treaty called the Hudaibiya Treaty. But, in 628 C.E. at the Khaidar Oasis, Mohammed killed them. The late Yasser Arafat often claimed that the Oslo Treaty is similar to the Hudaibiya Treaty which Mohammed violated with impunity when he was militarily stronger.

Mohammed never again mentioned the word Jerusalem in his compilation of Islam's "holy" book, the Koran and directed his "quibla" (prayers) to Mecca. If a Muslim happened to visit or pass through Jerusalem, it was called a "ziyara" unlike the holy pilgrimage to Mecca which was called by the honorific "Haj." A mandated visit to Mecca allowed the Muslim pilgrim to add Haj to his name.

For Mohammed, Jerusalem was a despised place of the Jews and had no place in his vision for his Islamic religion. It was as if he could not excise the Jewish essence from the holy Jewish City of Jerusalem, although it is said that he believed that the Last Judgment of mankind would issue from Jerusalem.

Mohammed spent his early years among the Jewish tribes particularly in and around Yathrib (Medina). It was, therefore, not unusual for Mohammed to include a pilgrimage to Mecca since the Jewish Torah called for the Jews to make three pilgrimages to Jerusalem each year on Sukkot, Pesach, and Shavuot. There is much in the Koran that finds its source in the Torah (Jewish Bible).

The photos taken in 1875 by the family Bonfils of Lebanon show that for centuries the Dome of the Rock and the el-Aksa Mosque were left unattended. No sign can be found of a flood of Muslim worshipers who would have come—if this was indeed the third holiest site in all of Islam. The buildings show decay and lack of repair. The weeds and grass grew up between the stone flooring, proving that few Muslim feet trod the Temple Mount. (Recall that Jews were prohibited by their rabbis from walking across the surface of the Jewish Temple Mount since, without intent, they might tread on the place where the Holy of Holies stood with the Ark of the Covenant.)

The Temple Mount was held by the Muslim Turks for several hundred years. Nothing was done to repair the walls or the roof tiles on the Dome of the Rock and the el-Aksa Mosque. There are no records of high Muslim clerics or kings paying homage to Jerusalem by visiting el-Aksa or the Dome of the Rock, nor is there evidence of caretakers or clerics to greet or preach to Muslims coming to worship during those hundreds of years. Granted, the Temple Mount was a magnet for conquerors seeking its power, but once in hand did not give up her secrets. Only the Jews seemed to want to stay and bask in its spiritual glow.

King Hussein of Jordan previously held the area for 19 years and did nothing to reclaim it. His only interest was to destroy the 58 Jewish synagogues, desecrate the ancient Mt. of Olives Jewish cemetery and drive the Jews out of what is now called East Jerusalem by the Arabs. King Hussein vented his fury by destroying everything Jewish (along with other Arab nations who lost the wars; they started to wipe out the Jewish State).

It wasn't until the Jews recaptured the Temple when they reunified Jerusalem in the 1967 Six-Day War that the Arabs paid any attention to the area. The Muslims who claim that the Temple Mount or Jerusalem is holy to Islam is a fallacy, based upon irrefutable historical evidence.

Before his death, Yasser Arafat found it quite easy to tell the big lie that Jerusalem belongs to the Muslims—since he received such positive support from the nations and the media. Strangely, he also received support from the Catholic Church who were willing to cut off the branch upon which their own religion rested. If, as Arafat claimed, there was no Jewish Temple, then

Jesus, the Jew, could never have thrown out the money changers from the Temple, not studied there or even existed.

Al Aqsa Mosque and Shrine of Omar were built at the site of the ancient Jewish temples. The Arabic name for Jerusalem "el-KuDS" is derived from the Arabic name "BeT el-MaKDeS," a translation of the Hebrew "BeiT ha-MiKDaSH," the name of the Jewish Temple.

Under Jordanian rule, Jewish holy sites were desecrated and the Jews were denied access to places of worship. Under Israeli rule, all Muslim and Christian sites have been preserved and made accessible to people of all faiths. The Western Wall (Wailing Wall) was a slum before the 1967 war and off limits to Jews and tourist groups.

To this day the Arabs control the Temple Mount and do not allow Jews to pray in the Temple Mount. Jews pray facing Jerusalem as the location of the Beit Hamikdash. Muslims pray facing their holy city Mecca with their backs toward Jerusalem. (Not exactly a reverent position to a place that they now claim is theirs.) Throughout all the ages the Arabs have essentially ignored The Temple Mount. Their intense interest is only a recent development due to their political interests and not because of a sacred religious history as they claim. The myth of Jerusalem as Islam's third holiest city based upon the mythical ascension of Mohammed from Al-Aksa to heaven has grown exponentially in the recent telling since 1967. When you tell a big lie and repeat it often, it achieves credibility and legs of its own.

In Islam, telling a lie to infidels for the sake of enlarging a Muslim's believer's faith or defeating the infidel is acceptable, even desirable. The terrorist state of Iran is doing just that regarding their intentions to create nuclear weapons. The Western "leaders" are pathetically ignorant when it comes to dealing with Islam's deceptive methods of negotiating.

Sheikh Ahmed Aladoan: Israel Belongs to the Jews

Israel Belongs to the Jews
Israel Today
Wednesday, February 19, 2014
By Yossi Aloni

Sheikh Ahmed Aladoan of Amman, a member of Jordan's well-known Adwan tribe, posted to Facebook this week that there is no such place as "Palestine," and provided references from the Koran to back up his assertion. One of the Koranic verses provided states that Allah gave the Holy Land to the sons of Israel until the Day of Judgment (Surah Al-Ma'ida, verse 21), and the other (Surah Al-Shara'a, verse 59) says that the land was bequeathed to the Jews.

The sheikh turned to those who "distort the words of the Koran," whom he labeled as liars, and questioned where they had even come up with the name "Palestine." He insisted their claims to the Land of Israel were forfeit because, "Allah is the protector of the children of Israel."

And if that wasn't enough, the sheikh went on to turn the tables on the anti-Israel propaganda machine by accusing the Palestinians of killing children, the elderly and women, of using human shields, and of having not an ounce of mercy for even their own children.

The sheikh's words caused a storm in the Arab media, and were picked up by the Israeli Embassy in Amman. The Arabic daily *Al-Quds Al-Arabi* further explained the sheikh's position, noting that he supports the notion that Jordan is Palestine, and insists that Arabs living both in Jordan and the Palestinian Authority-controlled territories would almost all love to be Israeli citizens.

The Adwan tribe issued a statement distancing itself from Sheikh Aladoan's remarks. But the sheikh was not intimidated, and insisted he would continue to make his voice heard on these matters.

Last year, Sheikh Aladoan visited Israel and spent time with the chief rabbi of Tsfat (Safed), Rabbi Shmuel Eliyahu. The sheikh informed Rabbi Eliyahu and his students that in the Koran, "There is no name 'Palestine' for this land, and therefore, the Arabs should not be fighting the Jews over control of this land."

Chapter Six

Israel's Future Glory

Jesus Promises to Return and Bless Israel

"And you shall remember the LORD your God, for *it is* He who gives you power to get wealth, that He may establish His covenant which He swore to your fathers, as *it is* this day" (Deuteronomy 8:18).

God's judgment and warning to unbelieving Israel and His requirement for her future acquisition of the Promised Land:

"I will lay your cities waste and bring your sanctuaries to desolation, and I will not smell the fragrance of your sweet aromas. I will bring the land to desolation, and your enemies who dwell in it shall be astonished at it. I will scatter you among the nations and draw out a sword after you; your land shall be desolate and your cities waste.

But if they confess their iniquity and the iniquity of their fathers, with their unfaithfulness in which they were unfaithful to Me, and that they also have walked contrary to Me, and that I also have walked contrary to them and have brought them into the land of their enemies; if their uncircumcised hearts are humbled, and they accept their guilt— then I will remember My covenant with Jacob, and My covenant with Isaac and My covenant with Abraham I will remember; I will remember the land.

But for their sake I will remember the covenant of their ancestors, whom I brought out of the land of Egypt in the sight of the nations, that I might be their God: I am the Lord" (Leviticus 26:31, 42, 45).

The Lord God Almighty has given His glory to Israel and will never take it from her or bestow it upon another:

> "For My name's sake I will defer My anger, and for My praise I will restrain it from you, so that I do not cut you off. Behold, I have refined you, but not as silver; I have tested you in the furnace of affliction. For My own sake, for My own sake, I will do it; for how should My name be profaned? And I will not give My glory to another" (Isaiah 48:9-11).

Israel became a minor nation after the civil war that split her into two nations because of her rebellion, rejecting her God Jehovah. When Solomon ruled, Israel was the greatest nation on earth. Then in the time of Rehoboam, the land was divided into two kingdoms—Israel to the north, Judah to the south. The Assyrians conquered the northern kingdom in 722 B.C. and then the Babylonians took the southern kingdom in 592 B.C. taking the people captive to Babylon (Iraq) in three waves – 597, 587 and 582.

When a remnant returned to Israel from Babylon seventy years later they established their nation, but it consistently remained an insignificant nation -- under the rule of the Medo-Persians, Greeks and then the Romans. Finally, in 70 A.D. the Romans destroyed the Temple with the legions of Titus and put an end to the nation of Israel. The people were scattered to the four winds and they remained a nation of refugees until May 14, 1948.

The early Church, then all Jewish, took the gospel throughout the world. This was a way that Israel gave God's glory to the world. Once again, God will take His gospel to the entire world during the Tribulation by commissioning 144,000 Jewish evangelists who will be supernaturally protected by God. They will lead millions of people to the Lord (Revelation 7:9-10; Matthew 24:14).

God has given the nation of Israel great gifts. Throughout the 20th century, Jews, more than any other minority, cultural or ethnic group have been recipients of the Nobel Prize in a world in which Jews number just a fraction of one percent of the population. Israel has also prospered as a nation.

Israel's Greatest Glory Is Yet to Come
(In the Future Millennial Kingdom)

In Ezekiel 37, the Valley of Dry Bones from 70 A.D. is illustrated as bones being scattered and buried in Israeli graves. "Can these bones live?" Ezekiel then prophesies and the bones come together. The nation of Israel was re-born in 1948 as foretold by the prophet Ezekiel, when they were in a state of unbelief; but they will not get the entire Promised Land until they are in a state of belief. When they repent and earnestly seek their Messiah, Jesus Christ, they will be in a position to inherit all the land promised to them in the millennial kingdom.

At the very end of the Tribulation the Lord will come back accompanied by His angels and saints to totally destroy Israel's enemies. Without God's intervention Israel will never be able to eradicate all of her enemies, even with the great might of the Israeli Defense Forces (IDF). Only the Lord can and will put an end to Israel's enemies that hover around her like persistent flesh-devouring wolves, methodically stalking their prey before an attack.

God is not going to fulfill His promise to expand Israel's borders and they cannot have the great nation that He promised until *after they confess their national sin*, repent, and plead for the return of their Messiah—Jesus Christ.

The nation of Israel was in total rebellion when judgment came in 70 A.D. Territorial gains have been severely hampered for Israel ever since that time because of her rebellious unbelief. It is not until the very end of the Tribulation that Israel will repent and cry out for her Messiah. Then, the Lord will return. He will refurbish the earth and the millennial kingdom will begin. Israel will then be a truly great nation as the Lord promised, and will at long last take her rightful place as the head of all the nations (Deuteronomy 28:13).

So Israel Will Lose the Promised Land
Of the Abrahamic Covenant and Then Get it Back?

Some commentators have the idea that Israel will gain some or all of the Promised Land *before* Jesus establishes His millennial kingdom. The boundaries of the land promised to the descendents of Abraham are clearly cited in the Bible. Not in the book of Genesis or anywhere else in the Bible can a single reference be found stating that Israel will have to fight and conquer to acquire the Promised Land. No mention of any kind of battle or war with or around Israel is cited as a requirement to bring about the fulfillment of the inheritance of that covenant land (from the Nile to the Euphrates). Nor is there a place anywhere in Scripture that tells us Israel will acquire the land promised in the Abrahamic Covenant and then—lose it!

When we look at the entire scope of end-time prophecy we know Scripture reveals that Israel will be facing tremendous challenges during the Tribulation. It will be the most horrific time for her. In no way would the anti-Semitic Jew-hating world allow Israel to hold on to expanded borders. Antichrist and his overt one world government would never let Israel have all that land. We know that the Jews in Israel will be fleeing from Antichrist at the halfway point of the Tribulation. And the Jews will not be holding onto their *Promised Land* or expanded borders of any kind when they are hiding from him trying to survive.

But Scripture *does say* that Israel will *no more be plucked up out of their land.* The idea that Israel will gain the Promised Land and/or greatly expand her borders in any way—prior to the Millennium—is a wishful thinking. Only by creating new doctrines—

> Nowhere in Scripture does it say that God will give Israel greatly expanded borders or all the land from the Nile to the Euphrates and then lose it!

which is forbidden by God, can an argument be made for such a scenario. To make such a claim is not sound exegesis. Rather it is eisegesis, which is the process of interpreting a text or a portion of text in such a way that the process introduces one's own suppositions, agendas or biases into and onto the text. This is commonly referred to as *reading into* the text.

The word eisegesis literally means "to lead into," which means the interpreter injects his own ideas into the text making it mean whatever suits his agenda. Eisegesis is a mishandling of the text which very often leads to a misinterpretation. However, exegesis is the exposition or explanation of a text based on a *careful, objective* analysis. The word exegesis literally means "to lead out of." That means that the interpreter is led to his or her conclusions by following the text; not inserting ideas into it. Eisegesis is best understood when contrasted with *exegesis*. While exegesis is the process of drawing out the meaning from a text in accordance with the context and discoverable meaning of its author, *eisegesis* occurs when a reader imposes his interpretation into and onto the text. As a result, exegesis tends to be objective when employed effectively—while eisegesis is regarded as highly subjective. Only exegesis does justice to the intended meaning of the text.

> "And I will plant them upon their land, and they shall no more be plucked up out of their land which I have given them, saith Jehovah thy God" (Amos 9:15).

As you have just read in Amos 9:15, the Lord declares that He will plant the Jews *upon their land and they shall **no more be plucked up**. When will the Lord give Israel the Promised Land of the Abrahamic Covenant? Scripture assures us that it will be at a time when the inhabitants of Israel will never again be uprooted (*plucked-up*), and when she does not have *any* enemies surrounding her: *And Jehovah gave them rest round about ... and there stood not a man of all their enemies before them.* That time can only be in the Millennium.

When will Israel have *rest* (peace) all around her? Only during the Millennium. And when will Jehovah God deliver *all of their enemies into their hand* as the Scripture states? At the end of the Tribulation—at the Second Coming—when Jesus *delivers all of Israel's enemies into their hand* (by defeating Israel's enemies at Armageddon). It is after that time that the Lord Himself will give Israel the Promised Land.

> "So Jehovah gave unto Israel all the land which he sware to give unto their fathers; and they possessed it, and dwelt therein. And Jehovah gave them rest round about, according to all that he sware unto their fathers: and there stood not a man of all their enemies before them; Jehovah delivered all their enemies into their hand. There failed not aught of any good thing which Jehovah had spoken unto the house of Israel; all came to pass" (Joshua 21:43-45 ASV).

Here is the same passage in the NSAB Version, emphasis added:

> "So the LORD gave Israel **all the land** which He had sworn to give to their fathers, and they possessed it and lived in it. And the LORD gave them **rest on every side**, according to all that He had sworn to their fathers, and **no one of all their enemies stood before them**; **the LORD gave all their enemies into their hand**. Not one of the good promises which the LORD had made to the house of Israel failed; all came to pass.

Israel is a great nation now *to some degree* but not in totality. She cannot be the great nation the Lord promised in her unsaved, unredeemed condition. Yes, the Abrahamic Covenant as a whole is without conditions—as far as the eventuality of its total fulfillment. But when we look at the whole counsel of God, we can see that the Lord does have a condition regarding when He can return to rescue Israel and the world. Israel must first repent and cry out to Him, which I have noted many times; and that will happen the last three days of the Tribulation.

Creating extra-biblical doctrines is not new; it has been a problem since the fall of Adam and Eve in the Garden when they were deceived by the serpent—the devil. False doctrines give rise to cults, aberrant sects of Christianity, and tremendous confusion in the Church due to the mishandling of the intended meaning of Scripture. Today, Scripture-twisting is more prevalent than ever. Commentators (including some "experts") publish books and articles misleading many by misapplying the meaning of words in Scripture, and conjuring up ideas that have nothing to do with biblical truth and sound exegesis. It seems that some of these confused Bible analysts may have watched too many episodes of *Mister Rogers' Neighborhood* in their formative years—where the very popular, Mr. Rogers, always encouraged the viewers to use their imaginations.

Jesus the Messiah: The Consolation of Israel

"And behold, there was a man in Jerusalem whose name was Simeon, and this man was just and devout, waiting for the Consolation of Israel, and the Holy Spirit was upon him" (Luke 2:25).

Simeon, a just and devout man waited for the "Consolation of Israel." He was waiting for the deliverance of the Jews by the coming of the Messiah. They did not as a nation receive Him, but a small number did and were consoled. And Israel will yet have the promised Consolation at the Second Coming.

A Key Hermeneutic Principle

No Prophecy of Scripture Is of Any Private Interpretation

"And so we have the prophetic word confirmed, which you do well to heed as a light that shines in a dark place, until the day dawns and the morning star rises in your hearts; knowing this first, that no prophecy of Scripture is of any private interpretation, for prophecy never came by the will of man, but holy men of God spoke *as they were* moved by the Holy Spirit" (2 Peter 1:19-21).

☆☆☆☆☆

Chapter Seven

Psalm 83, A Cry to God to Deal with Israel's Enemies

Psalm 83 is an imprecatory prayer for God to bring down judgment upon the enemies of Israel – Edom (Southern Jordanians), the Ishmaelites (Saudi Arabians), Moab (Central Jordanians), Hagarites (Egyptians), Gebal (Northern Lebanese), Ammon (Northern Jordanians), Amalek (Arabs south of Israel), Philistines (Palestinians of Gaza), inhabitants of Tyre (Southern Lebanese) and Assyria (Syria).

A Song—A Psalm of Asaph

83:1 O God, keep not thou silence: Hold not thy peace, and be not still, O God.

83:2 For, lo, thine enemies make a tumult; and they that hate thee have lifted up the head.

83:3 They take crafty counsel against thy people, and consult together against thy hidden ones.

83:4 They have said, Come, and let us cut them off from being a nation; that the name of Israel may be no more in remembrance.

83:5 For they have consulted together with one consent; against thee do they make a covenant:

83:6 The tents of Edom and the Ishmaelites; Moab, and the Hagarenes;

83:7 *Gebal, and Ammon, and Amalek; Philistia with the inhabitants of Tyre:*

83:8 *Assyria also is joined with them; they have helped the children of Lot. Selah.*

83:9 *Do thou unto them as unto Midian, as to Sisera, as to Jabin, at the river Kishon;*

83:10 *Who perished at Endor, who became as dung for the earth.*

83:11 *Make their nobles like Oreb and Zeeb; Yea, all their princes like Zebah and Zalmunna;*

83:12 *Who said, Let us take to ourselves in possession the habitations of God.*

83:13 *O my God, make them like the whirling dust; as stubble before the wind.*

83:14 *As the fire that burneth the forest, and as the flame that setteth the mountains on fire,*

83:15 *So pursue them with thy tempest, and terrify them with thy storm.*

83:16 *Fill their faces with confusion, that they may seek thy name, O Jehovah.*

83:17 *Let them be put to shame and dismayed for ever; yea, let them be confounded and perish;*

83:18 *That they may know that thou alone, whose name is Jehovah, Art the Most High over all the earth.*

Psalm 83 Is Not a War

Whenever we come to the Word of God we must remember there are hermeneutic principles by which we must interpret the Word of God. Nowhere in the imprecatory prayer of Psalm 83 does it say that Israel will go on a massive retaliation campaign and go after a vast coalition of nations that supposedly attack her.

> **"You shall not add to the word which I command you, nor take from it**, that you may keep the commandments of the Lord your God which I command you" (Deuteronomy 4:2).

> "In all things showing yourself *to be* a pattern of good works; in doctrine *showing* integrity, reverence, incorruptibility, sound speech that cannot be condemned, that one who is an opponent may be ashamed, having nothing evil to say of you" (Titus 2:7-8).

The imprecatory prayer of Psalm 83 describes the enemies of Israel who conspire against her. We have already heard many enemies curse Israel just as Asaph the psalmist relates in his imprecatory prayer—the prayer for God to pull down Israel's enemies. Some actually say that Psalm 83 is a direct call to the Israeli Defense Forces to defeat the Arab enemies around them, but that is not at all what the psalmist is conveying.

The IDF are not being called upon. God Himself is being called upon in the psalm. It is clearly a cry for God Himself to intervene and we find the overwhelming answer to that imprecatory prayer when the battle of Ezekiel 38 and 39 takes place when God Himself intervenes and saves Israel from the massive horde of intruders and later at the final battle at Armageddon.

I first wrote about this many years ago in 2009. Since that article was first published on a number of website and some commentators have picked-up on this important correlation—that the psalmist's plea is correctly an imprecatory prayer, which would be answered at the battle of Ezekiel 38 and 39 by Almighty God's supernatural intervention, and concluded at the final battle at Armageddon (when all of Israel's enemies will be destroyed at the Second Coming). I believe some Christian ministries will remember that article as it caused quite a stir with a number of people.

One of the common denominators in the imprecatory prayer of Psalm 83 and battle of Ezekiel 38 and 39 is to show the reason for the judgment upon Israel's enemies; that they may know whose name alone is the LORD, the Most High over all the earth (Psalm 83:18), and to magnify and sanctify Himself in the eyes of many nations; then they shall know that He is the LORD (Ezekiel 28:23). Both Psalm 83 and Ezekiel 38 and 39—exalt the LORD, and it is He who is directly called upon for justice and it is He who executes that justice victoriously.

God's Revelation Given to the Prophet Asaph

It is no secret that Asaph was a great prophet, although some people would like to make you believe that dedicated Bible students, teachers and great scholars don't know that.

Many commentators and analysts fail to discern that Asaph the prophet in Psalm 83 was carried *forward* in a vision by the Holy Spirit, and let down in time to where the Lord showed him the actual events taking place. He was carried forward to the time in which many nations are viciously calling for Israel's demise.

"They have said, "Come, and let us cut them off from *being* a nation, that the name of Israel may be remembered no more" (Psalm 83:4).

Those are the words we hear today, what the nations are saying today. The prophet Asaph foresaw those who would speak out boldly against Israel. Psalm 83 is prophetic in the sense that it is a progressive prophecy—expressed as an imprecatory prayer; not that Aspah had a hidden alternate meaning which is dissected by some commentators to be an actual war, and a "new revelation" that has bypassed great scholarly minds and dedicated Bible students for thousands of years. To believe such a thing about oneself takes quite a heaping spoon of self-indulgent arrogance and ignorance. To go against a mountain of accepted tried and true reliable biblical scholarship when referencing the imprecatory prayer of Psalm 83, and tag on new novel interpretations can only leave one confused and bewildered.

> "For prophecy never came by the will of man, but holy men of God spoke as they were moved by the Holy Spirit," which means Aspah was picked up and carried forward by the Holy Spirit Himself and was shown the actual events.

God's Revelation Given to the Prophet Ezekiel

Later in time, the prophet Ezekiel in chapter 38 was also carried forward in a prophetic vision to the time when the invasion actually *takes place.*

Psalm 83, therefore, is the imprecatory prayer for the enemies of Israel *today,* to be destroyed in the events of Ezekiel 38:1-39:16 and finally at the battle of Armageddon. Human conjecture or philosophy is not a Holy Spirit-led prophetic revelation.

Both Asaph and Ezekiel were given specific visions by the Holy Spirit of future events. They were not coming forth with their own interpretation of new "hidden" meanings of what "could be." That type of analysis alone should make a Bible believing, God-fearing Christian run very fast the other way. Mysterious new personal revelations added onto solid Scripture but revised and turned into something else all together—is nothing less than delving into the realm of New Age, New Spirituality.

This is also what all the founders of cults have done. They take the plain meaning of Scripture and twist it to give it new meanings—to suit their own corrupted concepts of God's true teachings. Sadly, a number of prophecy teachers in America have jumped onto the so-called Psalm 83 "war" fad, and are leading many sincere believers astray.

God-given discernment is lacking when Scripture is improperly used, causing much confusion—especially when sensationalized suppositions are inserted into the text. Breaking down which nations Asaph or Ezekiel named in their writings cannot be used as a test of truth as to exactly who will actually participate in the battle of Ezekiel 38 and 39. We must always keep in mind the Golden Rule of Interpretation. In this case the emphasis is on "unless the facts of the immediate context, studied in the light of *related passages* and axiomatic and fundamental truths, indicate otherwise."

By the time Ezekiel wrote God's revelations, long after Asaph's time, Israel's enemies had grown beyond the surrounding border nations. So any attempt to pick apart which nations will or will not be part of the battle of Ezekiel 38 and 39 cannot be a reliable method by which to try to support an argument, especially the uncovering of *new hidden* meanings (which is clearly unbiblical). Fussing about which nations are or are not listed in Psalm 83 or will take part in the battle of Ezekiel 38 and 39 is a moot point.

The Golden Rule of Interpretation

When the plain sense of Scripture makes common sense, seek no other sense; therefore, take every word at its primary, ordinary, usual, literal meaning unless the facts of the immediate context studied in the light of related passages and axiomatic and fundamental truths, indicates clearly otherwise.

When carefully reading passages from both Psalm 83 and Ezekiel 38 and 39, you will notice similarities that tie together the prophecies of both Asaph in Psalm 83 and Ezekiel in Ezekiel 38 and 39. The similarities between the war of Gog-Magog (the battle of Ezekiel 38-39) and the prayer of Psalm 83 distinctly show that Psalm 83 is a prayer for the fulfillment of God's wrath against Israel's enemies as will be demonstrated when the Gog-Magog war takes place. This call for God to destroy Israel's enemies will be concluded at the final battle at Armageddon.

In Psalm 83:9 the psalmist asks that the enemies of Israel be killed as the Midianites were—by God—who caused them to kill each other (Judges 7:22). The Russian led Muslim invaders will also be destroyed by God in this way (Ezekiel 38:21). In Psalm 83:14 the admonition is brought forth that these enemies will be destroyed by fire and that the Russian-led coalition will be destroyed in that same manner as cited in Ezekiel 38:22.

Similar Verses Found in Psalm 83 and Ezekiel 38 and 39

Psalm 83:13-17

"O my God, make them like the whirling dust; as stubble before the wind. As the fire that burneth the forest, and as the flame that setteth the mountains on fire, so pursue them with thy tempest, and terrify them with thy storm.

Fill their faces with confusion, that they may seek thy name, O Jehovah. Let them be put to shame and dismayed for ever; yea, let them be confounded and perish."

Ezekiel 38:21-22

"'And all men who *are* on the face of the earth shall shake at My presence. I will call for a sword against Gog throughout all My mountains,' says the Lord GOD. 'Every man's sword will be against his brother.

And I will bring him to judgment with pestilence and bloodshed; I will rain down on him, on his troops, and on the many peoples who *are* with him, flooding rain, great hailstones, fire, and brimstone.'"

Ezekiel 39:3-4

"'I will knock the bow out of your left hand, and cause the arrows to fall out of your right hand. You shall fall upon the mountains of Israel, you and all your troops and the peoples who *are* with you; I will give you to birds of prey of every sort and *to* the beasts of the field to be devoured.'"

✡ ✡ ✡ ✡ ✡

Psalm 83:18

"'That they may know that thou alone, whose name is Jehovah, Art the Most High over all the earth.'"

Ezekiel 38:23

"'Thus I will magnify Myself and sanctify Myself, and I will be known in the eyes of many nations. Then they shall know that I *am* the LORD.'"

Ezekiel 39:7

> "'So will I make my holy name known in the midst of my people Israel; and I will not *let them* pollute my holy name any more: and the heathen shall know that I *am* the LORD, the Holy One in Israel.'"

Obadiah's Prophecy

I have heard some people say that the book of Obadiah speaks of a future war prior to the Tribulation. Some tie it into the supposed Psalm 83 "war" and some do not. A problem exists with such a view, either way. Obadiah 1:15 is cited by some as a Pre-Tribulation verse when it is actually a Tribulation verse: "For the day of the LORD draws near on all the nations. As you have done, it will be done to you. Your dealings will return on your own head."

In verse 15, God definitively declares, "For the day of the LORD draws near on all the nations." Thus, the Lord has designated a particular period of His great plan for *all the nations*, a time when the various vestiges of human history, religion, culture, and thought terminate in confusion and rebellion against God; when He Himself steps up to the spotlight to resolve the satanic chaos. Though the Edomites have gloated over Israel's misfortune on other days in the past, it will recur most egregiously in this time of the end, causing God to decree, "As you have done, it shall be done to you... And no survivor shall *remain* of the house of Esau" (verses 15, 18).

The theme of this book is Obadiah's vision concerning Edom being punished in the immediate future, and also in the future day of the Lord for her sin of mistreating Israel. Edom had been very bitter against God's people, so He predicted the destruction of that nation in this prophecy, and the eternal possession of their land. This book demonstrates and predicts once more the blessings and curses of the Abrahamic Covenant—the promise to bless, and curse those who curse the descendants of Abraham (vv. 10-21 with Genesis 12:1-3).

In part of Obadiah's prophecy, he is carried forward in time when he sees that the day of the Lord is near. He tries to describe what will take place during the day of the Lord (Tribulation) when it comes. This certainly does not describe a Pre-Tribulation war as suggested by some commentators. Conservative scholars place the date of Obadiah's prophecy around the time of Babylon's invasion of Judah in 586 B.C. This also coincides with the exile of most Jewish people to Babylon for 70 years. Other prophecies in the Bible demonstrate Edom assisted Babylon in Judah's destruction at that time (Psalm 137:7; Jeremiah 49:9-16; Lamentations 4:21-22; Ezekiel 25:12-14; 35:1-15).

In this, the shortest book in the Old Testament, God appeals to these three groups: (1) An unidentified group of Judeans, probably the prophet himself, and the Jewish people taken into exile; (2) Edom, which helped Babylon conquer Israel; and (3) surrounding nations calling for war against Edom (Obadiah 1-2). Not unlike many nations today, Edom was proud and biased relentlessly persecuting those who lived nearby. The Edomites became overly secure believing themselves to be all-powerful because of what appeared to be a secure, vital location in the mountains of Seir.

Regardless, God Himself eventually judged Edom for helping the Babylonians destroy Judah (Psalm 137:7), using the Nabatean Arabs to destroy them and bring the Edomites under Nabeatean control (Jeremiah 49:7; Ezekiel 25:12-14). Edom was driven out of Seir and stripped of its land and national identity. The Edomites later settled in southern Judah where they became known by the Greek name *Idumeans*.

Despite the fact that Israel was robbed of her assets, God promises Israel a future, when she will experience "deliverance" (salvation), "possess their possessions" (recover her previously owned land and gain more in the millennial kingdom), be characterized by "holiness" (Obadiah 1:17), and destroy Esau's descendents (v. 18). God Almighty also promises the Jewish people will occupy all the territory which He promised them in the Abrahamic

Covenant (Obadiah 1:19-21; cf. Genesis 15:18-21) as an undivided people (Ezekiel 37:15-23). It is evident that the prophecies of Obadiah 1:17-21 will be fulfilled at Christ's return to set-up His millennial kingdom on earth, and not in a separate war anytime before His Glorious Appearing.

Conjecture Cannot Override God's Holy Word

We live at a time when philosophical speculation and conjecture far too often override sound biblical hermeneutics. Some people take speculation too far by injecting confusing ideas that cannot be biblically substantiated when *carefully* analyzed. Psalm 83 is not a missing prophecy with a new discovered hidden meaning that has eluded the discernment of great scholars.

In fact, great scholars who understand proper hermeneutics have consistently recognized Psalm 83 as an imprecatory prayer to bring down judgment against Israel's enemies. These dedicated men of God reject the heavy media sensationalism used to advance flawed hypothetical teachings which confuse and mislead many who are sincerely seeking the truth.

As I wrote in 2009, Psalm 83 is an imprecatory prayer, unfolding as a progressive prophecy; a fulfilled prophecy (83:3-4), a prophecy which continues to be fulfilled (83:3-4), and a prophecy that will be fulfilled when the battle of Ezekiel 38 and 39 takes place and again finally at the battle at Armageddon when the last remnants of hatred against Israel will be destroyed by God Himself—when He returns at the Second Coming. The battle of Ezekiel 38 and 39 will most likely be the next major biblically prophesied war against Israel.

"For we did not follow cleverly devised tales when we made known to you the power and coming of our Lord Jesus Christ, but we were eyewitnesses of His majesty.

> And *so* we have the prophetic word *made* more sure, to which you do well to pay attention as to a lamp shining in a dark place, until the day dawns and the morning star arises in your hearts.

> But know this first of all, that no prophecy of Scripture is a *matter* of one's own interpretation, for no prophecy was ever made by an act of human will, but men moved by the Holy Spirit spoke from God" (2 Peter 1:16, 19-20).

When we carefully *think* and stay true to Scripture we can be assured that the Lord God of Israel—not military armies on an expulsion mission—will fulfill His promise to tremendously expand Israel's territory during His millennial reign. Before that time, Israel will never be in the position to control a large extended parcel of land and its peoples. The huge numbers of enemies that surround Israel could not be placed in a position of total subjugation, even if their enormous populations were somehow decreased to some degree.

If a major war (a Psalm 83 "war") directly involving Israel were to happen prior to the battle of Ezekiel 38 and 39 and Israel acquired more land, how could the nations described in the Gog-Magog war attack Israel if *some of these major players* have already been subdued and Israel is in charge of them? Never mind the inner circle outer circle double talk myth. As I explained earlier, by the time Ezekiel wrote God's revelations—long after Asaph's time—Israel's enemies had grown beyond the surrounding border nations. Breaking down which nations Asaph or Ezekiel named in their writings cannot be used as a test of truth as to exactly who will actually participate in the battle of Ezekiel 38 and 39.

If a large-scale war took place and Israel conquered and destroyed the nations and its peoples acquiring their land before the battle of Ezekiel 38 and 39, Ezekiel's prophecy could not be fulfilled.

And placing an impossible hypothetical Psalm 83 war into the Tribulation makes no prophetic sense whatsoever. The one world government or ten nation coalition (ten kings) will be ruling and the Antichrist will never give

Israel the opportunity to wipe-out her surrounding enemies. The Jews will be seeking safety and hiding from the Antichrist. The Antichrist will have control of the world during the Tribulation and there is no way Israel is going to be able to greatly expand her borders at that time.

Israel will not be conquering anyone to expand her borders during the Tribulation or before. She is too busy protecting herself from the missile onslaughts from the Gaza terrorists and the rest of her enemies who call out, "Death to Israel."

It is an imaginary exercise to think that Israel will be invaded by a vast coalition of nations different from those who will participate in the battle of Ezekiel 38 and 39, and then overcome this supposed assault ultimately engaging in a conquest of those nations—occupying them and vastly expanding her borders before the Gog-Magog war or any time prior to Christ's Second Coming.

According to Scripture "those who dwell in the cities of Israel" (Ezekiel 39:9) will be fleeing half-way through the Tribulation trying to find a place of safety (Matthew 24:15-22; Revelation 12:6, 14). If Israel had large expanded borders, finding a place of refuge and safety during that time of hell on earth would not be necessary. But Scripture is absolutely clear that the inhabitants of Israel will be fleeing to save their lives from the Antichrist. Some commentators mistakenly believe and teach that only the "believing remnant" will be making a fast exit out of Israel. This teaching cannot be substantiated with Scripture. The idea that only believers will run and hide from the Antichrist is a creation outside of Scripture, an erroneous teaching that is injected into the text by those who overlook this obvious passage:

"Then those who dwell in the cities of Israel will go out and set on fire and burn the weapons, both the shields and bucklers, the bows and arrows, the javelins and spears; and they will make fires with them for seven years. They will not take wood from the field nor cut down *any* from the forests, because they will make fires with the weapons; and they will plunder those who plundered them, and pillage those who pillaged them," says the Lord GOD" (Ezekiel 39:9-10).

The Scripture reads: "Those who dwell in the cities of Israel" which would include everyone, not only a believing remnant. And Revelation 12:6 references the "woman" (Israel), not just *some* of Israel: "Then the woman fled into the wilderness where she had a place prepared by God, that they should feed her there one thousand two hundred and sixty days" (Revelation 12:6).

In Exodus 23:31 God promised that His Chosen People, Israel, would one day possess all of the land extending from the Red Sea to the Mediterranean Sea and from the desert to the Euphrates River. This is the land which today encompasses the lands of the Psalm 83 nations. The possession of this "Promised Land" has a clear chronological fulfillment in Scripture; the regeneration of Israel (at the Second Coming of Christ) is when God will fully carry out the promises of the Abrahamic Covenant concerning the Land. For the first time in all of Israel's history, she will possess all of the Promised Land.

"I will establish your borders from the Red Sea to the Mediterranean Sea and from the desert to the Euphrates River. I will give into your hands the people who live in the land, and you will drive them out before you" (Exodus 23:31).

In a *World Net Daily* commentary, author Joel Richardson, wrote an excellent article titled: "Which Nations Does Psalm 83 Really Include?" Joel states:

Among ardent students of biblical prophecy, there is presently a popular belief that Psalm 83 predicts an imminent invasion of Israel. Thus, according to this popular prophetic scenario, a coalition of nations, including Jordan, Egypt, Lebanon, Syria, Iraq, Saudi Arabia and the Palestinian peoples, will very soon join forces to attack Israel.

And I will add that according to those who teach the Psalm 83 war hypothesis, Israel will overcome this supposed attack, ultimately engaging in a conquest of these nations, occupying them and vastly expanding her borders. Because of this hypothetical Israeli military conquest over the surrounding Arab populations of the Palestinians, Syrians, Saudi Arabians, Egyptians, Lebanese, and Jordanians—Israel's borders will greatly increase; Israel will become richer and her national status will be much stronger. But this is pure conjecture. This scenario is simply not going to happen.

Amalek is listed as one of the offending parties in Psalm 83. However, the Psalm 83 "war" proponents *incorrectly* identify Amalek in the Psalm 83 war teaching by saying: "As correlating to the Sinai peninsula and thus Egypt." Joel corrects that incorrect teaching, "But again, if one simply examines any number of Bible atlases, he will see that the ancient land of Amalek is almost entirely contained within the borders of modern-day Israel."

Joel Richardson clarifies the problem when names in the Old Testament prophecies are incorrectly identified:

Another very important point must be emphasized here: When it comes to identifying the

Joel Richardson also points out, "For those familiar with the region, the idea of Israel actually occupying Egypt, Jordan, Syria and Saudi Arabia is quite a wild, if not a completely impossible scenario to imagine. Yet many students of prophecy have fully accepted this story line and are even eagerly anticipating its imminent fulfillment." He goes on to say, "While there are many problems with this interpretation on both a practical as well as an exegetical basis, one of its most glaring problems is that some of the key nations are simply not supportable by the historical or biblical record."

names in various Old Testament prophecies, conservative commentators and Bible scholars will almost universally advocate for utilizing the geographic-correlation method of interpretation. This method identifies the region where the particular peoples lived when the Psalm was written. It is also quite common, however, to find among untrained Bible teachers the effort to trace the migrations, intermarriages and movements of various peoples down through history in an effort to identify their modern day bloodline ancestors. This problem-fraught method of interpretation is responsible for numerous questionable prophetic beliefs, however, with Anglo-Israelism being among the most widespread and well-known.

It is apparent that Psalm 83 "war" hypothesis is a very confusing teaching. The advocates of this so-called war switch back and forth from one method to the other, from one name to another inconsistently, to try to make the idea work. Joel Richardson shows that the advocates of this hypothesis use both an ancestral-bloodline-lineage method to identify Edom as correlating to the Palestinians—but then only use the geographic-correlation method to point to Southern Jordan.

Joel further states:

Yet then, when it comes to the Ishmaelites, their identity is limited to modern-day Saudi Arabia. If one consistent method were used, then we would be forced to look to most of the Middle East and virtually all of northern Africa, which is largely inhabited by the Arab descendents of Ishmael today. But because using a consistent method would not work for this [Psalm 83 "war"] theory, the proponents of this myth must switch from one method to the next from name to name. In conclusion Joel states in emboldened font: **"It was important to demonstrate some of the ways in which the popular view of Psalm 83 is simply not in accord with the Scriptures."**

Chapter Eight

The Hijacking of Psalm 83

Great Scholars Recognize the Imprecatory Prayer of Psalm 83

If something is repeated enough times large numbers of people will accept it as truth—even if it is not. Propaganda and slick five-star salesmanship are nothing new. Consider the state of affairs in this nation, how the media blurts out so-called "news" that carries with it a very liberal agenda—and the masses believe it. Flood the Internet and as many media sources as possible, pushing an agenda, and people will believe it. Consider the vast number of cults that get their recruits by having a repeated presence everywhere we turn. "That must mean what I am being told can be trusted!"

No, that means people are being blindsided and not always carefully thinking things through and doing their homework by searching the Scriptures daily to find out whether these things are so (Acts 17:11). And that includes some Bible teachers with or without impressive academic credentials. Beware of those who claim to have the ability to uncover hidden meanings or "prophecies" in

Many good people with the best of intentions may have bought into a Psalm 83 "war" hypothesis simply because of their love for Israel. The thought of Israel having more land and being free of her surrounding enemies and their vicious attacks and verbal tirades, is of course a desired outcome for God's chosen people. We must think carefully and not participate in teachings that at first glance sound positive but when taken apart and carefully analyzed cannot be substantiated by Scripture and place Israel in danger.

the Bible—that great scholars have supposedly failed to identify. A frequent media presence and intense marketing promotions do not equal biblical truth.

We must not read into Scripture what is not there *before* God Almighty says it is time. In fact by placing Israel into a retaliatory position on a conquering mission could quickly bring about even more hatred toward her—as she would be seen as an aggressor. What is best for Israel is what God has already planned, in His own time. Israel's glory is guaranteed by God Himself. Nothing can change that.

All the marketing in the world to promote a hypothesis does not prove theological or biblical veracity. Video debates and TV interviews can be edited to make people look weak or strong. All it takes is a little splicing or asking just the right or wrong questions to make someone look good or bad. A highly educated scholar dedicated to the truth of God's Word is not necessarily a great orator. His focus is not on selling himself and gaining a personal following (while lining his pockets with silver and gold). His motive is staying true to Scripture and to serve the Lord. But a seasoned salesman and marketer can make arguments so appealing and convincing that he has sold the entire sinking bridge to the very people who are walking on it as they are about to drown.

The following is a sample of learned men whose teachings as a whole are reliable and grounded in the Holy Scriptures. Additional references to Psalm 83 classified as a national lament—an imprecatory prayer, can be found in vast numbers of Bibles, Bible commentaries, Bible dictionaries and varied published works. Here is a small sample:

J. Vernon McGee

Best known for: *Thru the Bible* worldwide radio program; the late, respected and beloved pastor, author and Bible teacher J. Vernon McGee wrote this:

Psalm 83 is an Imprecatory prayer, a cry for justice. The psalmist prays for God to deliver His people from their enemies in reference to those who have plotted the destruction of the nation of Israel. The psalm is retrospective in a sense saying, "Judge as you have done in the past. Do unto them as unto the Midianites; as to Sisera, as to Jabin, at the brook of Kison: Which perished at En-dor: they became dung for the earth. (Psalm 83:9-10, J. Vernon McGee, *Thru the Bible: Joshua through Psalms*, p. 806)

Dr. Thomas Ice
Executive Director of the Pre-Trib Research Center
Consistent Biblical Futurists Part XIII
Dr. Ice, a highly respected Bible scholar teaches that Psalm 83 is not a war. He "sounds the alarm" about a "so-called Psalm 83 war"

Dr. Thomas Ice goes on to say:

There will be a judgment of the nations at Armageddon in conjunction with our Lord's Second Coming at the end of the Tribulation and many of those mentioned in Psalm 83 are said by other prophets to be judged at that time.

If Psalm 83 can be made into a separate war, different from Tribulation events and the Gog and Magog invasion, then based upon the same logic, why not declare Psalm 2, or Psalm 79 and many others as separate phases of a much extended end-times?

This is just *some* of what Dr. Thomas Ice has to say on the topic and about those who teach the false Psalm 83 war hypothesis: "**What they teach is not really found in the Bible**. This is why I am sounding the alarm concerning the so-called Psalm 83 war. It is clear to me that Psalm 83 is an imprecatory request on behalf of the nation of Israel by Asaph 3,000 years ago. This is the reason that Psalm 83 is classified as a national lament. **There will be no Psalm 83 war!**"

There would be nothing to stop such a multiplication of events. Instead, Psalm 2, which actually has prophecy in it, is usually seen as being fulfilled via events included in the 70th Week of Daniel or the Tribulation period.

In my opinion, those who are willing to base their end-time views on mere speculation and inference will suffer the same fate as others who have played this game for the last 2,000 years—disrespect and distain.

Those who engage in such speculation will only bring shame to the cause of Christ and will serve to discredit our views of Bible prophecy. Consistent biblical futurism limits speculation to scenarios that flow out of a proper understanding of what the Bible teaches about end-time events. Futurists should not speculate about the meaning of biblical texts, as proponents of a so-called Psalm 83 war have done.

Dr. Ice's admonition should not be taken lightly. A dedicated and wise Christian is also a serious Bible student, and must realize *we are all accountable to God for what we teach and what we accept as truth*. Whoever criticizes, questions, challenges, subtracts from or adds to the complete canon of Scripture is ultimately undermining the divine authority of the Lord Jesus Christ placing the opinions of men in a place of authority instead of God (Revelation 22:18).

New discoveries or hidden meanings or prophecies forced upon God-breathed Scripture would fall into the category of usurping the inherent Word of God. Using the argument saying, "All those Bible scholars can't see it, but I can," should send every discerning Bible teacher or student running in the opposite direction. On the other hand, some believers seem to think if they tell others that they are unqualified to understand or comment on the Scriptures, they are being humble. They are not. They are exposing their foolish rebellion, their disobedience, disregarding God's admonition to study our Bibles *daily*, in order to be equipped to give an answer to everyone who asks the reason for our hope. We are not to be dependent on commentators, Internet and TV personalities, but the Word of God itself.

> "Be diligent to present yourself approved to God, a worker who does not need to be ashamed, rightly dividing the word of truth. But shun profane and idle babblings, for they will increase to more ungodliness. And their message will spread like cancer" (2 Timothy 2:15).

Dr. F. Kenton Beshore (D.D., Litt. D., D. Sac. Th., Ph. D., Th. D.) President and Executive Director World Bible Society

Dr. Beshore (Doc Beshore), an outstanding American scholar who has mentored great men of God. For example, he mentored Tim LaHaye for many years and was a tremendous help getting him started in his ministry work long before his *Left Behind* fame. Dr. Beshore has five doctorates, which includes a dissertation on the subject of hermeneutics. He has made nearly 19,000 daily broadcasts teaching the Word of God on the Bible Institute of the Air program which started in 1954. His proficiency in biblical hermeneutics is second to none. His knowledge and expertise are unsurpassed when it comes to understanding and teaching the Word of God. You have not been to a lecture until you have heard Dr. Beshore deliver the Word of God with his thorough detailed intricate exposition.

Dr. Beshore has also delivered more than 10,000 sermons as pastor. He is currently teaching a standing room only class at The Upper Room at Mariners Church. Doc Beshore has been active in preaching the gospel to the Jews by broadcasting from a powerful radio station on Mount Hermon, Israel since 1979. As founder and president of the World Bible Society, he has printed and distributed millions of Bibles, New Testaments and Bible study materials in over 120 countries. His writings and study tools have been translated into more than 60 languages.

Dr. Beshore unequivocally teaches Psalm 83 is an imprecatory prayer for God's victory over Israel's enemies; that the imprecatory prayer is a plea to God Himself to destroy the enemies of Israel as the Scriptures relate in Ezekiel 38 and 39; and not a request that gives Israel's armies a triumph over her enemies in place of God's miraculous intervention. Dr. Beshore strongly believes and teaches that the so-called Psalm 83 war is a heretical teaching, and should be exposed as such.

Dr. W.A. Criswell

(December 19, 1909 - January 10, 2002). The late W.A. Criswell was a beloved, great American pastor, author, and a two-term elected president of the Southern Baptist Convention from 1968 to 1970. Supporters have described him as one of the 20th century's greatest expository preachers and the patriarch of the "Conservative Resurgence" within the SBC.

Dr. Criswell pastored the First Baptist Church of Dallas for over fifty years. The W. A. Criswell Sermon Library has a collection of over 4100 of his sermons. Pastor Criswell taught Psalm 83 is an imprecatory prayer at the pulpit and as noted in his study Bible. (W. A. Criswell, W.A. *The Criswell Study Bible*. Nashville, Tennessee. Thomas Nelson Publishers. 1979. p. 686)

Dr. David Jeremiah
Shadow Mountain Community Church

Dedicated and popular pastor, Bible teacher and author, Dr. David Jeremiah teaches Psalm 83 is an imprecatory prayer. He does not confuse Psalm 83 with a separate so-called war. He states: "Psalm 83: 'Prayer to Frustrate Conspiracy against Israel,'" (*The Jeremiah Study Bible*, Dr. David Jeremiah, Worthy Publishing 2013, p. 761)

Bill Wilson
Christian Journalist and Commentator
Daily Jot

Bill Wilson has this to say on Psalm 83 in his article titled:
"Psalm 83 Confusion and Today's Middle East"

Following, are some excerpts:

The current U.S. assisted Middle East unrest spanning from Libya across Northern Africa through Egypt and north into Syria has inspired much talk and speculation about Psalm 83. There are many biblical commentators who believe that Psalm 83 is about a prophesied war that triggers several prophetic events, including the Rapture, the Tribulation, and the eventual return of Yeshua Ha Mashiach.

A careful reading of Psalm 83, however, will demonstrate that there is no war prophesied and that the psalm is not a prophecy [as in a new or hidden revelation], but rather a prayer against the enemies of Israel that could be used even today as the nation is surrounded by those mentioned when Asaph wrote the psalm.

Verses 1-5 say, "Keep not thou silence, O YHVH: hold not thy peace, and be not still O YHVH. For, lo, thine enemies make a tumult: and they that hate thee have lifted up the head. They have taken crafty counsel against thy people, and consulted against thy hidden ones. They have said, Come, and let us cut them off from being a nation; that the name of Israel may be no more in remembrance. For they have consulted together with one consent: they are confederate against thee."

Then Asaph names names—Ishmaelites who are Arabs; there is Edom, Moab, Ammon from Jordan; Gebal and Tyre from Lebanon; Hagarenes from Mesopotamia, Syria and Egypt; Amalek and Philistines from Gaza and Egypt; and Assur from Turkey and Iraq.

The rest of the Psalm asks YHVH to cause these enemies to perish by wind, fire, storm, even confusion, concluding with verse 18, "That men may know that thou whose name alone is

YHVH, are the most high over all the earth."

These nations that are prophesied as coming against Israel by the Old Testament prophets are consistent enemies of Israel and today they are followers of the most antichrist system in the world–Islam. It is no huge revelation that these traditional enemies of Israel will cause wars and rumors of wars from now until the end. Our generation may well see the end-time prophecies of the Bible play out before our very eyes.

But let us be ever mindful of false teachings and traditions of men that lead us astray. Don't take my word for it, or other teachers; don't get angry if what you have been taught over a lifetime is challenged. Read the Bible for yourself, in its context, and judge what is being taught. Yeshua told his followers repeatedly to not be deceived by Man.

William G. Heslop

Respected pastor, the late William G. Heslop wrote this in his "Sermon Seeds on the Psalms":

"Psalm Eighty-Three (83): The silence of GOD has always been misunderstood by Man. Instead of attributing such silence to his compassion and mercy, the wicked have imagined that He was unconcerned about their carnal and wicked ways.

The enemies of Israel had taken "crafty counsel" against them. They had "consulted" and conceived plans for the destruction of the people of GOD. They had passed resolutions, to destroy them as a nation and, Hitler-like, to blot out the very remembrance of them from the earth.

A confederation of men and nations had been formed to rid the world of the holy ones of the Most High. Fully cognizant of their wicked plans and purposes, the psalmist called upon Jehovah to speak and act on behalf of his own believing and trusting children.

The psalmist believed in both the power of prayer and the efficacy of praise. The imprecatory passages in this hymn can be understood only in the light of coming days." (Heslop G., William, Sermon Seeds on the Psalms, the Higley Press, Indiana, 1956)

The Baker Illustrated Bible Commentary

This reliable Bible commentary distinctly defines Psalm 83 as an imprecatory prayer:

"God destroy your enemies and ours! Asaph seeks God's help (83:1) because their mutual enemies have one terrifying purpose: annihilate Israel (83:2-5)."

Their enemy is formidable, consisting of Israel's neighbors to the east, south, and west—with Assyria (Syria) covering the northern flank (83:6-8). Aspah cites two decisive *victories that God achieved* over Midian—the first during Deborah's judgeship (83:9-10), the second during Gideon's (83:11-12). In both battles, Israel was at a great disadvantage [as they are today]. Asaph wants God, like wind, fire and storm, to shame Israel's enemies (83:16a, 17). So that the world seeing the destruction, *will recognize God's greatness* (83:16b; cf. 82:8).

And that is exactly what will happen at the Gog-Magog war (battle of Ezekiel 38 and 39). The entire world will recognize God's greatness. Notice that although actual battles took place that were referenced in the psalm, they were in reference to what GOD should do to Israel's enemies, and God's victories over Israel's enemies—not that Psalm 83 itself, is a war

The Asbury Bible Commentary Part II

The Old Testament, VI. taken Index to Treatment of Psalms in the Commentary—recognize Psalm 83 as an imprecatory prayer:

"A Prayer to Frustrate Conspiracy against Israel; a prayer:" An imprecatory prayer: "For Restoration from National Distress and Defeat." Other psalms that fall into this category are: Psalm 14, 44, 53, 60, 74, 79, 80, **83**, 85, 90, 108, 126, 129, 137.

NAVE'S Topical Bible (NASV)
Psalm 83 - Imprecatory Prayer

Psalm 83:13
O my God, make them like the whirling dust, like chaff before the wind.
Psalm 83:14
Like fire that burns the forest and like a flame that sets the mountains on fire.
Psalm 83:15
So pursue them with Your tempest And terrify them with Your storm.
Psalm 83:16
Fill their faces with dishonor, that they may seek Your name, O LORD.
Psalm 83:17
Let them be ashamed and dismayed forever, and let them be humiliated and perish.

Our first allegiance must always be to the Lord and His Scriptures, not Christian friends and cliques (while accepting very questionable and confusing ideas); especially hypotheses that have been called out to be false by great scholars who *understand* proper hermeneutic principles.

At some point in every believer's walk we have all had to rethink and reevaluate teachings as we are commanded to by the Lord (Acts 17:11 and 2 Timothy 2:15).

Israel is having enough trouble holding on to the land she has right now. To think that she will go forth knocking down one border nation after another and incrementally expanding her borders is a mental exercise in naiveté. Israel has given-up some land since she became a nation again in 1948:

Once a person becomes emotionally or psychologically attached to a premise or idea, it is understandable that one would have a tough time letting it go. Faithful believers who place the Lord first in their lives and are not concerned about following trends will carefully assess and even reevaluate what they accept as truth. This is something every believer should do periodically.

1. The Sinai Peninsula.
2. Gaza (a prophetic fulfillment, Zephaniah 2:1-7).
3. The Israeli people are constantly being pushed out of their homes to appease the Palestinians.

A good deal of confusion surrounds those who mistakenly think that Psalm 83 is an actual war. You might hear some talk by proponents of this hypothesis say that Israel will acquire a large amount of land incrementally, after Israel is supposedly attacked by the nations that they proclaim in a separate "war" (aside from the prophesied biblical teaching of the coming Gog-Magog war). Yet then even they admit, "No, well they won't get all that land until the millennial kingdom."

Their biggest hang-up is that they think the Gog-Magog incursion cannot happen until Israel is supposedly "safer" or living in peace. And they think that she will become safer by greatly expanding her borders. Then the hypothesis is that Israel will drop her guard and wham—Russia and the Islamic factions will strike. Those who teach the myth of a Psalm 83 war might also admit that Psalm 83 is indeed an imprecatory prayer, but then add on their own spin and try to sell their confusing teaching to the masses.

> "You shall not add to the word which I command you, nor take from it, that you may keep the commandments of the Lord your God which I command you" (Deuteronomy 4:2).

The supposed Psalm 83 war is a flawed and aberrant teaching, a hypothesis, which I pointed out in some detail in *A Better World Is Coming Soon - Don't Miss It* Expanded Edition (2013). I have included some of its content with additional annotations in Part Three of this book. It is my strong and studied opinion that Israel will NEVER let down her guard. She is as secure as she will ever be until the Lord returns. She will have to continue to fend off her enemies and do so from a defensive position. But Israel will have a stronger *false* sense of security for a time, after she signs the prophesied false covenant with the Antichrist. See Chapter Fourteen and read more including: "When Israel Is Living Securely" and "Unwalled Villages Defined."

The walls that surround that nation are not coming down, they are in fact part of what makes Israel secure today. Israel has secure borders now, even more secure than the U.S. southern border. Israel's borders have some security walls but the cities and towns or villages are not all individually surrounded by walls. Israelis are free to walk about, come and go as they please.

How can a so-called Psalm 83 war possibly take place?

The advocates of the manufactured Psalm 83 "war" cannot describe it or tell us what happens after this so-called war. Since their premise is that the Israeli Defense Forces ("an exceedingly great army") will conquer and exploit the resources of the nations mentioned in Psalm 83, *how* is that going to happen?

How is that going to happen? How can a so-called Psalm 83 war possibly take place?

If Israel took the nuclear option the Israelis would be removing God's role as identified in the psalm—an imprecation, a request for Him to destroy Israel's enemies. Psalm 83:13-18 are very strong verses. (Notice Asaph's plea is made directly to God, not to an army or nation.)

"O my God. Make them like the whirling dust, like the chaff before the wind! As the fire flame burns like the woods, and the flame sets the mountains on fire" (vv. 13-14).

"So pursue them with **Your** [God's] tempest, and frighten them with **Your** [God's] storm. Fill their faces with shame, that they may seek **Your** name, **O Lord**" (vv. 15-16).

"Let them be confounded and dismayed forever; yes, let them be put to shame and perish. That they may know that You [God], whose name alone *is* the Lord, *are* the Most High over all the earth" (vv. 17-18).

How would the Israeli Defense Army (IDF) do what is described in the previous verses? They can't. It would be a breach of prophetic Scripture. God will not allow this to happen. Prophecy must be fulfilled as it is written not as it is rewritten into something that it is not.

Those who teach a so-called Psalm 83 war have taken God out of the picture. Israel is made to be the victor *without* using God, by instead making the IDF the heroes; making Israel a nation that does not need God and straying far away from the pleadings of Asaph—for God Himself to deal harshly with Israel's enemies.

What on earth would Israel do with millions of people that they will supposedly defeat in a massive Arab-Israeli war?

The teachers of this flawed hypothesis cannot give a logical answer to how an army (IDF) is going to do what only God can do. The Psalm 83 proponents have made Psalm 83 Israel's war, and not a plea for God's intervention to *save* Israel from her enemies. And how would the Israelis go about defeating the surrounding nations? If Israel took the nuclear option or took on any other method of war to subdue and gain the territory of her enemies, she would be usurping God's role identified in the psalm—which is a plea for God Himself to destroy Israel's enemies.

What do the Psalm 83 "war" pitchmen see Israel doing with all these conquered nations? If this is a great war, the inventors of this contrived war have not solved the problem of what Israel will do with these nations once they are conquered. Making Israel into a retaliatory aggressor is not at all in keeping with the way Israel goes about doing things, historically or currently.

How could Israel possibly contain all the nations and its peoples? It is not possible for Israel to oversee huge numbers of "prisoner of war" detention camps as the Psalm 83 "war" advocates propose. Israel does not have enough manpower to contain millions of people and maintain prisoner of war camps. How would these people be fed, housed, looked after?

The merchandisers of the Psalm 83 war myth cannot solve this problem because there is no answer to support their hypothetical war. Israel simply could not conquer and contain millions of people. And I would say that the Israelis do not wish to take on such an outrageous quest. They simply want to live in peace.

What would Israel do with millions of people?

The so-called Psalm 83 war is a confusing and extra-biblical teaching placing Israel in a very ominous light by making her a potential antagonistic retaliatory predator. Once again, those who teach and promote a so-called Psalm 83 "war" have not solved the problem of what Israel will do with all the nations and its peoples once she supposedly gains possession of them. Israel would conquer these nations to what end?

Militarily: A So-Called Psalm 83 War Is a Strategic Nightmare

In order to conquer all the so-called Psalm 83 "war" nations, the Israeli military (IDF) would have to have an enormous supply chain. How many tanks, how much supply convoy, how many jets, how many trucks would be needed to keep front line forces supplied with men and materiel? What are the logistics required for a conquest and occupation of Israel's neighbors?

The logistics are incomprehensibly huge. The Israelis are too smart to undertake such a radical far-reaching campaign. They understand their limitations.

The one decisive resource the Israeli's do have is the Samson Option, which will only be used as an absolute last method of defense—if enemy attacks overwhelmingly threaten her very existence. The Samson Option is Israel's last resort wherein she would use nuclear weapons to stop an overpowering attack by enemy nations (if she thinks it is the only way to defeat them). Other than that, Israel cannot take on her Arab neighbors one after the other. And I would say the Israelis would not want to contain millions of prisoners in any way, shape or form. They simply want to be left alone and live in peace. But that peace will not come until after the Second Coming of her Messiah in the millennial kingdom. The Scriptures are very clear on this. It is men who complicate and convolute the Scriptures. God's Word is true and does not change (Hebrews 13:8; Malachi 3:6). Israel will not be preparing for an expansion campaign throughout the Middle East which would require an enormous amount of manpower and materiel.

Materiel (From the French *matériel* for equipment or hardware, related to the word material, and sometimes so spelled in English) is a term used in English for equipment and supplies in military and commercial supply chain management.

In a military context, materiel relates to the specific needs of a force to complete a specific mission. The term is also often used in a general sense ("men and materiel") to describe the needs of a functioning army. Materiel management consists of continuing actions relating to planning, organizing, directing, co-ordinating, controlling, and evaluating the application of resources to ensure the effective and economical support of military forces.

It includes provisioning, cataloging, requirements determination, acquisition, distribution, maintenance, and disposal. The terms "materiel management," "materiel control," "inventory control," "inventory management," and "supply management" are synonymous. Military materiel is often shipped to and used in severe climates without controlled warehouses and material handling equipment. Packaging and labeling often need to meet stringent technical specifications to help ensure proper delivery and final use.

Consider the Gaza Conflict in Relation to an Israeli Expansion Campaign

During the 2014 Gaza conflict (Operation Protective Edge) the IDF gave warnings before each attack to enable civilians to seek safe shelter. The Israelis did not behave like land-grabbing zealots. They simply did what they had to do to protect themselves from the bombardment of missiles inflicted by the Hamas terrorists. In early July 2014, Hamas started to send hundreds of missiles into Israel, more than their usual onslaughts. Israel's Iron Dome missile defense system was able to intercept them. A dramatic escalation in Hamas rocket fire forced Israel to take military action against the terrorists in Gaza -- because they had already launched more than 450 rockets at Israel (capable of reaching deep into the country) since the beginning of 2014.

The attacks sent thousands running into bomb shelters, threatening 3.5 million Israeli lives. Israel then launched what it called: Operation Protective Edge. Government officials said the aim was to secure and end weeks of Hamas rocket fire. Operation Protective Edge was the most intense military operation to have taken place in Gaza since the Gaza War in 2008–2009.

The name Iron Dome evokes an image of a protective bubble over a city. In practice, it targets incoming rockets, and fires an interceptor missile to destroy them in the air. Each battery has a firing-control radar to identify targets. It also has a portable missile launcher. The system is easily transportable, with just a few hours needed to relocate and set-up.

The missile is highly maneuverable. It is 3 meters, or almost 10 feet, long; has a diameter of about 6 inches (15 centimeters); and weighs 90 kilograms, or 198 pounds, the security analysis group *IHS Jane's* said in 2012. The warhead is believed to carry 11 kilograms, or 24 pounds, of high explosives, *IHS Jane's* said. Its range is from 4 kilometers to 70 kilometers, or 2½ miles to 43 miles. Iron Dome confronts multiple threats simultaneously, in all weather conditions, the military said. Israel credits "breakthrough technology" and the system's radar.

The radar detects a rocket launch and passes information regarding its path to the control center, which calculates the predicted point of impact," the IDF said. "If this location justifies an interception, a missile is fired to intercept the rocket. The payload of the interceptor missile explodes near the rocket, in a place that is not expected to cause injuries. The Israeli's are well-equipped to protect themselves which gives them a sense of security (secure borders) even when surrounded and attacked by their enemies.

As this conflict continued, more and more people blamed Israel for the deaths that inevitably resulted. It is evident that the hatred against Israel is growing; protests by the thousands in cities all over the world are trying to push Israel into a position of great danger. These uninformed and ill-informed Jew haters ignore the fact that Hamas hides its missiles under their own civilian buildings and fires them from civilian centers, and uses women and children as human shields. They ignore Israel's multi-tiered system when warning Palestinian civilians of impending attacks. They ignore Hamas' orders to its people to disregard Israel's warnings and deliberately stay in harms' way. Israel is blamed for this provocation brought on by Hamas by relentlessly firing their missiles into Israel. This is why we must continue to pray for Israel, speak out and remain informed.

Israel's careful destruction of the sophisticated tunnels posed a challenge causing a need to call forth more ground troops (16,000 reservists) early on to give relief and aid to those who have been fighting on the front lines. By August 20, 2014 Hamas fired over 3,800 rockets into Israel since Operation Protective Edge commenced on July 8th. This was the longest conflict to date between Israel and the Gaza-based Hamas militants—resulting in the death of 1,360 Palestinians and injuring more than 6,000, according to a spokesman for the Gaza health ministry.

Expect Hamas and all their Muslim allies to utilize the Islamic principle of Takiya: The right within Islam to fake peace when you're weak, so you can wait for better timing to conquer your enemy. There is a famous Arab saying: "When your enemy is strong, kiss his hand and pray that it will be broken one day." Moreover there is yet another Muslim technique they will use called: Tawriya ("Creative Lying") advocated by Muslims, a doctrine that allows lying in just about any circumstance. There is no need to warn Israel of false truces, they are well aware of the lies and deceit put forth by their enemies.

Paying careful attention to the difficulties in this one war alone, is a perfect example of why Israel's borders will not expand before the millennial kingdom—contrary to what the Psalm 83 "war" gurus teach. Wisdom and common sense go out the window when we do not carefully think through "new" revelations that do not add up to a viable undertaking ignoring the Golden Rule of Interpretation.

Imagine Israel going into all the nations which the Psalm 83 "war" proponents cite, undertaking an expansion campaign fighting battle after battle with even much more intense opposition and fighting than in the 2014 Gaza conflict. It is simply not going to happen. Israel is very strong but she does not have the manpower to knock down huge numbers of Islamic factions nation after nation, and certainly would not be able to contain them even if she could overtake them.

The militant Islamists are getting richer and more powerful throughout the Middle East day by day, and more organized—thanks to the huge debacles by the current U.S. administration. ISIS is getting a strong foothold in the Middle East region. They are highly equipped, very wealthy and an extremely brutal and dangerous group. As I have written a number of times, it is going to take God's intervention at the time of the Gog-Magog war to shake the foundations of the stronghold the Islamic terrorists hold in the region.

It is true that a number of reports have been made regarding what is perceived to be the hand God intervening in this Gaza conflict, when missiles carefully aimed by Hamas at specific points in Israel, instead, went into the sea or winds blew the missiles off course; and these claims were actually made by both Hamas terrorists and IDF soldiers. Reports like this have been made in nearly every war involving Israel. But this does not mean Israel will go out on a conquering expedition to expand her borders.

An excellent point made in an article published by Gatestone Institute on September 9, 2014 titled, "Conditions of Victory and Peace" by Shoshana Bryen. The author emphasizes the fact that neither Israel or the U.S. are willing to fight in the base of the enemy or "control enemy territory."

Before we get to excerpts from the article, let's address the section I just quoted referencing Israel. In other words, the Israeli's do not want their soldiers fighting in, or on permanent control inside Gaza. This sentiment is very much in keeping with what I have been saying in relation to the Psalm 83 war myth. The proponents of the myth come right out and say Israel will overtake and control large territories and establish detention camps. Really? The mindset of the Israelis is not to conquer nation after nation and create vast numbers of prisoner of war camps; that is not at all the Israeli ideology, not even in relation to the small area of Gaza.

Israel obviously has no intention or desire to conduct an expansion campaign, and then take on the burden of controlling the people and lands that she would supposedly conquer. The Israeli's (IDF) would have to be on permanent patrol inside those territories controlling millions of people. It is not possible. Just how many "detention" camps would they have? How would the Israelis feed such huge numbers of people? Would God send manna from heaven to feed the enemies (prisoners) of Israel?

Following is an excerpt from the aforementioned article, "Conditions of Victory and Peace":

> How do you defeat an armed ideological movement with a territorial base if you are unwilling to fight in that base? Neither Israelis nor Americans are prepared to control enemy territory as a means to determine the ultimate outcome. But that means there will be no destruction, no elimination of the enemy; control of territory and the ability to subject one's enemies to enforceable rules are the only known mechanisms for ending, rather than managing, a war.
>
> Neither Israelis nor Americans are prepared to control enemy territory as a means to determine the ultimate outcome. Their governments have correctly read the citizens – Americans are wary of "boots on the ground" and most Israelis acknowledge that they do not want their sons on permanent patrol inside Gaza, although they accept control of the periphery and occasional forays inside.

You have just read (emphasis added): "Americans are wary of 'boots on the ground' and most Israelis acknowledge that **they do not want their sons on permanent patrol** inside Gaza, although they accept control of the periphery and occasional forays inside." Yet we have commentators teaching a totally opposing objective; the myth that Israel is going to carry out a massive land expansion crusade, conquer millions of people—resulting in greatly expanded borders, and then hold captive her enemies in prisoner of war camps. Israel is not a ravenous nation and contrary to the very flawed thinking of fable-laden analysts; she is not going to mobilize a military border-expansion campaign.

Is the Gaza War Really Over?
Khaled Abu Toameh
Gatestone Institute
August 28, 2014

It is important to note that these cease-fire demands are not part of Hamas' or Islamic Jihad's overall strategy, namely to have Israel wiped off the face of the earth.

Many foreign journalists who came to cover the war in the Gaza were under the false impression that it was all about improving living conditions for the Palestinians by opening border crossings and building an airport and seaport.

These journalists really believed that once the demands of Hamas and the Palestinian Islamic Jihad are accepted, this would pave the way for peace between the Israelis and the Palestinians.

To understand the true intention of Hamas and its allies, it is sufficient to follow the statements made by their leaders after the cease-fire announcement this week. To his credit, Ismail Haniyeh, Hamas's leader, has never concealed Hamas's desire to destroy Israel. Hamas and its allies see the war in the Gaza Strip as part of their strategy to destroy Israel.

What Hamas and its allies are actually saying is this: "Give us open borders, an airport and seaport so we can use them to prepare for the next war against Israel."

Accountability and Endangering Israel

Understand, in no way is this book intended to be a personal attack on any who hold to the "Psalm 83 war" hypothesis. What is written here is simply to point out the serious and enormous problems with this troublesome and aberrant teaching—not only biblically—but for the nation of Israel and the Jewish population throughout the world. The dynamics taught in a so-called Psalm 83 "war" are completely out of character for Israel. We must avoid placing Israel into a heavy-handed despotic category by anticipating her to behave like an invasive retaliatory aggressor by turning the imprecatory *prayer* of Psalm 83 into a supposed war.

Those who support Israel should not foolishly make her into a people positioning to conquer and exploit the resources of her surrounding nations by reinventing Scripture to create a climate of an impending massive war. This would make Israel a nation of scheming oppressors and bring about even more anti-Semitism, which is the last thing Israel or any Jewish person needs.

Especially since the (2014) Operation Protective Edge Gaza conflict, and the accompanying ramped up anti-Semitic hatred launched against Israel from all over the world. France has been in an acute state of fear after the slaughter of four Jews by Muslims in a hostage stand-off at a kosher supermarket in Paris. They were among seventeen people killed in a wave of terror attacks carried out over a period three days in France (January 2015). European Jews are visibly shaken fearing what might come next. According to those who research and monitor social and political trends, not since World War II when some six million Jews were murdered in the Nazi Holocaust have European Jews felt this threatened. The terrorism in France was inflicted by Islamic militants claiming allegiance to the Islamic State extremist group and al-Qaida.

More Islamic terror shook Paris on November 13, 2015; the single dead-liest terrorist attack in French history. These barbaric acts were carefully coordinated multiple shootings and grenade attacks against all civilians, not only Jews. This bombardment of terror initially started with suicide bomb-ings at Stade de France stadium. Simultaneously dozens of people were shot and killed at restaurants and at a concert hall. The attacks left 130 people dead and more than 300 injured. As of November 24, French Health Minister Marisol Touraine said 161 people injured in the attacks remain hospitalized, including 26 in intensive care. ISIS claimed responsibility for the attacks and French President François Hollande named the Paris attacks an "act of war." Islamic terrorist attacks will continue and accelerate not only in France, but all over the world. This is outright war against Western civilization; an attempt by radical Muslims to take the entire world into a throwback seventh century caliphate. The true God of Abraham, Isaac and Jacob will not let that happen.

The demonization and irrational hatred toward Israel is getting worse day by day and so is worldwide terror brought on by Islam—Israel's great-est enemy. In the eyes of those who condemn Israel, the only thing Israel can do right is to stop existing as a nation and as a people. And that will never happen. Israel is here to stay like it or not. God will never aban-don Israel. In early 2016, Islamic terrorists were quickly escalating their killing sprees. We've already had the horrific Brussels attack in March of 2016, and in the same month additional attacks took place targeting Pakistan, Nigeria, Yemen, Iraq, Scotland, and Syria—killing and maim-ing hundreds of innocent victims. including children. And of course Israel is always victimized by the Islamic terrorists every month. Stabbings are more recently a popular way for the representatives of Islam to terrorize Israeli citizens as well as visitors to the Holy Land. Those who believe this type of terror will decrease before the Ezekiel 38 and 39 battle can take place are simply mistaken. Please read Chapter Fourteen in this book for detailed explanations: "When Israel Is Living Securely" and "Unwalled Villages."

A Gideon Comparison Works in Favor
Of the Imprecatory Prayer of Psalm 83

To try to compare Psalm 83 to what Gideon did in the book of Judges, as some do, would actually show that Psalm 83 is *not* a war, but an imprecatory prayer for God Himself to tear down Israel's enemies. In the book of Judges God instructed Gideon on how to go to war in great detail; and also how God led Gideon to reduce the size of his army to only three hundred men (Judges 7:7-8).

"The LORD looked at him and said, 'Go in this your strength and deliver Israel from the hand of Midian. Have I not sent you?' The LORD looked at him and said, 'Go in this your strength and deliver Israel from the hand of Midian. Have I not sent you?' He said to Him, 'O Lord, how shall I deliver Israel? Behold, my family is the least in Manasseh, and I am the youngest in my father's house.'

But the LORD said to him, 'Surely I will be with you, and you shall defeat Midian as one man.' So Gideon said to Him, 'If now I have found favor in Your sight, then show me a sign that it is You who speak with me. Please do not depart from here, until I come *back* to You, and bring out my offering and lay it before You.' And He said, 'I will remain until you return'" (Judges 6:14-18).

In Ezekiel 37:10 the prophet Ezekiel is describing: "an exceedingly great army" (not a small army of three hundred men). And this reference to an exceedingly great army is not in connection to any particular war. God was telling Gideon step-by-step what to do regarding the defeat of his enemies, but the psalmist, Asaph, in Psalm 83, wrote a heartfelt cry for God Himself to take out Israel's enemies:

"O my God, make them like the whirling dust, like the chaff before the wind! As the fire burns the woods, and as the flame sets the mountains on fire, so pursue them with Your tempest, and frighten them with Your storm" (Psalm 83:13-15).

No mention of armies or any one particular heroic person fighting on God's behalf or being used by God is even slightly alluded to in Psalm 83. The two events are totally different and opposite in their approach.

Gideon is clearly fighting a battle **specifically guided by God,** while Psalm 83 is a plea to God Himself to take out Israel's enemies; it is not a war. It speaks *about* war, about the demise of Israel's enemies by God Himself. When Psalm 83 was written, the prophet Asaph spoke about future verbal assaults against Israel as well as future destructive assaults that would involve God's supernatural intervention. We must think things through carefully before we accept new hypotheses apart from the infallible Word of God.

We can see Psalm 83 is briefly broken down into two parts: Verses 1-8: What the enemies of God and Israel are doing. Verses 9-18: What the psalmist wants (prays that) God will do. In verses 1-2, the psalmist says that God seems to be doing nothing while his enemies are getting ready to fight. They fight God by fighting his people Israel. They want everybody to forget that there ever was an Israel, in verse 4. Verses 6-8 tell us who these enemies are. Some are to the east, like Moab. Some are to the west like Philistia. Some are to the south and some are to the north. The Hagrites too, cast their power into the wrong arena, and with all their might sought the ruin of Israel.

The important thing is this: The enemies were all around Israel just as they are today. In verse 8, "the sons of Lot" means the countries that his children started. In verses 9-12, the psalmist speaks about people that **God destroyed**. Asaph is making the point of asking God to destroy Israel's enemies, not that Israel should go on an extensive war campaign to destroy her enemies. God Himself is being petitioned to take care of the destruction of Israel's foes.

Notice in verse 6: *The tents of Edom.* Leaving their rock built mansions for the tents of war; the Edomites invaded the land of Israel. Israel did not invade and attack the Edomites. (We know that Israel will be invaded by a Russian-led army at the battle of Ezekiel 38 and 39.) Edom was located in the region to the southeast of Israel. Mount Seir was a notable landmark in this region. The territory is currently controlled by Jordan.

I have actually heard that some teach the idea that people living in tents in Gaza is in reference to Psalm 83:6: "The tents of Edom and the Ishmaelites; Moab and the Hagrites." Exactly who the so-called Palestinians living in Gaza actually are, cannot be accurately identified. To assume they are "Edomites" is quite a stretch and pure conjecture.

Sisera is mentioned in verse 9. Sisera was the leader of his army but deserted his troops and fled on foot to the Northeast. He took refuge in the tent of Heber, near Kedesh, and there met his death at the hands of Jael, the wife of Heber.

Do unto them as unto the Midianites (v. 9). Faith delights to light upon precedents, and quote them before the Lord; in the present instance, Asaph found a very appropriate one, for the nations in both cases were very much the same and the plight of the Israelites very similar. Yet Midian perished, and the psalmist trusted that Israel's present foes would meet with the likely overthrow **from the hand of the Lord**, as they will in the battle of Ezekiel 38 and 39 when Israel is attacked.

As to Sisera, as to Jabin, at the river Kishon (v. 9). The hosts were swept away by the suddenly swollen torrent, and utterly perished; which was another instance of **divine vengeance upon confederated enemies of Israel**. When God wills it, a brook can be as deadly as a sea. Kishon was as terrible to Jabin as was the Red Sea to Pharaoh. How easily can the Lord smite the enemies of His people!

Notice in Judges 4:23 God intervened: "So God subdued on that day Jabin the king of Canaan before the children of Israel." Regarding verse 11, Oreb fell at the rock and Zeeb at the winepress: "And they captured two princes of the Midianites, Oreb and Zeeb. They killed Oreb at the rock of

Oreb, and Zeeb they killed at the winepress of Zeeb. They pursued Midian and brought the heads of Oreb and Zeeb to Gideon on the other side of the Jordan" (Judges 7:25).

The imprecatory prayer of Psalm 83 is a call directly to God to destroy Israel's enemies; Sisera, Jabin, Oreb, and Zeeb were destroyed and so were others. The mention of Sisera, Oreb or any other persons cited in Psalm 83 have no correlation to a massive conquering campaign resulting in expanded territories for Israel.

A further contortion of the Psalm 83 Scripture occurs when an attempt to interpret the phrase "hidden ones" is misconstrued to mean the Christian church; and then try to tie that phrase to the Rapture/Tribulation taking place before a so-called Psalm 83 "war." This is utter nonsense. Additionally, Hebrew poetry has a very distinctive flow, unlike American poetry, the thoughts and ideas rhyme, not the words. Hebrew poetry *is the rhyming of thoughts and ideas,* not words.

Psalm 83:1-3

"O God, keep not thou silence: Hold not thy peace, and be not still, O God. For, lo, thine enemies make a tumult; and they that hate thee have lifted up the head. Thy take crafty counsel against thy people, and consult together against thy hidden ones."

A consequence of this is that the Body of Christ has so much confusion, that credibility is lost

The words "thy people" and "hidden ones" are in reference to Israel. Asaph was making reference to Israel. When people take what they read in books or articles and **do not *think*** through the Scriptures that are used to try to sell a flawed argument, then we have one new invented doctrine after another—far removed from the true meanings intended in the Scriptures.

and the unsaved strategically use these inaccuracies of Scripture interpretation to make all Christians look and sound like egocentrics or illiterates. We must be careful what we accept as truth, especially in these last days when deception is at an all-time-high.

A lack of careful biblical hermeneutics causes much confusion. Some mistakenly view biblical hermeneutics as limiting our ability to learn "new truths" from God's Word or stifling the Holy Spirit's ability to reveal to us the meaning of God's Word. But this is not so. The goal of biblical hermeneutics is *to point us to the correct interpretation which the Holy Spirit has already inspired into the text.*

The purpose of biblical hermeneutics is to protect us from improperly applying a Scripture to a particular situation. Biblical hermeneutics points us to the true meaning and application of Scripture. Hebrews 4:12 declares, "For the word of God is living and active. Sharper than any double-edged sword, it penetrates even to dividing soul and spirit, joints and marrow; it judges the thoughts and attitudes of the heart." Biblical hermeneutics keeps the sword sharp.

All we need to do is turn on the Christian television networks and we will find all kinds of confusing, and contradictory doctrines being peddled. This makes it especially difficult for Bible teachers with the correct motives to teach and reach others. But God is not mocked and nothing remains hidden from God's eyes.

"But whoever wishes to become great among you shall be your servant; and whoever wishes to be first among you shall be slave of all. For even the Son of Man did not come to be served, but to serve, and to give His life a ransom for many" (Mark 10:43b-45).

"For nothing is hidden that will not become evident, nor anything secret that will not be known and come to light" (Luke 8:17).

God's Admonition in 2 Peter 3:16-18

"As also in all *his* letters, speaking in them of these things, in which are some things hard to understand, which the untaught and unstable distort, as *they do* also the rest of the Scriptures, to their own destruction.

You therefore, beloved, knowing this beforehand, be on your guard so that you are not carried away by the error of unprincipled men and fall from your own steadfastness, but grow in the grace and knowledge of our Lord and Savior Jesus Christ. To Him *be* the glory, both now and to the day of eternity. Amen."

Yes, to Him—God Almighty, be the glory and not to those who lead others astray for selfish-gain and personal glory. Such individuals are not serving the Church or Jehovah God by diligently studying the Bible, but are trying to create novel "cutting-edge" sensationalized hypothetical concepts to make themselves famous and rich.

"For such *are* false apostles, deceitful workers, transforming themselves into apostles of Christ" (2 Corinthians 11:13).

Israel's Fate Is Sealed

Another very important point to keep in mind is this: Israel's fate is sealed. It is clearly recorded in God's Holy Word. Tragically, Israel will suffer greatly, yet. And nowhere in Scripture does it say that Israel will gain vast parcels of land and gain the status of one of the most powerful nations in the world *before* the millennial kingdom. As I have already stated a number of times, Israel is struggling to hold on to the small amount of land she has now. To teach otherwise is irresponsible and an affront to Almighty God and His Holy Word.

Scripture Does Not Permit a Gap Between The Rapture and the Tribulation

According to those who promote of the Psalm 83 hypothesis, they proclaim that the Church will not be on earth when the so-called Psalm 83 war takes place. This would undoubtedly place a gap between the Rapture and the beginning of the Tribulation. But this is not possible. The Bible teaches that the Rapture and the Tribulation events will take place within the same 24-hour-day.

Jesus taught the Rapture and the start of the Tribulation take place on the same 24-hour day:

The only way the Psalm 83 "war" proponents can keep their hypothesis barely breathing is to prove there is a gap between the Rapture and the start of the Tribulation. But that is not possible because the Bible does not permit it. The Lord Himself illustrated there is no gap (Luke 17:27, 29). Paul also exemplified there is no gap (1 Thessalonians 5:3-4).

"And as it came to pass in the days of Noah, even so shall it be also in the days of the Son of man. They ate, they drank, they married, they were given in marriage, **until the day that** Noah entered into the ark, and the flood came, and destroyed them all. Likewise even as it came to pass in the days of Lot; they ate, they drank, they bought, they sold, they planted, they builded.

But in the day that Lot went out from Sodom it rained fire and brimstone from heaven, and destroyed them all: after the same manner shall it be in the day that the Son of man is revealed. In that day, he that shall be on the housetop, and his goods in the house, let him not go down to take them away: and let him that is in the field

153

likewise not return back. Remember Lot's wife. Whosoever shall seek to gain his life shall lose it: but whosoever shall lose his life shall preserve it" (Luke 17:26-33).

The flood began on the same 24-hour day that Noah entered the ark:

"In the **selfsame day** entered Noah, and Shem, and Ham, and Japheth, the sons of Noah, and Noah's wife, and the three wives of his sons with them, into the ark; And the flood was forty days upon the earth; and the waters increased, and bare up the ark, and it was lifted up above the earth" (Genesis 7:13, 17).

On the very same day that Lot fled Sodom, God brought judgment upon it; the day the Rapture takes place the seven-year Tribulation will begin.

"And when the **morning arose**, then the angels hastened Lot, saying, Arise, take thy wife, and thy two daughters that are here, lest thou be consumed in the iniquity of the city. But he lingered; and the men laid hold upon his hand, and upon the hand of his wife, and upon the hand of his two daughters, Jehovah being merciful unto him; and they brought him forth, and set him without the city" (Genesis 19:15-16).

The **sun was risen upon the earth** when Lot came unto Zoar. Then Jehovah rained upon Sodom and upon Gomorrah brimstone and fire from Jehovah out of heaven; and he overthrew those cities, and all the Plain, and all the inhabitants of the cities, and that which grew upon the ground. (Genesis 19:23-25).

The late J. Vernon McGee, a popular respected Bible teacher (Thru the Bible radio programs) taught the Tribulation (Day of the Lord) would begin *immediately* after the Rapture:

"The one event of the Rapture will end the day of grace and begin the Day of the Lord. It closes one day and opens another." (J. Vernon McGee, *Thru the Bible, Volume Five,* p. 400)

On the same page of the same book, J. Vernon McGee also discusses how the world will be expecting to enter a new era of peace, but instead will be "plunged" unexpectedly into the Tribulation, indicating that there will be a false peace just *prior* to the beginning of the Tribulation.

"While they are saying, 'Peace and safety!' **then destruction will come upon them suddenly** like birth pangs upon a woman with child; and they [unbelievers] shall not escape" (1 Thessalonians 5:3).

The late Dr. John Walvoord made the following statement:

"When the day of grace ends with the translation of the Church, the Day of the Lord [the Tribulation] begins at once." (*The Rapture Question,* page.162)

In 2006, the late Dave Hunt wrote in a newsletter:

Not only is it logical that Satan will act quickly once the Church is gone, but he must. Only the sudden, terrifying disappearance of perhaps 50-100 million persons from this earth could unite the entire world under Antichrist and cause the world to worship him. Nothing else could do it. Satan won't let that opportunity pass! So I believe that the Tribulation under Antichrist and the rule of Satan will begin immediately after the Rapture. (*The Berean Call,* January 6, 2006)

Scripture Does Not Permit a Gap

"They ate, they drank, they married, they were given in marriage, **until the day** that Noah entered into the ark, and the flood came, and destroyed them all" (Luke 17:27).

"But **on the day** that Lot went out from Sodom it rained fire and brimstone from heaven, and destroyed them all" (Luke 17:29).

The apostle Paul also wrote that there is no gap between the Rapture and the Tribulation:

"When they are saying, peace and safety, then sudden destruction cometh upon them, as travail upon a woman with child; and they shall in no wise escape. But ye, brethren, are not in darkness, **that this day should overtake you as a thief**" (1 Thessalonians 5:3-4).

A brief period of false "peace and safety" takes place immediately *before* the start of the Tribulation. Please note what Paul stated to Christians of the Church Age: **"Ye, brethren, are not in darkness, that this day** [Rapture/ Tribulation] should overtake you as a thief."

Many respected prophecy teachers have taught that there is no gap: Morgan Edwards, John Nelson Darby, Dr. John Walvoord, J. Vernon McGee, Harold Lindsell, Oliver Green, Dave Breese, Dr. F. Kenton Beshore, J. Dwight Pentecost, Salem Kirban, Perry Stone, Dr. Thomas Ice, Dave Hunt, Hilton Sutton.

Scripture is clear that the Tribulation begins when the Antichrist signs the covenant with Israel (Daniel (9:24-27). But that does not negate the Scriptures that tell us there is no gap between the Rapture and Tribulation. Some who want to place a gap between the Rapture and the Tribulation use a kind of double talk (Scripture twisting confusion) by saying that Scripture does not say the Tribulation begins with the Rapture, which is of course true.

But by saying that does not mean there is a gap. That is purely speculation. Where the gap zealots go wrong is when they ignore the obvious Scriptures that show us that very quickly after the Rapture on the "selfsame day" which means within a 24-hour hour period, the Tribulation begins. Therefore the signing of the covenant must take place, then.

The Rapture will be the perfect epic event that would set-in-motion the signing of the covenant. To be clear, I am not saying the Rapture triggers the Tribulation. I am saying the Rapture would trigger the signing of the Covenant, which then inevitably leads to the start of the Tribulation. After the Rapture those left behind are going to be in tremendous chaos and fear. A charismatic leader promising peace will be eagerly accepted by the world, and Israel will be ready to make a deal with such a man (Antichrist). Until the actual signing of the covenant the Antichrist's identity cannot be confirmed. But his likely established presence as a "leader" of sorts already on the world stage will make it easy for him to quickly sign a false peace covenant with Israel (2 Thessalonians). To try to place a gap between the Rapture and the Tribulation discredits the many Scriptures which disprove such a hypothesis.

For more on Psalm 83, see Part Two.

Chapter Nine

God Himself Protects and Defends Israel

The Battle of Ezekiel 38 and 39

When the battle of Ezekiel 38 and 39 (Gog-Magog war) takes place, God will cause those who come against Israel to turn and fight against each other. This particular war is given the most detailed description of any prophesied future war recorded in the Bible. The imprecatory prayer of Psalm 83 to bring down judgment upon Israel's enemies will be answered, and a large number of Israel's enemies will be destroyed. It is going to happen in the near future and the entire world will be affected by it. This war will bring about great devastation, but during and at the end of the Tribulation there will be utter destruction.

Russia Makes a Strong Move

Russian President Vladimir Putin has been making strong inroads in the Middle East, especially in Syria coming to the aid of the Assad regime. Israeli Energy Minister Yuval Steinitz on September 29, 2015 expressed growing concern over the presence of Iranian ground forces in neighboring Syria. It has been said and confirmed that the anti-Assad rebels (Free Syrian Army) have been trained by the CIA, which would have made Putin's launch against that group an indirect attack against the former Obama Administration's failed policies.

The Kremlin's jets that landed in Syria carried out a number of intense consecutive airstrikes in northern Syria. The campaign quickly escalated. Reports were coming in that China and Saudi Arabia were getting involved on some level. Russian combat forces increased fighting with motives that go far beyond saving what's left of the Bashar al-Assad dynasty from ISIS and the anti-Assad rebels. Since at least October of 2015, Russia fielded heavy artillery units near the cities of Homs and Hama, pounding targets there, according to a top U.S. State Department official. However, initially, Russia's firepower was at Latakia air base in western Syria which later expanded throughout the territory. The Russian decision to move artillery to the front lines was reported to be another development.

When this campaign began, Moscow officially denied that it had ground forces engaged in military operations in Syria, but a map shown by the Russian military on state television appeared to show that some Russian artillery contingents were operating on the ground in central Syria's Homs region. Moreover, the Russian army literally brought its big guns to the war in Syria. U.S. military analysts said the decision to add artillery to the battlefield indicated a number of key developments, including the Kremlin's growing influence in planning and executing Syrian military operations. It could be a sign that Russia is dedicated to a conventional *ground war at some point*—not just air strikes—in support of Syrian leader Bashar Al Assad, a staunch ally long supported by Moscow.

Business Insider reported on December 3, 2015 that Russia is building a second military airbase in Syria. Russia is planning on expanding an Assad regime air base in central Syria into a second base of operations for Moscow's air assets in the war-torn country, various sources report. The new base will be located southeast of Homs at the current Syrian military base of Shaayrat, AFP news reports citing an unnamed military official and a Syrian monitoring group. Russia is reportedly expanding the regime base into a location from which it can launch air strikes and house military helicopters.

Later, and suddenly, Vladimir Putin announced in mid-March of 2016 that Russia would be withdrawing its military involvement in Syria, which came as quite a surprise. Putin ordered the withdrawal of the main part of his military factions from the Syrian Arab Republic; but nevertheless, Russia asserted it will maintain a long-term presence in the country with bases in Latakia and Tartus. The BBC reported that Russia will continue air strikes in Syria despite the withdrawal of most of its forces. I would be very skeptical of this "withdrawal." Russia is involved in a master chess game and a very cunning strategic player.

Meanwhile, ISIS has been knee deep in selling stolen oil to Turkey. This has been openly reported by a number of news outlets worldwide. However, the U.S. media is quite silent on the matter. The former Obama Administration would have had to have been fully aware of this corrupt transfer, but it did nothing to stop it. Obama often claimed that the U.S. is fighting and defeating ISIS, but that is hard to believe since there has been a steady ongoing movement of vehicles carrying oil that ISIS has stolen going back and forth over the Turkish border (with his obvious approval). No evidence can be found that the U.S. was seriously fighting ISIS while Obama was in office; the terrorist group did not decrease in size but continued to expand its ruthless death cult around the world. Maybe Barack Hussein Obama does not want to see ISIS defeated.

The Russians also strategically edged close to Israel's borders using Ilyushin-20 super-surveillance planes to gather intelligence. The Russian bear is stalking its prey with determination. However, Prime Minister Benjamin Netanyahu stated on December 1, 2015 that Israeli forces have been operating in Syria, where the Iran-backed regime is battling rebels including ISIS. He said, "We occasionally carry out operations in Syria to prevent that country from becoming a front against us," Netanyahu told reporters during a visit to northern Israel. "We also do everything to prevent weapons, particularly lethal ones being moved from Syria to Lebanon," he added. Netanyahu (wisely) did not provide further details and his comments were the first public recognition that Israel has been active in conflict-riddled Syria. It has been reported that the Israeli's may have targeted Iranian arms transfers from Syria to Lebanon (destined for Israel's arch-foe, the Lebanese Shiite movement—Hezbollah.)

Russia has been a long time ally of Syria and said to be Iran's proxy. Russia has been a great ally and defender of Syria, arming the anti-Israel neighbor with missiles and other weapons. It is common knowledge in Christian prophecy circles that Russia will lead a mostly Islamic coalition against Israel. Russia is positioning itself to do just that. It appears that those who wish to destroy Israel are lining up to fulfill Ezekiel's prophecy, the battle of Ezekiel 38 and 39 (Gog-Magog war). Even so, we cannot say when this prophecy will be fulfilled. Considering the intense presence of Russia and other enemy nations in Syria, anyone who still thinks that a Psalm 83 "war" is going to take place, that Israel is going to knock down her neighbors one after another and greatly expand her borders, should think again. The Psalm 83 "war" proponents are asking the impossible of Israel. They have dug a hole for themselves making the imprecatory prayer of Psalm 83 into a so-called war that simply cannot happen. How they will dig themselves out of that hole remains to be seen.

We know that a number of intense Middle East wars have already taken place in our lifetime. Skirmishes and battles will continue. At this time, internally, Israel is very busy fending off militant Islamic terrorists within her borders with no end in sight. Yet some people teach and believe that Israel is about to go out and capture millions of people, imprison them and expand her borders? That is not going to happen. To some degree, war is constantly going on around Israel. The battle of Ezekiel 38 and 39 is the next biblically prophesied war on the horizon. Russia and its allies who march against her will be woefully defeated by God's miraculous intervention.

When Does This Invasion Take Place?

"Therefore prophesy, son of man, and say to Gog, 'Thus says the Lord GOD, 'On that day when My people Israel are living securely, will you not know *it*? You will come from your place out of the remote parts of the north, you and many peoples with you, all of them riding on horses, a great assembly and a mighty army; and you will come up against My people Israel like a cloud to cover the land. It shall come about in the last days that I will bring you against My land, so that the nations may know Me when I am sanctified through you before their eyes, O Gog'" (Ezekiel 38:14-16).

This invasion takes place when Israel is back in the land, regathered as a nation as she is today. This war is supernatural in nature and will take place when God Himself says it is time—when God in His sovereignty brings down the invaders. We need not look for any particular circumstances for God to decide to act. Israel does not need to be richer or bigger. She has plenty right now that her enemies would want to plunder.

"**I will** put hooks in your jaws and bring you down" (Ezekiel 38:4a).

Israel is right now in a position of "dwelling securely" (Ezekiel 38:8-11, 14). The Hebrew word to study **is not** SHALOM ("dwelling at peace"). The word to study is the Hebrew word, BATACH, meaning *dwelling securely*, with a *secure border*; which is essentially what Israel has today. Israelis will never forfeit their weapons by thinking they are suddenly "safer" because some people have the notion that having more land will lull their protective instincts to sleep. We must keep in mind that Scripture states "they shall dwell securely" (as in *secure borders*).

> "After many days thou shalt be visited: in the latter years thou shalt come into the land that is brought back from the sword, that is gathered out of many peoples, upon the mountains of Israel, which have been a continual waste; but it is brought forth out of the peoples, and **they shall dwell securely, all of them**" (Ezekiel 38:8).

As I have written many times before, the implements of that war are burned for seven years by the inhabitants of Israel who will be fleeing the Antichrist in the middle of the Tribulation. So, that war will likely begin at least 3.5 years *before* the Tribulation. To suggest that some non-Jews will stay behind and continue to burn the implements of war is a very unlikely prospect and nowhere does Scripture make that suggestion. When the Antichrist declares himself to be god at the second half of the Tribulation, Israel will be in total chaos.

Because of the seven-year time line we cannot ignore the Scriptures that alert us that the battle could very likely take place at least 3.5 years before the Tribulation begins—so the inhabitants of Israel can clean-up the damage within the seven-year period declared in Scripture, and *before* they flee from the Antichrist—when he is hunting them down halfway through the seven-year Tribulation (Matthew 24:15-16; Revelation 12:6, 14).

If the battle of Ezekiel 38 and 39 starts after the beginning of the Tribulation it would mean the weapons of war would be burned into the millennial kingdom which is not possible, because by Peter's account (2 Peter 3:10), at the very end of the Tribulation the Lord will destroy the earth and renew it. It will be burned up. In Ezekiel 39:9 we read:

> "They that dwell in the cities of Israel shall go forth, and shall make fires of the weapons and burn them for seven years."

In a popular book, *Charting the End Times*, p. 92, authors Tim LaHaye and Thomas Ice reinforce what I have been saying for many years:

> One of the major issues that any view of Gog and Magog must address is that seven months are required to bury the dead from the battle (Ezekiel 39:12-14) and seven years are needed to burn the weapons. In the second half of the Tribulation the Jews are fleeing and being persecuted, so they cannot be burying the dead at that time. Also, any other view places at least some of the burning of weapons beyond the seven-year Tribulation and into the Millennium, or even into the eternal state (which does not make sense).

At the midpoint of the Tribulation when the Antichrist enters the prophesied Tribulation temple and commits the abomination of desolation (declaring himself to be god), the inhabitants of the cities of Israel are commanded to flee to the mountains (Matthew 24:15-18). If the people of the cities of

Israel burn the weapons for seven years, Russia and its allies will most likely attack Israel *before* the Tribulation begins, since most of the Israeli population will not be living in the cities from the midpoint of the Tribulation on (Revelation 12:6, 14). The commentators who try to take the burning of the weapons into the Millennium perhaps have not thought through the relevant Scriptures.

Scripture specifically states: "They that dwell in the cities of Israel shall go forth and burn them for seven years." This does not leave room for anyone else to burn the weapons, only: "They that dwell in the cities of Israel." By the end of the Tribulation and even before, most of the people "that dwell in the cities of Israel" will be dead or in hiding from the Antichrist outside of Israel. Once again, we must *think* things through carefully before accepting confusing teachings.

Those who place the battle of Ezekiel 38 and 39 after the Rapture/Tribulation may mistakenly assume that because of the carnage and decimation brought about by God's Gog-Magog war, that life for the entire world will not be fairly "normal" and therefore could not fit into the "As in the days of Noah" Scripture. However, life overall, after the Gog-Magog battle could calm down relatively quickly and the world would be functioning in a manner where people are still "eating and drinking, marrying and giving in marriage" (Matthew 24:38). And not every nation will be devastated by this war; it will be primarily the godless Islamic nations and Russia. I think the emphasis of the Matthew 24 Scripture is that most people were not prepared for the Flood, just as most people will not be prepared for or anticipate the Rapture/Tribulation.

The Lord implores us to study and apply the entire counsel of God when identifying a doctrine, which of course includes the interpretation of the timing of the battle of Ezekiel 38 and 39:

"For I shrank not from declaring unto you the whole counsel of God" (Acts 20:27).

Living in Peace Is Not the Same as Living Securely

Some defenders of the flawed teaching of a so-called Psalm 83 war actually confuse the words "peaceful people" and "peace." They say the Gog-Magog war cannot take place until Israel is living in peace. But they are not reading Scripture as it is written. Ezekiel 38:11 states:

> "You will go up against a land of unwalled villages; I will go to a peaceful people, who dwell safely, all of them dwelling without walls, and having neither bars nor gates—"

The Scripture states a "peaceful people," not that Israel is living in "peace," as I pointed out in 2009 in my article about Psalm 83 and Ezekiel 38 and 39. These same people have the brazenness to come right out and say that scholars and those who do not support their erroneous teaching do not understand the meaning of the word "batach." Those of us who have not fallen for the confusing teaching of a so-called Psalm 83 war understand very well the meaning the Hebrew word batach. I found this interchange on an Internet blog between two people who intensely promote the so-called Psalm 83 war hypothesis:

First commentator: "You feel very strongly that Psalm 83 is likely to be waged before Gog and Magog?"

Second commentator: "I do, because Israel does not dwell securely right now. That is a prerequisite from Ezekiel 38:13."

First commentator: "Joel Rosenberg feels otherwise. Have you ever discussed this with him?"

Second commentator: "I've not had the opportunity to discuss it with Joel. And, Joel's not the only one that feels that way. There are other Bible prophecy teachers who believe that Ezekiel 38 is probably a more imminent event."

First commentator: "I don't see how they [those who reject the false teaching of a Psalm 83 war] can say that though when you consider the fact that Ezekiel says Israel will be living in peace. There's just no way that Israel is living in peace right now."

Second commentator: "These other eschatologists sort of redefine what I think the Hebrew word yashab batach means."

First commentator: "They must redefine what peace means as well."

Second commentator: "I think a lot of them believe that it is a sense of security that Israel would develop because they have comfort in their own Israeli Defense Forces and their ability to defend themselves. But, I just don't buy it. I don't buy it."

The first commentator needs to carefully reread and study the Ezekiel chapters. Nowhere in Ezekiel or anywhere else in the Bible does it say that Israel will be living in PEACE at the time of the Gog-Magog war as this commentator claims; he is making inaccurate assertions. The second commentator condescendingly alleges that "other eschatologists" do not know what the words "yashab batach" mean. (Apparently only he does.) Dr. Arnold Fruchtenbaum succinctly refutes what the second commentator tries to pass off as his own take on "scholarly" knowledge:

> They dwell securely (38:11, 14). This has often been misconstrued as meaning a state of peace, but this is not the meaning of the Hebrew root *batach*. The nominal form of this root means "security." This is not the security due to a state of peace, but a security due to

confidence in their, own strength. This, too, is a good description of Israel today. The Israeli army has fought four major wars since its founding and won them swiftly each time. **Today Israel is secure**, confident that her army can repel any invasion from the Arab states. **Hence, Israel is dwelling securely**. Israel is dwelling in unwalled villages (38:11). This is very descriptive of the present-day *kibbutzim* in Israel. (Arnold G. Fruchtenbaum, *Footprints of the Messiah*, pages 121-122.)

Notice here that Dr. Fruchtenbaum does not in any way say that Israel will be more secure or safer because she will conquer the enemy nations that surround her. He makes an accurate and excellent point that **Israel is already dwelling securely**.

Considering the timeline of seven years necessary to burn the implements of war, and if we consider the generation time span of 70-80 years detailed in Psalm 90, the prophetic fulfillment of the Gog-Magog war could take place within the next seven years (Ezekiel 39:9). Israel's rebirth was in 1948; we are close to reaching the 70-year generation mark (May 14, 2018), and after that Israel is only 10 years away from reaching the 80 year mark. No one can predict when this epic event will take place but we can have some reasonable idea that we are getting much closer to its fulfillment.

At some point in the not too distant future, God's wrath will pour down upon the Gog-Magog alliance, which will significantly and overwhelmingly change the world as we know it, accelerating last days events. Considering the anti-Israel, pro-Iran nuclear deal made by the former Obama Administration, the Gog-Magog war may not be too far off, especially since the ongoing threatened extinction of Israel by the Iranian demonically-infested thugs has now become a more imminent possibility. Iran is part of the Russian-led coalition prophesied by Ezekiel. In an article titled, "Gog's Evil Thought," author Daymond Duck makes this insightful statement (emphasis added):

> Some say "dwelling safely" means after the Antichrist confirms the seven-year covenant with many for peace in the Middle East (Daniel 9:27). But it doesn't have to mean that because **Israel is dwelling safely now under the protection of God who will not allow her to be defeated** (Amos 9:15).

Where Will the Gog-Magog Invasion Take Place?

Israel became a nation again in 1948 but did not get the mountains of Israel until the Six-Day War (that is after the 1967 borders). In the center of Israel there is a "hogback" of mountains between the Mediterranean Sea and the Jordan River. (The pre-1967 borders were all west of these mountains and Israel was at one point only nine miles wide.) This war takes place "upon the mountains of Israel" (Ezekiel 38:8).

What Happens?

God has plans for Russia and the death cult of Islam. Russia will lead a coalition of mostly Islamic nations against Israel. "You will ascend, coming like a storm, covering the land like a cloud, you and all your troops and many peoples with you" (Ezekiel 38:9). This sounds like conventional warfare, an air armada (paratroops to cover the land). In Ezekiel 38:4, a great army, horse and horsemen. We still speak of the power of an engine as in horsepower. The figure of speech is a METONOMY – "the thing for the thing signified" e.g.: "The pen is mightier than the sword." It is not a nuclear event; the fallout (radiation) would be too great afterward.

This war will occur before the Tribulation. It could begin as early as three and one-half years *before* the Tribulation begins or sooner. It will take seven years to clean-up the damage, and seven months to bury the dead (Ezekiel 39:9, 12). The Lord Himself will supernaturally intervene, and the majority of the ruthless aggressors will be obliterated. These warriors will turn against each other. God will shake the earth with tremendous power and the invaders will wish they had never even had a bad thought about Israel.

"Thus I will magnify Myself and sanctify Myself, and I will be known in the eyes of many nations. Then they shall know that I am the Lord'" (Ezekiel 38:23).

It is here during the battle of Ezekiel 38 and 39 that we have a major fulfillment of the imprecatory prayer of Psalm 83:

"O my God, make them like the whirling dust; As stubble before the wind. As the fire that burneth the forest, And as the flame that setteth the mountains on fire, So pursue them with thy tempest, and terrify them with thy storm. Fill their faces with confusion, that they may seek thy name, O Jehovah. Let them be put to shame and dismayed for ever; Yea, let them be confounded and perish; that they may know that thou alone, whose name is Jehovah, art the Most High over all the earth" (Psalm 83:13-18).

In keeping with a Pre-Tribulation/Rapture view regarding the timing and placement of the battle of Ezekiel 38 and 39, Tim LaHaye's reference to witnessing cited on the following page indicates the Church is still here after the Gog-Magog battle.

In a 1972 book, the late Timothy LaHaye stated:

> If the magnifying and sanctifying of the Lord, as indicated in Ezekiel 38:16, 23 and 39:7, 13, 22 does indeed mean a short period of time when men call upon the Lord as a result of his miraculous preservation of Israel, then we should work diligently to prepare for it. Since we can expect the period to be brief, we should begin now to train ourselves and find positions of service where we can reach a maximum number of people with the gospel. (*The Beginning of the End,* p. 84)

Scripture Tells Us This War Will Spread

Russia will burn and Islam will take a very hard hit. Islam will be seriously marginalized. What will be the effect of the Ezekiel war on the mind of the Islamic devotee of Allah? Utter defeat. The defeat will be recognized by the entire world (Ezekiel 39:21). The destruction of Russia, the decline of tyrannical Islamic domination and God's protection of Israel (Ezekiel 39:22-23) will be seen as a major historical event; a shift in geo-political policies worldwide will be inevitable. And Islam will be unable to deny the God who sovereignly intervened.

This event will change the dynamics of how Islam is viewed by the entire world. No doubt this defeat would be an intense repudiation of Islam, spiritually. The entire world will be forced to rethink their world views and spiritual beliefs that stray from the God of the Bible. But regardless, millions will eventually choose to follow a one world church during the Tribulation that will be comprised of a number of false religions led by the prophesied False Prophet.

> "And **I** [God] **will send fire** on Magog [Russia] and those who live in security in the coastlands. Then they shall know that I *am* the LORD.

So I will make My holy name known in the midst of My people Israel, and I will not *let them* profane My holy name anymore.

Then the nations shall know that I *am* the LORD, the Holy One in Israel" (Ezekiel 39:6-7).

The Destruction of Russia and Islam Bring About the Time Of "Peace and Safety"

The removal of Islamic domination will open wide the door for the time of "peace and safety" prophesied in 1 Thessalonians 5:3-5:

"For when they shall say, Peace and safety; then sudden destruction cometh upon them, as travail upon a woman with child; and they shall no wise escape. But ye, brethren, are not in darkness, that **that Day** [Tribulation/Rapture] should overtake you as a thief: for ye are all sons of light, and sons of the day: we are not of the night, nor of darkness."

This Scripture is another confirmation that the battle of Ezekiel 38 and 39 will most likely take place prior to the Tribulation ("that Day"). Islam is causing the most conflict and terror throughout the world today. Once Islam is marginalized, then a short period of "peace and safety" will be possible.

In Ezekiel 39 the name of God is magnified. Such a great miracle will take place when He protects Israel from Russia and the Islamic coalition coming against her, that the entire world will not be able to ignore the fact that the God of Abraham, Isaac and Jacob intervened. The fire on Russia (Ezekiel 38:6) includes Indonesia, a great Islamic area.

The entire world's geopolitical equation will change. A short revival will take place, but then later, all hell will break loose with the Tribulation as soon as the "son of perdition," the Antichrist, signs the false peace-covenant with Israel. It makes sense that the Gog-Magog war will take place prior to the Tribulation in order to fulfill this prophecy: "Then those who inhabit the cities of Israel will go out and make fires with the weapons and burn *them*, both shields and bucklers, bows and arrows, war clubs and spears, and for seven years they will make fires of them" (Ezekiel 39:9). This seven-year clean-up of the carnage and implements of war left from the battle of Ezekiel 38 and 39 may very well continue perhaps right up to the time the Jews flee from the Antichrist in the middle of the Tribulation (Ezekiel 39:9-11).

No one but God Himself will help rescue Israel when she is attacked. Without God's intervention, Israel will have no chance to survive this invasion. God *will* preserve His chosen nation. He will not be doing this for Israel's sake, but for His own sake, to make a powerful statement that He is in control, and that He is Almighty God and will no longer be ignored. God will actually bring these nations against Israel who has rejected Him—for His glory. It is a major wake-up call to the entire world, and primarily for Israel, that the God of Abraham, Isaac, and Jacob lives forever and is King.

Because of the undeniable miracles performed by the Lord during the battle of Ezekiel 38 and 39, Israel and the Jews as a whole will experience a huge resurgence in their quest for God—for their Messiah. The entire world will have a chance to see God in action as the true Protector of Israel, and many will come to salvation around that time. Scripture indicates the astonishing battle of Ezekiel 38 and 39 will take place before the prophesied Tribulation opening up tremendous opportunities to share the Word of God.

After this battle a significant segment of Israel will be saved (converted) and the nation of Israel will turn back to Jehovah God after having rejected Him for over 2,000 years. The Holy Spirit will be poured out on them bringing about a revival in Israel fulfilling the prophecies of Joel 2:28b-29, double referenced in (Acts 2:17-18), when the Jews will prophesy, dream dreams and see visions. In verse 29 Joel wrote: "And also upon the servants and upon handmaids in those days will I pour out My Spirit."

The prophet Joel is speaking about the Millennium in verses 21-28a, and then halfway through verse 28 he switches to the time prior to the Rapture and the Tribulation. The Joel 2:28b-29 prophecies are directed to the nation of Israel—to the Jews. It should be noted that earlier in verse 23, Joel's prophecies are specifically to the nation of Israel, to the "children of Zion."

In verses 28b-29 he is still making reference to the "children of Zion." These prophecies are about God pouring out His Spirit upon Jews. In the New Testament Peter takes an application of these passages in Acts 2:17-18. As mentioned earlier, nations throughout the entire world will witness and realize the miraculous supernatural intervention by God Himself (Ezekiel 38:23; 39:7, 21).

Furthermore, in Joel 2:30-32, Joel distinctly presents a case for the Pre-Tribulation Rapture. He describes *when* this outpouring of the Spirit upon the Jews will happen: Prior to the Rapture and the Tribulation. All believers, including the new converts will escape the Tribulation by way of the Rapture *before* the Tribulation begins.

Joel 2:30-32

"And I will show wonders in the heavens and in the earth: The sun shall be turned into darkness and the moon into blood, **before the great and awesome day of the LORD**. And it shall come to pass, that whosoever shall call on the name of Jehovah shall be delivered for in mount Zion and in Jerusalem **there shall be those that escape** as Jehovah hath said, and among the remnant those whom Jehovah doth call."

Keep in mind, that Scripture tells us that it will take Israel seven years to clean-up (burn) the implements of war left from the battle of Ezekiel 38 and 39.

"Then those who dwell in the cities of Israel will go out and set on fire and burn the weapons, both the shields and bucklers, the bows and arrows, the javelins and spears; and they will make fires with them for seven years" (Ezekiel 39:9).

Since the earth is burned up with fire at the very end of the Tribulation, it is not possible for the weapons left from that war to burn into the Millennium (2 Peter 3:10). We read in Isaiah 65:16 that after the earth burns at the end of the Tribulation "the former things are forgotten and hid from my eyes" by newly created material to cover up the old wrecked earth. It is inconceivable to believe that the Ezekiel 38 and 39 invasion would take place the second or third year of the Tribulation, taking the burning of the implements of war into the Millennium. Those who try to place this war into the Tribulation are simply not accepting what is written in Scripture.

No matter how much some individuals want to say, "God is God, He can do whatever He wants"—and use that kind of statement to try to turn the meaning of Scripture to support their own interpretations—God will not go beyond what His Word says. He cannot go against His righteous attributes. He will never lead us beyond what He has already revealed in His Word. Keeping that in mind, the seven years during which the implements of war will be burned clearly take us back before the beginning of the Tribulation because the Tribulation will last seven years. We also know that Antichrist will turn against Israel at the midpoint of the Tribulation causing the Jewish inhabitants to flee (Matthew 24:15-16; Revelation 12:6, 14).

Therefore, the inhabitants of Israel will not be able to burn those weapons during the second half of the Tribulation. They will not be there. Again, we can see another reason why those weapons will not be able to be burned into the Millennium. The point I am also making here is that Scripture gives us strong indication that the battle of Ezekiel 38 and 39 almost certainly may occur at least three and one half years *before* the Tribulation begins, in order to fulfill the prophecy of Ezekiel 39:9-11:

> **"Then those who inhabit the cities of Israel will go out and make fires with the weapons and burn them,** both shields and bucklers, and bows and arrows, war clubs and spears and **for seven years they will make fires of them.** And they will not take wood

> from the field or gather firewood from the forests, for they will
> take the spoil of those who despoiled them, and seize the plunder
> of those who plundered them, declares the LORD God."

The commentators who try to take the burning of the weapons into the Millennium perhaps have not thought through the relevant Scriptures. Scripture specifically states: "They that dwell in the cities of Israel shall go forth and burn them for seven years." This does not leave room for anyone else to burn the weapons, only: "They that dwell in the cities of Israel." By the end of the Tribulation and before, most people "that dwell in the cities of Israel" will be dead or in hiding from the Antichrist outside of Israel. Once again, we must *think* things through carefully before accepting hypothetical teachings.

A great (short) revival will follow the Gog-Magog war and many will turn to the Lord. This happens prior to the Tribulation and is the first stage of Israel's conversion as illustrated in Joel 2:28:

> "And it shall come to pass afterward that I will pour out My Spirit
> on all flesh; your sons and your daughters shall prophesy, your old
> men shall dream dreams, your young men shall see visions."

Please note that previously in verse 23, the prophet Joel was speaking to the "children of Zion." Joel 2:28 should never be interpreted as a picture of a revival among the Gentiles. This prophecy is about God pouring out His Spirit upon the Jews. This will be a great revival leading up to the Rapture. It will probably be short-lived.

> "And I will show wonders in the heavens and in the earth: blood, and
> fire, and pillars of smoke. The sun shall be turned into darkness, and the
> moon into blood, before the great and terrible day of Jehovah cometh."

How will people escape the Day of the Lord and be delivered from the Tribulation? By God Himself in the Rapture:

"And it shall come to pass, that whosoever shall call on the name of Jehovah shall be delivered; for in mount Zion and in Jerusalem there shall be those that escape. As Jehovah hath said, and among the remnant those whom Jehovah doth call" (Joel 3:32).

The second stage of Israel's conversion takes place early in the Tribulation with the 144,000 of Revelation 7. The third and final stage takes hold during the last three days of the Tribulation (Hosea 6:1-3).

"Come, and let us return unto Jehovah; for he hath torn, and he will heal us; he hath smitten, and he will bind us up. After two days will he revive us: on the third day he will raise us up, and we shall live before him. And let us know, let us follow on to know Jehovah: his going forth is sure as the morning; and he will come unto us as the rain, as the latter rain that watereth the earth."

The Western powers are still in existence when this invasion takes place prior to the Tribulation:

"Sheba, Dedan, the merchants of Tarshish, and all their young lions will say to you, 'Have you come to take plunder? Have you gathered your army to take booty, to carry away silver and gold, to take away livestock and goods, to take great plunder?'" (Ezekiel 38:13).

The meaning of the merchants of Tarshish is a reference to England. "With all the young lions therof" refers to the nations that have been colonized from England; the United States and Canada for example. The Western powers will not take a firm pro-Israel stand and will not help her when Russia and its allies attack Israel. Instead, it seems that the Western nations will offer only a mild protest:

"Have you gathered your army to take booty, to carry away silver and gold... and goods, to take great plunder?"

The Term "Rosh" in Reference to Russia

Highly respected Hebrew scholars have taken the term "Rosh" as a reference to Russia. This should not be underestimated. A notable example is Wilhelm Gesenius. His original Latin version of his lexicon titled, *Thesasurus Linguae Hebraeae et Chaldaeae Verteris Testamenti* contains nearly a page of notes dealing with the word "Roch" and with the Rosh people mentioned in Ezekiel 38-39.

Historical evidence has shown that the people known as Rosh, gave their name to the lands of Russia. Sometimes alternate spellings have been used such as Ros and Rux, all terms recognized in the ancient world, and located in the area now known as (modern) Russia.

Related to this, the Septuagint, the Greek translation of the Hebrew Old Testament that predates the time of Christ, translates, "Rosh" as "Ros." It is worth noting that the Septuagint is not much more than three centuries removed from Ezekiel's time. Moreover, evidence can be found of a people named Rosh/Rashu in the ninth through seventh centuries B.C. in Assyrian sources that predates the book of Ezekiel. So we have—quite early, evidence of a "Ros" people found that was geographically located in today's Russia.

Ros also appears as a place name in Egyptian inscriptions as Rash, dating as early as 2600 B.C. One inscription that dates to 1500 B.C. refers to a land called Reshu that was located to the north of Egypt (as is the case with modern Russia). Rosh or its equivalent is also found in a variety of other ancient documents.

Placing Rosh in the area today known as Russia has long been a tradition in the Christian church, as early as A.D. 438. In Ezekiel 39:2 Rosh is said to be "from the remotest parts of the north." The term "north" is to be understood in relation to Israel. If one draws a line from Israel and goes straight north, one ends up in Russia. An interesting matter to ponder in relation to the Gog-Magog war is this: The complex issues with Ukraine have been front page news since the spring of 2014. It is interesting to note the following King James translation (KJV) regarding Ezekiel 38:2:

"Son of man, set thy face against Gog, the land of Magog, the **chief** prince of Meshech and Tubal, and prophesy against him." (KJV)

What is the problem with this King James (KJV) translation?

It is the word *chief* – or, more specifically, the Hebrew word *rosh*. The King James Version gets it wrong. The King James claims that the Hebrew word *rosh* is an adjective, but Hebrew is very specific when it comes to adjectives, unlike English. If *rosh* was supposed to be an adjective, the Hebrew for chief prince would be:

ראשי נשיא

But, the prophet Ezekiel wrote it like this:

ראש נשיא

Notice see the difference; it's this one character: י

That's a *yood*, and it should appear at the end of *rosh* (Hebrew is written right-to-left), if it was a modifier of *nasi* (prince). Also, *nasi* ALREADY means chief prince. In fact, it is the word used in Israel to indicate the president. President Trump is the *nasi* of America. Putin is the *nasi* of Russia. Could he be Gog? We may find out soon.

The word *rosh* is obviously a proper noun – meaning, it's a name – and, it fits very nicely with the original name for the Ukraine – *Rus*. (Hebrew is very malleable in terms of pronunciation.) The Ukraine was once part of the Soviet Union (Russia). What does this mean? It means that the attempt by the U.S. to drag the Ukraine away from Russia is going to fail. It is highly likely that Ukraine will be involved in the Gog and Magog coalition that comes down to attack Israel. Furthermore, this attempt by the U.S. to meddle in Russian affairs will cause even more upset in the Kremlin.

An Israeli's Account of Israel's Secure Borders

Amir Tsarfati, whom I have often quoted as far back as 2009, is an Israeli born Jewish believer who resides in Jerusalem. He is a former deputy governor of Jericho and captain in the Israeli army. While Amir was deputy governor, the Israeli government entrusted him with what are now known as the famous Oslo Accords documents. This was long before his Israeli counterparts and the rest of the world knew anything about these important declarations regarding the Israeli-Palestinian conflicts.

Amir is highly aware of what is going on in Israel and her surrounding nations, and has many times declared publicly at his speaking engagements at various churches that nothing has to happen before the Gog-Magog invasion takes place. Even when Hamas is firing missiles into Israel, she is *secure* in her ability to retaliate and protect her citizens. Many Israeli citizens are armed and can protect themselves if necessary. Internal violence in Israel, particularly in Jerusalem brought on by Muslim aggressors is escalating but that does not negate the fact that Israel has *secure borders.*

More walls within Israel may be built to protect Israelis from Arab assaults but that will give them more *security.* We are primarily talking about the *borders around* Israel which are *secure.* But that does not mean internal violence from Muslim terrorists who reside in Israel will not increase. We can expect that it will. Those who are waiting for Israel to have peace or more safety *before* the Gog-Magog war will be very disappointed. Israel will never have true peace until Jesus the Messiah returns at the Second Coming.

In regard to Ezekiel 38:11: "And you will say, 'I will go up against the land of unwalled villages. I will go against those who are at rest, that live securely, all of them living without walls and having no bars or gates.'" To better understand what that verse means in its proper context please read the section in Chapter Fourteen titled, "Unwalled Villages Defined."

It is no secret that Israel has secure borders and has a strong military; the requirement for Ezekiel's prophecy to be fulfilled (chapters 38-39). It is completely illogical and foolish to think that Israel will have true peace any time before Jesus rescues her at Armageddon. Especially since the overall condition in the Middle East is getting worse and more dangerous each day.

As soon as Russia and the Islamic hordes march against Israel fulfilling the Ezekiel 38 and 39 prophecies, those who are waiting for Israel to be "safer" or more at peace as a prerequisite for the Gog-Magog war will realize they have not understood the meaning of the Hebrew word batach ("to trust in," "to be secure," "be careless") and that the Psalm 83 war hypothesis is a distortion and misapplication of Scripture.

Sunny Shia and Bible Prophecy
Behold Israel Blog
June 27, 2014
Amir Tsarfati

The Middle East Is Burning While Israel Is Prospering

Many of you are hearing daily incidents between Sunni and Shia Muslims. The division between Shia and Sunni dates back to the death of the Prophet Muhammad, and the question of who was to take over the leadership of the Muslim nation.

Sunni Muslims agree with the position taken by many of the Prophet's companions, that the new leader should be elected from among those capable of the job. This is what was done, and the Prophet Muhammad's close friend and advisor, Abu Bakr, became the first Caliph of the Islamic nation. The word "Sunni" in Arabic comes from a word meaning "one who follows the traditions of the Prophet."

On the other hand, some Muslims share the belief that leadership should have stayed within the Prophet's own family, among those specifically appointed by him, or among Imams appointed by God Himself.

The Shia Muslims believe that following the Prophet Muhammad's death, leadership should have passed directly to his cousin/son-in-law, Ali bin Abu Talib. Throughout history, Shia Muslims have not recognized the authority of elected Muslim leaders, choosing instead to follow a line of Imams which they believe have been appointed by the Prophet Muhammad or God Himself.

The word "Shia" in Arabic means a group or supportive party of people. The commonly-known term is shortened from the historical "Shia-t-Ali," or "the Party of Ali." They are also known as followers of "Ahl-al-Bayt" or "People of the Household" (of the Prophet).

Today, Iran is the guardian of Shia Islam while Saudi Arabia is the guardian of Sunni Islam. Thus much of what is going on in Iraq and Syria is the manifestation of the real struggle for power between the two countries. More than any Islamist nation in the world, it is Saudi Arabia that fears the possibility of a nuclear armed Iran.

Pay attention to Damascus on one hand as I believe it will pay the price of this struggle, and to the fading out of the USA and the rise to power of Russia in the Middle East. Ezekiel 38 is literally around the corner. Believers—Rejoice for our soon salvation of the body from this world! Non-believers—great tribulation is ahead. God wants your attention.

Egypt Is Destroyed Before the Tribulation Begins

The fulfillment of the prophecy found in Scripture regarding Egypt's destruction is on the near horizon. As we read the news headlines and watch the extreme aggression and resulting bloodshed, the relentless fighting is destroying the entire nation. In the book of Isaiah, chapter 19 speaks of God's judgment against Egypt. The prophet Ezekiel also wrote about Egypt's total demise, which would take place prior to the Tribulation. Notice the Scripture "For the day is near, even the day of Jehovah is near" [the Day of the Lord].

> "The word of Jehovah came again saying unto me, saying, Son of man, prophesy, and say, **Thus saith the Lord Jehovah: Wail ye, Alas for the day! For the day is near, even the day of Jehovah is near**; it shall be a day of clouds, a time of nations. And a sword shall come upon Egypt; and they shall take away her multitude, and her foundations shall be broken down.
>
> Ethiopia, and Put, and Lud, and all the mingled people and Cub, and the children of the land that is in league, shall fall with them by the sword. Thus saith Jehovah: they also that uphold Egypt shall fall and the pride of her power shall come down" (Ezekiel 30:1-8).

For more on the battle of Ezekiel 38 and 39 see Chapter Fourteen in Part Three of this book.

God's Wisdom Brings Understanding and Discernment

"For the LORD gives wisdom; from His mouth *come* knowledge and understanding; He stores up sound wisdom for the upright; *He is* a shield to those who walk uprightly" (Proverbs 2:6-7).

**Dr. and Mrs. F. Kenton Beshore and the late
Israeli Prime Minister Ariel Sharon**

**Dr. and Mrs. F. Kenton Beshore and Israeli
Prime Minister Benjamin Netanyahu**

Chapter Ten

A Message to Christian Evangelicals From Israel's Leaders

During the first Gulf War Israel was asked by President George H. W. Bush to stay out of that war. Although the Israeli's were methodically being fired upon with scud missiles by Saddam Hussein's military, Israel complied and stayed out of the war. Around that same time, the Israeli government, through the Israel Ministry of Tourism invited Dr. F. Kenton Beshore, president of the longstanding renowned World Bible Society and some of his staff on a full-expense paid trip to "Bless the Land of Israel."

Dr. Beshore and his small entourage were greeted at the Ben Gurion International Airport by gas masks, a personal driver (to act as a guide) and a car. They traveled throughout Israel praying over the Land of Israel. It was a very special trip giving Dr. Beshore the opportunity to better understand firsthand the government of Israel's position on some important matters—including some observations pertaining to evangelical Christians.

At that time, Benjamin Netanyahu was in his first term of office. Prime Minister Benjamin Netanyahu invited Dr. Beshore along with some of his staff into his office in Jerusalem, which turned out to be a lengthy meeting. They discussed many issues relating to Israel's safety, sovereignty and future. Prime Minister Netanyahu expressed great concern regarding how dangerous it would be for Israel to ever go back to the pre-1967 borders.

"I have set watchmen on your walls, O Jerusalem; they shall never hold their peace day or night. You who make mention of the LORD, do not keep silent, and give Him no rest till He establishes and till He makes Jerusalem a praise in the earth" (Isaiah 62:6-7).

On that same trip, Dr. Beshore met with Knesset members who expressed their gratitude for Christian evangelicals. They all said that they appreciate evangelicals standing with Israel and appreciate that they don't picture Israel, and these are the words they used: "As predatory or expansionist."

Years later, the late Prime Minister Ariel Sharon was invited to and attended a reception in Beverly Hills, California sponsored by the World Bible Society. While hosting the reception for the prime minister, Dr. Beshore welcomed him to "occupied territory." Prime Minister Sharon replied, "What do you mean?" Dr. Beshore replied by saying that the United States took this country fair and square from England, we took Georgia from the Cherokees and Texas from Mexico. He then said, "Mr. Prime Minister, the next time our U.S. State Department tries to tell you to give back the 'disputed territories' you tell them you will glad to do so when America gives back the 14 colonies."

Their spokesman said, "We are simply trying to maintain defensible borders and live at peace with our neighbors. We have no desire to expand into Lebanon, Syria, Jordan or Egypt. We want to live in peace with our neighbors and to show good faith, that is why we gave back the Sinai to Egypt."

At that reception, Prime Minister Sharon commended Christian evangelicals for loving Israel. However, he expressed a serious, new concern:

We have a problem with you evangelicals saying we will get all the land from the Nile to the Euphrates. Please be careful because we do not want to be seen as, "predatory or expansionist." (The same words used by the leading Knesset member years earlier.) Prime Minister Sharon continued to say, "We want to make it clear that the land is only to be given in the days of Messiah – and even talk about the Temple is very dangerous because it could lead to a Holy War.

The last thing Israel wants is for Christian evangelicals to portray Israel as "expansionist," as that would put her in a very bad light with the other nations worldwide, perpetuating increased anti-Semitism and bring on even more hatred toward the nation and Jews everywhere. Our love for Israel should not portray her as a land grabber or a nation that would take advantage of her enemies when they are weak and fighting amongst themselves—which could create an open door for land confiscation.

In this ungodly world where ruthless competition and over-the-top self-indulgence is glorified, we can rejoice knowing that Israel—the devil's prime target of annihilation—is destined to be the premiere nation during the millennial kingdom. Israel's phenomenal destiny is already promised. When Jesus the Messiah returns, not only will that be a time of great glory for Israel, it will be a time of great glory for Christ and all His redeemed. The devil surely knows his final knockout punch is coming soon. Be sure you know the Lord God of Israel so you can participate in the great glory He has prepared for His beloved nation, and all those who belong to Him.

> "For there will be peace for the seed: the vine will yield its fruit,
> the land will yield its produce, and the heavens will give their dew;
> and I will cause the remnant of this people to inherit all things"
> (Zechariah 8:1).

Please notice in Chapter Four of this book the entry, "Myth: Israel sought War in 1967 to Conquer Territory," which documents that even according to the 1993 Oslo accords with the Palestine Liberation Organization and their provisions for final status talks by 1998 on the West Bank and Gaza Strip (much of which were to be administered by the new Palestinian Authority), likewise **confirmed that the Six-Day War *had not* been launched for territorial conquest**. This too, shows that Israel is not predatory and expansionist but simply wants to live in peace. But we know from Scripture Israel has some extremely tough days ahead, not a massive land grab of victory where she will have power greater in scope and magnitude than that which she has now.

As noted earlier, Israel will receive all the blessings promised to her from Jesus Himself during the Millennium. Then she will be the preeminent nation where Jesus the Messiah, the King of kings and Lord of lords will rule and reign.

Those who teach the hypothesis of a supposed Psalm 83 war are creating a serious problem for Israel. They are making her out to be predatory and expansionist portraying Israel as she has never behaved in the past and is it not today. Have the proponents of the hypothetical teaching of a Psalm 83 war ever considered how they are negatively undermining Israel? Apparently not.

> The hypothetical teaching of a Psalm 83 "war" places Israel in a very unattractive light making her appear as if she wants to, and will go after all her enemies and subjugate them. This teaching could create a serious backlash against Israel and cause people to become even more anti-Semitic—fearing that Israel will attack the surrounding nations.

A Relevant Point: On June 22, 2014 in Prime Minister Benjamin Netanyahu's address, he told journalists that in conflicts like Syria where al-Qaida-inspired extremists are battling Iranian-backed Syrian troops there is no good choice, and it is best for Israel to sit back and let its enemies weaken each other. "This is a fault line between civilization and savagery," Benjamin Netanyahu said. He made it clear that Israel's position is not to go forth pummeling other nations to take possession of them, which once again shows that the premise of a so-called Psalm 83 war is based on flawed calculations and assertions.

Impressions of a Devout Christian

"While I was in Israel, I was struck by the people of Israel and those who surround them. As a people in general, Arabs are arrogant and prideful. They hate the Israelis and covet their land. The Israelis simply go about life, holding onto what's theirs, just wanting to live in peace. Israelis maintain a courageous dignity, outnumbered but not overwhelmed or despairing. These are my impressions of the people." —Patrick Wyett, a former Defense Contractor for the U.S. Military

✡✡✡✡✡✡

Chapter Eleven

Stabbing Israel in the Back

"For thus says the LORD of hosts; He sent Me after glory, to the nations which plunder you; for he who touches you touches the apple of His eye" (Zechariah 2:8).

Never before has Israel—the only democracy in the Middle East, received as much pressure and derogatory interference from the "Washington elite" as she did under the former Obama Administration. No one has the right to tell the people of Israel to give up land, stop building homes, or stop breathing air in their God-given land. The United States has always been Israel's greatest ally until Obama changed those dynamics. That long-term friendship was on very shaky ground during his presidency, thanks to the increased nefarious, busybody posturing of his administration. It is foolhardy to conspire against Israel.

"I will bless those who bless you, and I will curse him who curses you; and in you all the families of the earth shall be blessed" (Genesis 12:3).

If you reread the previous Scripture, notice, "in you [Israel] all the families of the earth shall be blessed." In other words, the blessings for all nations and people, "the families of the earth," are contingent on how Israel is treated. This includes, of course, the United States. One only has to look at the daily news to see how Israel is being verbally decimated by one news anchor after another. Former President Obama has aggressively worked to undermine and defeat allied leaders he does not like, and Israel was at the top of his list.

Obama's Campaign Against Israel

It is common knowledge that in January 2015, Obama sent a team of high-powered campaign operatives to Israel to work to defeat Benjamin Netanyahu in the March 2015 elections. He sent an entourage of his own campaign operatives to try to bring about the destruction of the conservative government and replace it with a leftist one that would give Obama more influence in dismantling God's chosen nation. The danger that a leftist government would be formed supported by a large and powerful Arab party that would be more influential than ever, proposed a real danger. As the election drew near there seemed to be a worldwide effort to defeat Netanyahu. When I saw the pictures of thousands of protestors rallying together in Tel Aviv against the prime minister, all I could think of is this: *Obama's ruthless Chicago-style community organizing has reached Israel.* The hatred Obama holds toward Israel and Prime Minister Netanyahu is not new and became glaringly obvious over the years. Thankfully, Obama's plan to defeat Netanyahu did not work. I expect this former American "president" will become even more hostile toward Israel in the future as a civilian.

Now that we have a new pro-Israel president—President Trump, how the USA will be placed into the position of fulfilling the prophecy of Ezekiel 38:13, when the Western powers do not take a firm pro-Israel—when Russia and its allies attack her, is unknown. The prophesied scenario can come about by any number of unknown ways. Scripture tells us that the Western nations will offer only a mild protest.

As the 2015 Israeli election results were coming in I was busy writing this article which we immediately published on various websites on the Internet.

God's Victory

The leftist coalition sent to Israel has fallen apart (for now). Despite the Obama Administration's intense interference, Obama's Chicago-style radical Alinsky sanctioned attempts to destroy Prime Minister Netanyahu, and Israel's sovereignty—did not work. The shameful interference of the White

House has been circumvented by God Almighty. Make no mistake about it, God should be given all the credit and glory for this important win. In this extremely intense battle between good and evil, God has given us this gift of great encouragement in these very trying, last days.

The Obama Administration's attempt to transform Israel into a leftist menagerie has been given a good swift kick. All good Christians and Jews should be celebrating Netanyahu's victory; for it is God's victory. And the same God of the Bible has sent a very strong message: God is not mocked and despite all the efforts of the devil's representatives, He rules like no other.

We have been given hope in these dark days when out-of-control liberalism (which is nothing less than a serious mental and spiritual disorder), has seeped into every nook and cranny of our lives. The moral depravity engineered by Satan's representatives may be having a field day throughout the world but their days are numbered.

The King of kings and Lord of lords is alive and well. *I wonder if the angels in heaven are cheering.* I can only imagine the disdain and shock of the leftists who tried to dismantle Israel. All the money and manipulations used by the Obama Administration were made ineffective by God Himself. The problem for the administration and those who oppose Israel's sovereignty is this:

They do not understand they are opposing the God of the universe, the Great I AM, God Almighty, the Creator of heaven and earth. The radical vermin are totally out of their league. They are fighting a losing war, a war they ultimately cannot win. They will win some skirmishes and battles but we all know that they will never defeat God and His prophetic plan for Israel and mankind.

I ask all those who love our Messiah Jesus, the great Messiah of Israel, to fall on your knees and praise Him and thank Him for we have been given a small glimpse of a heavenly victory.

We know Israel has some very rough days ahead during the coming Tribulation. But the fact that God did not allow, at this time, the radical leftists from Obama's cadre of godless cohorts to tear apart His Holy Land—should give us all hope. Hope, that when it is all said and done every prophetic utterance in the Bible will be fulfilled exactly as intended by God.

Consider Netanyahu's win in the Israeli elections a preview of one of God's soon coming attractions—when he tears down all those who oppose Him and His beloved Israel—when the battle of Ezekiel 38 and 39 takes place. All these same anti-Semitic, anti-Israel, anti-God elitists will be shaken to the core when God intervenes and saves Israel from the Russian-led Islamic coalition.

This coalition of nations will be destroyed by God Almighty Himself—who stops them in a spectacular divine action (Ezekiel 38:22). The defeat of this coalition will be so unbelievable that the nation of Israel will get a serious wake-up call that God is alive, and many will come to understand that YAHWEH is their God (Ezekiel 38:23; 39:7, 22, 28). The defeat of these enemy nations that vastly outnumber Israel will also show the people of the world that their destruction was a divine act.

"'And all men who *are* on the face of the earth shall shake at My presence. I will call for a sword against Gog throughout all My mountains,' says the Lord GOD. 'Every man's sword will be against his brother. And I will bring him to judgment with pestilence and bloodshed; I will rain down on him, on his troops, and on the many peoples who *are* with him, flooding rain, great hailstones, fire, and brimstone'" (Ezekiel 38:21-22).

"And I [God] will send fire on Magog [Russia] and those who live in security in the coastlands. Then they shall know that I *am* the LORD. So I will make My holy name known in the midst of My people Israel, and I will not *let them* profane My holy name

196

anymore. Then the nations shall know that I *am* the LORD, the Holy One in Israel" (Ezekiel 39:6-7).

So get ready, Jesus is coming soon! In Jesus' Name. Amen.

✡✡✡✡✡✡

On March 1, 2015 it was reported that the Bethlehem-based news agency *Ma'an* had cited a Kuwaiti newspaper report, that U.S. President Barack Hussein Obama thwarted an Israeli military attack against Iran's nuclear facilities in 2014 by threatening to shoot down Israeli jets before they could reach their targets in Iran. Following Obama's threat, Prime Minister Benjamin Netanyahu was reportedly forced to abort the planned Iran attack that was obviously intended to protect Israel from Iran's never-ending vilification to destroy God's chosen nation.

According to *Al-Jarida*, the Netanyahu government took the decision to strike Iran some time in 2014 soon after Israel had discovered the United States and Iran had been involved in secret talks over Iran's nuclear program, and were about to sign an agreement in that regard behind Israel's back. An unnamed Israeli minister with good ties with the U.S. administration "revealed the attack plan to John Kerry."

This report surfaced just prior to Prime Minister Netanyahu's speech at a joint session of the U.S. Congress on March 3, 2015. He delivered a multi-tiered indictment of Iran's regime and the dangerous negotiations Obama was engaged in with the terrorist nation. Obama's deal was the worst possible. Not only does Iran get a clear path to the bomb but it gets sanctions lifted, all pressure removed and international legitimacy. Obama in his typical narcissistic style once again arrogantly snubbed and insulted the Israeli prime minister refusing to meet with him. He even stated that the prime minister had not said anything new in his speech and offered no solutions. This is absolutely false. Benjamin Netanyahu detailed why Obama's deal is a very bad one: "This deal has two major concessions: one, leaving Iran with a vast nuclear program and two, lifting the restrictions on that program in about a decade. That's why this deal is so bad. It doesn't block Iran's path to the bomb; it paves Iran's path to the bomb."

The prime minister then offered a workable alternative which Obama apparently did not (want to) hear:

> We can insist that restrictions on Iran's nuclear program not be lifted for as long as Iran continues its aggression in the region and in the world. Before lifting those restrictions, the world should demand that Iran do three things. First, stop its aggression against its neighbors in the Middle East. Second, stop supporting terrorism around the world. And third, stop threatening to annihilate my country, Israel, the one and only Jewish State.

Israel did not and need not to bow down to any demands from the failed former President Obama and his surrogates. Israel's economy is technologically advanced by global standards, and has shown outstanding growth for many years. This growth also serves American interests. When the U.S. cut support to Israel during the economic crisis, Israel found that she got by very well without U.S. assistance. The support given by the U.S. signifies about one and a half percent of the Israel gross national product and if that is decreased or eliminated all together it will not harm Israel. The Israelis do not need to buckle under pressure from the Obama or from anyone else. Let's go back to May 19, 2011 when former President Obama unreasonably, and some would say diabolically, made a public plea to Israel that she should return to her 1967 borders relinquishing her precious land; which would leave her utterly vulnerable in the face of her many enemies.

Media reports have stated that the former Obama Administration was pressuring Israeli Prime Minister Benjamin Netanyahu to publicly adopt Obama's view that Israel's pre-1967 border should be the basis for future peace talks.

The request by the White House in the spring of 2011 for Israel to surrender her land to her enemies actually goes beyond the pre-1967 borders, which was reposted by Jennifer Rubin in the *Washington Post* on June 12, 2011 in an article titled, "Obama Bullies Israel; So Much for His Promises at AIPAC."

I can only imagine what our Lord and Savior, the Messiah of Israel might be preparing for those who come against His chosen nation, Israel. The former Obama Administration was obviously not on the side of Israel. Dividing her God-given land is something Obama and his lackeys methodically worked toward. Obama's dealings with Iran are essentially emboldening and perhaps accelerating the Ezekiel 38 alliance to strike Israel. Israel will be victorious and all those who have undermined Israel will get a much needed comeuppance when they witness God Almighty's protective intervention.

Issue no. 5 of Women in Green's *Sovereignty Journal* published March 3, 2015 states: "Do not divide the land under an economic pretense. The heads of Women in Green, Yehudit Katsover and Nadia Matar, stress the importance of publishing the issue especially these days, in the days of the final stretch before the elections, when it seems that the public is engrossed by social, economic matters, while behind these matters hides the open attempt by the Left at regime change, in order to speed up the political process toward establishing a Palestinian terror state in the heart of the Land of Israel."

Economic Minister Naftali Bennett added this to the publication:

"A Palestinian state would collapse the Israeli economy. Ben Gurion Airport would be paralyzed, there would be no tourism, there would be no commerce, we would return to the economic collapse of the days of the second intifada and they would run away from here. The Left thinks that the economy would flourish if there would be peace here, but this is simply not true... Annexation of Judea and Samaria is not a distant vision, but something practical that is possible to achieve with enough political and public power. We must really believe in it."

The Boycott Divestment and Sanctions Movement (BDS)

The Boycott, Divestment and Sanctions Movement is expanding all over the world. The intention of this intensely anti-Semitic group is to apply massive pressure both economically and politically until Israel ends their so-called Israeli occupation and colonization of Palestinian land. (That will never happen.) Israel is God's chosen nation no matter what the naysayers say and do. Those who foolishly boycott Israel will not be able to force Israel to give in to their demands. Little do they know they are fighting the God of the universe.

Paper Details Obama Admin's Alleged Secret Note Sent to Iran: If Israel Attacks, We Won't Get Involved - September 3, 2012 [Excerpt]:

Israeli newspaper *Yediot Ahronot* published a startling report Monday detailing a message it says was conveyed by the Obama Administration – via two European countries – to Iranian officials. The request: If Israel decides to strike Iranian nuclear facilities, the U.S. will not support it and the Islamic Republic should refrain from retaliating on U.S. military installations in the Persian Gulf.

Wall Street Journal - Israeli's Are Right Not to Trust Obama September 1, 2012 [Excerpt]: "Though President Obama likes to say he has Israel's 'back,' "his administration tries to sell to the public a make-believe world in which Iran's nuclear intentions are potentially peaceful, sanctions are working and diplomacy hasn't failed after three and half years."

Barack Obama: Israel's Most Dangerous Enemy
Published: 08/06/2014
P. J. Media. com
Roger L. Simon

Barack Obama is apparently very angry with Bibi Netanyahu [again]. We have known for some time, via hot-mic and other methods, that neither he nor his secretary of state much care for the Israeli prime minister. But – perhaps exacerbated by a multiplicity of foreign and domestic policy failures, plus atrocious poll numbers, including a recent CNN poll showing Romney beating him handily were the election held today – Obama seemed more irked than usual.

Obama needed someone to beat up since the world was beating *him* up. And the Israelis had just hugely embarrassed his secretary of state (and by extension Obama) by pointing out their absurd bias in favor of Hamas in cease-fire negotiations; so absurd in fact that they outraged even Israel's most famous liberal/left politician, Tzipi Livni, who would normally do almost anything for a chance for peace. (Ironically, the details of the pro-Hamas negotiations in which Israeli security concerns – the tunnels, demilitarization, etc. – were ignored were exposed by Barak Ravid in Israel's most liberal newspaper, *Haaretz.*)

Further, they had outraged the Egyptians, who were dumped from the negotiations by Obama and Kerry in favor of Turkey and Qatar. Our administration seems to have a preference for the more extreme Islamist/Muslim Brotherhood societies, although you would think, given their professed loyalty to women's and gay rights, these cultures would be anathema to them Never mind. Obama is an equal opportunity narcissist and everything's fine, unless you cross him.

Which, according to sources in Israel, is where Netanyahu found himself when the American president called to admonish him about Gaza. Obama reportedly used or implied the threat of withholding the resupply of weapons – don't know if this includes the Iron Dome itself – if Israel didn't fall into line and stop attacking Gaza immediately.

What Obama was doing, in effect, was saving Hamas. It's almost mind-boggling to think, but it's true.

The standard excuse is that if Hamas is obliterated, what replaces it will be even worse. Oh, really? ISIS or similar may be waiting in the wings to step in, but it's doubtful if Israel (given its huge 87 percent public support for the current war) will ever let something like that happen, at least in the near future.

That is, if Israel is allowed to finish the job. Obviously, Obama is doing everything he can to make sure it's otherwise. Part of this may stem from his deep-seated identification with the Third World, some from a buried (agnostic's version) sympathy for Islam and some may be merely personal or fashionably anti-Semitic (see the Khalidi Tapes … oops, sorry, they're stuck in a vault at the L.A. Times), but it's very much there. Obama may be on the rocks, but he's quite willing to take us all – and I mean the global *all* – down with him.

In the final analysis, he may be seizing on Israel-bashing as a way to distract from his failures and resurrect his reputation as a "good man." No more callous behavior toward dead or dying veterans, no more endless lies about Obamacare, no more blindness as ISIS runs roughshod over Syria and Iraq, or Libya (his supposed triumph) turns into a giant Islamist nightmare, not to mention armies of illegal aliens streaming over our borders in numbers no one could conceivably count and with missions no one could possibly guess.

No, Obama can't man up and take responsibility for his failures, all of this is somehow Israel's fault. ("See how the Jews over-reacted, killing all those innocent Arab children!")

In this, of course, Obama always has the eager compliance of the mainstream media, who loathe to show what Hamas really is and only reluctantly report the unprecedented lengths Israel goes not to harm civilians. But for those who are still undecided, videos on the Internet will surely convince you.

You will see the Hamas group that Barack Obama is trying to save. Morally challenged, he and Kerry are oblivious to the obvious – that only a total victory by Israel over Hamas can save the miserable lives of the Gaza Palestinians.

Fortunately, if Obama follows through on his threats, veiled or otherwise, about restricting Israeli arms, he and his party will probably suffer mightily for it in November. Unfortunately, that is not near punishment enough.

PJ Media has been running non-stop stories on the terrorist crisis in Gaza, including our recent photo essay, "Fourteen ways Hamas weaponizes women, children, animals against Israel" and our recent look at how "Hamas boasted about its capture of IDF soldier … then backtracked four times."

Obama Administration Blocks Missile Shipments to Israel
August 2014

Obama "support" of Israel includes blocking arms. He exposes his true feeling toward Israel in this unprecedented move. The Obama Administration confirmed on August 14, 2014 reports that it had, in an unusual move, pro-actively stepped in to hold up arms shipments to Israel for further review as the current conflict in the Gaza strip continues.

State Department spokeswoman Marie Harf confirmed to reporters the accuracy of reports published in both the United States and Israel revealing that the White House was subjecting to further review Israeli requests for ammunition shipments, which typically have not needed explicit White House approval.

The added reviews on the munitions shipments prompted accusations that the White House is punishing Israel and injecting partisan politics into a military process typically unaffected by diplomacy issues between the two allies.

Furthermore, a new *Wall Street Journal* report reveals that President Barack Obama's Administration blocked a shipment of missiles to Israel in late July and tightened additional weapons shipment procedures to Israel, revealing increasing tensions between the two governments.

The U.S. decision to tighten arms transfers to Israel comes as the UK threatens similar actions. Recently, the British government announced the suspension of 12 arms export licenses to Israel if fighting resumed in Gaza.

The report cites officials in the Obama Administration who say Israel had requested a large number of Hellfire missiles directly through military-to-military channels, for which no additional administration approvals are required. An initial batch of the missiles was about to be shipped, according to sources in Israel and the U.S. Congress.

At that point, the administration stepped in and put the transfer on hold. Top White House officials instructed various U.S. military agencies to consult with the U.S. State Department before approving any additional arms requests from Israel.

The decision to clamp down on future transfers was the equivalent of "the United States saying 'the buck stops here. Wait a second…It's not okay anymore,'" said one official.

An Israeli defense official confirmed the reports, saying, "The U.S. delayed a shipment of Hellfire missiles to the Israeli air force" in the face of "national tension" with Israel.

Obama has not been on the same page as Israel in terms of Israel's operation in Gaza, making various attempts to press Israel into accepting a truce with Hamas, even under terms unpalatable to the Israeli government.

After one instance where America allegedly pressured Israel into a ceasefire that was violated within 90 minutes by a Hamas attack which killed several Israeli soldiers, Prime Minister Benjamin Netanyahu reportedly told the administration "not to ever second guess me again."

According to U.S. officials cited in *The Wall Street Journal* report, a recent phone call between Obama and Netanyahu was "particularly combative."

A turning point appeared to be Israel's July 30 IDF strike on terrorists adjacent to a UN school, which the U.S. slammed as "disgraceful."

In response, the IDF confirmed it targeted Islamic Jihad terrorists in the vicinity of the school and provided video evidence that Hamas had fired rockets from inside schools.

The U.S. administration has since required White House and State Department approval for even routine munitions requests by Israel, officials say.

Instead of being handled as a military-to-military matter, each case is now subject to review, slowing the approval process, and signaling to Israel that military assistance once taken for granted is now under closer scrutiny. This is an obvious attempt to undermine Israel by the Obama Administration.

Journalists Slam Hamas for Censoring the Press During Operation Protective Edge

Sound familiar? Government censorship is a growing trend everywhere around the world, not only abroad but also here in the U.S., especially under the former Obama Administration.

"You belong to your father, the devil, and you want to carry out your father's desires. He was a murderer from the beginning, not holding to the truth, for there is no truth in him. When he lies, he speaks his native language, for he is a liar and the father of lies" (John 8:44).

In an August 11 statement, the Foreign Press Association (FPA) condemned Hamas for holding international journalists under threat and for censoring stories about Hamas war crimes and terror activities in Gaza during Israel's Operation Protective Edge.

The FPA berated Hamas for forcing journalists to underplay or ignore the terror group's activities in the Gaza Strip to make Israel look bad. It claimed forceful threats were used against its journalists, the first such claims by an official organization. (*Ynet*)

"The FPA protests in the strongest terms the blatant, incessant, forceful and unorthodox methods employed by the Hamas authorities and their representatives against visiting international journalists in Gaza over the past month," the organization stated.

Some journalists, including a France 24 group, released damning evidence about Hamas' war crimes, but only upon their exit from Gaza. The FPA now reports that several reporters were "harassed, threatened or questioned" about stories released through their news outlets. (*Times of Israel*)

Hamas has "put in place a 'vetting' procedure that would, in effect, allow for the blacklisting of specific journalists. Such a procedure is vehemently opposed by the FPA," the FPA statement adds.

Islamic Factions to Unite and Gang-Up on Israel?

Iranian Supreme Leader Ali Khamenei: "The Islamic world should set aside all differences. Let us unite and carry out our religious and human duty in order to help the people in Gaza."

Iran's New Strategy Of Diversion: Persuading
The Sunni Camp to Fight Israel, Not Iran
Behold Israel, August 4, 2014
A. Savyon and Y. Carmon

Recently, the Iranian regime has launched a campaign for arming the Palestinians in West Bank and Israel's Arab citizens; the campaign is being led by Iranian Supreme Leader Ali Khamenei.

On July 23, 2014, on the eve of Iran's Qods (Jerusalem) Day, Khamenei said that "the only solution [for Israel] is its annihilation and liquidation. Of course, until that time [when this happens], the determined and armed Palestinian resistance, and its spread to the West Bank, are the only way to deal with that bestial regime... Therefore, it is my belief that the West Bank should be armed just like Gaza. Anyone who cares about the fate of Palestine, and who is capable of doing something, should act in this matter in order to reduce the suffering and torment of the Palestinian people by means of their strong hand..."

This campaign played a role in Iran's strategy, in two vital areas that are completely unconnected to the war in Gaza or to the Palestinian cause: a) It serves the Iranian regime in its struggle against the Sunni world, which has ratcheted up its pressure on Iran, and b) it serves the Iranian regime in its struggle against the opposition, i.e. the pragmatic camp, at home, that has recently escalated its attacks on the ideological camp. See MEMRI series on "The Struggle Between Khamenei and Rafsanjani over the Iranian Leadership."

While the policy of annihilating Israel is one thing that the ideological and the pragmatic camps in Iran have in common, as it is a founding tenet of the regime, the move to arm the West Bank Palestinians and Israel's Arab citizens is a new element that the regime is stressing in recent days, and by all possible means. In every major speech and announcement, regime spokesmen emphasize the need for the Sunni world to stop fighting Shi'ites and join Iran in its fight against Israel. The regime also is highlighting the need for unity at home, which is actually a demand that the pragmatic camp accept the authority of the ideological camp.

It should be noted that on the internal level, this tactic has been successful, as expected; the pragmatic camp has hastened to stand with the regime on this matter.

However, the effort to divert the Sunni camp from its struggle with Iran and the Shi'ites has as of yet yielded no results. Apparently, the Sunni world understands Iran's gambit and is not going along with it; it is also stepping up its pressure on the Shi'ites in Iraq and elsewhere in the Middle East.

It should be clarified that this strategy of diversion is not just talk – the Iranian regime is working to implement it in coordination with the leaders of Hizbullah and of the Palestinian factions. But the main importance of this effort for Iran is that it serves both Iran's existential interest against the external Sunni threat and also the interest of the Iranian regime at home against the opposition.

This paper will review statements by senior members of the Iranian leadership calling on the Sunni world to forget about its fight against the Shi'ites and about the Sunni-Shi'ite schism and to instead unite with the Shi'ites against Israel.

Khamenei: "The Islamic world should set aside all differences… Let us unite and carry out our religious and human duty in order to help the people in Gaza."

In a July 29, 2014 speech to Muslim countries' ambassadors in Iran, Khamenei stressed the need for the Islamic world – that is, both Sunnis and Shi'ites – to unite and act together against Israel: "The Islamic world should set aside all differences, and use all its capabilities to meet the needs of the people in Gaza while fighting against the shameful crimes of the Zionists, and while despising and renouncing their supporters, particularly America and Britain.

Unfortunately, and contrary to the instructions of Islam, the Islamic ummah is today in a schism, because of politics and power-seeking. The leaders of the Islamic countries must set aside such motives and establish a united, strong, and mighty nation. If power-seeking, dependence [on the West], and corruption cannot divide the Islamic world, no arrogant power [i.e. the U S. and the West] will dare attack the Islamic states, to extort their governments…

In order to realize this goal, all the Islamic governments must abandon the political and non-political disputes among themselves, and everyone together must hasten to the aid of the oppressed who are palpitating in the claws of the bloodletting Zionist wolf… Let us unite and carry out our religious and human duty in order to help the people in Gaza overcome the obstacles that the Zionists are setting [before them]. Fighting the perpetrators of the historic oppression in Gaza is the second duty of the Islamic world…"

President Rohani: "In order to solve these difficult problems" of "The Suppurating Tumor[s]" of ISIS and the Zionist Regime, "We have No option except to unify the Islamic world."

At the same July 29, 2014 meeting with the ambassadors of Muslim countries, Iranian President Hassan Rohani compared the "suppurating tumor" of the Islamic State (IS, formerly the Islamic State in Iraq and Syria, or ISIS) – that is, the murder of Shi'ites by Sunnis in Iraq – to the "Zionist suppurating tumor." He stated that they have shared roots, and stressed that the only thing that could solve this problem was Sunni-Shi'ite unity:

> In order to solve these difficult problems, we have no option except to unify the Islamic world, explain the merciful [kind of] Islam, and distance ourselves from stagnation and fixation [in the Shi'ite-Sunni dispute]. The global strategy of the Islamic Republic of Iran is peace and justice, and in the Islamic world [the Iranian strategy is] brotherhood and unity, and the establishment of a single Islamic ummah.

> Those who dream of weakening Islam and the Muslims will take that aspiration to their grave. The Islamic Republic of Iran is mobilizing all its strength and all its means, for establishing stability and security, and for preventing massacres and bloodshed and creating peace and justice in the region. The Islamic world will triumph by virtue of the [Islamic] awakening, vigilance, and unity, with God's help.

Also on July 29, at a government meeting for 'Eid Al-Fitr, Rohani said: "The leaders of the regime have gone into action with all their might on the issue of Palestine and Gaza; we see this as part of our religious and human duty... I hope that all the Muslims in the world will fulfill their human and Islamic duty, in light of the savage attacks of the Zionist regime."

Other Regime Spokesmen Call for Arming
West Bank and Israel's Arab Citizens

On July 26, Ahmad Vahidi, former defense minister under president Mahmoud Ahmadinejad and former commander of the Qods Force in Iran's

Islamic Revolutionary Guards Corps (IRGC), said: "Arming the West Bank is the strategic policy of the Leader [Khamenei], and its implementation will change the arena of the developments in Palestine. The arming of the West Bank will be a golden card in the hands of the resistance of the Palestinian people. The Islamic governments and the supporters of the Palestinian people must use all their efforts for the sake of arming the West Bank, and even the region occupied in 1948. As the Leader [Khamenei] said, Iran supports Palestine with all its might and in all dimensions; it is expected that the required effort will be carried out in order to implement [Khamenei's] policy on the arming of the West Bank."

On July 28, a number of officials made similar statements in interviews with the Fars news agency, among them Hossein Sheikh Al-Islam, head of the Committee for the Support of the Palestinian and advisor to Majlis Speaker Ali Larijani; Hossein Kna'ani-Moqadam, former top IRGC official; and Fathollah Hosseini, Majlis National Security Committee member. Also, the July 25 editorial of the daily *Kayhan,* which is affiliated with Khamenei, was titled "Resistance in Gaza, Intifada in the West Bank."

Amir Mousavi, former advisor to the Iranian defense minister, said in a July 25 interview with Al-Mayadeen TV that Iran had discovered more efficient routes for transferring weapons to the Palestinians, including via Jordan and the Golan Heights, as a result of the Shi'ites' fight against the takfiri organizations. He added that because of the West Bank's proximity to Tel Aviv and Haifa, short-range missiles would be sufficient (see MEMRI TV Clip. No. 4377).

On July 24, Majlis National Security Committee member Ismail Kowsari made similar statements to Fars in an interview, and on the same day the Basij released a communique calling on the government to urgently submit a bill to the Majlis on arming the Palestinians in the West Bank in accordance with Khamenei's statements.

Supporting Hamas over Israel
The Daily Jot
Tuesday August 5, 2014
Bill Wilson

It is truly a sign that the world is upside down when you have people protesting Israel's right to defend itself. People, let's get real. Hamas is a terrorist organization whose goal is to kill every Jewish man, woman, and child. There are people who support this madness? Reuters reports Turkey's Prime Minister Tayyip Erdogan declared Sunday "They kill women so that they will not give birth to Palestinians; they kill babies so that they won't grow up; they kill men so they can't defend their country. They will drown in the blood they shed." He compared the Jews to Hitler. This is one of the occupant of the Oval Office's primary foreign policy partners. What does this say about the times we live in? A lot.

The U.S. "president's" ally makes an outrageous statement comparing Jews to Hitler and there is no response or rebuke from the White House. That tells us a lot. This statement by Erdogan should have been met with outrage by world leaders. The facts are that Hamas had been raining down missiles on Israeli civilians for months without Israeli retaliation.

As soon as Israel moves to defend itself, the news media and the politicians cry foul. Hamas parades out all the civilians that Israel's mighty military has "murdered" and the world begins to side with one of the most brutal and single-focused terror agents on earth. America's Secretary of State tries to broker peace by involving Turkey and Qatar, trusted Hamas funders.

When Hamas agrees to ceasefires. Israel does its part, even sends medical supplies and aid to the enemy. All the while, Hamas is using the time of ceasefire to regroup for yet another assault. This is standard operating procedure. Meantime, Hamas and its ally al Qassam Brigades posted some 60-plus pictures of Israelis the organization has killed, saying, "We killed 150 Zionist soldiers. Here's photo of killed soldiers which the Zionist Enemy, Israel officially recognized." CNS News reported July 28 that House Minority Leader Nancy Pelosi said, "And we have to confer with the Qataris, who have told me over and over again that Hamas is a humanitarian organization." The Hamas leader operates out of Qatar.

So-called "leaders" like Nancy Pelosi should be run out of office. Hamas should not be considered anything but an enemy to humanity. Let us remember when President George W. Bush forced Israel to evacuate Gaza. He and his globalist buddies set up "free elections" in Gaza. The people there elected Hamas to represent them.

So much for a "Palestinian" state living side by side with Israel in peace. Israel gives every civilian ample opportunity to get out of the way of war when it strikes. They choose to stay because they support Hamas. Politicians, some Americans, Islamists living in America who support Hamas are supporting brutal terrorists. Jesus said in Matthew 24:4, "Take heed that no man deceive you."

Wars on Israel
Behold Israel Blog
July 31, 2014
Gary Bechor

Op-ed: Ban on flights to Israel was just another attempt by U.S. administration to force Israel to accept difficult conditions in Gaza. President Barack Obama: Artificial sweet talk in public and stabs in the back behind the scenes – that's how we should describe the attitude of U.S. President

Barack Obama's Administration toward us. From now on we can also call it "Obama's wars on Israel."

The first war was in the 2011 Arab Spring, when this American regime tried to portray the events as a sort of marvelous democratic uprising, compared to the obsolete Israeli democracy which is lagging behind. This is the way the Arab uprising was explicitly described by some members of Obama's staff, all Jews of course.

Then came reality and it hit Obama in the face, as the Arabs – all of them – collapsed: Syria died, Iraq died, Libya died, and an Arab democracy remained solely in the American hallucinations.

The second war was Secretary of State John Kerry's desperate attempt in 2013 to reduce Israel's size to the point of putting it in existential danger. He forced Israel and Mahmoud Abbas into futile but dangerous negotiations, which evoked destructive Islamic urges and deteriorated the security situation both in the Palestinian Authority and in Israel.

Encouraged by Kerry, the Palestinians' imagination began going wild: They would receive Jerusalem, the return of the refugees, the Jordan Valley, lands, prisoners – and the result was arrogance, and therefore violence, defiance and self-destruction.

Of course those American diplomats rushed to blame Israel for all the world's troubles, at their master's order, but that war failed too. Israel insisted on its right to exist, and not to turn Judea and Samaria into Gaza.

Where is that Kerry today, the man wanted to hand Judea Samaria over to Arab sovereignty? Why everything that is happening in Gaza would have happened here, and that would have been the end of Israel.

Fortunately, the Gaza war broke out now, because it illustrates what would have happened if, God forbid, we would have transferred more lands to the Arab terror.

The third war is taking place now, and we must admit that the Obama regime is not giving up: An attempt to force Israel to accept difficult conditions in the Gaza Strip, including through the outrageous ban on flights to Israel. The ban was issued by the American FAA, a federal administration subject to the U.S. secretary of transportation. As opposed to previous wars, in which the administration warned against an intifada or European boycott – it is now attacking Israel directly and openly, and trying to suffocate it.

This administration is closer today to Qatar and the Muslim Brotherhood or to Iran, which encourage terror, than to Israel. This is an astonishing blindness, an abandonment of the West's leadership and a cultural decline at an inconceivable magnitude.

This isn't the first time Kerry is caught smiling at Israel while inciting against it behind the scenes. But not just towards Israel. This is also a betrayal of the moderate axis of the Middle East – Egypt, Jordan and Saudi Arabia – as well as encouraging and rewarding jihadist terror, and a betrayal of all the real American values.

Israel will manage to free itself of this attack too, and the American curse will turn into a blessing also here – because the Palestinian sides are collapsing as it is, and going back to being portrayed as terrorists in the world.

But before the upcoming elections, every American citizen should know how this American administration treats its only ally in the Middle East – and vote accordingly.

John Kerry Pretty Much Threatens Israel to Concede
Key Issues to Palestinians
LI Legal Insurrection
Posted by William A. Jacobson
Thursday, November 7, 2013 at 2:48pm

John Kerry's public warning to Israel that it will face a 3rd Intifada and international de-legitimization, unless it relinquishes "illegitimate" settlements and a final peace deal does not leave a single Israeli soldier in the West Bank, was a clear threat. The threat took place in an interview with Israeli and Palestinian television, as reported by The Times of Israel, "Kerry slams Israel's West Bank policies, warns of third Intifada."

U.S. Secretary of State John Kerry launched an unusually bitter public attack on Israeli policies in the West Bank Thursday, warning that if current peace talks fail, Israel could see a third intifada and growing international isolation, and that *calls for boycott, divestment and sanctions would increase*. Kerry made the comments during a joint interview with Israel's Channel 2 and the Palestinian Broadcasting Corporation.

"The alternative to getting back to the talks is the potential of chaos," Kerry said. "I mean does Israel want a third Intifada?" he asked. "Israel says, 'Oh we feel safe today, we have the wall. We're not in a day to day conflict,'" said Kerry. "I've got news for you. Today's status quo will not be tomorrow's..." Israel's neighbors, he warned, will "begin to push in a different way."

The secretary went on: "If we do not resolve the issues between Palestinians and Israelis, if we do not find a way to find peace, there will be an increasing isolation of Israel, there will be **an increasing campaign**

of de-legitimization of Israel that's been taking place on an international basis."

Turning to settlements and Israel's presence in the West Bank, he added: "If we do not resolve the question of settlements, and the question of who lives where and how and what rights they have; **if we don't end the presence of Israeli soldiers perpetually within the West Bank**, then there will be an increasing feeling that if we cannot get peace with a leadership that is committed to non-violence, you may wind up with leadership that is committed to violence."

The emboldened words have a lot of meaning in the context of the dispute, particularly with regard to BDS and de-legitimization.

As Israel-hating, Hezbollah-loving Lebanese commentator Sharmine Narwani notes, in arguing against Israel's right to exist, Israel is just "a lone UN Security Council veto" away from international de-legitimization — something Kerry surely knows as it has been dangled over Israel's head by the Obama Administration for years.

So too the final agreement issue of Israeli military presence along the Jordan river valley — a military necessity given there are fewer than a dozen miles at some points between the formerly Jordanian illegally occupied West Bank and the sea.

Kerry is not just criticizing, he is dictating the terms of a final agreement, and hanging threats over Israel's head if it does not capitulate. Israeli officials recognized that, per the Times article:

Israel's Channel 2 news quoted unnamed officials in Jerusalem responding bitterly to the secretary's remarks. Israel, said one official, would not "give in to the intimidation tactics" of the secretary, and would not compromise on its vital security needs. The official also reportedly noted that Kerry's comments would not "encourage" the Palestinians to compromise.

By taking sides publicly, Kerry encourages Palestinian intransigence and escalating demands.

Evelyn Gordon at Commentary Notes

Kerry has been actively encouraging the Palestinians' bad faith. On his current trip, for instance, he publicly and repeatedly denounced Israeli construction as "illegitimate" and "disturbing," even though it doesn't violate any Israeli commitments—including those five signed agreements, not one of which mandated a construction freeze.

Yet he hasn't said a word about PA actions that explicitly violate previous commitments, such as its ongoing campaign of incitement (barred by all its signed agreements) and push for international boycotts and sanctions against Israel. And Europe, needless to say, has been even worse.

The result is that Palestinians have concluded they can violate any agreement with impunity. And Israelis wonder why, in that case, they should ever bother signing one.

Kerry Has Declared a War on God
Write Hard-Line Rabbis in Letter
Jerusalem Post, Jeremy Sharon
02/05/2014

A group of rabbis, including the founder of the far-right, Our Land of Israel party, wrote in an open letter to U.S. Secretary of State John Kerry that he had declared war against God through his current mediation efforts between Israel and Palestinian negotiators, and said he must cease such activities to avoid divine punishment.

The letter was sent by the Committee to Save the Land and People of Israel, founded by Rabbi Sholom Dov Wolpo, who also founded the Our Land of Israel party, as an activist group to oppose political accords with the Palestinians involving territorial concessions. "Your incessant efforts to expropriate integral parts of our Holy Land and hand them over to Abbas' terrorist gang, amount to a declaration of war against the Creator and Ruler of the universe! For G-d awarded the entire Land of Israel to our ancestors, Abraham, Isaac and Jacob, in order that they bequeath it, as an everlasting inheritance, to their descendants, the Jewish people, until the end of all time," the letter reads.

The rabbis argue that Kerry's plans endangers Israeli Jews by bringing them within close range of potential rocket and missile fire from the West Bank should it be ceded by Israel to the Palestinians. "If you continue on this destructive path, you will ensure your everlasting disgrace in Jewish history for bringing calamity upon the Jewish people." continued the rabbis "By the power of our Holy Torah, we admonish you to cease immediately all efforts to achieve these disastrous agreements – in order to avoid severe heavenly punishment for everyone involved," they threatened.

The letter was signed by Rabbi Wolpo, along with four other rabbis including Rabbi Yisrael Ariel, the founder and Chairman of the Temple Institute; Rabbi Yigal Pizam, the Dean of a Yeshiva and a leader of the Chabad community in the Haifa neighborhood of Kiryat Shmuel; Rabbi Gedalya Axelrod, the emeritus head of the Haifa Rabbinic Court; and Rabbi Ben Tziyon Grossman from the town of Migdal Haemek.

U.S. Ramping Up Diplomatic Pressure on Israel
February 5, 2014
Prophecy News Watch
Darrel Gleason

U.S. Secretary of State John Kerry is exerting great pressure on Israel to accept the framework of his peace plans with the Palestinian Authority.

According to published reports, Kerry is eager to advance the peace talks, believing that they will fall apart if a framework agreement isn't in place by April.

As part of his strategy for brokering an agreement the Secretary of State has resorted to using scare tactics against Israel, such as new waves of Palestinian uprisings, international boycotts and increased isolation from the global community.

Kerry, who touted a resumption of peace talks between the Israelis and the Palestinians last July after a three-year lull, has been shuttling between the two sides in recent months as part of his diplomatic efforts. The U.S. has begun to push the talks on a higher level out of concern that they may fall apart over Israel's continuing settlement construction and its insistence on tough security demands. Reports indicate that the U.S. framework document outlines the future peace talks on the condition of pre-1967 borders and land and Israeli compensation of Palestinian refugees who ran away from their homes in the midst of the 1948 war.

Kerry, having become known as "Mr. Interim Agreement" in diplomatic circles for his partial deals with Iran in its nuclear enrichment program and Syria's chemical arsenal, attended the Munich Security Conference Saturday, Feb. 1.

While at the conference, Kerry criticized Israeli Prime Minister Benjamin Netanyahu for his claim to have steered Israel toward a period of relative calm.

Kerry called Netanyahu's claims "an illusion." DEBKAfile, an Israeli military intelligence website, said Kerry's statements are a clear signal that the U.S. is prepared to use a heavy dose of coercive tactics against Israel in order to reach a final accord with the Palestinians.

In comments Sunday February 2, Netanyahu attempted to shoot down the idea that Israel might buckle under U.S. pressure.

"Boycotts of Israel are amoral and unjustified and will not achieve their aims," said Netanyahu. "First of all, they cause the Palestinians to become entrenched behind their intransigent positions and push peace farther away, and secondly, no pressure will cause me to give way on Israel's vital interests, first and foremost the security of its citizens."

Netanyahu's statements were quickly denounced by the U.S. State Department. A State Department spokesman said that Kerry was "merely describing the situation exactly as it is ... and his record of dedication to Israel's security goes back three decades."

Nonetheless, DEBKAfile, citing reliable sources, reports that since Kerry last year warned Israel of new rounds of Palestinian uprisings, terrorist strikes against Israeli targets have spiraled upward for the first time in recent years.

The U.S. has set an April deadline for the first round of talks between the Israelis and Palestinians. Kerry is hoping that a framework agreement between the two sides will extend the talks until the end of the year.

Reports say that Kerry and his diplomatic team are pushing to reach the framework agreement before the upcoming release of another group of Palestinian prisoners. The next group of prisoners will be the fourth to be released out of an overall 104 Palestinians. Israel agreed to free Palestinian prisoners when peace negotiations renewed six months ago.

Meanwhile, as Kerry squeezes Israel to accept terms of his peace plan, a new poll indicates that a vast majority of Americans support the Jewish State on virtually every issue concerning the Israel/Palestinian situation, while opposing the Administration.

The National Omnibus Poll, conducted by McLaughlin and Associates, surveyed a cross section of 1,000 Americans. It found that by a ratio of 3.5 to 1 (58 percent to 17 percent), Americans believe that any future Palestinian Arab state would be hostile to Israel and support terrorism. Moreover, 47 percent of the Americans polled said they believe Jews have a right to settle in Israel's West Bank.

The poll was commissioned by the Zionist Organization of America.

ZOA National President Morton A. Klein said, "Large majorities of Americans clearly understand that a Palestinian state, if established, will not live in peace with Israel and will simply be another Mideast terrorist state."

As the U.S. continues to broker talks between the Israelis and Palestinians, European businesses and organizations have begun imposing bans against Israelis businesses in protest of Israel's construction in the West Bank and East Jerusalem settlements. The contested areas are part of land Israel annexed in the 1967 war.

Attempts to Subvert Israel

Obama has done more to delegitimize and undermine Israel's position in the world than any other U.S. president. This is a serious problem because it is in the strategic interest for the U.S. to have Israel as an ally. The first section of this chapter explains why Israel is in the strategic interest of the United States. The second section describes Obama's actions that have betrayed and berated Israel, actions that have been clearly anti-Israel. These anti-Israel actions violate a first principle of American foreign policy, which is to stand firm by our friends.

Israel Is in the Strategic Interest of the United States

The United States relies on Middle East oil. To be able to purchase that oil, the Middle East has to be stable. To help the Middle East be stable, the United States has to have accurate intelligence about what is going on in the various Arab countries of the Middle East. Israel has been providing such counter terrorism and intelligence to the United States. Israel has been providing access to unique Israeli technology capabilities in key niche areas. Indeed the U.S. is spending around $1.5 billion dollars a year to purchase Israel military technology. Included in these purchases are:

- Short-range unmanned aircraft systems that have seen service in Iraq and Afghanistan.
- Unmanned aerial systems, a technology that has contributed to the U.S. drones used in Afghanistan.
- Targeting pods on hundreds of Air Force, Navy, and Marine strike aircraft.
- A revolutionary helmet-mounted sight that is now standard in nearly all frontline Air Force and Navy fighter aircraft.

- Lifesaving armor installed in thousands of MRAP armored vehicles used in Iraq and Afghanistan.
- A gun system for close-in defense of naval vessels against terrorist dinghies and small-boat swarms.
- The Israeli and American joint production of the Iron Dome which is the world's first combat-proven counter-rocket system.

Obama Humiliates Netanyahu at the White House

In March 2010 Netanyahu was in the United States spending two days with senior Republicans and members of Congress. He had also received a standing ovation from the American Israel Public Affairs Committee, one of the most influential lobby groups in the United States. On the third day he was invited to come to the White House to meet with Obama.

Obama walked in and gave Netanyahu a list of 13 demands. When Netanyahu did not give in to his agreement, Obama abruptly walked out telling Netanyahu that he was going to have dinner with Michelle and the girls. Netanyahu and his advisors were left over an hour alone.

Benjamin Netanyahu was left to stew in a White House meeting room for over an hour after. Furthermore, Obama banned all TV cameras, a level of humiliation almost completely unique in modern White House practice. The United States would not ever receive third world tyrants in such a rude fashion. Plain and simple, Obama displayed arrogant disdain to Netanyahu.

Obama's power move failed. Netanyahu left understanding that he cannot count on the United States and proceeded to set forth a policy for Israel more independent of the United States. In other words, the United States now has a less influence on Israel than before Obama.

Obama's State Department Speech

In May 2011, Obama gave a speech at the State Department. Relative to Israel Palestinian issue. He said:

> So while the core issues of the conflict must be negotiated, the basis of those negotiations is clear: a viable Palestine, and a secure Israel. The United States believes that negotiations should result in two states, with permanent Palestinian borders with Israel, Jordan, and Egypt, and permanent Israeli borders with Palestine. The borders of Israel and Palestine should be based on the 1967 lines with mutually agreed swaps, so that secure and recognized borders are established for both states. The Palestinian people must have the right to govern themselves, and reach their potential, in a sovereign and contiguous state.

Netanyahu replied to that speech by stating that the 1967 border proposed by Mr. Obama as a basis for negotiating the outlines of a Palestinian state was a nonstarter. In other words, we have another power play by Obama suggesting a basis for negotiation that is impossible for Israel. The 1967 borders would leave—in the middle of Israel, a narrow stretch of land about 8 miles across that would enable an enemy to easily cut Israel in two. It would make the borders of Israel indefensible.

Obama Excludes Israel from the Global Counterterrorism Forum

The U.S. sponsored the first Global Counterterrorism Forum, an international meeting of countries concerned about terrorism. In June of 2012 the Global Counterterrorism Forum had its first meeting in Istanbul. Who did Obama invite? Countries with a history of sponsoring radical Islamic ideology. For example, Saudi Arabia was at the meeting. The Saudi kingdom's government embraces and spreads the radical Wahhabist ideology to which many terrorists adhere.

Who did Obama not invite? Israel. The lack of Israel's presence at the Istanbul meeting is incredulous. Israel has a long track record of combating terrorism. Having a global counterterrorism forum and not including Israel, is like having a global technology conference and excluding the United States of America. The State of Israel has more experience at combating terrorism or educating civilians about it.

Israel, a victim of constant Hamas and Hizbullah terrorism, was blatantly excepted from the meeting. This exclusion of Israel was clearly the Obama Administration's acquiescence to the will of the Islamic leaders. By discriminating against Israel, the United States government has once again emboldened the Islamic countries responsible for worldwide terrorism and diminished its position as Leader of the Free World.

Israel remains the closest ally of the United States so that the U.S. has become its own enemy. No matter how we strive to comply with Islamic directives, these countries have made it perfectly clear, through the Muslim Brotherhood, their Koran, and the terrorist or stealth agents they send to invade the globe, that they will conquer and Islamize, enslave or kill.

Obama Erases Jerusalem from State Department Documents

In 2011, Obama's White House scrubbed all references to Jerusalem being part of the Jewish state from a collection of photos on its website. Captions of photos that had Jerusalem, Israel were changed to Jerusalem.

In Omri Ceren's Commentary article of May 8, 2012, he writes about altered documents on the State Department Web servers:

In August 2011, the administration was caught digitally altering archived historical documents of previous White Houses in order to suggest, falsely, that past administrations had had the same policy. The administration had erased parts of publicly available documents in a brazen attempt to trick people into thinking that other administrations had taken positions they had not.

Two documents listing the locations of American consulates, one from 2002 and one from 2003, placed the U.S. consulate in Jerusalem in "Israel." Some time, after the controversy began in 2011, somebody went back to those documents and scrubbed them to read only "Jerusalem." A search on the piquantly named Internet Wayback Machine, which periodically captures time-stamped snapshots of websites, quickly confirmed as much.

Thus, while some administration officials were telling reporters and the public that there were no Bush-era documents referencing "Jerusalem, Israel," other administration officials were busy scrubbing Bush-era documents referencing "Jerusalem, Israel." Such digital alteration is no small task. Somebody at the State Department had to go back to the original 2002 and 2003 documents, convert them into PDF files, then upload the new ones to the State Department servers under the same file names as the old documents.

Obama's Anti-Israel Agenda

Nobody believed former President Obama when he claimed that he "has done more for the security of the State of Israel than any previous administration." That's because he hasn't and because President Obama and his administration repeatedly acted to weaken the security of the State of Israel.

Jeffrey Kuhner, February 18, 2011, expressed the following point of view:

Mr. Obama's decision to betray Israel should come as no surprise. He is a privileged liberal who reflects the values and prejudices of the academic left.

The cultural milieu of his intellectual formation was steeped in hatred of America and the West. His father was an anti-colonial socialist determined to destroy European imperialism. His mentor was Frank Marshall Davis, an avowed communist. His pastor was the Reverend Jeremiah Wright, a black-nationalist known for his Jew-baiting.

His seminal intellectual influences were revolutionary Marxists such as Frantz Fanon and Edward Said. They championed the belief -- prevalent among college radicals -- that Israel symbolizes Western subjugation of Third World peoples. In their view, it is a militaristic, quasi-fascist state based on oppression and Zionist expansion. In other words, for the hard left, Palestine is a continuation of the anti-imperial struggle -- a mass movement for liberation from Western occupation. That is why progressives have only two real enemies: the United States and Israel.

Obama Snubs Israel at the UN

Obama's anti-Israel Agenda has reached new heights. During the week of September 23, 2012, various leaders of the countries of the world addressed the UN. Netanyahu, the Prime Minister of Israel requested a meeting with Obama for that week when both would be in New York, Obama refused the meeting. Then when on Thursday, September 27, Netanyahu spoke to the UN General Assembly, Susan Rice, the U.S. Ambassador to the UN walked out just before his talk.

U.S. Secretary of State Hillary Clinton called a luncheon meeting with the foreign minister of the five permanent members of the UN Security Council to conflict with the time Netanyahu would speak at the UN. So not only was the U.S. Ambassador to the UN not present, but the U.S. Secretary of State was not present, and the other four Foreign Ministers of the permanent members of the UN Security Council were not their either.

Congratulations Obama! Your policy with respect the U.S.'s most loyal friend in the Middle East is wrong for the U.S., and history will record your policy as a disaster for the U.S. The Obama message is loud and clear: The world would be a safer, simpler, and more peaceful place if not for the troublesome Jewish State.

Obama to Advance Palestinian State by January 2017

U.S. President Barack Obama and Secretary of State John Kerry intend to advance recognition of an independent Palestinian state by January 20, 2017 -- the end of Obama's second term -- regardless of how adversely it will affect national and homeland security. According to Obama and the U.S. foreign policy establishment, a Palestinian state would enhance stability, moderation, peace and democracy.

After regaining control of the mountain ridges of Judea and Samaria in 1967, Israel dramatically upgraded its posture of deterrence and transformed from a consumer to a producer of means to ensure national security. Against the backdrop of the rising conventional and unconventional Islamic threats to the U.S., Israel increasingly resembles the largest and most critical U.S. aircraft carrier, one which does not require a single U.S. boot on board, deployed in a most vital area for U.S. military and economic interests.

The establishment of a Palestinian state on the mountain ridges of Judea and Samaria would dramatically erode Israel's posture of deterrence, which currently extends the strategic hand of the United States, sparing the need to deploy additional U.S. troops to the Middle East. This enhances the national security of pro-U.S. Arab regimes – especially Jordan -- which consider Israel to be an effective life insurance policy. The proposed Palestinian state cannot exist simultaneously with U.S. values and national security interests. (*Israel Hayem* newsletter)

IRAN SAYS: DEATH TO ISRAEL AND JEWS

February 5, 2012 Iran's Ayatollah Khamenei Calls for Destruction of Israel, Jews

Ayatollah: KILL All Jews, Annihilate Israel
By Reza Hahlil
World Net Daily Exclusive

Iran lays out a legal case for genocidal attack against "cancerous tumor." The Iranian government, through a website proxy, has laid out the legal and religious justification for the destruction of Israel and the slaughter of its people. The doctrine includes wiping out Israeli assets and Jewish people worldwide.

Top Commander Reiterates Iran's Commitment to Full Annihilation of Israel

Tehran Fars News Agency (FNA) May 20, 2012 - Chief of Staff of the Iranian Armed Forces Major General Hassan Firouzabadi said threats and pressures cannot deter Iran from its revolutionary causes and ideals, and stressed that the **Iranian** nation will remain committed to the full annihilation of the Zionist regime of Israel to the end.

Let's Fast Forward to 2015

A new book written by Ayatollah Ali Khamenei, Iran's supreme religious leader, makes Iran's plans for the destruction of the Jewish State of Israel very clear. The 416-page book titled *Palestine* leaves no doubt about the Ayatollah's intention to take Israel from the hands of the Jews. Coming rapidly on the heels of the Iran nuclear deal, this represents an escalation in the threat to Israel from Iran.

In a recent article about the book, Iranian-born author and journalist Amir Taheri wrote, "Khamenei insists that he is not recommending 'classical wars' to wipe Israel off the map. Nor does he want to 'massacre the Jews.' What he recommends is a long period of low-intensity warfare designed to make life unpleasant if not impossible for a majority of Israeli Jews so that they leave the country. His calculation is based on the assumption that large numbers of Israelis have double-nationality and would prefer emigration to the United States and Europe to daily threats of death," he added.

My question is this: Is the Ayatollah's book a smokescreen to take away attention from Iran's nuclear threat by saying Israeli Jews will leave Israel because they will be constantly badgered by the Islamic factions? I would not trust anything a radical hate-filled Mullah says. After all, it is a badge of honor to lie in Islam to fool the infidel. According to Taheri's assessment, the publication of Khamenei's book placed former U.S. President Barack Obama and former Secretary of State John Kerry in difficult positions, when they tried to defend an increasingly unpopular nuclear deal with a country whose most important religious leader openly announced his goal is to destroy Israel.

Beware of Anti-Israel "Christian" Leaders and Groups

Although much of the following information was published in various news venues and blogs many years ago, Israeli-support has not improved from these groups. In fact, more professing Christians are speaking out against Israel. Sadly, the false teachers who are against Israel are leading the masses in the wrong direction—away from God's chosen nation. Apparently reading and studying the Bible is something these professing Christians do not have high on their priority list.

The worst offenders against Israel in the West are those who actually openly speak the name of the Lord, "Yahweh" (the God of the Bible in Hebrew—**the Holy One of Israel**). And yet in their next breath condemn Israel with great disdain and hatred. What's worse, some of these people believe they are well-informed because they unreasonably buy into the lies, the distortions, the intentional anti-Israel propaganda fabricated and underwritten by Israel's sworn enemies, "news" that finds its way into the mainstream media all over the world. These people are contributing to the growing worldwide anti-Semitism.

Petra News Agency Monday, June 18, 2007
WCC Chooses Jordan to Launch Initiative to Put
End to Israeli Occupation
The World Churches Council (WCC) has chosen Jordan to launch an international initiative that calls on international churches to put an end for Israeli occupation of the Palestinian and Arab lands to reach just and comprehensive peace in the region. Choosing Jordan, conferees said, was because of the WCC confidence in the initiatives of His Majesty King Abdullah II, which they described as "precursor in seeking to achieve peace in the Middle East."

This was announced during the World Council of Churches International Peace Conference, which kicked off today in Amman. The conference aims to call all churches and related organizations to work together and put an end for the Israeli occupation of the Palestinian and Arab lands, according to the General Secretary of the WCC Samuel Kobia. Kobia highlighted importance of ending the Palestinian-Israeli conflict according to the international legitimacy resolutions.

One must ask: Why does, the **WCC** chose to meet in Amman Jordan rather than Jerusalem, city of our God?

How does the **WCC** justify propagating the Humanist political worldview rather than the Bible worldview and seeking a secular political solution instead of God's will?

When did the **WCC** become an arm of the **UN**?

Where did **WCC** pick up their terminology? **WCC** claims to be representing millions of Christians - do you have any say in their agenda? Is **WCC** representing you in its pronouncements?

It is important to note that the World Council of Churches has approximately 1.2 million members in 5,100 churches in the USA. Their overall track record thus far is convoluting the facts, therefore taking a very pro-Palestinian attitude and in turn berating Israel to no end.

EAPPI

The Ecumenical Accompaniment Programme in Palestine and Israel is, effectively, the outreach arm of the WCC to spread their anti-Israel message around the churches by visiting and recounting their stories and activism in the West Bank. For instance, the Wednesday morning club in our church was recently addressed by Stan Rowe of Hereford on. "The Trouble with Jerusalem." This sounds innocuous enough; just a local man telling his story, he doesn't appear in a Google search. When he arrived we found out that he represents EAPPI and came to share his loathing for Israel and recount all the Palestinian lies about Israel.

The Ecumenical Accompaniment Programme in Palestine and Israel (EAPPI) brings internationals to the West Bank to experience *life under occupation*. Ecumenical Accompaniers (EAs) provide protective presence to vulnerable communities, monitor and report human rights abuses and support Palestinians and Israelis working together for peace. When they

return home, EAs campaign for a just and peaceful resolution to the Israeli/
Palestinian conflict through an end to the occupation, respect for international law and implementation of UN resolutions.

Although they speak of "Palestinians and Israelis working together for
peace" and "peaceful resolution to the Israeli/Palestinian conflict" their
baseline assumptions are revealed by their use of "under occupation"
and "international law" and UN "resolutions." All of these terms refer
to the Palestinian narrative version of history, the Palestinian version of
International Law and of UN Resolutions. It must also be remembered that
the United Nations is not God's arbiter of international affairs but a heavily biased worldly pressure group.

Their forthcoming World Week for Peace in Palestine Israel is to encourage concerned communities and individuals to make a common witness by
participating in worship, educational events and acts of advocacy in support
of a just peace for Palestinians and Israelis. sounds laudable and will doubt-
less recruit plenty of Christians to pray against Israel. But, if they seek a
just peace for Palestinians and Israelis, why do they show no concern for the
suffering and terrorism suffered by the Israelis?

Who pays their activists to go to the disputed territories and bring back their
tales to their local churches? Is it the churches that support Christian Aid
and related organizations?

More than 100 church-based relief and development organizations worldwide, including Christian Aid in the UK, have formally united under an umbrella group.
ACT Alliance, created through the leadership of the World Council of Churches.

The "Christian" community that is working against Israel is highly pro-
fessional, highly organized and very well funded. But Christians who

believe that Israel not only has a right to exist but is part of God's plan for completing world salvation are largely enthusiastic amateur individuals.

Seeing all the recent advertising campaign for Christian Aid Week on TV, posters, buses and everywhere, have you wondered how much of your money is spent on advertising, misguided political activism and how much actually finds its way to acts of charity in the name of Jesus?

Christian Aid

Christian Aid has been running a long campaign against Israel, wholeheartedly propagating the Palestinian Authority version of events. Its fall 2004 magazine was a particularly blatant example of its obsession with Israel. Of its 24 pages, the following all referred to the campaign against Israel.

World Vision

Blogger, Kristy Walker, reported in August of 2011, that she attended a World Vision sponsored presentation in a local church to view the documentary, *With God on Our Side*. She was startled to learn of the anti-Israel bias of the organization. The film was introduced as providing a "missing narrative" of the Middle East conflict, and that it was a fair, if controversial, representation of the real situation "on the ground" in Gaza and the West Bank.

Kristy Walker learned that the documentary does not attempt to provide a balanced explanation of the conflict in the Middle East; rather, it simply condemns the Jewish state and Christians who support Israel. *With God On Our Side* contains serious errors and bias, gives a narrow, overly simplistic view of the Arab-Israeli conflict, and lays the blame for the suffering of the Palestinian people solely at the feet of Israel. It also attacks a section of the Christian church, namely Christian supporters of Israel, identified in the documentary as "Christian Zionists." (http://israel.co.nz/)

International Red Cross Plants Trees to Honor Palestinian Terrorists
In a ceremony celebrating its 150th anniversary, the International Red Cross together with the Palestinian Red Crescent planted 150 trees bearing the names of "veteran prisoners." The Palestinian Authority uses the term "veteran prisoners" to refer to those who have been in jail the longest, and in most cases are serving life sentences for murder or multiple murders. Giorgio Ferrario, representative of the International Federation of Red Cross and Red Crescent Societies, participated in this ceremony honoring terrorists, which was named "My Honor Is My Freedom."

The Emergent Church Is Infiltrating Various Denominations
A drop in support for Israel has been detected concurrently with the rise of the Emergent Church movement. Roger Oakland (www.understandthetimes.org) observed that this *purpose-driven* view of establishing global utopia may be a plan, but it is "driven" by humanistic reasoning and not led by the Holy Spirit. While it is of course good, to do good, unto others, all the goodness that we can do—will not be good enough. Pastors and church leaders who get involved in such man-driven programs can usually be identified by certain characteristics:

- Sound biblical doctrine is dangerous and divisive, and the experiential (i.e. mystical) is given a greater role than doctrine.
- Bible prophecy is no longer taught and is considered a waste of time.
- Israel becomes less and less important and has no biblical significance.
- Eventually the promises for Israel are applied to the church and not Israel (Replacement Theology).
- Bible study is replaced by studying someone's book and his methods.
- Church health is evaluated on the *quantity* of people who attend.
- The truth of God's Word becomes less and less important.
- God's Word, especially concepts like hell, sin and repentance, is eventually downplayed so the unbeliever is not offended.

Churches Disenfranchising

A succession of churches have voted, in their governing assemblies, to withdraw all investment from companies who have trade arrangements involving Israel, and to *promote boycott* of all Israeli products. Apart from the fact that these moves will hit the Palestinians as hard as the Jews, these churches appear to be distancing themselves from God's blessings and inviting His cursing. The level of hatred for Israel in church publications on Israel is staggering.

2008 Methodist UMC

A report on Israel produced by the United Methodist Church is "distorted and mendacious," the Anti-Defamation League has charged.

The 225-page report, Israel-Palestine: A 2007-2008 Mission Study likens Jews to "monsters" and compares the actions of Israelis to Nazis, the group said. The group also criticized the report for using the word "terrorism" to describe Israeli actions, while the actions of Palestinian Arabs are described as "activism."

In a statement, ADL officials called on the church to repudiate the report. The study "repeatedly twists history and employs inciting language to denigrate Israel and Jews," the group's national director, Abraham Foxman, said in a statement. Church officials defended the study.

The United Methodist Church is not neutral on the question of military occupations," officials said in a statement. "The mission study's perspective is in keeping with the thoughtful, informed, and consistent position of the United Methodist Church on the occupation of Palestinian territories."

United Church of Christ (UCC)

Known as a liberal Protestant church, UCC's sweeping decision signals a major win for the anti-Israel Boycott, Divestment and Sanctions (BDS) movement. In total, the UCC pension board and investment fund control some $4 billion United Church of Christ Divests from Israel. Top officials of the United Church of Christ (UCC) voted on Tuesday June 30, 2015 to divest from companies that conduct business in Judea and Samaria.

During the church's annual meeting in Cleveland, the groups General Synod endorsed the move with a final vote of 508-124 with 38 abstentions. Unlike a similar vote last year by the Presbyterian Church USA, which voted to sell of its stocks in companies whose products are widely used in Judea and Samaria, the UCC vote is more comprehensive. Delegates of the church are calling on its financial officers to sell off all stock in companies which "have been found to profit from the occupation of the Palestinian territories by the State of Israel." The church also agreed to boycott all products made in the territories.

Presbyterian Church of USA (PCUSA)
In 2004 PCUSA voted to begin a process of phased, selective divestment from companies operating in Israel. In May of 2008, a remarkable document appeared on the PCUSA website titled: "Vigilance Against Anti-Jewish Ideas and Bias."

While church members had already spoken on this topic with their votes in 2006, this document was the first response from the leadership of PCUSA to concerns (expressed by both Jews and significant numbers of Presbyterians) that church language and action regarding the Middle East was tarnished by incorrect or biased information, one-sided accusations, and even anti-Semitic theology.

This was a remarkable work in many ways. Rather than talk in bland generalities, the church document stated outright that: "We are aware and do confess that anti-Jewish attitudes can be found among us."

"Anti-Jewish theology can unfortunately be found in connection with PC (USA) General Assembly overtures."

"One finds characterizations of Zionism that distort that movement."

"The problems and suffering of the Palestinian people are attributed solely, and inaccurately to Zionism alone."

Most significantly, the statement asked church members to reflect carefully on analysis of the Middle East delivered through the prism of "liberation theology," a reference to the work of those such as the Sabeel Ecumenical Liberation Theology Center.

"VIGILANCE AGAINST Anti-Jewish Ideas and Bias" was celebrated by the church's interfaith partners as well as by PCUSA's harshest internal critics. And then, with no fanfare, no announcement, without even an explanation, this document was quietly replaced by an "updated" version, one which stripped the work of any acknowledgement that the church continues, as it does, to traffic in retrograde theology and stances.

Gone was direct acknowledgement of problems with the stands that the church is currently taking, and gone was the reference to Israel's sole responsibility for Palestinian suffering as being "inaccurate," replaced by broad generalizations and hints that criticism of PCUSA had more to do with misinterpretation of good intentions than with actual error.

As one Internet critic put it: "It is as though a liberation theologian came upon the original paper, 'Vigilance Against Anti-Jewish Ideas and Bias,' took out a pair of scissors and started hacking away at it."

Not all Presbyterians agree with the stance some radicals within their organization take:

In the early part of 2014, anti-Semitic extremists within the Presbyterian Church USA asserted themselves with the publication of a new "study guide" on the Israeli-Palestinian conflict. This "guide" was released by the "Israel/Palestine Mission Network of the Presbyterian Church (USA)" and is titled "Zionism Unsettled." It comes with a companion DVD.

In its self-promotion, the "study guide" states its purpose this way:

> What role have Zionism and Christian Zionism played in shaping attitudes and driving historical developments in the Middle East and around the world? How do Christians, Jews, and Muslims understand the competing claims to the land of Palestine and Israel? What steps can be taken to bring peace, reconciliation, and justice to the homeland that Palestinians and Israelis share?
>
> Zionism Unsettled embraces these critical issues fearlessly and with inspiring scope. The booklet and companion DVD draw together compelling and diverse viewpoints from Jews, Muslims, and Christians in Israel, Palestine, the U.S. and around the globe. By contrasting mainstream perceptions with important alternative perspectives frequently ignored in the media, Zionism Unsettled is an invaluable guide to deeper understanding.

This is hardly a guide to deeper understanding because it outright rejects the right of the Jewish people to a state of their own, calls Zionism a "pathology," "heretical" and "a doctrine that promotes death rather than life." It accuses Israel of "ethnic cleansing," calls it an "apartheid state" and charges that Israel, despite being the only democracy in the Middle East, is inherently discriminatory towards non-Jews.

The guide ignores historical context altogether and shows no sympathy towards the Jewish victims of war and terror, nor does it justify Israel's legitimate security concerns based on one hundred years of hostility against it. The guide even says that Jews have no inherent right to defend themselves.

The same anti-Semitic faction that produced this guide attempted at the last national conference of the Presbyterian Church USA to pass a resolution supporting the "Boycott, Divestment, and Sanctions" (BDS) movement, but failed by a small margin. This group intends to bring a BDS resolution again to the June national conference, not motivated as a protest against certain Israeli policies in the West Bank, but against the very existence of the State of Israel.

Thankfully, there are many fair-minded and decent Presbyterians who have condemned the guide, reaffirmed their friendship with the Jewish people, support for the State of Israel and for a two-state solution to the Israeli-Palestinian conflict.

Among Israel's greatest defenders is the revered Chris Leighton, who serves as the Executive Director of the Institute for Christian and Jewish Studies and is an ordained Presbyterian minister. He has heavily critiqued this guide in "An Open Letter to the Presbyterian Church."

He writes in part:

> The condemnation of Zionism, in all its forms, is not merely simplistic and misleading; the result of this polemic is the theological de-legitimization of a central concern of the Jewish people... Even a cursory study of history reveals the varied and complex forms that Zionism has taken over the centuries.

> The yearning for their national homeland has been woven into the Jewish community's daily life for millennia. The Torah (Deuteronomy)

and the Tanakh (2 Chronicles) both end with images of yearning to return to the land; synagogues face Jerusalem; the Passover Seder celebrated annually concludes with the prayer, "Next year in Jerusalem."

To suggest that the Jewish yearning for their own homeland—a yearning that we Presbyterians have supported for numerous other nations—is somehow theologically and morally abhorrent, is to deny Jews their own identity as a people. The word for that is "anti-Semitism," and that is, along with racism, sexism, homophobia, and all the other ills our church condemns, a sin."

This guide does not contribute to dialogue or mutual understanding between American Christians, American Jews, American Muslims, or any of the parties in the Middle East because it is a vicious polemic against one of the principle actors in the Israeli-Palestinian drama, and against the position of anyone who would support the fundamental right of the Jewish people to a state of their own.

The Vatican

In 2014 the Pope officially recognized the "State" of "Palestine." This is an odd turn of events considering there is no such place as the state of Palestine. "More significantly, the Vatican signed a treaty in June with "Palestine" in which the Holy See switched its diplomatic relations from the Palestinian Liberation Organization to the "State of Palestine." This treaty is the first legal document negotiated between the Holy See and the Palestinian state and as such, constitutes an official recognition. One of the strategic goals of Palestinian leadership has been to convince as many nations, governments and institutions as it can to endorse a fictional "state" to create a sense of inevitability that will pressure Israel into acquiescence. And while the United nations or certain European governments are perfunctorily anti-Zionist (or worse), the Pope yields far too much moral authority to be similarly dismissed.

Israeli Prime Minister Netanyahu Sounds Off

In June of 2014 Israeli Prime Minister Benjamin Netanyahu criticized the Presbyterian Church (USA) for its recent decision to sell its stock in U.S. businesses that operate in Judea and Samaria (the West Bank). By a 310-303 vote, the PC (USA) voted on Friday to sell an estimated $21 million in stock in Hewlett-Packard, Motorola Solutions, and Caterpillar.

Netanyahu called the vote "disgraceful," saying Israel is the only democracy in the Middle East that protects human rights, including those of Christians, in a region filled with religious hatred and immense savagery.

"It should trouble all people of conscience and morality because it's so disgraceful," Netanyahu charged. "You know, I would suggest to you, those Presbyterian organizations to fly to the Middle East, come and see Israel for the embattled democracy that it is, and then take a bus tour, go to Libya, go to Syria, go to Iraq and see the difference. And I would give them two pieces of advice. One is, make sure it's an armor-plated bus, and second, don't say that you're Christians," he said. Netanyahu also said he wonders why they single out Israel for such treatment.

Extracted from the Jerusalem Post
Christian Literature - John Hube

Much Christian literature is tainted by Replacement Theology. Regular, sloppy, references to Jesus living in Palestine only serve to reinforce in people's minds the ownership claims made by the Palestinian Authority. The term "Palestine" was not coined until 70 CE to spite the Jews by reference to their enemies, the Philistines. (The Philistines were European, not Arab or even Semitic.) The Palestinians did not assume that name until 1967, and are mostly Jordanian.

One book titled, *Blood Brothers* by Elias Chacour is marketed as an inspiring story about Christian love. It was disappointing to find it is actually a very rosy picture of a childhood spent in the Galilee establishing that the Palestinians had been there since before Jesus came.

This idyll is contrasted with the coming of the Israeli army. Admittedly, loving and understanding words are used about the Jewish enemy, but the book appears to rehearse all the Palestinian grievances against Israel but gloss over the Muslim persecution of Palestinian Christians, and violence against Israel which causes ordinary Palestinians such misery.

Christians reading this book, who don't know better, might be inspired by the author's life, but would at the same time be absorbing the propaganda of the Palestinians who are actually seeking to destroy Jesus' race and take over God's Holy Land for Allah.

Sabeel

Sabeel is a group of Palestinian Christians (only some; not all) who hold to a Replacement Theology, which they describe as an Ecumenical "Palestinian Liberation Theology," "nourished by the hopes, dreams and struggles of the Palestinian people." That is, seeking liberation from Israeli "occupation, violence, discrimination and human rights violations."

This group appears to hold that anything leading toward the destruction of Israel is good. A very strange position for any Christian to hold about any nation; especially one quoting Matthew 5:9, "Blessed are the peacemakers..." The director of Sabeel is Dr Naim Ateek.

This organization has "friends" and official support within the Anglican church in the United Kingdom. (Rev John Gladwin - Bishop of Chelmsford and Rev. Michael Langrish - Bishop of Exeter) and International Patron the

Most Rev. Desmond Tutu. By the way, Sabeel is a Christian Aid partner, another group that is against Israel.

Liberation Theology

Liberation Theology appears to say that Christians should always champion the underdog. In some situations this could be applicable, but the "underdog" is not necessarily in the right or worthy of being championed. Liberation Theology is effectively harnessed by the Palestinian activists by portraying Palestinians as underdogs, oppressed by the powerful Israelis, and calling upon Christians to fight their cause.

Sadly, many Christians buy into this without noticing that the "Palestinians," however real the individual suffering of the chosen subjects, are actually the aggressors who are seeking to destroy Israel. Thus we see Christians siding with Islam in its campaign against the people of our Lord Jesus.

Exodus 23:1-2 says: "You shall not circulate a false report. Do not put your hand with the wicked to be an unrighteous witness. You shall not follow a crowd to do evil; nor shall you testify in a dispute so as to turn aside after many to pervert *justice*."

Jesus the Palestinian in Palestinian Propaganda

Jesus and His crucifixion are misappropriated to bring Christians on side with the Palestinian (Islamic) campaign against Israel and the Jews.

Peace Organizations

Pax Christi is an international "Catholic Movement for Peace" which is well-known and respected by many for its work in "Israel/Palestine." Its international president is Michael Sabbah, who is mentioned in the book, *Why*

I Left Jihad by Walid Shoebat (an ex-Palestinian Terrorist), now a Christian and a lover of Israel and the Jews,

Many organizations call for peace, yet in reality they support the utter destruction of the State of Israel. Emil Salayta, who heads the Latin Patriarchate schools in Jerusalem, once spoke on "peace" at the Presbyterian Church in Walnut Creek, California. I attended and challenged him. "Could peace be achieved by bombing Israeli buses?" I asked. I have his answer on tape. "Israel must be eliminated, by whatever means," he replied. No one else seemed concerned.

Palestinian Mentors Associated with Willow Creek [Church] Association and Religious Left's War on Israel:

Stakelbeck on Terror
By Jim Fletcher – Israel Watch
April 23, 2012

My friend Erick Stakelbeck, a courageous reporter and TV host (CBN's *Stakelbeck on Terror*) is superb at connecting the dots. He is also fearless, a much-needed trait in today's harrowing world.

Today he posted an article about the nefarious work of Media Matters, the left-wing watchdog group that targets Christians and Israel. Not surprisingly, Media Matters is close to the White House.

Part of Erick's research uncovered the following:

"It is common for news and commentary by the press to present viewpoints that tend to overly promote a conservative,

Christian-influenced ideology," the group said in its application for non-profit status with the IRS.

This is an absurd statement, and a good example of the brazenness of the left to peddle lies. It's quite obvious to anyone paying even the slightest attention that media don't "promote" conservative Christian worldviews.

The opposite is true. David Brog, executive director of Christians United for Israel, thinks Media Matters' targeting of Christians is influenced by its (MM) anti-Israel bias.

Erick makes an important point about Media Matters' former senior foreign policy fellow, M.J. Rosenberg:

"Rosenberg routinely uses the label, 'Israel Firsters,' implying that American supporters put the interests of Israel above the United States. It's a charge commonly made by Neo-Nazis and anti-Semitic groups."

It is interesting to note that Media Matters promotes the same kind of rhetoric as that of the American religious left, particularly those who are calling themselves evangelicals. This is an ongoing story that will get much bigger, as more facts come to light regarding the players and agendas involved.

There is plenty of evidence, for example, that Rick Warren has already aligned himself with a whole host of anti-Israel friends, in his purposeful drive toward pluralism. And he's been at it a long time. Readers will simply have to figure out if supporting Israel is reason enough to oppose what Warren is about.

In 2008, Rick Warren's Saddleback Community Church hosted presidential candidates Barack Obama and the Republican ringer, John McCain. Warren of course proposed a balanced set of questions, ranging from the environment to poverty—all softball issues in such a forum.

But the group he selected to help him come up with questions for the candidates was most revealing: Faith in Public Life. Self-described as "a strategy center for the faith community advancing faith in the public square as a powerful force for justice, compassion and the common good," this multi-denominational religious group was founded by, among others, Jim Wallis (Sojourners); and Bob Edgar (former head of the National Council of Churches).

Among the board members and advisers for Faith in Public Life: Elizabeth Letzler, member of the PCUSA's Mission Responsibility Through Investment committee and the Israel-Palestine Network (i.e., an Israel divestment proponent); Jim Winkler, General Secretary of the United Methodist Church's General Board of Church and Society—he also sits on the board (with Communist Party USA leader Judith LeBlanc) of the U.S. Campaign to End the Israeli Occupation; and Dr. Nazir Khaja, chairman of Islamic Information Service.

One would have had to have been aware for some time (as I have been) of the anti-Israel views of people like Winkler—a key mover in United Methodist circles—and Mission Responsibility Through Investment committee and the Israel-Palestine Network (i.e., an Israel divestment proponent); Jim Winkler, General Secretary of the United Methodist Church's General Board of Church and Society—he also sits on the board (with Communist Party USA leader Wallis, in order to fully understand the implications of Warren working with them).

What we now have, you see, is a man who is perhaps the most identifiable evangelical in the world linking arms with avowed opponents of a sovereign Jewish State to administer its own defense against relentless terrorism. Fellow "evangelical" Brian McLaren also referenced recently on his blog:
(http://brianmclaren.net/archives/blog/proisraeli-and-propalestinian.html) the efforts of Aaron Niequist to be "Pro Israel and Pro Palestinian."

And who is Niequist?

He is the son-in-law of Bill and Lynne Hybels, founders of the monolithic Willow Creek Church outside Chicago. Willow Creek is a huge association of like-minded churches around the country. At 9,000 member churches—Hybels certainly has the attention of many thousands of evangelical Christians. And he and his wife were mentored by a Palestinian beginning in the 1970s, so their animus toward Israel is not new.

I'm going to make a bold statement, but one I think that is backed with common sense: It is not possible that those 9,000 churches do not share Bill and Lynne Hybels' attitudes about modern Israel.

In August 2011, Lynne Hybels hosted a "Summit Lunch" titled: "Leading Toward Peace in Israel and Palestine." The tip-off of course that this was to be a left-wing gathering comes in the now ubiquitous use of the term "Palestine," as if they are describing a sovereign nation.

The main presenter was Dr. Gary Burge, a Wheaton College professor and author, whose anti-Israel bias goes way back. It is almost an afterthought to note that Rick Warren and Bill Hybels are chums. They share the same interests and goals.

In other words, what we now takes me back to the beginning of this column, to point out that groups like Media Matters are no longer really New York-based groups (and thus far removed in every way from Middle America); they are ideological bedfellows of the leading Christian speakers and writers today.

Rick Warren's associations are the same in many respects as groups like Media Matters. What I've written is the tip of the iceberg in the new war on Israel from the Religious Left in America. Watchmen like Erick Stakelbeck are heavily out-numbered by the above-mentioned individuals and groups, and more, but I still believe that personal courage and a passionate commitment to truth will win the day.

Brian McLaren's Liberal Agenda

Notice what the anti-Israel Brian McLaren wrote on his blog in July 2014 in response to a couple's question about finding an "emergent" church:

Your question about finding a church is one I hear often. As more and more Evangelical (and Catholic) churches hold firm or double down with a kind of fierce conservatism, more and more moderate and progressive Evangelicals (and Catholics) feel they don't fit.

Often they end up in Mainline Protestant churches - Episcopal, UCC, DOC, Presbyterian, Lutheran, Methodist, etc. In addition, some evangelical and charismatic churches are changing -

becoming less fearful and more accepting of science (relating to evolution and global warming and sexual orientation), more committed to social justice, more reflective and less rigid theologically. There are websites that help people locate churches that are committed to LGBT equality, for example... some of these groups, like The Fellowship, are forming networks that make them easier to find.

Not only is McLaren anti-Israel, he is into evolution, global warming, he embraces homosexuality and condones "feel good" liberal theology—all the things that go directly against God's Holy Word—the very apostasy prophesied in 2 Thessalonians 2:3 (the falling away from the faith).

This brief overview has touched on some of the problems with some who dare to call themselves evangelicals or Christians. Their anti-Semitic, anti-Israel stance is very disturbing and very anti-biblical. And so are their apostate teachings. Do these "Christians" never read their Bibles? Israel is God's chosen nation. His Holy Book is filled with references to His beloved Israel—which He demonstrates through His promises and prophetic fulfillments of His Word.

Even long after we come to a saving faith in Christ we must be very much on guard for questionable and unsound teachings found *within* the Christian church. We are living in the last days when "falling away from the faith"—the apostasy—is steadily increasing, just as Jesus foretold in 2 Thessalonians 2:3. For example, some individuals will try to convince others that emotional "experiences" are credible tests of biblical, spiritual authenticity.

Experience alone, apart from adhering to the accuracies of Scripture cannot be a reliable gauge by which to test the spirits (1 John 4:1). This is the same lie that keeps many New Agers bound to false doctrines. Some spiritual experiences or encounters are God-given and some are not. Satan has a counterfeit deceptive action for many of God's teachings (2 Thessalonians 2:9; 2 Corinthians 11:14).

The devil's aim is to cause confusion and mayhem and he is doing a superlative job. Many "sheep in wolves clothing" are deliberately infiltrating the Christian church offering confusing, distorted teachings spanning from the emergent church movement, "contemplative prayer" trends to "seeker-sensitive" doctrines. They are dangerously compromising the gospel by attacking the very basic, core-truths of Scripture. Substitutes for God's redemptive work are running awry—propelled by those who do not accept the authority, inspiration and inerrancy of the Bible.

Because they do not like or want to accept the truths of the Bible. A deceptive tactic used by some "evangelicals" who compromise the Scriptures is to say that the true meanings of Scripture are "unclear" in an attempt to appear modest and gain popular favor with their target audience; when in truth, they are casting doubt upon God's inerrant Word.

Today Christians Are the Most Persecuted People Worldwide

On a similar note, not only is the world anti-Israel and anti-Semitic but Christian persecution, including that of children is exponentially increasing. Christians are abducted, raped, jailed, tortured, beheaded—slaughtered in any manner that suits their terrorist captors' agendas. Christians are being displaced from their homes by ISIS and other Muslim factions that are fighting for their false god—Allah. At this time in history Christians are being targeted and exterminated more radically and aggressively than Jews or any other group of people.

Both Jews and Christians are high on the expulsion list when it comes to Allah's henchmen. Only Jesus Christ, the Jewish Messiah, will be able to put an end to all of these demonically-underwritten attacks when He returns at the Second Coming and puts an end to the devil's atrocities.

Former U.S. President Obama did nothing to eliminate ISIS and help stop the torture and slaughter of Christians in the Middle East. But Obama does have an affinity for relocating Islamic "refugees" into this country; individuals who cannot be properly vetted, putting our nation at further risk. Obama turned his back on Christians in the Middle East, whose numbers have dwindled in the face of ISIS, which forces Christians to convert to Islam, pay a special tax or face execution in the territories it controls within Iraq and Syria.

A Gatestone Institute report verified that since the start of 2015, more than 4,200 Muslims were admitted into the U.S. from Iraq, but only 727 Christians—making it a ratio of around 5 to 1, despite the fact that Christians are a heavily targeted "infidel" minority. Nearly two dozen brutalized Iraqi Christians who fled ISIS and crossed into the U.S. from Mexico seeking religious asylum were denied protection, and were shamefully denied asylum by the former Obama Administration. How much more obvious can Obama's hatred for Christians be? He always favors Muslims and has even mocked Christians here in America. Jeremiah Wright, Obama's pastor of at least twenty years (up to the time he first campaigned to become president) recently stated, "Jesus was a Palestinian." Here we have the blind leading the blind. Or is it one devil's representative leading another?

In a *World News Daily* article titled, "Obama Stunner: 31 Christians vs. 2,000 Muslims" it was reported on December 27, 2015 by Leo Hohmann that Christians continue to be the most persecuted religious people in the world. He noted that "Despite President Obama's recent comment that it would be un-American to apply a 'religious test' for refugees seeking a safe haven in the United States, it appears his administration has already applied such a test, at least for Syrian refugees. Christians make up 10 percent of the Syrian population, and about 350,000 of them have been run out of their homes. Their property has been stolen by Muslims affiliated with ISIS, al-Nusra Front and other Islamic factions. Their men have been beheaded or summarily shot, their women raped and forced into submission."

The article points out the "dismal numbers" all throughout 2015, that the U.S. only managed to take in 31 Christians, or 1.4 percent of the total Syrian contingent that has been resettled by Obama's State Department. "This is even more concerning when considering the fact that the U.S. government pays nine private agencies to do its resettlement work – and six of the nine are affiliated with Catholic, Lutheran, Episcopal, evangelical and Jewish organizations. These groups are paid hundreds of millions of taxpayer dollars to resettle Muslims into 180 U.S. cities and towns. The U.S. has resettled 2,192 Syrian refugees in 2015, according to the federal database for refugee resettlement." Here is the breakdown of Syrian refugees by religion:

- 2,149 Muslims (98 percent) – including 2,089 Sunni, eight Shiite.
- 31 Christians (1.4 percent).
- Two atheists.
- Six Zoroastrians.
- Two Bahai.
- One "other."
- One listed no religious affiliation.

Former President Barack Hussein Obama has many times over proven to be unmoved by the torture and deaths of Christians all over the world—primarily executed by Islamic terrorists. However, he consistently shows himself to be a Muslim sympathizer, which includes radical Jihadist sects. His attitude is not unlike a "would be" closet Muslim. While in office, Obama seemed to be doing everything in his power to advance a dangerous radical 7th century Islamic invasion into our endangered Constitutional Republic—the United States of America.

On April 13, 2016, Leo Hohmann, again, reported for *World Net Daily* that Obama had implemented a surge of Syrian "refugees" (358 per week) which will total about 10,000 in this fiscal year (September 30, 2016). This includes thousands of men of military age. Since his report more news clips are coming in exposing how Obama worked with international organizations attempting to circumvent Congress to bring in many *more* improperly vetted or unvetted Syrian "refugees" (under-the-radar-routes), by expediting their entry through special visas and university scholarships. If this invasion of unvetted Syrians and the unvetted illegal entry of those from Mexico and Central America continues, this time in American history may be remembered as the open door gateway for terrorist Trojan Horses—facilitating the breakdown of American culture and sovereignty. And the U.S. president is leading the charge.

The *Washington Examiner* reported on May 2, 2016 that when Obama was still "president" he budgeted $17,613 for each of the estimated 75,000 Central American teens that were *expected to illegally* cross into the United States in the latter part of 2016; $2,841 more than the average annual Social Security retirement benefit, according to a new report. The total bill to taxpayers: $1.3 billion in benefits to "unaccompanied children," more than double what the federal government spent in 2010, according to an analysis of the administration's programs for illegal minors from the Center for Immigration Studies. (The average Social Security retirement benefit is $14,772.)

We are without a doubt living in an age of lawlessness; in an age of unprecedented deception and betrayal on a criminal level—beginning in the very top ranks of government and global organizations. It seems that acts of *treason* are not news worthy concerns in the (obviously) government-controlled mainstream media; only alternative news sources bravely reveal tyrannical movements of the globalists who are entrenched in all aspects of the take-down of the American way of life and our national sovereignty.

The Balkanization and Selling Out of America

Patriotic and pro-Israel Americans deeply concerned for their national sovereignty, liberty, safety and economic stability are also getting stabbed in the back—by leftist open borders advocates which includes the U.S. administration. On March 26, 2016 Tom Tancredo wrote this brilliant report for *Brietbart News Network*:

The ISIS Barbarians Are Already Inside the Gate

The religion of peace has struck again. As the FBI well knows, ISIS is already inside the United States. Guarding our gates is still necessary, but it is not enough when thousands of Islamist jihadists are already here, and being aided by Muslims attending a friendly neighborhood mosque near you.

The unpleasant, politically incorrect truth is that ISIS is only the point of the spear, the jihadist with the suicide belt and the duffle bag bomb, but that messenger was sent by Islam itself.

In Brussels, police have said that some of the murderers who carried out the Paris attacks were hidden and aided for months by the Muslim communities in Brussels. ISIS "cells" cannot survive and build their bombs and conduct their attacks without help from a broader network of sympathizers.

After each terrorist attack carried out by Islamist militants, we are told that the religion of Islam is blameless and we are lectured and warned against the evils of "Islamophobia." No one is permitted by the PC police to hold the "religion of peace" and its mosques and imams accountable for crimes committed for the greater glory of Allah.

To the American left and its willing collaborators in the media and the halls of power, "Islamophobia" seems a greater threat than ISIS. This moral confusion violates Sun Tzu's first principle of warfare: know thy enemy. Effective war planning and countermeasures are impossible if you are more concerned with political correctness than defeating the enemy.

Common sense says don't let the enemy inside the gate. Political correctness says put out the welcome mat. The evidence of collective insanity is all around us. Is it any wonder citizens are rebelling against the establishment when willful blindness is praised as a humanitarian virtue?

Our political establishment, including the business community, continues to tolerate and excuse open borders despite overwhelming public support for halting all illegal entry.

Our leaders continue to import new Islamist refugees from Syria—adding to the half-million already here from Somalia and other Muslim nations—despite ISIS's documented success in infiltrating its trained jihadists among those refugees.

Our leaders and our media continue to criticize growing European efforts to curtail the movement of over two million Muslim "refugees" into Europe despite the cultural conflict accompanying that chaotic movement.

Our limited military action against ISIS strongholds in Iraq and Syria is designed to silence domestic critics, not to destroy ISIS. Killing ISIS's top commanders one by one is like killing cancer cells one by one.

It's bad enough that this idiotic code of silence is enforced by the mainstream media, the universities, and the Obama Administration, but it is nothing but sheer stupidity wrapped in cowardice when Republican leaders and conservative pundits fall into line and censor themselves. It is not "radical Islam" that has declared war on us, it is orthodox Islam as defined and taught in Islam's holiest texts, the Quran and the Hadith.

What Obama insists on calling "extremists" or "radicals" are Muslims who are devout in their adherence to Islam's doctrines. "Moderate Muslims" are the less devout who do not follow Islam's teachings.

It is Islam's basic worldview that inspires hatred of the West, not grievances against U.S. foreign policy or lack of economic opportunity in Muslim societies. The Muslim Brotherhood was founded in 1928, not 1988, decades before any American soldier set foot in Kuwait.

Why then is it "Islamophobic" to speak the truth about Islam's hostility to Western values? Self-censorship is the main obstacle to effective steps to halt ISIS in its tracks, and people who preach such nonsense, and the Quislings who tolerate it—are aiding ISIS and need to be called out for it.

It is well known that the FBI has over 900 active investigations underway of ISIS sympathizers in every state, and it is only the lack of manpower that limits that number.

Yet the leftist Mayor of New York City has dismantled a surveillance program aimed at radical mosques and Islamist organizations—all in the name of preserving civil liberties, and such moral idiocy is applauded.

Meanwhile, tens of thousands of Somali-born migrants living in towns in Minnesota, Texas and California are demanding their own courts, their own schools, and are electing their own mayors, as well as sending young men to Syria to be trained as ISIS warriors.

And what is the response of our government? The Obama State Department wants to bring MORE Somali and Syrian refugees, and the Republican Congress refuses to halt the insanity.

What is the source of this willful blindness? To say it is political correctness run amok only raises the question, why the popularity of policies that are so obviously suicidal?

Our future safety and security depends on waking up from a suicidal expansion of Islamic communities inside our country. Until we do that, doubling or tripling the number of air strikes against ISIS enclaves 6,000 miles away is whistling past the graveyard.

Israel's Sovereignty

9 B'Av March and Rally Attended by
Thousands, a Huge Success
Women in Green
August 5, 2014

Last night in Jerusalem to renew the traditional march around the walls of Jerusalem's Old City on the night of Tisha B'Av.

"Some people may ask us, what are we looking for in Gaza? But Gaza is a part of Israel, and it gave us vegetables, flowers, and fruit trees. And then we abandoned it, and it turned into a hornet's nest that seeks to destroy us," Struk said. She then reiterated her commitment to her efforts toward obtaining sovereignty.

Last, but not least, was Chairman Gershon Mesika, Chairman of the Samarian Regional Council, who said, "On this day, all Jews the world over are in mourning for the things that have taken place on this day for the past 2,000 year. We march around the Temple Walls, around the Temple Mount, and we are surrounded by blood-thirsty foxes, while the Israeli government, out of weakness, relinquishes control to them."

"Every Jew knows of the glory that was on the Temple Mount, and the work done there, and of the burning of both the First and Second Temples. Sovereignty must be restored, and it is upon us to demand that the Israeli government bring sovereignty not only to the Temple Mount, but to each and every place in Israel," he stated.

Outstanding Accomplishments by the Israelis

"Since Abraham will surely become a great and mighty nation, and all nations on earth will be blessed through him" (Genesis 18:18).

God has greatly blessed Israel. This is only a very small sample of Israel's tremendous contributions to the world:

1. The Middle East has been growing date palms for centuries. The average tree is about 18-20 feet tall and yields about 38 pounds of dates a year. Israeli date trees are now yielding 400 pounds/year and are short enough to be harvested from the ground or a short ladder.

2. Israel the 100th smallest country, with less than 1/1000th of the world's population, can take credit for a long list of accomplishments.

3. The cell phone was developed in Israel by Israelis working in the Israeli branch of Motorola, which has its largest development center in Israel.

4. Most of the Windows NT and XP operating systems were developed by Microsoft-Israel.

5. The Pentium MMX Chip technology was designed in Israel at Intel Both the Pentium-4 microprocessor and the Centrino processor were entirely designed, developed and produced in Israel.

6. The Pentium microprocessor in your computer was most likely made in Israel.

7. Voice mail technology was developed in Israel.

8. Both Microsoft and Cisco built their only R&D facilities outside the U.S. in Israel.

9. The technology for the AOL Instant Messenger ICQ was developed in 1996 by four young Israelis.

10. Israel has the fourth largest air force in the world (after the U.S, Russia and China). In addition to a large variety of other aircraft, Israel's air force has an aerial arsenal of over 250 F-16's. This is the largest fleet of F-16 aircraft outside of the U.S.

11. Israel's $100 billion economy is larger than all of its immediate neighbors combined.

12. Israel has the highest percentage in the world of home computers per capita.

13. According to industry officials, Israel designed the airline industry's most impenetrable flight security. U.S. officials now look (finally) to Israel for advice on how to handle airborne security threats.

14. Israel has the highest ratio of university degrees to the population in the world.

15. Israel produces more scientific papers per capita than any other nation by a large margin – 109 per 10,000 people – as well as one of the highest per capita rates of patents filed.

16. In proportion to its population, Israel has the largest number of startup companies in the world. In absolute terms, Israel has the largest number of startup companies than any other country in the world, except the U.S. (3,500 companies mostly in hi-tech).

17. With more than 3,000 high-tech companies and startups, Israel has the highest concentration of hi-tech companies in the world — apart from the Silicon Valley, U.S.

18. Israel is ranked #2 in the world for venture capital funds right behind the U.S.

19. Outside the United States and Canada, Israel has the largest number of NASDAQ listed companies.

20. Israel has the highest average living standards in the Middle East.

21. The per capita income in 2000 was over $17,500, exceeding that of the UK.

22. On a per capita basis, Israel has the largest number of biotech startups.

23. Twenty-four per cent of Israel's workforce holds university degrees, ranking third in the industrialized world, after the United States and Holland and 12 per cent hold advanced degrees.

24. Israel is the only liberal democracy in the Middle East.

25. In 1984 and 1991, Israel airlifted a total of 22,000 Ethiopian Jews (Operation Solomon) at risk in Ethiopia, to safety in Israel.

26. When Golda Meir was elected Prime Minister of Israel in 1969, she became the world's second elected female leader in modern times.

27. When the U. S. Embassy in Nairobi, Kenya was bombed in 1998, Israeli rescue teams were on the scene within a day — and saved three victims from the rubble.

28. Israel has the third highest rate of entrepreneurship — and the highest rate among women and among people over 55 – in the world.

29. Relative to its population, Israel is the largest immigrant-absorbing nation on earth. Immigrants come in search of democracy, religious freedom, and economic opportunity. (Hundreds of thousands from the former Soviet Union.)

30. Israel was the first nation in the world to adopt the Kimberly process, an international standard that certifies diamonds as "conflict free."

31. Israel has the world's second highest per capita of new books.

32. Israel is the only country in the world that entered the 21st century with a net gain in its number of trees, made more remarkable because this was achieved in an area considered mainly desert.

33. Israel has more museums per capita than any other country.

34. Medicine…Israeli scientists developed the first fully computerized, no-radiation, diagnostic instrumentation for breast cancer.

35. An Israeli company developed a computerized system for ensuring proper administration of medications, thus removing human error from medical treatment. Every year in U. S. hospitals 7,000 patients die from treatment mistakes.

36. Israel's Given Imaging developed the first ingestible video camera, so small it fits inside a pill. Used to view the small intestine from the inside, cancer and digestive disorders.

37. Researchers in Israel developed a new device that directly helps the heart pump blood, an innovation with the potential to save lives among those with heart failure. The new device is synchronized with the camera which helps doctors diagnose heart's mechanical operations through a sophisticated system of sensors.

38. Israel leads the world in the number of scientists and technicians in the workforce, with 145 per 10,000, as opposed to 85 in the U. S., over 70 in Japan, and less than 60 in Germany. With over 25% of its work force employed in technical professions. Israel places first in this category as well.

39. A new acne treatment developed in Israel, the Clear Light device, produces a high-intensity, ultraviolet-light-free, narrow-band blue light that causes acne bacteria to self-destruct — all without damaging surrounding skin or tissue.

40. An Israeli company was the first to develop and install a large-scale solar-powered and fully functional electricity generating plant, in southern California's Mojave desert.

41. All these achievements were undertaken while engaged in regular wars with an implacable enemy that seeks its destruction, and an economy continuously under strain by having to spend more per capita on its own protection than any other county on earth.

New Israeli Device Helps People Better Understand The Physical World

Tel Aviv's Consumer Physics, Inc. has created a device called SCiO that will give ordinary people insight into the physical world in which we live. It uses Near Infra-Red Spectroscopy to provide instant information about the chemical make-up of just about anything and sends it directly to the user's Smartphone.

The device works by shining a light onto the surface of the object, which reflects back onto the device sensor along with the object's molecules, creating a unique molecular optical signature for that object.

The SCiO (Latin for to know or understand) provides the user with practical information about food, plants, and medicines.

For instance, this handheld molecular sensor can be pointed at food and provide nutritional facts, caloric content, and the degree of ripeness.

Pointing it at a plant will provide in-depth data such as its well-being, hydration, and soil analysis.

Pointing it at medicine will identify the name and make-up of a pill.

Although this method of analysis is not new, the capacity to bring this technology to such a small, affordable device is.

While the device can currently be used for the analysis of foods, plants, and medicines, plans are in place to increase its analytical capabilities.

Perhaps it will eventually have some practical lifesaving applications, such as testing for the safety of food and water or analyzing evidence at a crime scene. The device currently detects materials in concentrations of 1% or higher, although "concentration levels of 0.1% or less may also be feasible for some materials."

As information is uploaded to the SCiO database, creating a massive storage of knowledge regarding all types of objects, its capabilities will grow over time. The goal of its developers is to create a "world database of matter," not a modest objective. As the entire Internet community will be joining in to provide Smartphone apps and other possible uses when it reaches the market in December 2014, its potential can only grow.

The Top Ten Israeli Inventions Since 2003

Israel is one of the smallest countries in the world, with less than eight million citizens. But Israel is far from small in its contributions to the world. From breakthrough research in the medical world, to its advances in solar energy, for such a small country, Israel is doing fascinating things. Here is a list of the top ten Israeli Inventions since 2003.

1. Pythagoras Solar is just one of many Israeli inventions in solar energy. Over 80% of Israeli homes use solar energy, the highest percentage of any country in the world! Pythagoras Solar is the newest break-through invention for solar energy, its model being duplicated worldwide.

    It is the world's first solar window, combining energy efficiency, transparency and power generation through use of photovoltaic glass, reducing energy consumption and generating power for homes.

2. Netafim was started by Israeli engineer Simcha Blass and is now operating in over 113 countries and 13 factories worldwide! The company (owned and run by Kibbutz Netafim) has been a huge success in the fields of water preservation and agriculture. Netafim use drip irrigation, which releases water in controlled, slow drips for precise crop irrigation, saving water and producing more plants.

3. The cherry tomato was invented in Israel, through Hazera Genetics, a project of the Hebrew University of Jerusalem. The project yielded the cherry tomato, eaten and enjoyed worldwide. The cherry tomato ripens slowly and holds a longer period of time than regular tomatoes. The

project started as a means of developing produce that would not rot in shipment and was successful in their goal.

4. Better Place is the first of its kind, having created electric cars that rely on battery exchange spots. Israel is the first country to adapt and provide this service nation-wide. Shai Agassi's company has skyrocketed, with cooperation worldwide and reshaping the future of electric cars.

5. The Disk-on-Key was invented by Dov Moran and is trademarked by SanDisk. Through use of flash memory and USB interface, the portable storage device is used worldwide on computers. Who doesn't have one?

6. Mazor Robotics is the innovated creator of spine assist, surgical robots that are transforming spine surgery freehand procedures. By use of surgical robots, precision and less use of radiation allow for advances in spinal surgeries and medicine. The spine assist is the first break though invention of Mazor Robotics, and has led to several new inventions in the medical field.

7. BabySense was designed to prevent cribs deaths. Created by HiSense, the device monitors baby's movement and breathing while they are sleeping. The non-touch, non-radiation device notifies with a visual and auditory alarm if a baby stops breathing for more than 20 seconds or if their heart rate slows.

8. PillCam, known to many as capsule endoscopy, was created by Given Imaging. The capsule, used for intestinal visualization, is a camera that is pill sized and reports images that are used in detecting disorders of the GI tract. PillCam is used worldwide and is one of many inventions by Given Imaging in the medical world.

9. Leviathan Energy are the masterminds behind the Wind Tulip, a silent, vibration-free wind turbine, providing clean energy at lower costs. They also invented the Wind Lotus that can be used for both urban and rural locations. The wind lotus has a generation capacity of 5 kilowatts, making it the smallest, but most powerful wind turbine on earth.

10. HydroSpin provides electricity for water monitoring and control systems in remote areas, through its developed internal pipe generator. The pipe generator provides energy from water flow inside distribution pipes. It is used in areas that have no access to electricity and is used in many countries worldwide as humanitarian aid.

Israel Helps Protect U.S. Southern Border

It was October 2012. Roei Elkabetz, a brigadier general for the Israel Defense Forces (IDF), was explaining his country's border policing strategies. In his PowerPoint presentation, a photo of the enclosure wall that isolates the Gaza Strip from Israel clicked onscreen. Swimming in a sea of border security, the brigadier general was, however, not surrounded by the Mediterranean but by a parched West Texas landscape. He was in El Paso, a 10-minute walk from the wall that separates the United States from Mexico.

In February 2014, Customs and Border Protection (CBP), the Department of Homeland Security (DHS) agency in charge of policing our borders, contracted with Israel's giant private military manufacturer Elbit Systems to build a "virtual wall," a technological barrier set back from the actual international divide in the Arizona desert. That company, whose U.S.-traded stock shot up by 6 percent during Israel's massive military operation against Gaza in the summer of 2014, will bring the same databank of technology used in Israel's borderlands—Gaza and the West Bank—to Southern Arizona through its subsidiary Elbit Systems of America.

Chapter Twelve

Key Future Prophetic Events That Will Affect Israel

The Appearance of Elijah

Before the Tribulation begins the return of Elijah is prophesied in Malachi 4:5-6:

> "Behold, I am going to send you Elijah the prophet **before the coming of the great and terrible day of the LORD**. He will restore the hearts of the fathers to *their* children and the hearts of the children to their fathers, so that I will not come and smite the land with a curse."

Some commentators confuse the return of Elijah with John the Baptist, but Elijah is assured in Scripture before the Second Coming of the Lord and before the Tribulation years begin. John the Baptist was the forerunner before the First Coming of Messiah Jesus as stated in Malachi 3:1 and Isaiah 40:3-5. When one studies the verses in Matthew 17:9-13 it is abundantly clear that John the Baptist is not Elijah. Families were once very strong, for many centuries but as these last days have taken hold there has been a breakdown in the family system. It will be Elijah's mission to help recover and restore God's plan for family unity. Elijah's ministry appears to be one of restoration of the family structure in preparation for the important work of the 144,000 during the Tribulation and to prepare for Jesus' Second Coming.

Interpreting 2 Thessalonians 2

This is a key Scripture because it tells us the order of the Rapture, the Tribulation and Christ's Second Coming. The Rapture is portrayed in verse 1; the Tribulation in verses 3-8, and the Glorious Appearing of Christ in the Second Coming in verse 8, NOT verse 2 as some mistakenly teach.

> "Now we beseech you, brethren, touching the coming [the Rapture] of our Lord Jesus Christ, and our gathering together unto him; to the end that ye be not quickly shaken from your mind, nor yet be troubled, either by spirit, or by word, or by epistle as from us, as that the day of the Lord [the Tribulation] is just at hand (2 Thessalonians 2:1-2).

As you just read, Paul was reassuring the Thessalonians not to think that they were living in the Tribulation. He was telling them what would take place *before* the Tribulation, and that is the Rapture of the Church. The "day of the Lord" is always in reference to the Tribulation. In the King James translation instead of "day of the Lord" the verse was transcribed as "day of Christ" which some pastors and Bible teachers are unaware of and incorrectly use to teach that verse 2 is the reference to the Second Coming. As we continue on to verse 3, Paul points out two other things that would take place before the Tribulation begins:

> "Let no man beguile [or, deceive] you in any wise: for it will not be, except the falling away come **first**, **and** the man of sin be revealed, the son of perdition" (2 Thessalonians 2:3).

According to Paul's account (2 Thessalonians 2:3) the Antichrist is revealed (recognizable) *before* the Tribulation "**for it will not be** unless the falling away [the apostasy; falling away from the faith] comes first **and the man of sin is revealed**." These two prophecies declared in 2 Thessalonians 2 do not negate the idea of an "imminent" return of Christ within the context of that verse. The moment of the Rapture in relation to the growing apostasy and the revealing of the man of sin—the Antichrist, could happen very quickly—which would then bring about an imminent Rapture. As the apostasy increases and a personality emerges who can be recognized as the "son of perdition," the Lord's descent from heaven to rapture His Church could happen suddenly with great synchronicity, as ("a thief in the night" 1 Thessalonians 5:2). Nevertheless, Paul exhorts us to be alert so we are not totally surprised, "But you brethren are not in darkness, that the day would overtake you as a thief":

> "For you yourselves know full well that the day of the Lord will come just like a thief in the night. While they are saying, 'Peace and safety!' then destruction will come upon them suddenly like labor pains upon a woman with child, and they will not escape. But you, brethren, are not in darkness, that the day would overtake you like a thief; for you are all sons of light and sons of day. We are not of night nor of darkness; so then let us not sleep as others do, but let us be alert and sober" (1 Thessalonians 5:2-6).

The apostasy, the falling away from the faith—is already well underway and will continue to get much worse. The reference in 2 Thessalonians 2:3 to "and the man of sin is revealed" does not necessarily mean identified or recognized for *who he really* is *before* the Tribulation. Christians may have an idea of who this man is but will not know for sure because all true believers will be taken up to heaven in the Rapture *before* the signing of the false covenant with Israel (Daniel 9:27). It is at that time the Antichrist's identity (the man of sin), can be without a doubt identified and the Tribulation will begin. Halfway through the Tribulation the Antichrist's *true character* will be revealed.

In his book, *Footsteps of the Messiah* on page 123, Dr. Arnold Fruchtenbaum has this to say regarding 2 Thessalonians 2:1-3:

> The Antichrist's rise to power before the Tribulation is a biblical necessity. That there was to be a revelation of the identity of the Antichrist before the Tribulation is clear from 2 Thessalonians 2:1-3.

In this passage two events are said to occur before the day of the Lord, which always refers to the Tribulation. The first is the apostasy. The second is the revelation of the man of sin and the son of perdition. The revelation as to the identity of the Antichrist will come before the Tribulation, and it will come after the world has been divided into ten kingdoms.

The Antichrist's rise to power before the Tribulation is a biblical necessity. Since the Tribulation begins with the signing of the seven-year covenant between Israel and the Antichrist, it is necessary for the Antichrist to be in sufficient political power to sign such a covenant.

The Tribulation will be the most devastating time like never before in world history. A very mesmerizing leader will become the world ruler. He will emerge promising peace, hope, change, and prosperity for everyone. It will look like he will be able to solve all the world's problems. He will even appear to succeed in making a "peace" deal (a covenant) with Israel and her enemies. He will promise to protect Israel. But this man will be the *greatest enemy* the nation of Israel has ever had and he will turn against her, breaking his promise.

Halfway through the seven-year Tribulation, this charismatic leader, the Antichrist, will become indwelt by Satan himself (Revelation 13:3-4). The timing of this indwelling coincides with Revelation 12:7-12, when a war breaks out in heaven during the midpoint of the Tribulation and Satan and his angels are cast down to earth, never again to have access to the heavenly realms. It is at this time that Satan literally takes over the body of this charismatic leader. Antichrist will then enter the rebuilt temple in Jerusalem and declare that he is God. He will demand to be worshiped. Those who refuse to do so will be put to death.

From this point on, planet Earth will become increasingly deluged with unfathomable demonic activity. When Antichrist first appears, he will deceive millions into following him because of his beguiling, cult of personality. Instead of bringing peace, he will bring tyranny like never before. Life will become unbearable. It will be hell on earth. When Antichrist signs the false covenant with Israel, the Tribulation will begin in full force. Israel will be deceived by Antichrist and will in fact be signing a covenant with death. The rebuilt temple that will be defiled by Antichrist is not the same temple that will be built by the Lord for the Millennium (Zechariah 6:13).

In Joel 2 we learn that an army of robotic-like beings—the "overflowing scourge" that will strike terror in Israel and throughout the Middle East. The prophet Joel saw and described the following events that take place; it seems shortly *before* the Tribulation begins. Keep in mind that in the following verse Joel stated: "For day of the Lord *is coming,* for it is at hand" (certain). The "day of the Lord" is in reference to the Tribulation.

Joel 2:1-11:

"Blow the trumpet in Zion, and sound the alarm in My holy mountain! Let all the inhabitants of the land tremble; **for the day of the LORD is coming, for it is at hand**: A day of darkness and gloominess, a day of clouds and thick darkness, like the morning *clouds* spread over the mountains. A people *come*, great and strong, the like of whom has never been; nor will there ever be any *such* after them, even for many successive generations.

A fire devours before them and behind them a flame burns; the land is like the Garden of Eden before them. And behind them a desolate wilderness; surely nothing shall escape them. Their appearance is like the appearance of horses; and like swift steeds so they run. With a noise like chariots over mountaintops they leap, like the noise of flaming fire that devours the stubble. Like a strong people set in battle array.

Before them the people writhe in pain; all faces are drained of color. They run like mighty men, they climb the wall like men of war; every one marches in formation, and they do not break ranks. They do not push one another; everyone marches in his own column. Though they lunge between the weapons, they are not cut down, they run to and fro in the city, they run on the wall; they climb into the houses, they enter at the windows like a thief.

The earth quakes before them, the heavens tremble; the sun and the moon grow dark, and the stars diminish their brightness. The LORD gives voice before His army. For His camp is very great; for strong *is the One* who executes His word. For the day of the LORD *is* great and very terrible; who can endure it?"

The army of robotic-like beings described in Joel continues into the Tribulation for an unspecified period of time. This army is not related to the demonic hordes referenced in Revelation chapters nine or sixteen. When Antichrist advances to power he may very likely dominate and take control of the "overflowing scourge" promising to stop the onslaughts of the robotic-like beings which will lead to Israel signing the prophesied covenant. It seems that Antichrist will keep the "overflowing scourge" tame but for only a limited time. When the nation of Israel signs the covenant with the Antichrist, they may be given the impression that he will hold back the "overflowing scourge."

"Because ye have said, We have made a covenant with death, and with Sheol are we at agreement; when the overflowing scourge shall pass through, it shall not come unto us; for we have made lies our refuge, and under falsehood have we hid ourselves" (Isaiah 28:15).

"And he will make a firm covenant with the many for one week [7 years]; but in the middle of the week [3.5 years] he will put a stop to sacrifice and grain offering; and on the wing of abominations *will come* one who makes desolate, even until a complete destruction, one that is decreed, is poured out on the one who makes desolate" (Daniel 9:27).

It is the signing of this covenant that actually begins the Tribulation. The Antichrist adheres to the stipulations in the covenant for a time, but then allows the overflowing scourge to take up its crusade of terrifying and brutalizing Israel as well as other Middle Eastern nations:

"Because you have said, 'We have made a covenant with death, and with Sheol [hell] we are in agreement. When the overflowing scourge passes through, it will not come to us, for we have made lies our refuge, and under falsehood we have hidden ourselves.' Your covenant with death will be annulled, and your agreement with Sheol will not stand; when the overflowing scourge passes through you will be trampled down by it" (Isaiah 28:15, 18).

One World Rule

I edit and revise a lot of articles—literally *thousands* over the past five years. I find myself shaking my head every now and then. Some confusion exists regarding what many believe to be a "revived" Roman Empire, and the *order* of events regarding the coming one-world government.

The prophet Daniel prophesied that there would be a one-world government in the last days.

> "Thus he said, The fourth beast shall be a fourth kingdom upon earth, which shall be diverse from all the kingdoms, and shall devour the whole earth, and shall tread it down, and break it in pieces. And as for the ten horns, out of this kingdom shall ten kings arise: and another shall arise after them; and he shall be diverse from the former, and he shall put down three kings" (Daniel 7:23-24).

In verse 23 reference is made to, "the whole earth." This final kingdom will be similar to the first world kingdom under Nebuchadnezzar. Almighty God gave Nebuchadnezzar rule over the entire world (Daniel 2:36-38). Although he did not actually rule over all the kingdoms on earth, he was given the entire earth to rule over. The final world government will not only be given power over all the nations, it will also *rule over* them.

The Ten Kings Arise
Out of the One World Government

Daniel indicated that out of "this kingdom" [one-world rule], the group of ten ("ten kings") will "arise" and *out of* that group of ten the Antichrist will "arise." I don't know why so many people get this backward. The verse clearly states that the "ten kings" will arise *out of* "this kingdom." This prophecy is not necessarily in relation to any current ten nation coalition or ten divisions of any kind we hear about in news reports today. It is always a bad idea to try to squeeze (force) news headlines into biblical prophecy. After the Gog-Magog war when the eastern balance of power collapses with the fall and destruction of Russia and its Islamic allies, the door will open wide for an overt one world government.

By Stealth We Already Have a One World Government

Some people believe we already have a covert one-world ruling entity (one world government) because of the corporate lobbyists, shadow bankers—the World Bank (WB), International Monetary Fund (IMF), the Global Monetary Authority (GMA), the Financial Stability Board (FBS), the Bank for International Settlements (BDS)—out of which the FBS operates. The BDS pulls the strings of the world's monetary system and can create a boom or bust in a country. If a nation is not doing what the money lenders want; then all they have to do is sell their currency (a not so nice stranglehold technique). This is nothing less than a planetary financial dictatorship.

The Bank for International Settlements is completely above the law operating as a sovereign state located in Switzerland; no taxes are levied on the BDS or on personal salaries. The grounds of the bank are sovereign as are the buildings and offices. The Swiss government has no legal jurisdiction over this ruling bank and no government or authority has oversight over its operations. Additionally, the proposed Trans-Pacific Partnership (TPP) is a giant leap forward to secure an overt one world government—a corporate global governance of the world. TPP has been in the process of negotiations for several years in

Dr. Arnold Fruchtenbaum agrees that this is the correct interpretation of Daniel 7:24; that the one world government comes first and is then split-up into ten kingdoms covering the entire world, not only the Common market or the European Union. The world will fall under the one world government first and then after, the one world government is divided up into ten kingdoms. This will begin *before* the Tribulation. This ten kingdom group will continue into the middle of the Tribulation (part of the sixth birth pang). See *Footsteps of the Messiah*, pp. 125-126.

secret by corporate lobbyists and special interest groups without any oversight by the U.S. Congress. The "partnership" denies Congress any input or knowledge of the contents of the "partnership." This treaty is said to be a proposal for a multi-national free-trade agreement but is in fact an anti-sovereignty agreement. The globalist takeover is well underway, aided and abetted by the Executive branch of the United States government.

The ten kings [divisions] cited in Daniel come out of "this kingdom" [world government]. "Out of this kingdom shall ten kings arise." The prophesied ten divisions do not come *before* "this kingdom."

> "And as for the ten horns, out of this kingdom [world government] shall ten kings arise [ten divisions]: and another shall arise after them [Antichrist]; and he shall be diverse from the former, and he shall put down three kings" (Daniel 7:24).

Daniel Spoke of Types of Governments Not Geographic Locations

Most prophecy commentators say the seven heads represent the seven great empires of the world; Egyptian, Assyrian, Babylonian, Medo-Persian, Greek, Roman and the Antichrist. This idea is flawed. The seven heads are the seven *types* of government. John wrote the book of Revelation around 95 A.D. By the time he had written it Rome had undergone five different types of governments: Tarquin kings (753-509 B.C.) a republican type of government (509-300 B.C.), a plebeian government (300-264 B.C.), a consular (264-60 B.C.), and a triumvirate (60-27 B.C.). John went on to say essentially that not only had the five types of government come and gone, but *one is.* That was the government in John's time – Caesarean imperialism which started with Augustus beginning in 27 B.C. a few years after he defeated Mark Antony at the Battle of Actium in 31 B.C.

John continued ... *the other is not yet come; and when he cometh, he must continue a little while* (Revelation 17:10). The seventh type of government will be a worldwide alliance which will not last very long. It will break apart into a smaller group of ten nations. Rome had undergone five types of government before John's time; one during John's time, and the seventh to follow which will be the one-world government: a Roman type of government. The ten horns will be the ten kings who rule with the Antichrist for a short time (Revelation 17:12).

Historically speaking, Rome, as a type of government has continued throughout the Christian dispensation. The Roman Empire type of government never ceased to exist; it has simply evolved into a different form as it exists today, which will become the one world government of Daniel 7:23. Today, some Bible expositors are expecting the revival of the old Roman Empire, anticipating a geographical revival of the old Roman Empire. However, Rome as a *type* of government does not need to be revived; therefore it is not necessary to be looking for Rome to reappear in its old geographical location, or to confuse something like the European Common Market with the "ten kings" of Daniel 7:24.

The Roman *type* of government portrayed in Daniel has never stopped existing. In his prophecies, the prophet Daniel was speaking of types of governments, *not* geographical locations of governments. Each of the metals represents a different type of government. The image represents time, consecutively from Nebuchadnezzar's era until the Second Coming of Christ. It also represents the types of kingdoms that will emerge. The legs of iron in the metallic image of Daniel 2 continue all throughout the Christian dispensation until the Second Coming of Christ, which is pictured by the stone smashing the image at its feet.

"You **continued looking until** a stone was cut out without hands, and it struck the statue on its feet of iron and clay and crushed them" (Daniel 2:34).

The "stone" symbolically represents Jesus Christ (Matthew 21:42, 44). He will destroy the dictatorial rule of the Tribulation years, and set up His millennial kingdom over which He will reign and rule.

> "And in the days of those kings the God of heaven will set up a kingdom which will never be destroyed, and *that* kingdom will not be left for another people; it will crush and put an end to all the kingdoms, but it will itself endure forever. Inasmuch as you saw the stone was cut out of the mountain without hands and that it crushed the iron, the bronze, the clay, the silver, and the gold, the great God has made known to the king what will take place in the future; so the dream is true, and its interpretation is trustworthy" (Daniel 2:44-45).

The "ten kings" come out of the one world government. Therefore, looking for "ten kings" or ten nations that will fulfill the prophecy of Daniel 7:24 before the one-world government is established—is untimely and pointless. Scripture does not teach us how long it will be before the "world government" is divided into ten divisions. The world government comes into place *before* the "ten kings." Notice in Daniel 7:24 cited previously that the Antichrist "shall arise after them" meaning after the ten kings [ten divisions] come to power out of the collapsed world government.

A further collapse of the nation states as we know them will be a strong clue that the Antichrist is close to making his grand center stage entrance onto the world scene. Scripture is unclear how long after the ten divisions are created that the Antichrist will emerge. But when he does arrive on the prophetic scene, this man will be so charismatic and convincing that most of the world will fall for his lies.

The prophesied Antichrist will be seen as the answer to the world's pressing economic and social problems, not for the narcissistic monster he will later prove to be. His agenda to subvert God will go forward at super-sonic speed. The Tribulation will shift into gear when he convinces Israel to sign the covenant of Daniel 9:27. The Tribulation will then begin and accelerate at greater intensities right up until the Lord returns.

As I stated earlier, believers will not see Israel sign the covenant (Daniel 9:27) with the Antichrist because they will have been taken up in the Rapture earlier. But they should see preparation for the signing of the impending covenant.

Who Are the 144,000 of Revelation Seven? Where Do They Come From?

One of the purposes of the Tribulation is to bring about worldwide revival. The identity of the 144,000 is distinctly derived from twelve tribes: 144,000 Jews who will be supernaturally sealed for protection from the judgments brought down by God, and from the persecutions against believers. They are special emissaries who will declare the gospel during the first half of the Tribulation.

The 144,000 will be scattered worldwide and are men from the lineage of the twelve tribes of Israel. Although we do not specifically know who these Jews are, God chooses them and seals them for their worldwide ministry. However, Scripture is clear that these witnesses cannot be angels or supernatural beings who suddenly appear from heaven. These witnesses are real men; very anointed learned men who will speak various languages as they reach others with the gospel all around the world. They may actually be given supernatural ability to speak the various languages—just as the apostles did on the day of Pentecost. These men are not part of the Church taken previously in the Rapture.

Scripture does not tell us how these men actually become born-again believers but God Himself anoints these special redeemed emissaries and they survive the Tribulation. They are all chaste men who are saved on earth, none of them are married, Revelation 14:4-5:

> "These are they that were not defiled with women; for they are virgins. These are they that follow the Lamb whithersoever he goeth. These were purchased from among men, to be the firstfruits unto God and unto the Lamb. And in their mouth was found no lie: they are without blemish."

These special anointed men are unmarried male virgins and their calling is to evangelize the world throughout the Tribulation as led by the Lord (the Lamb). The 144,000 are shown with Jesus on Mount Zion here on earth in a vision of the Millennium when Jesus returns at the Second Coming which tells us that they accomplish their mission for Christ and survive the Tribulation.

> "And I saw, and behold, the Lamb standing on the mount Zion, and with him a hundred and forty and four thousand, having his name, and the name of his Father, written on their foreheads" (Revelation 14:1).

Revelation 7:1-8

> "After his I saw four angels standing at the four corners of the earth, holding the four winds of the earth, that no wind should blow on the earth, or on the sea, or upon any tree. And I saw another angel ascend from the sunrising, having the seal of the living God: and he cried with a great voice to the four angels to whom it was given to hurt the earth and the sea, saying, 'Hurt not the earth, neither the sea, nor the trees, till we shall have sealed the servants of our God on their foreheads.' And I heard the number of them that were sealed, a hundred and forty and four thousand, sealed out of every tribe of the children of Israel:

Of the tribe of Judah were sealed twelve thousand:

Of the tribe of Reuben twelve thousand; of the tribe of Gad twelve thousand.

Of the tribe of Asher twelve thousand; of the tribe of Naphtali twelve thousand; of the tribe of Manasseh twelve thousand.

Of the tribe of Simeon twelve thousand; of the tribe of Levi twelve thousand; of the tribe of Issachar twelve thousand.

Of the tribe of Zebulun twelve thousand; of the tribe of Joseph twelve thousand; of the tribe of Benjamin were sealed twelve thousand."

Those who are saved during the Tribulation is a result of the efforts of the 144,000. In the following passage we read, "After these things" (the work of the 144,000) and of "a great multitude" who are saved and martyred during the Tribulation; those who stand before the throne of God in heaven expressing their awe-inspired praise for our great and glorious King.

Revelation 7:9-14

"After these things I looked, and behold, a great multitude which no one could count, from every nation and *all* tribes and peoples and tongues, standing before the throne and before the Lamb, clothed in white robes, and palm branches *were* in their hands; and they cry out with a loud voice, saying, 'Salvation to our God who sits on the throne, and to the Lamb.'

And all the angels were standing around the throne and *around* the elders and the four living creatures; and they fell on their faces before the throne and worshiped God, saying, 'Amen, blessing and glory and wisdom and thanksgiving and honor and power and might, *be* to our God forever and ever. Amen.'

Then one of the elders answered, saying to me, 'These who are clothed in the white robes, who are they, and where have they come from?' I said to him, 'My lord, you know.' And he said to me, 'These are the ones who come out of the great tribulation, and they have washed their robes and made them white in the blood of the Lamb.'"

The work of the 144,000 Jews will bring about the final fulfillment of Jesus' Matthew 24:14 prophecy:

"And this gospel of the kingdom will be preached in all the world as a witness to all the nations, and the end will come."

The Two Witnesses of Revelation Eleven

During the first half of the Tribulation the Lord will bring to power two, yet unknown Jewish men who will have a special anointing from the Lord. They will have the ability to kill men by fire, withhold rain and cause droughts, turn water into blood and cause other plagues that will startle and frighten the masses. Their ministry will be located in Jerusalem which is quite different from the 144,000 whose ministry covers the entire globe:

"And I will grant *authority* to my two witnesses, and they will prophesy for twelve hundred and sixty days, clothed in sackcloth." These are the two olive trees and the two lampstands that stand before the Lord of the earth.

And if anyone wants to harm them, fire flows out of their mouth and devours their enemies; so if anyone wants to harm them, he must be killed in this way.

These have the power to shut up the sky, so that rain will not fall during the days of their prophesying; and they have power over the waters to turn them into blood, and to strike the earth with every plague, as often as they desire" (Revelation 11:3-6)

The Two Witnesses will be active for the first 3.5 years of the Tribulation (1,260 days). The ministry of the Two Witnesses will also be a fulfillment of Zechariah 4:11-14. A calculated attempt on the part of the Antichrist to use the Two Witnesses to his advantage will backfire. These two men will have used their supernatural powers to shake the earth and no one can destroy them until God allows the Antichrist to succeed in killing the two men (in Jerusalem). The media and those who suffered from the judgment plagues inflicted by the two men will celebrate their death.

The dead bodies of the Two Witnesses will be displayed in the streets of Jerusalem (Antichrist's trophies). But after 3.5 days God will resurrect the Two Witnesses and take them to heaven shocking the world (Revelation 11:11-12). An intense earthquake will follow the ascension of the Two witnesses killing seven thousand and causing great damage to the city. Many will then realize that the God of heaven cannot be overruled and will praise Him. But nevertheless, many will foolishly worship and follow the Antichrist to their ultimate and total demise.

Revelation 11:7-13

"When they have finished their testimony, the beast that comes up out of the abyss will make war with them, and overcome them and kill them. And their dead bodies *will lie* in the street of the great city which mystically is called Sodom and Egypt, where also their Lord was crucified.

Those from the peoples and tribes and tongues and nations *will* look at their dead bodies for three and a half days, and will not permit their dead bodies to be laid in a tomb.

And those who dwell on the earth *will* rejoice over them and celebrate; and they will send gifts to one another, because these two prophets tormented those who dwell on the earth.

But after the three and a half days, the breath of life from God came into them, and they stood on their feet; and great fear fell upon those who were watching them. And they heard a loud voice from heaven saying to them, 'Come up here.'

Then they went up into heaven in the cloud, and their enemies watched them. And in that hour there was a great earthquake, and a tenth of the city fell; seven thousand people were killed in the earthquake, and the rest were terrified and gave glory to the God of heaven."

Who Are the Two Hundred Million of Revelation Nine?

Israel will be in a very tough position once the Tribulation begins. To convey even more details about how serious and frightening the Tribulation will be, I am going to briefly discuss John's vision regarding the Sixth Trumpet Judgment beginning with Scripture from Revelation 9:13-21:

"Then the sixth angel sounded: And I heard a voice from the four horns of the golden altar which is before God, saying to the sixth angel who had the trumpet, 'Release the four angels who are bound in the great river Euphrates,' So the four angels who had been prepared for the hour and day and month and year were released to kill a third of mankind" (Revelation 9:13-15).

"Now the number of the army of the horseman was two hundred million; I heard the number of them. And thus I saw the horses in the vision: those who sat on the horses in the vision: those who sat on them had breastplates of fiery red, hyacinth blue, and sulfur yellow; and the heads of the horses were like the heads of lions; and out of their mouths came fire, smoke and brimstone.

By these plagues a third of mankind was killed—by the fire and the smoke and the brimstone which came out of their mouths "For their power is in their mouth and their tails for their tails are like serpents, having heads; and with them they do harm" (Revelation 9:16-19).

A popular theory which started at least several decades ago claims that Red China can gather into action an army of two million soldiers and fulfill the prophecy given in Revelation 9:16-19. This interpretation is significantly flawed. The previous description in Revelation 9 portrays the heads of the horses to resemble the heads of lions. Fire, smoke and sulfur come out of their mouths. Their tails are like snakes that inflict harm on people. The riders wear breastplates that are fiery red, dark blue and yellow.

It is obvious that the creatures are not horses and men. These are demons riding demonic creatures. It is not difficult to understand from the language used in the verses that these creatures are not symbolic entities. They are exactly what they are described to be and they are not men, certainly not Red Chinese soldiers. No humans could possibly resemble the description given of the demonic beings. Throughout Scripture, the east is consistently in reference to Mesopotamia (Assyria and Babylonia), which also applies to the verses here (Revelation 16). China cannot be part of this equation. China cannot be properly interpreted to represent "the kings of the east."

Moreover, if Scripture is alluding to a human army, which it is not, the nation of India could just as easily fulfill the number requirement. "The kings of the east" of chapter sixteen of Revelation are not the Red Chinese. They are "Mesopotamian" kings. Modern day Mesopotamia would include Iraq, parts of eastern Iran, southwest Iran and southeast Turkey. It should be remembered that any passage in Revelation or any book of the Bible that does not show itself to be symbolic is to be taken literally, unless the word or words are used symbolically elsewhere. The following examples will clarify this statement. In Revelation 17:1-8 the great whore is described. Then in verses 9-18 the angel explains who the whore is as well as the kings, their kingdoms, the beast, the Lamb and the waters. In Revelation 13:1-8 the beast that comes out of the sea is described. He has seven heads and ten horns, and looks like a leopard, bear and lion. The heads, horns and beasts are not explained in this chapter, but they are explained in chapter 17 and in Daniel 7:17-26.

The demonic army of Revelation nine is not related to the events of Revelation sixteen. The demonic army of two million is part of the Trumpet judgments, and the events of chapter sixteen are part of the Bowl judgments when the Euphrates River will be dried up (v. 12) for the purpose of making it easier for the Antichrist to assemble his forces for the Armageddon campaign. (The drying up of the Euphrates is not for the purpose of making a pathway for a Red Chinese army to march to the Middle East, contrary to popular teachings.)

These two judgments occur at two different (separate) times during the Tribulation years and have no relation to one another..

The two hundred million are in a Trumpet judgment but the *kings of the east* ("the sunrising") are in a Bowl judgment and *cannot* be combined into the same event; they are two different judgments. These shocking revelations, the events just described are very difficult to comprehend. We would certainly like to think they must be symbolic. But Scripture is precise and tells us that there will be heavy demonic involvement during the Tribulation and some inconceivably frightening events will transpire during that time.

Outstanding Bible scholars including Arnold Fruchtenbaum are in agreement that the Red Chinese cannot comprise the two hundred million army of Revelation nine or Revelation sixteen, and that there is no correlation between the events of Revelation nine and Revelation sixteen. And that the *two hundred million* are demons *not* men (*Footsteps of the Messiah*, 1993, p. 310).

The Falling Away—The Apostasy

Scripture gives us more information on what we can expect prior to the Tribulation. During the Tribulation Israel will be challenged like never before. The Day of the Lord is in reference to the Tribulation years. We already touched upon the Antichrist cited in the following Scripture. Now let's look at the meaning of *apostasy*. The nation of Israel has been in a rebellious condition for a long time rejecting Christ, but that will change incrementally and finally at the end of the Tribulation. The word *apostasy* is in reference to a *falling away* from the faith.

> "Now we request you, brethren, with regard to the coming of our Lord Jesus Christ, and our gathering together to Him, that you may not be quickly shaken from your composure or be disturbed either by spirit or a message or a letter as if from us, to the effect that the day of the Lord has come, Let no one deceive you, for it [the Tribulation] will not come **unless the apostasy comes first, and the man of lawlessness is revealed**, the son of destruction [the Antichrist]" (2 Thessalonians 2:1-3).

Some individuals try to translate the Greek word "apostasia" to mean a reference to the Rapture by using the word "departure." The Greek word "apostasia" stems from "aphistemi" which means *to stand away from a body of truth.* When Paul used the word *apostasy (apostasia)* in 2 Thessalonians 2:3 it was in reference to *a falling away from,* a *departure from the faith.* The Scriptures tell us that the Tribulation will not come until the apostasy (the falling away from biblical truth) and "the man of lawlessness is revealed" (Antichrist). His identity will be recognizable, but his true character will not be known until the midpoint of the Tribulation.

The word *departure* must be used carefully in its proper context. It needs to be qualified and defined within a discourse. The Rapture is an involuntary action (a snatching up, a taking away). But a *departure* is a voluntary act, as in packing ones bags for a vacation. Or a decision to depart from a belief. Departure and "the snatching away" have opposite meanings. To try to use the word *departure* to mean the Rapture of the Church is inserting something into the text that is not there. The word *departure*, therefore cannot be used as a reference to the Rapture.

> "The Lord Himself will descend from heaven with a shout; with the voice of an archangel, and with the trumpet of God. And the dead in Christ will rise first. Then we who are alive *and* remain shall be caught up together with them in the clouds to meet the Lord in the air. And thus we shall always be with the Lord" (1 Thessalonians 4:16-17).

The passage above describes the Rapture event—when God *calls away* all true believers. When the Church is "caught up," the Lord comes down to meet His Church in the air and off she goes. This is an sudden involuntary taking away totally based on the efforts and timing of God Himself. But a *departure,* as in the departure from the faith, used in that context puts the decision voluntarily on the part of the person(s) departing; as in *departing from the faith*—apostasia: defection, revolt. (#646 *Strong's Concordance*)

Another important point is this: In 2 Timothy 4:6 Paul uses the word *departure*: "For I am already being offered, and the time of my departure is come." The Greek word for *departure* is *analusis.* Paul is speaking about the end of his life in that passage; that he fought the good fight, that he was about to leave (depart) from this earth and go to be with the Lord, that his time had come. He did not use the word *apostasy* (*apostasia*) to make that point. He used the word *departure* (*analusis*), which shows the word apostasy *apostasia* must not be used to refer to the Rapture. In 2 Timothy 4:10 Paul uses the word *departed*: "For Demas hath forsaken me, having loved this present world, and is departed unto Thessalonica; Crescens to Galatia, Titus unto Dalmatia." Once again we see a form of the word *departure used as a voluntary act*, not an involuntary abrupt exit. Therefore we conclude that *apostasia* means *a forsaking of a body of truth.*

We must also keep in mind that 2 Thessalonians was written before 2 Timothy. Why would Paul then later use the word *departure* (*analusis*) to make the point of his anticipated leaving (death) instead of *apostasy* (*apostasia*), "the falling away" which he used earlier in 2 Thessalonians 2:3? Clearly Paul's intention, his word usage in each context have two different meanings. *Apostasy* in the Greek means *to stand away from a body of truth*; when using the word *departure* in reference to *apostasy* (*apostasia*), it means to *depart from a previous standing* not a physical departure. The Greek word *analusis* means departure, as in physically leaving.

Strong's Concordance
359. analusis analusis: a loosing, departure
Original Word: ἀνάλυσις, εως, ἡ
Part of Speech: Noun, Feminine
Transliteration: analusis
Phonetic Spelling: (an-al'-oo-sis)
Short Definition: departing, departure from this life
Definition: a loosing, departing, departure (from this life)

The Greek definition of the word "apostasy" means "a defection; a renunciation." *Strong's* #646: apostasia (pronounced ap-os-tas-ee'-ah) feminine of the same as *Strong's* #647; defection from truth (properly, the state) ("apostasy"): falling away, forsake. *Strong's* #868 aphistémi: to lead away, to depart from. *Strongs* #646 apostasía (from 868 /aphístēmi, "leave, depart," which is derived from 575 /apó, "away from" and #2476 /histémi, "stand") – properly, departure (implying *desertion*); *apostasy* – literally, "a leaving, from a *previous standing*."

Archibald Thomas (A.T.) Robertson (November 6, 1863 – September 24, 1934) was a Southern Baptist preacher and a highly esteemed Bible scholar whose work focused on the New Testament and Koine Greek. A.T. Robertson clearly wrote that the Rapture, "the coming of our Lord Jesus Christ and our gathering together unto him" is Paul's reference to the Rapture in 2 Thessalonians 2 verse 1, not verse 3 as many commentators contend. He also carefully analyzed the meaning of *apostasy (apostasia)* in verse 3 shown next:

> **Except the falling away come first** (εαν μη ελτηι η αποστασια πρωτον — *ean mē elthēi hē apostasia prōton*). Negative condition of the third class, undetermined with prospect of determination and the aorist subjunctive. *Αποστασια — Apostasia* is the late form of *αποστασις — apostasis* and is our word apostasy.

Plutarch uses it of political revolt and it occurs in 1 Maccabees 2:15 about Antiochus Epiphanes who was enforcing the apostasy from Judaism to Hellenism. In Joshua 22:22 it occurs for rebellion against the Lord.

It seems clear that the word here means a religious revolt and the use of the definite article (η — *hē*) seems to mean that Paul had spoken to the Thessalonians about it. The only other New Testament use of the word is in Acts 21:21 where it means apostasy from Moses.

It is not clear whether Paul means revolt of the Jews from God, of Gentiles from God, of Christians from God, or of the apostasy that includes all classes within and without the Body of Christians. But it is to be **first** (πρωτον — *prōton*) before Christ comes again. Note this adverb when only two events are compared (cf. Acts 1:1).

(See Appendix B for A. T. Robertson's entire treatise on 2 Thessalonians. 2:1-3.)

Webster's Dictionary, the 1928 Edition provides a solid definition for the word apostasy, "An abandonment of what one has professed; a total desertion or departure from one's faith or religion." Not a spatial, physical departure up into the air as in the Rapture.

The *Liddell and Scott Greek Lexicon,* 7th Edition defines "apostasia" as, "the late form of apostasis, defection." Apostasia, as defined by Liddell and Scott makes no reference to "physical departure" or "disappearance." They also offer no secondary definition. They do offer definitions for the Greek word *apostasis,* of which *apostasia* is a later form:

Apostasis (aphistami) *a standing away from*, and so:

1. Defection, revolt *apo timos* or *tinos Herodotu,* Thucydides*; pros tins* Thucy.
2. Departure, *Biou* Euripides.
3. Distance, interval, Plato.

Note the word "departure" is given a *secondary* meaning in the lexicon, and to the later form of the Greek word *apostasies.* Therefore it is not the primary dominant meaning and certainly not a core, root meaning. In the *Holman Illustrated Bible Dictionary,* the first definition for "apostasy" is:

> Act of rebelling against, forsaking, abandoning, or falling away from what one has believed. The English word "apostasy" is derived from a Greek word (apostasia) that means, "to stand away from."

Also, in that same dictionary under the New Testament category for the word "apostasy" we find the following notations:

> In 2 Thessalonians 2:3 Paul addressed those who had been deceived into believing that the day of the Lord had already come. He taught that an apostasy would precede the day of the Lord. The Spirit had explicitly revealed this falling away from the faith (1 Timothy 4:1). Such apostasy in the latter times will involve doctrinal deception, moral insensitivity, and ethical departures from God's truth.

> Associated NT (New Testament) concepts include the parable of the soils, in which Jesus spoke of those who believe for a while but "fall away" in time of temptation (Luke 8:13). At the judgment those who work iniquity will be told to depart" (Luke 13:27). Paul "withdrew" from the synagogue in Ephesus (Acts 19:9) because of the opposition he found there, and he counseled Timothy to "withdraw" from those who advocate

a different doctrine (1 Timothy 6:3-5). Hebrews speaks of falling away from the living God because of "an evil heart of unbelief" (3:12).

Furthermore, according to Greek New Testament language experts D.A. Carson and J.P. Louw *form* does not determine *meaning*. The meaning of a word is determined by usage, or *semantically*. The meaning is not derived because it does or does not agree with the presumptive root meanings or constituent parts. It is not possible to move from *form* to *meaning* to determine the meaning of a word accurately. Also, if one was to assign the meaning of a word based *completely on etymology*, by the root or roots of a word, that method of interpretation is not a reliable guideline.

J.P. Louw affirms this important principle:

> It is a basic principle of modern semantic theory that we cannot progress from the form of a word to its meaning. Form and meaning are not directly correlated. Just as we cannot explain the English term 'understand' as meaning 'under'+'stand,' so we cannot explain diaxeirzo in Acts 5:30 as 'to lay hand upon vehemently.' The word only means 'to kill.' How it was done is a matter of context, not lexicography. (*Semantics of New Testament Greek*, page 29)

D.A. Carson states:

> One of the most enduring errors, the root fallacy presupposes that every word actually has a meaning bound up with its shape or components. In this view, meaning is determined by etymology; that is by the root or roots of a word. Normally we observe that any individual word has a certain limited semantic range, and the context may therefore modify or shape the meaning of a word only within certain boundaries. The total semantic range is not permanently fixed, of course; with time and novel usage, it may shift considerably.

Even so, I am not suggesting that words are infinitely plastic. I am simply saying that the meaning of a word cannot be reliably determined by etymology, or that a root once it is discovered, always projects a certain semantic load onto any word that incorporates that root. Linguistically, meaning is not an intrinsic possession of a word; rather, "it is a set of relations for which a verbal symbol is a sign." We cannot responsibly assume that etymology is related to meaning. We can only test the point by discovering the meaning of a word inductively. (*Exegetical Fallacies*, pages 28, 32-33)

In 2 Thessalonians 2:1-3 Paul is making a differentiation of what precedes and what follows. The "gathering together" (Rapture) in verse 1, and then the coming "day of the Lord" (the Tribulation) follows, "for it" will not come unless the apostasy comes first and the revealing of the man of lawlessness (Antichrist) takes place. Even learned, respected men who interpret the word "apostasy" to be a physical "departure" would have Paul essentially saying, "The Rapture cannot happen until the Rapture happens." But Paul is explicitly warning of certain events as signs that must take place before the Lord's return. Christ's return. Paul is giving a warning about deception. Paul in his writings refers to "deceptions" of all kinds, expressing the need to be very discerning.

In 2 Thessalonians 2:3 the word "apostasy" (*apostasia*) comes from the Greek verb *aphistemi,* which literally means, "to depart," "revolt" or "stand away from a body of truth." Paul spoke of this falling away in (1 Timothy 4:1) and used the same Greek word. However, in 1 Timothy 4:1 Paul *added the words* "depart from the faith" (KJV, NKJV) instead of using the word "depart" by itself, specifically defining the phrase. Paul states the reason for the falling away is because some are listening to demons; deceiving spirits. So some are being deceived by teachings that are in opposition to the Word of God and this is taking place within the Christian church.

Another important point to keep in mind is the order of the passages, the distinct succession of the verses in 2 Thessalonians 2:1-3: *Let no one in any way deceive you by any means*, implies that attempts to deceive are at play. Immediately after that verse we read: *For it come unless the apostasy comes first*, implying: defection, caused by what is stated in the previous verse: "deceive" (deception). After the deception, comes the *apostasy*, the falling away.

Continuing on, simple logic tells us that out of *the apostasy the son of destruction* (the Antichrist) will emerge—as a result of the falling away, the **apostasy**. His appearing will be preceded by the "great apostasy." He will continue to perpetuate the apostasy and take it to new heights. His rise, his revealing will be in relation to a great falling away from the faith, and it is he who will primarily carry it on and continue to promote false religious doctrines (one-world church) by using deception ("lying wonders") until he finally goes into the temple halfway through the Tribulation declaring himself to be God.

To illustrate further, consider the end-times apostasy in the parable of the leaven showing that the apostasy is going to take place in the last days, and that the infiltration of corrupt doctrines into the church will result in *total* apostasy. In Matthew 13 and 16, the "leaven" is the end-times apostasy (false doctrines) as shown by Jesus in the parable of the leaven. Jesus warned about false doctrines:

"Another parable He spoke to them: 'The kingdom of heaven is like leaven, which a woman took and hid in three measures of meal till it was all leavened'" (Matthew 13:33).

"Then Jesus said to them, 'Take heed and beware of the leaven of the Pharisees and the Sadducees.' How is it that you do not understand that I did not speak to you concerning bread?—*but* to beware of the leaven of the Pharisees and Sadducees.

Then they understood that He did not tell *them* to beware of the leaven of bread but of the doctrine of the Pharisees and Saduccees" (Matthew 16:6, 11-12).

Jesus' parable of the leaven is concerning apostasy in the last days. It is a warning about false teachings and false doctrines, a "standing away from faith." By the Lord's own account, leaven is false doctrine. In Thessalonians 2:3, Scripture teaches that the explosion of false doctrines in the last days will take hold, making the way for Antichrist. The following verses clearly show that some will teach false doctrines that contradict the true teachings of the Bible.

"Now the spirit expressly says that in latter times some will depart from the faith, giving heed to deceiving spirits and doctrines of demons, speaking lies in hypocrisy, having their own conscience seared with a hot iron" (1 Timothy 4:1-2).

"For many deceivers have gone out into the world who do not confess Jesus Christ *as* coming in the flesh. This is a deceiver and an antichrist. Whoever transgresses and does not abide in the doctrine of Christ does not have God. He who abides in the doctrine of Christ has both the Father and the Son. If anyone comes to you and does not bring this doctrine, do not receive him into your house nor greet him; for he who greets him shares in his evil deeds" (2 John 7, 9-11).

Popular author, the late Cris Putnam explained in an interview (and in various blogs) how he had spent a great deal of time tracing the use of the word *apostasia,* and it *never* means *a physical departure*, but rather *a departure from faith*; it means apostasy in the Church, the *falling away from the faith.* The word *apostasia* in the Greek Old and New Testaments always refers to a "departure from faith" and never to a "catching away" or "bodily resurrection."

The great Bible scholar, the late Dr. David L. Cooper, founder and president of the esteemed Biblical Research Society commented on the interpretation of the Greek word *apostasia*:

> "One could not find anywhere that the word *apostasia* had taken on the meaning of *departure* before the Sixth Century A.D."
>   —*Biblical Research Monthly*, October 1948

Therefore as consistent Bible students we must follow the Golden Rule of Interpretation by following the primary, ordinary, usual literal first century meaning of *apostasia* defined as, "A departure from a body of truth," and not as a reference to the Rapture of the Church.

Part Two

Longing for the Millennial Reign of Christ

Jeremiah 24:6-8

"For I will set My eyes on them for good, and will bring them back to this land; I will build them and not pull *them* down, and I will plant them and not pluck *them* up."

Peace on Earth at Last

Isaiah 11:6-11

"And the wolf will dwell with the lamb, and the leopard will lie down with the young goat, and the calf and the young lion and the fatling together; and a little boy will lead them. Also the cow and the bear will graze, their young will lie down together, and the lion will eat straw like the ox.

The nursing child will play by the hole of the cobra, and the weaned child will put his hand on the viper's den. They will not hurt or destroy in all My holy mountain, for the earth will be full of the knowledge of the LORD as the waters cover the sea.

Then in that day The nations will resort to the root of Jesse, Who will stand as a signal for the peoples; and His resting place will be glorious.

Then it will happen on that day that the Lord will again recover the second time with His hand the remnant of His people, who will remain, from Assyria, Egypt, Pathros, Cush, Elam, Shinar, Hamath, and from the islands of the sea."

✡✡✡✡✡

Chapter Thirteen

Will Believers Rule and Reign with Christ?

The Antichrist's reign of terror during the Tribulation fueled by Satan and assisted by the False Prophet (the unholy trinity) will end with the physical, literal return of Jesus the Messiah. Accompanied by His army of believers and holy angels Jesus will annihilate the Antichrist and his armies, which will have surrounded Jerusalem (Zechariah 14:2). The surviving population and nations will be judged. This judgment is by Christ as described in the Olivet Discourse (Matthew 25:31-46). The Antichrist and the False Prophet will be cast alive into the lake of fire.

> "Then the beast was captured, and with him the false prophet who worked signs in his presence, by which he deceived those who received the mark of the beast and those who worshiped his image. These two were cast alive into the lake of fire burning with brimstone" (Revelation 19:20).

All those who survive the Tribulation will be gathered before the Lord and judged. Those who believe in Him through the witness of the 144,000 and their converts will enter into the millennial kingdom. These people are referred to as the sheep (Matthew 25:33). Everyone who refused to believe in Jesus will be judged for their sins, found guilty and cast into the lake of fire to join the Antichrist and the False Prophet.

> "Then He will also say to those on the left hand, 'Depart from Me, you cursed, into the everlasting fire prepared for the devil and his angels: And these will go away into everlasting punishment, but the righteous into eternal life'" (Matthew 25:41, 46).

This group of unsaved people standing before the Lord will not be cast into hell (Hades, Sheol, abode of the dead), as were the unrepentant that have died before them. They will be thrown directly into the lake of fire where they will exist in this eternal penitentiary with the devil and the fallen angels. The dominion of the final world kingdom will be taken away, consumed and destroyed, replaced at long last first by the Lord's 1000-year millennial kingdom, then followed by the eternal order (Revelation 20:11; 21:1).

> "And in the days of these kings the God of heaven will set up a kingdom which shall never be destroyed; and the kingdom shall not be left to other people; it shall break in pieces and consume all these kingdoms, and it shall stand forever" (Daniel 2:44).

The saints will inherit the earth:

> "Then the kingdom and dominion, and the greatness of the kingdoms under the whole heaven, shall be given to the people, the saints of the Most High. His kingdom *is* an everlasting kingdom, and all dominions shall serve and obey Him. This *is* the end of the account. As for me, Daniel, my thoughts greatly troubled me, and my countenance changed; but I kept the matter in my heart" (Daniel 7:27-28).

The entire rejuvenated earth will be given to believers to rule over. We will rule over those saved during the Tribulation years including their descendents from generation to generation.

> "No more shall an infant from there *live but a few* days, nor an old man who has not fulfilled his days; for the child shall die one hundred years old, but the sinner *being* one hundred years old shall be accursed" (Isaiah 65:20).

Believers will rule with Jesus the Messiah who will be the Sovereign Ruler:

> "And he who overcomes, and keeps My works until the end, to him I will give power over the nations—He shall rule them with a rod of iron; They shall be dashed to pieces like the potter's vessels—as I also have received from My Father" (Revelation 2:26-27).

The rule and reign of believers with Christ will last throughout all of eternity:

> "And He will reign over the house of Jacob forever, and of His kingdom there will be no end" (Luke 1:33).

After the 1,000-year millennial kingdom there will be a pause when God will judge the wicked, those who have been waiting in hell (Great White Throne Judgment). They will be judged for every sin they have ever committed in thought, word, deed and motive. They will have to give an account for every sin. Because they rejected Christ as Lord and Savior they will of course be found guilty and cast into the lake of fire. This punishment will continue for eternity never, ever to end.

If you do not know Jesus Christ as your Lord and Savior, please understand there is little time left before the Tribulation begins—when all hell breaks loose on this earth—a time so terrible people will be begging for rocks to fall upon them to escape the horrors they face. Revelation 6 tells us that people will be begging to die for the wrath of God will be so fierce and intense:

> "And the kings of the earth, the great men, the rich men, the commanders, the mighty men, every slave and every free man, hid themselves in the caves and in the rocks of the mountains, and said

to the mountains and rocks, "Fall on us and hide us from the face of Him who sits on the throne and from the wrath of the Lamb! For the great day of His wrath has come, and who is able to stand?" (Revelation 6:15-17).

As the old saying goes, "Tomorrow is promised to no one." Anyone of us could take our last breath this very day. Death can be a very imminent event. Ruling and reigning with the King of kings and Lord of lords is a God-given promise to all those who will have placed their trust in the Messiah of Israel. Chasing after riches and power in this life will soon come to an abrupt halt. Nothing in this life can remotely compare to the glory that the Lord has prepared for all those who belong to Him.

Please don't wait to make a decision for Christ if you have not, yet. Satan is working overtime to deceive every man, woman and child into believing that the God of the Bible is a fictional character and that hell doesn't exist. Much of the world is in a hypnotic-stupor blinded by the father of lies, the devil (John 8:44). Let go of the fleeting thrills of this world and fully commit your life to Christ.

Jesus warned, "Let no man deceive you" (Matthew 24:4).

"But even if our gospel is veiled, it is veiled to those who are perishing, whose minds the god of this age has blinded, who do not believe, lest the light of the gospel of the glory of Christ, who is the image of God, should shine on them" (2 Corinthians 4:3-4).

In the book of Luke there is a true story of a greedy rich man suffering eternal torment upon death, while Lazarus was comforted and carried to a place of rest by the angels, when he died. The rich man desperately wanted to get out of hell but could not—it was too late for him to repent.

In the story of the death of the rich man and Lazarus, which was not a parable, Jesus taught about the reality of heaven and hell. He explained what happened to the rich man when he died to show the horrors of hell. He contrasted the agony of the rich man with the rest, contentment and peace of Lazarus who was taken to Paradise. Abraham, the father of the nation of Israel, was the protector of Paradise. This is why it is called Abraham's bosom.

Luke 16:22-26

"There was a certain rich man who was clothed in purple and fine linen and fared sumptuously every day.

But there was a certain beggar named Lazarus, full of sores, who was laid at his gate, desiring to be fed with the crumbs which fell from the rich man's table.

Moreover the dogs came and licked his sores. So it was that the beggar died, and was carried by the angels to Abraham's bosom.

The rich man also died and was buried. And being in torments in Hades, he lifted up his eyes and saw Abraham afar off, and Lazarus in his bosom.

Then he cried and said, 'Father Abraham, have mercy on me, and send Lazarus that he may dip the tip of his finger in water and cool my tongue; for I am tormented in this flame.'

But Abraham said, 'Son, remember that in your lifetime you received your good things, and likewise Lazarus evil things; but now he is comforted and you are tormented.

And besides all this, between us and you there is a great gulf fixed, so that those who want to pass from here to you cannot, nor can those from there pass to us.'"

How Do We View This Life?

Countless people in this life wear themselves out to achieve fame, celebrity and recognition amongst their peers on various levels; they want and think they need to be on the "winning" side. Sadly, these same dynamics can be found within some popular Christian circles where there are those who exude superiority over other believers forgetting we are to be humble servants before God not emulating the movers and shakers of this fallen world. Treating fellow believers with deliberate disrespect and rude disregard is symptomatic of a haughty spirit, which the Lord abhors.

Can an honest self-inventory by those who post multiple pictures of themselves and their lives all over the Internet—reveal they are doing it for God's glory? Of course not. They are doing it to draw attention to themselves: "Look at me!" (I have detailed this type of preoccupation with oneself in the first chapter of *A Better World Is Coming Soon - Don't Miss It*, Updated Expanded Edition, World Bible Society, 2013.)

Winning, power and control issues motivate far too many people. The majority of the wealthiest most powerful and influential people on earth today deny the truth of Christ. Unless they genuinely repent from their unbelief before they die, they will have a terrifying future like the rich man described in Luke 16.

If you want to be a real winner, choose the side of Almighty God who created you. He died to save you from eternal damnation, to give you a phenomenal life in a place where even the streets are pure gold. In Christ we are already victorious. Striving and never really arriving is a futile energy-zapping way of living. As overwhelmingly frustrating and painful as this life can be, we must focus on the promises of Christ and know this is not our true home, and that His future plans for us are extraordinarily abundant and real.

"The twelve gates *were* twelve pearls: each individual gate was of one pearl. And the street of the city *was* pure gold, like transparent glass" (Revelation 21:21).

Perhaps in this life you haven't quite made it to the "top" in your field. Maybe you are very distressed by this. Let go of the world's mantras and expectations and realize they are meaningless. Nothing in this life outside of what we do for Christ matters once we physically die. And die we will unless the Rapture comes first. Our eternal existence and fate rest on the decisions we make while we are alive—whether we accept or reject Christ for who He says He is: Our "great God and Savior" (Titus 2:13).

After we die, our souls remain completely conscious and enter immediately into heaven or hell. If you are a believer, another exit from this life apart from physical death is in the coming Rapture when we will receive our perfect glorified immortal bodies (1 Corinthians 15:51-52; 1 Thessalonians 4:16-18). In Christ's future kingdom every believer will have a significant role of importance, eternally. All believers are considered heirs of God, a much higher calling than even the highest-ranking positions found in the power structures of this present world-system. As a redeemed child of the living God, who better to work for than your Heavenly Father, the triumphant King of the universe?

Place your trust and faith in Him and Him alone. Allow the Lord to pull you out of the wretched strongholds of this life and carry you into His eternal kingdom where you will live a life of royalty. Run to Him while there is still time, cry out to the Lord so you too, will have a special place in His coming glorious kingdom, forever, in the awesome joyful presence of the Great "I AM."

"For you did not receive the spirit of bondage again to fear, but you received the Spirit of adoption by whom we cry out, 'Abba, Father.' The Spirit Himself bears witness with our spirit that we are children of God, and if children, then heirs—heirs of God and joint heirs with Christ, if indeed we suffer with *Him,* that we may also be glorified together" (Romans 8:15-17).

Yes, all true born-again believers will rule and reign with Christ and that magnificent time cannot come soon enough. Even so come Lord Jesus!

Israel in All Her Glory—At Long Last

The Millennial Reign of King Jesus

Jesus the Christ, Yeshua Ha Mashiach, will dwell in the midst of Israel and His everlasting glory will fill the temple during His 1,000-year millennial reign:

> "The Spirit lifted me up and brought me into the inner court; and behold, the glory of the Lord filled the temple. Then I heard Him speaking to me from the temple, while a man stood beside me.
>
> And He said to me, 'Son of man, this is the place of My throne and the place of the soles of My feet, where I will dwell in the midst of the children of Israel forever.
>
> No more shall the house of Israel defile My holy name, they nor their kings, by their harlotry or with the carcasses of their kings on their high places'" (Ezekiel 43:5-7).

Jerusalem and Jesus the Messiah

These Scriptures tell us that Jesus the Messiah will be literally *dwelling* in the midst of Jerusalem; God's glory will prevail all throughout the earth:

> "Thus says the LORD, 'I will return to Zion and will dwell in the midst of Jerusalem. Then Jerusalem will be called the City of

Truth, and the mountain of the LORD of hosts *will be called* the Holy Mountain'" (Zechariah 8:3).

"'Sing for joy and be glad, O daughter of Zion; for behold I am coming and I will dwell in your midst,' declares the LORD. 'Many nations will join themselves to the LORD in that day and will become My people.

Then I will dwell in your midst, and you will know that the LORD of hosts has sent Me to you. The LORD will possess Judah as His portion in the holy land, and will again choose Jerusalem'" (Zechariah 2:10-12).

Jesus will be literally *ruling* the rejuvenated earth from Jerusalem:

"Thus says the LORD of hosts, *'It will* yet *be* that peoples will come, even the inhabitants of many cities. The inhabitants of one will go to another, saying, Let us go at once to entreat the favor of the LORD, and to seek the LORD of hosts; I will also go. So many peoples and mighty nations will come to seek the LORD of hosts in Jerusalem and to entreat the favor of the LORD.' says the LORD of hosts, 'In those days ten men from all the nations will grasp the garment of a Jew, saying, Let us go with you, for we have heard that God is with you'" (Zechariah 8:20-23).

Zechariah 14:6-11

"It shall come to pass in that day *that* there will be no light; the lights will diminish. It shall be one day which is known to the LORD—neither day nor night. But at evening time it shall happen *that* it will be light.

And in that day it shall be *that* living waters shall flow from Jerusalem, half of them toward the eastern sea and half of them toward the western sea; in both summer and winter it shall occur.

And the Lord shall be King over all the earth. In that day it shall be—'The Lord *is* one,' and His name one.

All the land shall be turned into a plain from Geba to Rimmon south of Jerusalem. *Jerusalem* shall be raised up and inhabited in her place from Benjamin's Gate to the place of the First Gate and the Corner Gate, and *from* the Tower of Hananel to the king's winepresses.

The people shall dwell in it; and no longer shall there be utter destruction, but Jerusalem shall be safely inhabited."

The Nations Will Worship King Jesus
During the 1000-Year Millennium

Zechariah 14:16-21

"And it shall come to pass *that* everyone who is left of all the nations which came against Jerusalem shall go up from year to year to worship the King, the Lord of hosts, and to keep the Feast of Tabernacles.

And it shall be *that* whichever of the families of the earth do not come up to Jerusalem to worship the King, the Lord of hosts, on them there will be no rain.

If the family of Egypt will not come up and enter in, they *shall have* no *rain;* they shall receive the plague with which the Lord strikes the nations who do not come up to keep the Feast of Tabernacles.

This shall be the punishment of Egypt and the punishment of all the nations that do not come up to keep the Feast of Tabernacles.

In that day 'HOLINESS TO THE LORD' shall be *engraved* on the bells of the horses. The pots in the LORD's house shall be like the bowls before the altar.

Yes, every pot in Jerusalem and Judah shall be holiness to the LORD of hosts. Everyone who sacrifices shall come and take them and cook in them.

In that day there shall no longer be a Canaanite in the house of the LORD of hosts."

These Scriptures bring us exceedingly good news. The LORD shall be the ruling King all over the newly rejuvenated earth. And Jerusalem shall be safely inhabited. This is prophetic biblical proof that the LORD God of Israel will literally rule and reign during the millennial kingdom—after He cleans-up the wreckage from the Tribulation. What an awesome future awaits all believers. Amir Tsarfati, the Israeli believer and lecturer whom I have often mentioned has titled his website, *Behold Israel*. I could not say it better: Behold Israel! And get ready for the Lord to interject Himself into this cor-rupt degenerate world and bring glory to Himself and His beloved Eretz Israel (Hebrew for the Land of Israel).

When Adam sinned he brought the curse of sin not only to his descen-dants, but to the entire planet—the ground and the animal kingdom. During the millennial kingdom that curse will be removed not only from mankind and the ground, but also from the animal kingdom (Hosea 2:18; Isaiah 65:25; Ezekiel 34:27). The earth itself and all of mankind had to be redeemed by Jesus' sacrifice on the cross. This is symbolically portrayed in His wearing of the crown of thorns. God cursed the ground causing *thorns* and *thistles* to spring up (Genesis 3:17-19). The wearing of the crown of thorns means that Christ took the curse He had placed on the earth upon Himself, redeeming the planet. During the millennial kingdom when Jesus removes the curse, the deserts shall blossom and the entire planet will be turned into a utopian paradise like the Garden of Eden (Isaiah 35:1-7; Amos 9:13).

During the Millennium, Israel will be the nation from which divine blessings, favor, prosperity and peace will radiate into the other nations. All of God's divine blessings during the millennial kingdom with go forth from Israel. Peace and prosperity will reach all the nations—from Israel. God's favor will be so rich and plentiful upon Israel that Scripture shows us, as noted earlier, that "ten men from all the nations will grasp the garment of a Jew, saying, 'Let us go with you, for we have heard God is with you'" (Zechariah 8:23).

In Isaiah 60:3-5, 10-11 we learn that kings, queens, statesmen and presidents will come to Israel. When God glorifies Israel, the Jewish nation will become the center from which magnificent blessings and prosperity will flow into the nations. Isaiah prophesied that "the sons of those who afflicted you, and all those who despised you will bow themselves at the soles of your feet; and they will call you the city of the Lord, the Zion of the Holy One of Israel" (Isaiah 60:14-15). Nothing will be lacking in the millennial kingdom; nations and kings (leaders) will come to Israel to bask in its light. Fear, anti-Semitism, oppression of any kind and war—will never exist again. Instead, God's peace, righteousness, and holiness will fill the earth.

Scripture tells us when God makes Jerusalem a praise in the earth, the Jewish people will "take root, blossom and sprout." They will fill the entire world with fruit (Isaiah 27:6). Isaiah prophesied that God will make Jerusalem "a crown of beauty in the hand of the LORD, and a royal diadem in the hand of your God" (Isaiah 62:3). When God glorifies Israel the nation will be a place of unprecedented joy and gladness. Israel will no longer be a nation constantly threatened by war and extermination: "Whereas you have been forsaken and hated with no one passing through, I will make you an everlasting pride, a joy from generation to generation" (Isaiah 60:15).

When God made the covenant with Abraham, He said, "I will give you and your descendents after you, the land of your sojournings, all the land of Canaan, for an *everlasting possession*" (Genesis 17:8). The borders of the land of Israel are to extend from "the river of Egypt as far as the great river, the river Euphrates" (Genesis 15:18). The only time Israel came even close to possessing all of that territory was during the time of King David and King Solomon (1 Chronicles 18:3).

When Jesus the Messiah returns and sets up His millennial kingdom and makes Jerusalem His headquarters, Israel's land will then be greatly extended. Isaiah stated, "You have increased the nation, O LORD. You have increased the nation, You are glorified; You have extended all the borders of the land" (Isaiah 26:15). The Jewish people will possess the promised covenant land and the Lord will transform the Middle East into an righteous area of holiness, even restoring the damage done over many thousands of years caused by the hate-filled animosity between Isaac and Ishmael.

After the Second Coming of Christ there is a short interval of 75 days (Daniel 12:11-12) when the judgment of the nations takes place (Matthew 25:31-33). This is when the Lord gets the Millennium organized as described in Matthew 25:31-46. Then His one thousand year reign will begin. The Millennium is the *better world* that *is* coming soon.

> "And the LORD shall be King over all the earth.
> In that day it shall be—'The LORD *is* one,'
> And His name one." —Zechariah 14:9

After the Millennium, the Great White Throne Judgment, will take place and then the eternal kingdom will begin—as referenced in Revelation 21 and 22. But before these events take place, all born-again believers will be taken up to heaven in the Rapture, immediately followed by the seven-year Tribulation (Day of the Lord). Jesus said "until **the day** that Noah entered into the ark, and the flood came, and destroyed them all" (Luke 17:27), and "in **the day** that Lot went out from Sodom it rained fire and brimstone from heaven, and destroyed them all" (Luke 17:29). He then said, "After the same manner shall it be in the day that the Son of man is revealed" (Luke 17:30).

In Revelation 20:4-6, John wrote that Messiah Jesus is going to be literally, physically ruling upon the earth during the one-thousand-year Millennium. All true believers in their new, immortal glorified bodies will be assisting Him.

Some teachings confuse a number of events and characteristics of the Millennium with those of the eternal kingdom described in Revelation 21 and 22. At the end of the Millennium heaven and earth will pass away, as if they simply disappear or cease to exist. Then the Lord will make **all things anew**. John describes this as "fled away." But at the end of the Tribulation, the earth is burned up. These are noticeably two different events. In the book of Revelation, John described what he saw:

> "And I saw a great white throne and Him who sat upon it, from whose presence earth and heaven fled away, and no place was found for them" (Revelation 20:11).

By Peter's account (2 Peter 3:10), at the very end of the Tribulation the earth will be destroyed in a different way—by intense heat. It will be burned up. Peter goes on to say in 2 Peter 3:13, "according to His promise, we look for new heavens and a new earth." How did Peter get that idea? It could not have been from the reference to a "new heaven and new earth" declared in Revelation 21 and 22, because Revelation had not been written yet. His reference came from Isaiah 65:16-20. At the very end of the Tribulation the Lord creates "new heavens and a new earth" (Isaiah 65:17), which will last for the entire one-thousand-year millennial reign of Messiah Jesus.

This is what Peter wrote:

> "But the day of the Lord will come like a thief; in which the heavens shall pass away with a great noise, and the elements shall be dissolved with fervent heat, and the earth and the works that are therein

shall be burned up. Seeing that these things are thus all to be dissolved, what manner of persons ought ye to be in all holy living and godliness, looking for and earnestly desiring the coming of the day of God, by reason of which the heavens being on fire shall be dissolved, and the elements shall melt with fervent heat? But according to his promise, we look for new heavens and a new earth, wherein dwelleth righteousness" (2 Peter 3:10-13).

The prophet Isaiah wrote about God's promise of the new millennial heavens and millennial earth in Isaiah 65:16-19:

"So that he who blesseth himself in the earth shall bless himself in the God of truth; and he that sweareth in the earth shall swear by the God of truth; because the former troubles are forgotten, and because they are hid from mine eyes. For, behold, I create a new heavens and a new earth; and the former things shall not be remembered, nor come into mind. But be ye glad and rejoice for-ever in that which I create; for, behold, I create Jerusalem a rejoicing, and her people a joy. And I will rejoice in Jerusalem, and joy in my people; and there shall be heard in her no more the voice of weeping and the voice of crying."

In Isaiah 65:18 we see the word "forever."

"But ye be glad and rejoice forever in that which I create; for, behold, I create Jerusalem a rejoicing, and her people a joy."

A person looking at the previous verse not knowing or thinking about the Old Testament Hebrew meaning of the word "forever" would say this verse must be referring to eternity, an indefinite, endless span of time, easily mistaking what the prophet Isaiah wrote in Isaiah 65:18-19 to be referring to eternity because of the word "forever" used in verse 18. And without careful scrutiny, also assume those verses refer to the same "new heaven and a new earth" in Revelation 21. However, the Hebrew meaning of the word is often determined by its context, but in Greek the meaning of the word determines the *meaning* of its context. In the Old Testament, in the Hebrew language the word "forever" is Ad Olam. Below, we see that it takes three English words to relate or to express the meaning:

1. Continuity;
2. Perpetuity (an indefinite period of time);
3. Duration (which can refer to endlessness).

The Hebrew word "Ad Olam," does not mean "forever" as we know it in English. For example, in 1 Kings 2:11a, we learn, "And the days that David reigned over Israel for *were* forty years" indicating "continuity." In 1 Chronicles 28:4a we read, "Yet the LORD, the God of Israel, chose me from all the house of my father to be king over Israel forever." King David did not rule "forever" as we use the term in every day English. In actuality David ruled for forty years. "Forever" in these passages means that David ruled forty years without a break in his reign: "continuity." "Duration" is the length of time that he actually reigned, and "perpetuity" would be *until* David died.

The application, the use of the Old Testament word "forever," in Hebrew— Ad Olam, is demonstrated in Isaiah 32. The prophet Isaiah spoke of the seven-year Tribulation in verses 9-18 indicating once the Tribulation begins it will continue without stopping, without any break. However the word "forever" is used in the following passage in reference to the seven-year Tribulation, which is a definitive span of time: "Because the palace has been abandoned, the populated city forsaken. Hill and watch-tower have become caves **forever**, a delight for wild donkeys, a pasture for the flocks" (Isaiah 32:14).

Immediately in the next verse, verse 15, Isaiah referenced the one-thousand-year Millennium using the word "forever," even though one thousand years is a definite span of time, not forever (endless) as we know it in the English language.

"Until the Spirit is poured upon us from on high, and the wilderness becomes a fruitful field, and the fruitful field is counted as a forest, then justice will dwell in the wilderness, and righteousness remain in the fruitful field.

The work of righteousness will be peace, and the effect of righteousness, quietness and assurance **forever**. My people will dwell in a peaceful habitation, in secure dwellings, and in quiet resting places" (Isaiah 32:15-18).

Clearly the word "forever" does not always mean a lengthy or an endless duration of time. We also see by reading Isaiah 32 that the word "forever" in verse 14 is in reference to the seven-year Tribulation, and then following in verse (18) the word "forever" is referring to the subsequent one-thousand-year Millennium. Neither of these events last an endless duration of time, "forever" as we know it in the English language. Therefore, the Hebrew term "forever" has its meaning determined by the context which is evidenced in Isaiah 32.

Another verse from Isaiah 65 that is often misinterpreted is verse 19. Many Bible "teachers" take that verse and try to tie it to Revelation 21:4. In Isaiah 65:19 the Lord is precisely speaking specifically about those in Jerusalem, not the entire millennial population:

"And I will rejoice in Jerusalem, and joy in My people; there will be no more the voice of weeping and the voice of crying."

During the Millennium there will still be some problems with sin. Some tears will be shed and there will be death. In the eternal kingdom spoken of in Revelation 21, there will be no more death, and no one will have tears or pain. Isaiah 65:19 addresses the millennial reign of Christ, and Revelation 21:4 is in relation to the eternal kingdom. Once again, these are two distinctly different events with two different time references. However, many make the mistake of thinking that Isaiah 65:19 is speaking about the same event stated in Revelation 21:4. Isaiah 65 is in reference to the millennial kingdom, and Revelation 21 deals with the eternal kingdom.

> "And he shall wipe away every tear from their eyes; and death shall be no more; neither shall there be mourning, nor crying, nor pain, any more" (Revelation 21:4).

The key verse here to understanding the passages in 2 Peter (3:10-13) is found in Isaiah 65:16. The burned up, damaged earth is created anew; re-surfaced. Scripture indicates it will not be totally destroyed. Isaiah wrote: "the former troubles are forgotten, and because they are hidden from My [God's] sight!" "Forgotten and hidden" do not mean destroyed completely and do not mean vanished or "fled away" as will be the case *after* the Millennium when God makes "all things new" for the eternal kingdom (Revelation 21:5).

After the Tribulation God will hide (conceal) the damaged earth and the heavens, and change their condition with newly created acts, newly created material. We must be careful to take every passage according to related passages. Isaiah 16 must be taken into account before interpreting verses 17-19, or else the true meaning of the subsequent passages is lost. The prophet Jeremiah also wrote about the condition of the heavens and the earth at the end of the Tribulation supporting Isaiah 65:16-17:

> "I looked on the earth, and behold, *it was* formless and void; and to the heavens, and they had no light. I looked on the mountains, and behold, they were quaking, and all the hills moved to and fro.

> I looked, and behold there was no man, and the birds of the heavens had fled. I looked and behold, the fruitful land was a wilderness; and all its cities were pulled down before the LORD, before His fierce anger.

For thus says the LORD, the whole land shall be a desolation, yet **I will not execute a complete destruction**; for this the earth shall mourn, and the heavens above be dark, because I have spoken, I have purposed, and I have not changed My mind nor will I turn from it" (Jeremiah 4:23-28).

Notice, that the Lord said He "will not execute a complete destruction" of the earth and "the heavens will be dark." This again is not the same "fled away" condition of the heavens and the earth that takes place at the end of the Millennium when God will make "**all things new**." In the 1901 American Standard Version of the Bible, verse 27 reads: "For thus saith Jehovah, the whole land shall be a desolation; **yet will I not make a full end**."

In Zephaniah 1:18 we also read:

"Neither their silver nor their gold will be able to deliver them in the day of Jehovah's wrath; but the whole land shall be devoured by the fire of his jealousy: for he will make an end, yea, a terrible end, of all them that dwell in the land."

Once again, we see a reference to the land being "devoured" by fire, which does not translate as "fled away" as John described in Revelation 21. The verse states that the Lord will make "a terrible end" of those who "dwell in the **land**." He will end the existence of all those who have corrupted this world. The **land**, which is the surface of the earth will be "devoured," not the entire earth. The prophet Isaiah further wrote that "the inhabitants of the earth are burned" and that *few* men would be left at the end of the Tribulation:

"Therefore the curse has devoured the earth, and those who dwell therein are found guilty: therefore the inhabitants of the earth are burned, and few men left" (Isaiah 24:6).

Keeping these things in mind, earlier we discussed that Scripture tells us that it will take Israel seven years to clean-up (burn) the implements of war left from the battle of Ezekiel 38 and 39 (Ezekiel 39:9). Since the earth is burned up with fire at the very end of the Tribulation, it is not possible for the weapons left from that war to burn into the Millennium. They would never survive the fire of the earth. We also know that Antichrist will turn against Israel at the midpoint of the Tribulation causing the Jewish inhabitants to flee (Matthew 24:15-16; Revelation 12:6, 14).

Therefore, the Jews will not be able to burn those weapons during the second half of the Tribulation. They will not be there. Again, we can see another reason why those weapons will not be able to be burned into the Millennium. The point I am also making here is that Scripture gives us strong indication that the battle of Ezekiel 38 and 39 discussed in length earlier, may very well occur at least three and one half years *before* the Tribulation begins, in order to fulfill the prophecy of Ezekiel 39:9-11:

> "Then those who inhabit the cities of Israel will go out and make fires with the weapons and burn them, both shields and bucklers, and bows and arrows, war clubs and spears and for seven years they will make fires of them.
>
> And they will not take wood from the field or gather firewood from the forests, for they will take the spoil of those who despoiled them, and seize the plunder of those who plundered them, declares the LORD God."
>
> It will come to pass in that day *that* I will give Gog a burial place there in Israel, the valley of those who pass by east of the sea; and it will obstruct travelers, because there they will bury Gog and all his multitude. Therefore they will call *it* the Valley of Hamon Gog."

Now regarding more on the Millennium; we have already established that the Lord will make Israel the preeminent nation during the His 1,000-year millennial reign (Isaiah 62:1-4), and the curse will be lifted. Therefore Israel will not need to burn the "plundered" weapons during the Millennium.

> "And He said to me, "Son of man, *this is* the place of My throne and the place of the soles of My feet, where I will dwell in the midst of the children of Israel forever" (Ezekiel 43:7a).

Another distinction between the millennial reign of Christ and the eternal kingdom is the sin factor. In Isaiah 65:20, which references the millennial kingdom, we learn: "and the sinner being a hundred years old shall be accursed." In eternity no sin will abound. Once again we see the millennial kingdom is not the same as the eternal kingdom. But Messiah Jesus will physically, literally be on His throne, in the temple on top of Mt. Zion bringing sinners to salvation, and righteousness will reign. During the Millennium those who are in their natural bodies will still have a carnal sin nature, and sin will still exist. Each person will have to chose whether to accept Jesus or reject Him.

Scripture is filled with distinct differences between the millennial city and the eternal city (the New Jerusalem, the holy city which will descend from heaven). For example, both cities have flowing rivers. The total measurement of the millennial city where Messiah Jesus will dwell will be ten miles square (Ezekiel 48:30-35). The eternal city (New Jerusalem) will be foursquare, a cube with the height, length and breadth being equal, that is, measuring about 1500 miles long, wide and high (Revelation 21:15-17). The eternal city in Revelation 22:1 has no temple, but there is a river that comes from the throne of God. In the millennial city, there is a river that emanates from the millennial temple (Ezekiel 47:1-12). During the Millennium, the twelve tribes of Israel will have land partitioned for them with the sea as the western boundary (Ezekiel 47:15-20). In the eternal city, there is no sea (Revelation 21:1b)

The Millennium and then continuing on into the eternal kingdom are the future homes for all those who place their faith and trust in Messiah Jesus. We are given glimpses of these places throughout Scripture. In reference to the millennial kingdom:

Zechariah 6:13a; 8:3:

> "Yes it is He [the Lord Himself] who will build the temple of the LORD, and He who will bear the honor and sit and rule on His throne. Thus says the LORD, I will return to Zion and will dwell in the midst of Jerusalem. Then Jerusalem will be called the City of Truth, and the mountain of the LORD of hosts will be called the Holy Mountain."

Zechariah 14:10-11:

> "All the land shall be turned into a plain from Geba to Rimmon south of Jerusalem. *Jerusalem* shall be raised up and inhabited in her place from Benjamin's Gate to the place of the First Gate and the Corner Gate, and *from* the Tower of Hananel to the king's winepresses. *The people* shall dwell in it; and no longer shall there be utter destruction, but Jerusalem shall be safely inhabited."

Messiah Jesus will return at the end of the Tribulation, reestablish the earth and the heavens, set-up His millennial kingdom, and sit upon the throne of His glory, the throne of David. His righteous order will be implemented. Israel will be leveled at the beginning of the Millennium (Isaiah 40:4), and Mount Zion will be a high mountain (Isaiah 2:2). The millennial city of Jerusalem will be at the top of Mount Zion. Messiah Jesus will continue to cleanse from sin those who receive Him during the Millennium.

Those who survive the Tribulation, the burning fire of the earth, and do who not take the mark of the beast, and get saved at the end of the Tribulation will enter the Millennium in their natural bodies. Some will not get the gospel in its fullness until they actually see the Lord as Matthew told us: "But he who endures to the end shall be saved" (Matthew 24:13).

In the following passage, Isaiah gives a description of the fire and horrors of the Tribulation and the small number who will survive:

"The sinners of Zion are afraid; trembling hath seized the godless ones; who among us can dwell with the devouring fire? Who among us can dwell with everlasting burnings? He that walketh righteously, and speaketh uprightly; he that despiseth the gain of oppressions, that shaketh his hands from taking a bribe, that stoppeth his ears from hearing of blood and shutteth his eyes from looking upon evil; he shall dwell on high; his place of defense shall be the munitions of rocks; his bread shall be given *him*; his waters will be sure" (Isaiah 33:14-16).

Out of the ravages and ruins of the Tribulation emerge those who survive. The Lord will separate the saved and the unsaved. The unsaved will go into "everlasting punishment" and the saved into the Millennium, graciously blessed with eternal life with the Lord (Matthew 25:31-46). During the Millennium Messiah Jesus will literally rule the earth and its inhabitants.

All believers in their new glorified bodies will be given responsibilities according to their faithful service and devotion to the Lord, as recorded in: Luke 19:11-27; Revelation 20:2-6; Revelation 2:26-28; 3:12, 22; 1 Corinthians 6:2-3.

The overall curse put upon mankind since the fall of Adam and Eve will be removed. An ecologically, biologically superior environment will prevail, including fresh produce filled with complete nutrition and organic perfection, clean healthy air, pure water and every good thing imaginable, and much, much more will be part of the millennial blessings.

It will not be quite the perfection of the eternal order following the Millennium, but the millennial years will be richly blessed and righteousness will prevail because of the rule of Jesus Christ. Social justice (transformation) will prevail without the fear of anyone being robbed or hurt in anyway. A strong and constant sense of the presence of the Lord, and His majesty will cover the entire earth (Isaiah 11:9).

"For *there will be* peace for the seed: the vine will yield its fruit, the land will yield its produce, and the heavens will give their dew; and I will cause the remnant of this people to inherit all *things*" (Zechariah 8:12).

"Then justice will dwell in the wilderness, and righteousness remain in the fruitful field. The work of righteousness will be peace, and the effect of righteousness, quietness and assurance forever. My people will dwell in a peaceful habitation, in secure dwellings, and in quiet resting places" (Isaiah 32:16-19).

"And many peoples will say, 'Come, let us go up to the mountain of the LORD, to the House of the God of Jacob; that He may teach us concerning His ways, and that we may walk in His paths.'

For the law will go forth from Zion, and the word of the LORD from Jerusalem. And He will judge between the nations, and will render decisions for many peoples; and they will hammer their swords into plowshares, and their spears into pruning hooks. Nation will not lift up sword against nation, and never again will they learn war" (Isaiah 2:3-4).

Every person born during the Millennium will be considered a child until he or she is one hundred years old. If by the age of one hundred that person has not yet accepted the Lord Jesus as Savior, he will be rejected by Him and suffer the same fate as all those who has rejected Him in this life (Isaiah 65:20). The children born during the Millennium are the offspring of those who physically survive the Tribulation, those who realize the truth of Messiah Jesus and receive Him as their Savior during that horrible seven-year ordeal. Those individuals will be allowed to enter the Millennium. They and their descendents will populate the millennial earth. During the Millennium predators will no longer hunt down their victims. Animals of all types will live together in perfect harmony.

Isaiah 11:6-9

"The wolf also shall dwell with the lamb, the leopard shall lie down together with the young goat. The calf and the young lion and the fatling together; and a little child will lead them. The cow and the bear shall graze; their young ones shall lie down together; and the lion shall eat straw like the ox.

The nursing child shall play by the cobra's hole, and the weaned child shall put his hand in the viper's den. They shall not hurt nor destroy in all My holy mountain, for the earth shall be full of the knowledge of the LORD as the waters cover the sea."

The vast majority of people will be saved up until the last years of the Millennium. At the end of the thousand years, Scripture tells us that Satan, who was bound in the bottomless pit, is then loosed for a short time at the end of the Tribulation (Revelation 20:7). He deceives the unsaved and some of the final millennial generation into one last great rebellion against the Lord. He will gather together for battle nations from all over the world to attack the camp of the saints and the beloved city (Jerusalem). It is unfathomable to think that while Jesus is ruling and reigning on earth that there will be those who will reject Him. Even with Christ ruling the earth, wicked mankind is deceived. The camp of the saints and the beloved city will be surrounded, but fire from heaven will quickly devour the rebellious attackers (Revelation 20:9).

Gog-Magog in Ezekiel 38 and 39: Not the Same As the Gog Magog Reference in Revelation 20

The names "Gog" and "Magog" used in Revelation 20:8 and are not to be confused with the Gog-Magog war of Ezekiel 38 and 39 which takes place prior to the Tribulation. The term Gog-Magog is used as a reference point in Revelation 20 as a way to indicate once again God's great supernatural defeat against His enemies. God will destroy the rebellious millennial attackers in terms of the original Gog-Magog war in Ezekiel 38 and 39, and Satan will finally meet his eternal demise. (This is when he is cast into the lake of fire to join the Antichrist and the False Prophet for all eternity.) This great defeat is likened to the battle of Ezekiel 38 and 39 (Gog-Magog war) because once again by God's intense supernatural intervention these enemies are destroyed, just as the Russian led invaders were defeated by His extraordinary spectacular intervention.

The Great White Throne Judgment

"For it is written, as I live, saith the Lord, to me every knee shall bow, and every tongue shall confess to God. So then each one of us shall give account of himself to God" (Romans 14:11-12).

After the one-thousand-year millennial kingdom, the Great White Throne judgment will take place when everyone who died in their sins is judged those who never accepted Messiah Jesus as Savior and Lord. It will be too late for salvation in Christ for those who did not want to receive the truth while they were still alive.

"And I saw a great white throne, and him that sat upon it, from whose face the earth and heaven fled away; and there was no place found for them. And I saw the dead, the great and the small, standing before the throne; and books were opened: and another book was opened, which is *the* Book of Life: and the dead were judged out of the things which were in the books, according to their works" (Revelation 20:11-12).

"And the sea gave up the dead that were in it; and death and Hades gave up the dead who were in them: and they were judged every man according to their works. And death and Hades were cast into the lake of fire. This is the second death, *even* the lake of fire. And if any was not found written in the Book of Life, he was cast into the lake of fire" (Revelation 20:13-15).

As we have just read we learn those who die in their sins without accepting Christ's free gift of salvation will actually be judged from a written record found in books and "according to their works" (Revelation 20:12). It will be too late for those who die in their sins to repent and receive Christ. All born-again believers will not be part of this judgment because of Christ's sin pardon.

The New Jerusalem
(The Eternal Kingdom)

"There shall be no night there: They need no lamp nor light of the sun, for the Lord God gives them light. And they shall reign forever and ever" (Revelation 22:5).

After the Great White Throne Judgment, the eternal kingdom will begin. No sin or corruption will exist ever again. Everything passes away (Revelation 21:1), and the entire universe is recreated:

Revelation 21:1, 3-6

"And I saw a new heaven and a new earth: for the first heaven and the first earth are passed away; and the sea is no more. And I saw the holy city, New Jerusalem, coming down out of heaven from God, made ready as a bride adorned for her husband. And I heard a great voice out of the throne saying, Behold, the tabernacle of God is with men, and he shall dwell with them, and they shall be his peoples, and God himself shall be with them, and be their God.

And He shall wipe away every tear from their eyes; and death shall be no more; neither shall there be mourning, nor crying, nor pain, any more: the first things are passed away. And He that sitteth on the throne said, 'Behold, I make all things new. And He saith, write: for these words are faithful and true.' And He said to me, 'They are come to pass. I am the Alpha and the Omega, the beginning and the end. I will give unto him that is athirst of the fountain of the water of life freely.'"

In Revelation 21:2 the apostle John reveals that the New Jerusalem comes down from heaven to take its place on the new earth. This city is holy and nothing unclean shall ever enter in (Revelation 21:8, 27). This is the city that Abraham looked for in faith (Hebrews 11:10). It is the place where God will dwell with His people eternally (Revelation 21:3). The Father and the Lamb dwell in the New Jerusalem (Revelation 21:22).

Angels are at the gates (Revelation 21:12). This magnificent city will be filled with God's redeemed children and will have all tears wiped away (Revelation 21:4). The New Jerusalem will be a place of unimagined blessings. The curse of the old earth will be gone (Revelation 22:3). In the city are the tree of life "for the healing of the nations" and the river of life (Revelation 21:1-2). The New Jerusalem is the ultimate fulfillment of all God's promises. The New Jerusalem is God's goodness made fully manifest.

The Lord has a special place throughout eternity for the Jewish people. Scripture teaches that upon walking into the holy city of the New Jerusalem, individuals will have to walk under and over the name of a Jew:

"And he carried me away in the Spirit to a mountain great and high, and showed me the holy city Jerusalem, coming down out of heaven from God, having the glory of God: her light was like unto a stone most precious, as it were jasper stone, clear as crystal; having a wall great and high; having twelve gates, and at the gates twelve angels; and names written theron, which are *the names* of the twelve tribes of the children of Israel: three gates on the east, three gates on the north, three gates on the south, and three gates on the west" (Revelation 21:10-12).

The eternal city—the New Jerusalem will have streets of pure gold, clear like glass and phenomenal jewel laden gates and walls. The city will not have or need the light of the sun or the moon because the Lamb—the Lord Jesus, will be the light (Revelation 21:23). Revelation 21:24, shows that new nations will be created for the eternal kingdom that will glorify the Lord. Their inhabitants will not be sinful beings.

The term *New Jerusalem* occurs twice in the New Testamenthttp://en.wikipedia.org/wiki/New_Testament, in Revelation 3:12 and 21:2. A large portion of the final two chapters of Revelation deal with John of Patmos' vision of the New Jerusalem. He described the New Jerusalem as "the Bride, the wife of the Lamb" where the river of the water of life flows (Revelation 22:1).

After John witnessed the new heaven and a new earth "that no longer has any sea" an angel took him "in the Spirit" to a vantage point on "a great and high mountain" to observe the New Jerusalem's descent. The enormous city comes out of heaven down to the New Earth. John's detailed description of the New Jerusalem retains many features of the Garden of Eden and the paradise garden, such as rivers, a square shape, a wall, and the tree of life.

The apostle John described the New Jerusalem as "pure gold, like clear glass" and its "brilliance [is] like a very costly stone, as a stone of crystal-clear jasper." The streets of the city is also made of "pure gold, like transparent glass." The base of the city is laid out in a square and surrounded by a wall made of jasper. It says in Revelation 21:16 that the height, length, and width are of equal dimensions - as were the Holy of Holies in the Tabernacle and First Temple, and they measure 12,000 furlongshttp://en.wikipedia.org/wiki/Furlongs which is approximately 1500.3 miles).

John wrote that the wall is 144 cubits, which is assumed to be the width since the length is mentioned previously; 144 cubits are about equal to 65 meters, or 72 yards. It is important to note that 12 is the square root of 144. The number 12 was very important to early Jews and Christians, representing the 12 tribes of Israel and 12 Apostles of Jesus Christ. The four sides of the city represented the four cardinal directions (North, South, East, and West.)

In this way, New Jerusalem was thought of as an inclusive place, with gates accepting all of the 12 tribes of Israel from all corners of the earth. There is no temple building mentioned in the New Jerusalem. God and the Lamb are the city's temple, since they are worshiped everywhere. Revelation 22 goes on to describe a river of the water of life that flows down the middle of the great street of the city from the Throne of God. The tree of life grows in the middle of this street and on either side, or in the middle of the street and on either side of the river. The tree bears twelve fruits, or kinds of fruits, and yields its fruit every month. According to John, "The leaves of the tree were for the healing of the nations." This inclusion of the tree of life in the New Jerusalem brings to mind the Garden of Eden. The fruit the tree bears may be the fruit of life.

In the New Jerusalem the "servants of God" shall see His face and have His name on their foreheads. Night will no longer fall, and the inhabitants of the city will "need no lamp nor light of the sun, for the Lord God gives them light." John ends his account of the New Jerusalem by stressing its eternal nature: "And they shall reign forever and ever."

There are twelve gates in the New Jerusalem in the wall oriented to the compass with three each on the east, north, south, and west sides. There is an angel at each gate, or gatehouse. These gates are each made of a single pearl, giving them the name of the "pearly gates." The names of the twelve tribes of the children of Israel are written on these gates. Here, the apostle John (John the Revelator) does his best to try to describe what he is shown:

Revelation 21:10-21

"And he [an angel] carried me away in the Spirit to a great and high mountain, and showed me the great city, the holy Jerusalem, descending out of heaven from God, having the glory of God. Her light *was* like a most precious stone, like a jasper stone, clear as crystal.

Also she had a great and high wall with twelve gates, and twelve angels at the gates, and names written on them, which are *the names* of the twelve tribes of the children of Israel: three gates on the east, three gates on the north, three gates on the south, and three gates on the west.

Now the wall of the city had twelve foundations, and on them were the names of the twelve apostles of the Lamb. And he who talked with me had a gold reed to measure the city, its gates, and its wall.

The city is laid out as a square; its length is as great as its breadth. And he measured the city with the reed: twelve thousand furlongs. Its length, breadth, and height are equal.

Then he measured its wall: one hundred *and* forty-four cubits, *according* to the measure of a man, that is, of an angel.

The construction of its wall was *of* jasper; and the city *was* pure gold, like clear glass.

The foundations of the wall of the city *were* adorned with all kinds of precious stones: the first foundation *was* jasper, the second sapphire, the third chalcedony, the fourth emerald, the fifth sardonyx, the sixth sardius, the seventh chrysolite, the eighth beryl, the ninth topaz, the tenth chrysoprase, the eleventh jacinth, and the twelfth amethyst.

The twelve gates *were* twelve pearls: each individual gate was of one pearl. And the street of the city *was* pure gold, like transparent glass."

Revelation 21:22-27

"And I saw no temple in it, for the Lord God, the Almighty, and the Lamb are its temple. And the city has no need of the sun or the moon to shine upon it, for the glory of God has illumed it, and its lamp *is* the Lamb.

And the nations shall walk by its light, and the kings of the earth shall bring their glory into it. And in the daytime (for there shall be no night there) its gates shall never be closed.

And they shall bring the glory and the honor of the nations to it; and nothing unclean and no one who practices abomination and lying, shall ever come to it, but only those whose names are written in the Lamb's Book of Life."

Perfection and exquisite beauty will be found everywhere in the Lord's eternal kingdom. Any dream or imagined thought we might have of a perfect world will seem utterly insignificant when compared to the magnificent glory of the Lord and His eternal provisions.

John describes more as we read on into Revelation 22:1-3:

"And he showed me a river of the water of life, clear as crystal, coming from the throne of God and the Lamb, in the middle of its street. And on either side of the river was the tree of life, bearing twelve *kinds of* fruit, yielding its fruit every month; and the leaves of the tree were for the healing of the nations."

And in conclusion, John leaves us with some final messages:

> "And he said unto me, these words are faithful and true: and the Lord, the God of the spirits of the prophets, sent his angel to show unto his servants the things which must shortly come to pass" (Revelation 22:6).

> "I, Jesus have sent My angel to testify to you these things for the churches, I am the Root and the Offspring of David, the Bright and Morning Star" (Revelation 22:16).

Synopsis

At the end of the seven-year Tribulation Christ will return at the Second Coming. He will fight and win the battle of Armageddon destroying Israel's enemies for good (Revelation 19:11-21). Scripture reveals when the Lord appears at the final battle, the world leader (the beast)—who is the Antichrist—his demons, and his cohort, the False Prophet—the world religious leader, along with all the nations will try to physically fight off the Lord, the God of the universe!

He will immediately put a stop to the burgeoning siege. "Now out of His mouth goes a sharp sword, that with it He should strike the nations" (Revelation 19:15a). He will defeat Antichrist and all the blood thirsty, power-hungry hordes. He will rescue Israel and the entire planet from complete annihilation; then and only then will there be peace on earth.

> "And then the lawless one will be revealed, whom the Lord will consume with the breath of His mouth and destroy with the brightness of His coming" (2 Thessalonians 2:8).

At the Second Coming, Satan, the devil will be cast into the bottomless pit and he will be bound for a thousand years (for the duration of the Millennium, Revelation 20:1-3). Christ will then resurface and rejuvenate the damaged earth where the Redeemed will reign and rule with Him for one thousand years (Revelation 20:6).

After the millennial reign of Christ, Satan will be released from his prison, the bottomless pit (Revelation 20:7), and will go out to deceive the nations of the earth to gather them together to battle. (One last time, which shows us that even when Christ is ruling and reigning on earth there will be those who will rebelliously reject Him.) But God will very quickly destroy them (devour them) by sending fire down from heaven.

The devil, who deceived the rebellious millennial nations will be cast into the lake of fire where the beast (Antichrist) and the False Prophet already reside at that point. Scripture tells us they will be tormented day and night forever and ever (Revelation 20:10). The Great White Throne judgment will commence for all those who have rejected Christ. They will be cast into to the lake of fire for eternity. There will be no escape.

Beginning in Revelation 21:9, John recorded his vision of the New Jerusalem where all true Christians will spend eternity (the eternal heaven), which takes place after the fulfillment of the previous prophecies of 1 Thessalonians 4:15-17, Revelation 19:17-21; 20:1-10; 11-15. In Revelation 21:1-8 the new heaven and the new earth are created, and God the Holy Father will bring heaven to earth in the New Jerusalem where all believers will dwell with God for all eternity.

Part Three

Psalm 83, the Ezekiel Prophecies, Islam and the Palestinians

What Will God Do When Israel Is Attacked?

Ezekiel 38:18-22

"This is what will happen in that day: When Gog attacks the land of Israel, my hot anger will be aroused, declares the Sovereign LORD.

In my zeal and fiery wrath I declare that at that time there shall be a great earthquake in the land of Israel.

The fish of the sea, the birds of the air, the beasts of the field, every creature that moves along the ground, and all the people on the face of the earth will tremble at my presence.

The mountains will be overturned, the cliffs will crumble and every wall will fall to the ground.

I will summon a sword against Gog on all my mountains, declares the Sovereign LORD. Every man's sword will be against his brother.

I will execute judgment upon him with plague and bloodshed; I will pour down torrents of rain, hailstones and burning sulfur on him and on his troops and on the many nations with him."

✡✡✡✡✡

Chapter Fourteen

When God Deals With Islamic World Dominance

The Battle of Ezekiel 38 and 39 (The Gog-Magog War)

An important prophesied war is on the near horizon. Of course, Israel will be the target. In the Bible, the battle of Ezekiel 38 and 39 (Gog-Magog war) is given one of the most *detailed* descriptions of any prophesied future war. It is going to happen soon and the entire world will be affected by it. This war will bring about great devastation, but during and at the end of the Tribulation there will be utter destruction.

Russia will lead a coalition of mostly Islamic nations against Israel. This war will most likely occur before the Tribulation. It could begin as early as three and one-half years *before* the Tribulation. It will take seven years to clean-up the damage, and seven-months to bury the dead (Ezekiel 39:9, 12). Halfway through the Tribulation the Jews will have fled Israel and will no longer be able to bury the dead. In order to fulfill the prophecy of Ezekiel 39:9, 12) this battle will most likely happen at least three and one half years before the Tribulation begins.

An important point to keep in mind is this: In Genesis 15 the Lord tells us that the cup of iniquity of the Amorites was not yet fulfilled but when it was, God dealt with them. It is the same for Islam. God is still allowing them to wreak havoc (for now). But He has some intense plans for blasphemous Islam. The day is soon coming when God will no longer tolerate Islam's fanaticism, and He will pour out His judgment upon the followers of Allah—at the battle of Ezekiel 38 and 39, when hordes of Islamic troops will march against Israel, led by Russia.

The great miracle in the Old Testament is the Exodus but it will pale in comparison to what happens as a result of the Gog-Magog war (Jeremiah 16:14). When God saves Israel, and Allah is nowhere to be found during this epic battle, surviving devotees of Islam throughout the world will no longer be so willing to fight for Allah's sake. It will shake their radical psychopathic fanatical mantras to the core.

The Lord Himself will supernaturally intervene in this war and the majority of the caustic aggressors will be obliterated. These warriors will turn against each other. God will shake the earth with tremendous power and the invaders will wish they had never even had a bad thought about Israel. Scripture tells us this war will spread (Ezekiel 39:6-7):

> "And **I** [God] **will send fire** on Magog [Russia] and those who live in security in the coastlands. Then they shall know that I *am* the LORD. So I will make My holy name known in the midst of My people Israel, and I will not *let them* profane My holy name anymore. **Then the nations shall know that I** *am* **the LORD, the Holy One in Israel.**"

No one but God Himself will help rescue Israel when she is attacked. Without God's intervention, Israel will have no chance to survive this invasion. God *will* preserve His chosen nation. He will not be doing this for Israel's sake, but for His own sake, to make a powerful statement that He is in control, that He is Almighty God and can no longer be ignored. God will actually bring these nations against Israel who has rejected Him—for His glory.

It is a major wake-up call to the entire world, and primarily for Israel, that the God of Abraham, Isaac, and Jacob lives forever and is King. Everyone should realize that without Him, they are condemned. Followers of Allah will be left scrambling trying to figure out how they can possibly continue claiming that Allah is God. Allah will be nowhere to be found when these heavily numbered, primarily Muslim forces march against Israel.

The "coastlands" referred to in the previous Scripture are also destined to experience the wrath of God for participating in the offense against Israel, indicating that the Muslim population will significantly decrease. The coastlands are maritime regions in the Middle East with heavy Muslim populations. These are homelands to those who will assist Russia against Israel with their fleets and troops. The "coastlands" extend to what would actually encompass global Islam, reaching all around the world, including Indonesia.

One of the results of this war points to be the removal of a significant portion of Islamic domination. It is also very likely that Mecca, the al-Aqsa Mosque and the Dome of the Rock will to be severely damaged or destroyed by the tremendous earthquake cited in Ezekiel 38:19. It will not be possible for a one-world government, a one-world church and a one-world economic system to take hold unless the influence of Islam is tremendously reduced or removed. If not, we will have an Ayatollah type one-world government, economic system and world church.

It is apparent to me that it would be nearly impossible for the prophesied one-world government, a world economic system, and a world church to be established while Islam is standing in the wings of worldwide dominance.

From studying Scripture, it is my point of view that an ecumenical, apostate one-world church is much more likely than an Islamic religious take-over. Although at the moment, it certainly does appear that Islam, because of its enormous population, wealth, and outrageous aggressiveness—could rule the entire world.

In keeping with the premise that the death cult of Islam has to be subdued before they will participate in a one-world church, an insightful statement was made in an article published on a number of blogs on January 19, 2015. The article is titled, "World Apostate Religion: A New False Islam":

> For Satan's master plan of a one-world apostate religion to become a reality, a complete purge of fundamental Islam and fundamental Christianity must take place. The main goal of this mission is to facilitate the signing of the false peace treaty between Israel and the rest of the world (Daniel 9:27). —Dan Payne

Scripture reveals there is a point when God will no longer sit quietly on the sidelines and allow His holy name to be desecrated—as described at the beginning of this chapter when referencing Ezekiel 39 and 39.

Furthermore, let's look at the two legs on the image of Daniel in chapter two. The two legs represent the two divisions of the Roman Empire, which were divided into those two legs in 400 AD upon the death of Theodosius; the western capital in Rome and the eastern capital in Constantinople. The western leg with its capital in Rome was broken

> If fundamental Islamic world dominance is not removed, then the Antichrist will be Muslim, the world church will be Muslim and the one world government will be a caliphate. But that is not what Scripture describes.

and not restored until 800 AD when the pope crowned Charlemagne king of the holy Roman Empire. That empire then was overrun by the Huns and that type of government went up into Germany under Kaiser Wilhelm.

The eastern leg stayed intact until 1453 and then it was overrun by the Muslims. So we have a choice then, of either taking the Antichrist, the world government and one-world religion out of that eastern division/Islam, or the western division. I choose the western division because of typology. Antiochus Epiphanes, a Greco-Syrian is given in Daniel as a type of Antichrist, and he was a European. The Antichrist will be from the western or European side and therefore not a Muslim.

Moreover, the Antichrist is seen riding, from the west to the east as he makes his capital in ancient Babylon. And the one who rides that beast today is the Vatican or the Western side of the old Roman Empire (the Roman Catholic Church from the western leg). And the world church is not Islamic because it comes from Nimrod with the worship of little baby Tammuz in Semiramis' arms (Nimrod's Babylon/the Roman Catholic Church).

The Israelites worshipped the Babylonian god Tammuz whom the Canaanites addressed as Adonai (my lord). The summer festival of Tammuz celebrated the death of nature and revival in the spring. Tammuz was associated with the Babylonian deity Ishtar (Astarte), (who was later called Adonis by the Greeks). He was also associated with Aphrodite, the Greek goddess, who was worshipped by the Romans.

Notice God's attitude toward those who engaged in the worship of Tammuz: "Therefore will I also deal in wrath; mine eye shall not spare, neither will I have pity; and though they cry in mine ears with a loud voice, yet will I not hear them (Ezekiel 8:18). God said He would not hear anyone who carried out the idolatrous worship of Tammuz.

The church in Rome was once a very fine church. The apostle Paul wrote one of his greatest letters to that church; in it he mentioned their faithfulness. Then corruption set in and the Roman Empire outlawed Christianity, and the true Christian church was forced to go underground. The authentic and faithful Christian church was heavily persecuted by the Roman government. When Constantine came into power as the Roman ruler, he was converted to Christianity (at the beginning of the fourth century), which slowed down the persecution of true Christians. Christianity until that time was outlawed, but Constantine declared Christ Jesus to be the only true God, and Christianity became the official religion. He declared that the heathen temples had to be destroyed. By that time, temples had been built all over the known world to the "Queen of Heaven," the virgin-mother goddess pictured with the little boy Tammuz in her arms.

Then Christianity became the only legal religion. Constantine said Tammuz and the Queen of Heaven could not be worshipped. When this declaration was made, the priests in the temple of Ishtar-Innini committed abominable acts by chiseling the names of Ishtar and Tammuz off these idols (pictures and statues) and chiseled the names of Jesus and Mary onto these same statues. This distortion of the true Jesus and Mary continues to be propagated all over the world today, mostly by the Roman Catholic Church. The roots of the end-time world church will be a survival from the background of Babylonian mysticism: Mystery Babylon, an ecumenical compilation of apostate religions.

God's Mighty Presence

Israel is the "apple of God's eye." Jerusalem *is* the capital of Israel. Although it is rumored that the push to internationalize Jerusalem *is* clandestinely and swiftly gaining ground, encouraged and led by Pope Francis, former U.S. President Barack Obama, Tony Blair, Rick Warren and others who want to force their one-world agenda on Israel and on the all nations. Of course this slap in God's face is all being done under the guise of "peace" and bringing humanity together. Some of the participants are biblically illiterate useful idiots and apostate sell-outs while others are demonically driven globalists (Satan's representatives).

Aaron Klein reporting for *World Net Daily* (WND): "White House map 'erases' Jerusalem, biblical territories" and that an Obama Administration video highlighting the president's plans for his Mideast trip in 2013 depicted Jerusalem, the Golan and the West Bank – also known as Judea and Samaria – as non-Israeli territory.

The Obama White House actually released a map of Israel and JERUSALEM was not a part of Israel, nor its capital. Bible prophecy is steadily moving forward gaining speed as these significant events are part of the last days scenario before Christ's Second Coming.

The Dome of the Rock is located in Jerusalem on the Temple Mount, along with the al-Aqsa Mosque. These Muslim representations are an insult and disgrace to the God of Abraham, Isaac and Jacob. The irreverent Islamic inscriptions on the Dome of the Rock of course deny that Jesus is the Son of God, and attempt to reduce His identity to a mere messenger and a servant to the god they refer to as, Allah. Another one of their inscriptions denies the blessed Trinity.

Notice the Islamic inscription (translated) etched at the Dome of the Rock on the Inner Face of the Octagonal Arcade, blaspheming Almighty God:

"The unity of God and prophecy of Muhammad are true. The Sonship of Jesus and the Trinity are false." —*Biblical Archaeology Review*, July 2006

In the Bible we learn the truth about the Trinity: 1 John 5:7, "and these three are one." Also, in the same verse, Jesus the Messiah is addressed as the "Word." When the apostle John described the Second Coming of Christ in Revelation 19:13, another reference again is made to Jesus as: "The Word of God." Jesus *is* the Word of God.

> "For there are three that bear witness in heaven; the Father, the Word [Jesus], and the Holy Spirit; and these three are one" (1 John 5:7).

> "And He is clothed with a robe dipped in blood, and His name [Jesus] is called The Word of God" (Revelation 19:13).

Scripture is clear that the God of Abraham, Isaac and Jacob will cause the world to know He is in control. The battle of Ezekiel 38 and 39 will also open the door for the continuing fulfillment of key prophetic Scriptures that will lead to the Tribulation and the final battle of Armageddon.

> "I will set My glory among the nations; all the nations shall see My judgment which I have executed, and My hand which I have laid on them. So the house of Israel shall know that I am the LORD their God from that day forward" (Ezekiel 39:21-22).

> "Therefore behold, the days are coming, says the LORD, that it shall no more be said, 'The LORD lives who brought up the children of Israel from the land of Egypt, but the LORD lives who brought up the children of Israel from the land of the north and from all the lands where He had driven them.' For I will bring them back into their land which I gave to their fathers" (Jeremiah 16:14-15).

God and God alone should get all the credit for saving Israel from the determined invaders. His indisputable presence *will* be revealed. It will be obvious to the entire world that He subverted the advancing armies and that the

Israelis could not have survived the assaults without His supernatural hand reaching out to save them. The nations will know that God interjected His awesome might into that precise time in history.

No longer will He be identified as the God who saved the Old Testament Jews from Egyptian enslavement. But because of the Lord's overwhelming miracles during the battle of Ezekiel 38 and 39 will override even those of the Exodus, He will be known as the God "who brought up the children of Israel from the land of the north and from all the lands" (Jeremiah, 16:14-15; 23:8).

"You will come up against My people Israel like a cloud, to cover the land. It will be in the latter days that I will bring you against My land, so that the nations may know Me, when I am hallowed in you, O Gog, before their eyes" (Ezekiel 38:16).

"And I will bring him to judgment with pestilence and bloodshed; I will rain down on him, on his troops, and on the many peoples who *are* with him, flooding rain, great hailstones, fire, and brimstone.

Thus I will magnify Myself and sanctify Myself, and I will be known in the eyes of many nations. Then they shall know that I *am* the LORD" (Ezekiel 38:22-23).

Notice the verse says the Lord will intervene and execute His judgment on the invading troops with "pestilence and bloodshed" and by using extremely intense weather patterns and natural elements: Flooding rain, great hailstones, fire, and brimstone. Because of this intervention by God Almighty, no one will be able to deny that it was He, who saved Israel from the descending armies.

Footnote:
Dr. Arnold Fruchtenbaum also supports the view that the Gog-Magog invasion will take place prior to the Tribulation, *Footsteps of the Messiah*, page 121 (f. The Pre-Tribulation View).

Does Scripture Reveal Middle East Nuclear Wars Before the Tribulation?

Some students and commentators of Bible prophecy suggest that there will be a nuclear exchange during the Gog-Magog battle and even attempt to derive a nuclear holocaust from the passages in Ezekiel 39:1-16; pure speculation which cannot be substantiated. We dare not allow any commentators to take away from God the great victory of this battle.

Scripture tells us in no uncertain terms that it is He who will be magnified. Scripture tells us that it is distinctly God who will obliterate the enemy. Radioactive material from the nuclear weapons would affect not only the invading troops, but the Israelis as well. Even if nuclear weapons could be used successfully *only* against the enemy, then those who would deliver them would receive the credit, and not the Lord.

If we stop and think things through carefully, it would become obvious that when anyone takes *any* particular Scripture and tries to turn it into a massive Middle East nuclear war before the Tribulation, he or she is doing so based on nothing but one's own imagination or hypotheses determined outside of the Scriptures. If a nuclear war takes place *before* the Tribulation the radioactive contamination would linger and create so much damage (fallout) that too many areas would be affected and even rendered uninhabitable. The nations prophesied to invade Israel in the Gog-Magog incursion would be greatly affected and could not fulfill Ezekiel's prophecy.

Some commentators mistakenly believe a nuclear incursion will happen *during* the battle of Ezekiel 38 and 39 (Gog-Magog), and some go so far out on a nonsensical limb saying a major nuclear event will happen in the Middle East even *before* the battle of Ezekiel 38 and 39, and *before* the Tribulation. But does that make sense? ISIS is the most vicious dangerous Hitlerian group on the planet today—frightening. It is true, ISIS is sending out messages that they are planning a nuclear holocaust somewhere. Only God can know where these demonically possessed maniacs would do such a thing.

We must trust what Scripture teaches. No one, including ISIS can stand in the way of the fulfillment of God's prophetic Word. Prophecy must be fulfilled as it is written, and the Gog-Magog war is a major prophecy that must take place. It will change the entire dynamics of the Middle East—when God destroys Russia from the North and Islam, "those who dwell securely in the isles [coastlands] Ezekiel 39:6). When God sends fire upon the invaders, the destruction will be far-reaching. If you look on a map you can see that there is a densely populated Islamic ring completely surrounding the globe. At that point I think God will have had about enough of Allah's terror loving followers who desecrate and blaspheme his holy Name.

It makes more sense that if ISIS does fire off nuclear weapons it would be possibly in the U.S., Europe or another part of the world. They are too hell-bent on taking over the world to destroy themselves, and the key players of ISIS in the Middle East are not about to become martyrs and lose all the impact they have already made. If ISIS detonates a nuclear bomb in the Middle East the fallout would affect them too much or even destroy them.

Tactical Nukes Are Tactical Insanity

Recent threats asserting Russia will use a tactical weapon against Turkey is very unlikely for the reasons discussed in this chapter, and also because Scripture tells us that at some point Turkey will join Russia in attacking Israel in the Gog-Magog war; they will become allies against Israel along with many other nations. Some strongly proclaim Israel will destroy Damascus (Isaiah 17:1) before the Tribulation by using tactical nuclear weaponry. In other words, those who teach this type of tactical nuclear attack (nuclear neophytes) are saying Israel would be *the one* who will push the nuclear button. God forbid! Only if Israel has no other option to survive, will she use the Samson option.

> Jerusalem is only a short 134 miles from the city of Damascus. There is no guarantee nuclear fallout would not affect Israel or other areas located far beyond Damascus.

A tactical nuclear war is tactical insanity. It could unleash a nuclear holocaust in the Middle East and Israel would be viewed *as the nation* that did the unthinkable; that Israel pushed the nuclear button first! Once again, I thank God Israel is smarter than those who come up with such blatantly flawed and dangerous ideas.

Let's talk about tactical nuclear weapons. There is no precise definition of the "tactical" category, neither considering range nor yield of the nuclear weapon. The yield of tactical nuclear weapons is generally lower than that of strategic nuclear weapons, but larger ones are still very powerful, and some variable-yield warheads serve in both roles. Modern tactical nuclear warheads have yields up to the tens of kilotons, or potentially hundreds, several times that of the weapons used in the atomic bombing of Hiroshima and Nagasaki.

Use of tactical nuclear weapons against similarly-armed opponents carries a significant danger of quickly escalating the conflict *beyond* anticipated boundaries, from the tactical to the strategic. Small, low-yield tactical nuclear warheads can dangerously encourage forward-basing and pre-emptive nuclear warfare, as nuclear weapons with destructive yields of 10 tons of TNT (e.g., the W54 warhead design) are less reluctantly used at times of crisis than warheads with yields of 100 kilotons.

Consider the huge opposition Israel received from the world press during the Gaza war during the of summer 2014. The pundits were falsely reporting that Israel used "disproportionate" responses when defending herself against the Hamas terrorists. Nothing could be further from the truth If Israel used tactical nuclear weapons against any nation unless she had no other choice—she would be accused of being a blood-thirsty predator and ruthlessly expansionist. Anti-Semitism would dangerously rise to an all-time high.

Jeremiah 49

Twisting the meaning of Scripture to make a case for a nuclear event cannot be claimed as a new discovery revealed by the leading of the Holy Spirit. For example, the verses from Jeremiah 49:34-39 are used by some with over active imaginations to fabricate outlandish suppositions claiming a

The battle between Israel and Iran is not a battle of brawn which must result in nuclear devastation prior to the Tribulation; it is a battle of moxie and brain power. Israel is clearly superior in those areas.

massive nuclear war will *precede* the Tribulation and the Gog-Magog war. We have claims for yet another over-looked "prophecy!" Biblical scholars of old must have been a dumb old bunch to have missed that one. No doubt, Iran's nuclear program is a major threat. If Israel does have to attack Iran for self-preservation it would make much more sense that she would use bunker buster bombs but even *much more likely*, subterfuge, such as a Stuxnet type operation.

Some commentators try to make case for Elam to be identified as to-day's northern Iran and say that the entire Jeremiah 49:34-39 passage relates to today's Iranians. Most probably because one of Iran's nuclear facilities is located in the area once called Elam. Iran's nuclear reactor in Bushehr lies on the eastern shore of the Persian Gulf in the area of ancient Elam. But what does history say and what do the Scriptures say? Only one verse cited in Jeremiah 49, verse 39, could possibly be a future prophecy, "the latter days." Substituting Iran for Elam in Jeremiah 49:34-39 is tenuous speculation at best. As recorded in the *Inscription of Darius the Great at Naqsh-e-Rostam*, Persians and Elamites are not the same two names for the same people. After Persia conquered Elam the original inhabitants of Elam, according to Jeremiah's prophecy, were scattered to the "four winds" and absent from historical writings for over 2,500 years.

> *Inscription of Darius the Great at Naqsh-e-Rostam*: 2f (8-15): I am Darius the Great King, King of Kings, King of countries contain-ing all kinds of men, King in this great earth far and wide, son of Hystaspes, an Achaemenian, a Persian, son of a Persian, an Aryan, having Aryan lineage.

Prophecy mania seems to override common sense far too often. We should not try to create new prophecies by disregarding or misinterpreting historical events that have already been fulfilled. In verses 36-37, the Elamites were defeated and scattered among the nations as Jeremiah prophesied.

Daniel 8:2 identifies Shushan as being in the province of Elam, indicating it was already a part of the Persian Empire at the time. From this brief history it appears that all but possibly the last verse of Jeremiah's prophecy was fulfilled in the Assyrian and Persian conquests. Because of the Bushehr nuclear reactor, some commentators propose these verses to be an imminent nuclear event. Substituting present day Iran for the Elam prophecy in Jeremiah 49:34-39 cannot be declared as fact and is a wildcard supposition.

Elam was defeated and ceased to exist. Nowhere in Scripture is there any mention of that nation since. But some want to take these verses into today creating an entirely new meaning for God's Scriptures.

Once again, I say, be on guard when you hear commentators present a case for "new hidden meanings" of Scripture claiming that they were led by the Holy Spirit to try to justify and authenticate their hypothesis. That is what all cult leaders do. Jeremiah 49:38 is a thought-provoking verse and makes perfect sense when keeping verses 34-38 as fulfilled prophecies:

> "'I will set My throne in Elam, and will destroy from there the king and the princes,' says the LORD" (Jeremiah 49:38).

It is one thing to observe signs leading up to the Tribulation but molding Scripture to try to fit passages into current news headlines is not sound biblical exegesis. For example, in Zechariah 14:12 the prophet Zechariah forewarned of an event that sounds like it could be a nuclear event during the Tribulation years. But is it? We cannot be sure. The Lord Jesus is certainly capable of delivering devastating results upon peoples and nations with His breath alone. We cannot be sure how these passages will be fulfilled, but we know the people described in these passages will suffer extremely harrowing afflictions. We must not underestimate God's wrath administered directly by Him when the time comes. Notice some key words in the Scripture: "The LORD will smite." Not a "Nuke will smite."

We must take the time to study the Word of God on our own without the influences of popular rhetoric. We must study our Bibles and think carefully before accepting sensationalized "revelations" or newly discovered meanings as truth. A frequent media presence does not translate into biblical truth.

"And this shall be the plague wherewith the LORD will smite all the people that have fought against Jerusalem; their flesh shall consume away while they stand upon their feet, and their eyes shall consume away in their holes, and their tongue shall consume away in their mouth" (Zechariah 14:12).

Separating Truth from Fiction

We must rely on God and His Holy Scriptures and not the musings of men when determining the authenticity of claims made by those who even use the name of the Holy Spirit to try to support their newfound hypotheses. Christian journalist, Bill Wilson made some interesting points in one of his columns. He essentially said that teachers, preachers, and others who self-proclaim their church offices will not stand in your place before the Lord on Judgment Day. It will be you, and you alone. Quoting the *opinions* of some Bible commentators ("experts") in your defense will not be an option. It will be about your relationship with the LORD and your biblical faithfulness. With the exponential increase in events that can be related to prophecy and the desire of the masses to chase after the newest opinion on Scripture, keep in mind what apostle Paul wrote in Philippians 2:12: "Work out your own salvation with fear and trembling."

Escalating Middle East Strife

Before the Tribulation begins, there will be great devastation in Egypt as shown in the following passages. Considering what we currently hear and read in the daily news headlines, this prophecy (possibly tied in with the battle of Ezekiel 38 and 39) is nearing its time of fulfillment. Egypt is plagued with problems, protests and extreme political upheaval.

> "The word of Jehovah came again unto me, saying, Son of man, prophesy, and say, thus saith the Lord Jehovah: Wail ye, Alas for the day! **For the day is near, even the day of Jehovah is near**; it shall be a day of clouds, a time of nations, and a sword shall come upon Egypt, and anguish shall be in Ethiopia, when the slain shall fall in Egypt; and they shall take away her multitude, and her foundations shall be broken down, Ethiopia, and Put [Libya], and Lud and all the mingled people, and Cub, and the children of the land that is in league, shall fall with them by the sword. Thus saith Jehovah: They also that uphold Egypt shall fall; and the pride of her power shall come down" (Ezekiel 30:1-8).

We know that a number of intense Middle East wars have already taken place in our lifetime. To some degree, war is constantly going on around Israel.

The Timing of Isaiah 17

The destruction of Damascus is foretold in the book of Isaiah and Jeremiah. It is possible that Isaiah's prophecy could be fulfilled at the time of the Gog-Magog war, and actually be destroyed when God unleashes His mighty power as detailed in Ezekiel 38 and 39. Although it does seem like the destruction of Damascus could happen at any time, especially since Syria is engulfed in internal fighting. ISIS is on the move and the entire country is in serious trouble.

Some people think Damascus will be destroyed by a nuclear attack—which is possible during the Tribulation. But a major nuclear attack prior to the Tribulation would cause a great deal of radioactive fallout and cause too much damage in the entire area. Jerusalem is only 134 miles from Damascus. Even a tactical nuclear weapon could easily cause serious problems. Verse 1 states, "Damascus will be a ruinous heap." How this cataclysmic prophecy will be fulfilled is unknown. We cannot say for sure how this will happen or what God's plans are for the fulfillment of this prophecy.

ISIS and Muslim rebels have surrounded the ancient city of Damascus, and the entire country is in serious crisis barely holding on. (Since March 2015, Assad has steadily lost territory in the northwest, south, and central Syria to an array of groups including the Islamic State, the Al Qaeda-linked Nusra Front, and rebels who profess a more moderate vision for Syria.)

Damascus is known to be a major hub for terrorists. Syria's involvement in the ongoing aggression to eliminate Israel will bring catastrophe to that nation. Additionally, current news reports point to extreme political and civil devastation continues to grow within Syria. As far back as 2007, Israeli intelligence discovered that in the desolate Syrian Desert, a facility was in the process of manufacturing nuclear weapons. It was being aided by North Korea. Of course, Israel did what she had to do and sent a few jets overhead to take care of the problem. The Israelis were able to unscramble the radar so the visit was a complete surprise to the Syrians and everyone else involved, including Iran. It is often said that Syria is just Iran's proxy. Russia also, is a great ally and defender of Syria arming the anti-Israel neighbor with missiles and other weapons.

In February of 2011, Western Intelligence agencies discovered another nuclear plant in Syria, in a Damascus suburb. In addition, a German newspaper, the *Süddeutsche Zeitung (SZ)*, reported that it received photos of the site, but will not publish them because inferences can be made as to when they were taken, and thus to who leaked them. In addition, Washington's Institute for Science and International Security (ISIS) published photos on February 23, 2011 of one of three more sites that are believed to be connected to the Al-Kibar facility destroyed in 2007, as reported in *Arutz Sheva, Israel National News* on February 24, 2011.

Never Underestimate Israel When Dealing with Iran

An incident involving some destruction of Iran's nuclear facilities is very possible in the near future, even before the Gog-Magog incursion. As difficult and challenging as it may seem strategically, Israel may find a way to take out the areas that house Iran's nuclear weapons programs such as the Fordo site located deep in the mountains of Iran, near the city of Qom or the area where the Bushehr nuclear plant that resides in Iran (Elam).

I have heard reports given by Amir Tsarfati, that Israel has been going into Syria, Iran's strategic ally, taking out some of their caches of weapons. It has been reported for years that Israeli war planes have targeted military sites including Dimas, 25 kilometers (15.5 miles) northwest of Damascus and located on the Damascus-Beirut road at the foothills of the Anti-Lebanon Mountains. They also targeted Damascus International Airport, 25 kilometers east of the capital. Perhaps the Israeli's have some other clever clandestine strategies in mind to put an end to Iran's potential nuclear holocaust. I would not underestimate the Israeli's when it comes to protecting their homeland and their very existence.

Intense uprisings in the Middle East countries are quickly escalating. Iran is gaining more control of the entire region while its leaders are continuing to loudly threaten Israel and all Jews with comments like: "The Zionist regime will be wiped soon." Radicals are gaining strength, while traditional moderate Arab leaderships are weakening. Egypt has fallen apart and is in total chaos—a dangerous situation that most likely leading to an Iranian type extremist hard-line government—leading to its complete demise. Lebanon, Israel's neighbor to the north has essentially been taken over by Iran gaining much closer proximity to Israel. Iraq is on the verge of being taken over by pro-Iran Shiite factions. It is very possible that Israel will defend herself against Iranian nuclear threats by using subterfuge or some kind of creative preemptive defense measures even *before* the battle of Ezekiel 38 and 39 takes place. We certainly are living in very perilous times in these last days.

It is impossible to keep up with the fast-moving events involving the Middle East. No doubt some of these situations are being methodically manipulated by those who have diabolical, hidden agendas and want to bring about "change." Change, that is not in the best interest of freedom-loving people. But God cannot be outwitted. He has the final say regardless of what governments, terrorists or pompous elitists try to do.

The Importance of Psalm 83

Psalm 83 is an imprecatory prayer important in relation to end-times events and recognized as such by scholars throughout history. Psalm 83 has been especially near and dear to my heart for a long time because it is a plea to save Israel—a prayer asking God to tear down her enemies. Psalm 83 is an imprecatory prayer to bring down judgment against the enemies of Israel, to protect Israel and bring about the fulfillment of the battle of Ezekiel 38 and 39.

The straightforward correlation between Psalm 83 and the coming battle of Ezekiel 38 and 39 is evident upon studying the Scriptures. The passages that tie together the imprecatory prayer of Psalm 83 to the verses describing the battle of Ezekiel 38 and 39 are good examples of the Lord's intricate message system woven throughout the Bible.

Some of the nations mentioned in Psalm 83 are not specifically mentioned with those in Ezekiel 38 and 39, but this is not unusual. Throughout Scripture there are instances when only *some* nations are listed when making reference to a war. This can be found when studying the final war of Armageddon. For example, Joel 3:1-18 is relating to when God judges the nations during the battle of Armageddon. Some of the primary nations that will participate in that war are not mentioned in those passages. Psalm 83 is not a war, it is an imprecatory prayer calling down judgment upon Israel's enemies and the answer to that prayer is when God destroys Israel's enemies in the battle of Ezekiel 38 and 39.

At some point in the near future, Russia will gather its Muslim allies and go after Israel. Israel does not need to have expanded borders to place her in a position of living more securely or have more wealth so her enemies can take a greater "spoil" in order for this war to occur. What the Jew-hating coalition will be going after are the *people* of Israel (Ezekiel 38:16). However, after the Lord returns at the end of the Tribulation, Israel *will* have much greater boundaries because she will be a major part of the coming millennial kingdom (Isaiah 62:1-4; Daniel 7:27).

Another matter to keep in mind when reading and interpreting the imprecatory prayer of Psalm 83 is to keep the psalm in its *proper* context. An imprecatory prayer is a prayer for God to bring down judgment against one's enemies. By attempting to turn the verses in the imprecatory psalm into something entirely different is disregarding the *core premise* of the psalm—turning the inspired infallible Word of God from an imprecatory prayer into something it is not (taking away from the Word and adding to it). Psalm 83 is Israel's prayer to God for *protection* from an impending war, not a war in and of itself.

This basic fact cannot be ignored and it is as basic as English Comprehension 101. The psalmist is pleading with the Lord for help from those who are conspiring (ganging up) against Israel, preparing to destroy

Israel, "O my God, make them like the whirling dust, like chaff before the wind, like fire that burns the forest and like a flame that sets the mountains on fire" (Psalm 83:13). And we see the answer to that prayer in the battle of Ezekiel 38 and 39, and ultimately again at the final battle at Armageddon.

This imprecatory prayer should be given the full-respect it deserves and not be disparagingly dismissed as *just a prayer*. Scripture teaches that prayer is a powerful spiritual tool. The Word of God is more powerful than a two-edged sword (Hebrews 4:12). Almighty God asks us to *communicate* with Him. Psalm 83 is an intense *imprecatory prayer* for God Himself to bring about the demise of Israel's enemies in an impossible situation—when surrounded by enemies on every front. Psalm 83 is an imprecatory *prayer* for protection from Israel's enemies, for God Himself to intervene. All proposed hypothetical statements and equations become null and void regardless of how many suppositions are presented in an attempt to turn this imprecatory psalm into a war—**when it is explicitly a prayer for the enemies of Israel to be destroyed by God Himself**.

The premise of Psalm 83 is an imprecation so no matter how you spin it, Psalm 83 is not a war. It is an imprecatory prayer for God to come to the aid of Israel and save her from impending doom, which some well-meaning critics sadly fail to understand and without careful contextual reading and thinking, assumptively disregard.

Philosophical conjecture cannot transcend the correct laws of scholarly biblical hermeneutics (the Golden Rule of Interpretation). If one needs an analogy, imagine driving a car but then suddenly deciding the car is an airplane. No matter how many ways one tries to turn the car into a airplane, the car will not fly and will always be a car and not an airplane.

Psalm 83 is the imprecatory prayer that points to the events of Ezekiel 38-39:16—for the destruction of the invaders to take place; for the Lord to intervene because of the insurmountable situation Israel faces as she is surrounded by enemies. The participants in the battle of Ezekiel 38 and 39 are many of the same nations emphatically expressing their hatred against Israel today.

The Lord implores us to "rightly divide the word of truth" (2 Timothy 2:15) which includes detecting seriously questionable teaching regardless of who is delivering the message and not blindly accepting a postulation simply because it is popular, regardless of how many books or articles are written supporting a widely accepted hypothetical premise.

Two wars are actually prophesied in Ezekiel. The first is the battle of Ezekiel 38 and 39 which takes place before the Tribulation begins (Ezekiel 38-39:16) and then in verse 39:17 by the law of double reference (Revelation 19:20-21) Ezekiel shifts to describing the final battle of Armageddon. It will become very evident after the coming battle of Ezekiel 38 and 39 when the Russian-led army falls "upon the mountains of Israel" (Ezekiel 39:2), that Psalm 83 is indeed an imprecatory prayer for God to bring down judgment against Israel's enemies and *not* a separate newly invented event: a Psalm 83 "war."

Some Bible commentators use the passages from Ezekiel 38:8 from the New International Version (NIV) of the Bible to try to support a hypothetical "Psalm 83 war." The New International Version's translation for Ezekiel 38:8 is a simplified, modernized translation. Some of the verses translated in the NIV are acceptable, but I rarely use that translation. In this case the translation of Ezekiel 38:8 is problematic and can be misleading. In that verse, Ezekiel describes how the Jews are regathered into their land in the latter days (since 1948). In Psalm 83, the psalmist describes Israel's cries to the Lord for help as countless enemies conspire against her—which ultimately results in the coming battle of Ezekiel 38 and 39 and then later, at the final battle of Armageddon.

A very important point: Yet some commentators try to use the New International Version of the Bible to make a case for a large regional war apart from and prior to the battle of Ezekiel 38 and 39. The NIV translation of Ezekiel 38:8 states, "In future years you will invade a land that has recovered from war" instead of "brought back from the sword" or "restored from the sword." The more accurate translations are as follows:

King James Version:

> "After many days thou shalt be visited: **in the latter years thou shalt come into the land that is brought back from the sword**, and is gathered out of many people, against the mountains of Israel, which have been always waste: but it is brought forth out of the nations, and they shall dwell safely all of them."

New American Standard Bible:

> "After many days you will be summoned; **in the latter years you will come into the land that is restored from the sword**, whose inhabitants have been gathered from many nations to the mountains of Israel which had been a continual waste; but its people were brought out from the nations, and they are living securely, all of them."

The 1901 American Standard Version of the Bible, translated out of the original tongues:

> "After many days thou shalt be visited: **in the latter years thou shalt come into the land that is brought back from the sword**, that is gathered out of many peoples, upon the mountains of Israel, which has been a continual waste; but it is brought forth out of the peoples, and they shall dwell securely, all of them."

Israel has *already* been ("brought back from the sword"). Additionally, another obvious and important fact—simple fourth grade math and common sense show—that population growth disproves the possibility of a large regional Israeli conquest (war) against the Arab nations. Israel has about 7.8 million people including women and children (75.3% are Jews). The total population of the Arab countries encircling Israel is over 280 million! The Jewish population is dramatically outnumbered and could not *control* those nations.

The overall tone emanating from the Israeli people is that they simply want to live in peace in their God-given land. They are not ravenous wolves scheming to lead a Genghis Khan type, conquering-binge to expand their borders. To think that there must be some sort of large regional war prior to the Gog-Magog event to expand Israel's borders and supposedly create a stronger sense of peace and security is pure conjecture and makes no sense.

However, I would say that we could very well be closer to the eruption of the battle of Ezekiel 38 and 39 than some might think. Since the Six-Day War of 1967, Israel has regained her "mountains" (Judea and Samaria, also known as the West Bank) leaving no further land acquisitions necessary for the prophetic battle of Ezekiel 38 and 39 to be fulfilled.

I am including a published article I wrote in 2009 because it contains some additional, detailed points relevant to what you have just read. You will recognize some information I have already touched on. You will also see how the prophetic Word of God is very precise, and how Scripture is intricately interwoven. When you read the article you will see how some aspects of the prophetic *imprecatory prayer* have *already* been fulfilled; we have the formation of the Arab League and the constant verbal threats to destroy Israel. Israel's enemies conspiring together *are being fulfilled* today—leading up to the fulfillment of the battle of Ezekiel 38 and 39 and also the final war at Armageddon (both are God's battles to win). But first, please read through the entire imprecatory prayer of Psalm 83, imploring God to confound Israel's enemies.

Psalm 83

God Is Implored to Confound His Enemies
A Song—a Psalm of Asaph

"O God, do not remain quiet; do not be silent and, O God, do not be still. For behold, Your enemies make an uproar, and those who hate You have exalted themselves. They make shrewd plans against Your people, and conspire together against Your treasured ones.

They have said, 'Come, and let us wipe them out as a nation, that the name of Israel be remembered no more. For they have conspired together with one mind; against You they make a covenant.

The tents of Edom and the Ishmaelites, Moab and the Hagrites; Gebal and Ammon and Amalek, Philistia with the inhabitants of Tyre; Assyria also has joined with them; they have become a help to the children of Lot. Selah.

Deal with them as with Midian, As with Sisera *and* Jabin at the torrent of Kishon, who were destroyed at En-dor, who became as dung for the ground. Make their nobles like Oreb and Zeeb and all their princes like Zebah and Zalmunna, who said, Let us possess for ourselves the pastures of God.

O my God, make them like the whirling dust, like chaff before the wind. Like fire that burns the forest and like a flame that sets the mountains on fire. So pursue them with Your tempest and terrify them with Your storm. Fill their faces with dishonor, that they may seek Your name, O LORD.

Let them be ashamed and dismayed forever, and let them be humiliated and perish, that they may know that You alone, whose name is the LORD, are the Most High over all the earth.'"

Psalm 83 and the Battle of Ezekiel 38 and 39

"But know this first of all, that no prophecy of Scripture is *a matter* of one's own interpretation" (2 Peter 1:20).

Psalm 83 is an imprecatory prayer, an imprecatory psalm—it seems very obvious to me. Some popular hypotheses regarding the meaning of Psalm 83 are circulating claiming the psalm is an unfulfilled prophecy, describing a major separate war that will take place before the battle of Ezekiel 38 and 39. Accompanying that particular interpretation is a belief that the Israeli Defense Forces (IDF) will successfully defeat Arab enemies, therefore getting all the credit for defeating the Arab nations that surround Israel.

It is true that in Ezekiel 37:10, an "exceedingly great army" is mentioned, but the verse does not say that a great army will be responsible for the destruction of Israel's enemies. The Arab states mentioned in Psalm 83 are the modern Arab states who are members of the Arab League. Their agenda is to reduce Israel to nothing. In reference to Psalm 83, verse 5, the word "confederacy," berith, in Hebrew can be translated into the word "league" from Hebrew to English. Also, according to the *New Strong's Exhaustive Concordance of the Bible*, the Hebrew word berith is translated "covenant" in the English Bible. The concordance also states the word berith appears 227 times in the Old Testament, and means "confederacy, league or covenant." Psalm 83 is a progressive prophecy and a prophecy that will be fulfilled when the battle of Ezekiel 38 and 39 takes place; and completely fulfilled when Jesus the Messiah returns at Armageddon and personally destroys the nations that come against Him and Israel. The battle of Ezekiel 38 and 39 is the next major biblically prophesied war in the Middle East.

By carefully comparing Psalm 83 with Ezekiel 38 and 39, Psalm 83 is an imprecatory prayer *for Israel*, and certainly relates to current events. Both Christians and Jews have been praying for God's intervention—to stop Israel's enemies from the continuous barrage of threats and assaults from those who also happen to be members of the Arab League.

This fervent appeal can be witnessed today. Every time Israel is threatened, prayers go before the throne of God on Israel's behalf. An imprecatory prayer is pleading with God to bring down judgment upon a dangerous enemy. To imprecate means to call God's judgment down upon a people. The following verses sound like what the enemies of Israel are saying today, including those who are members of the Arab League:

"They have taken crafty counsel against Your people, and consulted together against Your sheltered ones. They have said, Come and let us cut them off from being a nation, that the name of Israel may be remembered no more. For they have consulted together with one consent, they form a confederacy against You" (Psalm 83:3-5).

Psalm 83 speaks about a "confederacy" and some of the nations listed in that psalm are part of the Arab League, whose members are frequently calling for Israel's demise. The political leader of Iran, Mahamoud Ahmadinejad, is well known for spewing his hatred for Israel and calling for its total destruction.

Psalm 83 is a *prayer* to circumvent the conspiracy against Israel. I would further say that Psalm 83 describes and correlates what will happen during of the battle of Ezekiel 38 and 39, when the nations of the world will know God and God alone will save Israel from the Russian-led invasion. To imply that the Israeli Defense Forces will liberate Israel from Islamic threats cannot be confirmed or supported by any Scripture found in Psalm 83, or Ezekiel 38 and 39. If the IDF is given the credit for winning that war, then God will not be known for saving Israel.

Where does it say in Psalm 83 that man-made military forces will save Israel? Where does it say in Ezekiel 38 and 39 that an army will save Israel? Only God will save Israel during the judgments *described* in Psalm 83 and Ezekiel 38 and 39. There will be no mistaking His supernatural intervention when He rescues Israel. This event will be a monumental, defining moment in history. The entire world will see God in a new light, in a different way because of His undeniable, supernatural miraculous intervention. Weapons of war will of course exist but God will somehow make them inoperable or skew them away from the Israelis sending the enemy into frenzied confusion. The invaders will turn against each other (Ezekiel 38:21).

Psalm 83 is not a war, but an imprecatory prayer calling for Ezekiel 38 and 39 to be fulfilled., as well as the final battle at Armageddon. The circumstances of the battle of Ezekiel 38 and 39 will surpass even the historic miracles of the Exodus. The Exodus will take a back seat in comparison to what God will do at the battle of Ezekiel 38 and 39. God's new historic identity will be, "The Lord who brought up the children of Israel from the land of the north," based on Jeremiah 16:14:

> "Therefore behold, the days are coming," says the LORD, "that it shall no more be said, 'The LORD lives who brought up the children of Israel from the land of Egypt,' but, 'The LORD lives who brought up the children of Israel from the land of the north and from all the lands where He had driven them.' For I will bring them back into their land which I gave to their fathers'" (Jeremiah 16:14-15).

Approximately one million Jews have already immigrated to Israel from Russia (the north). The Islamic population will be tremendously decreased because of that war. Russia will be destroyed:

> "And I will send fire on Magog [Russia] **and on those who live in security in the coastlands**. Then they shall know that I *am* the LORD" (Ezekiel 39:6).

According to Ezekiel 38:13, Saudi Arabia (ancient Sheba and Dedan) will not participate in the Ezekiel 38 and 39 invasion of Israel. Even now the Saudi's are leading the central banking group into pressuring Israel into a land-for-peace deal, and most probably will keep pushing for that deal, rather than joining the future Russian-led Islamic forces when Israel is attacked.

The Saudi's appear to be leaning in the direction of those who form the Mediterranean Union, pressuring Israel to make land-for-peace concessions. The prospect of a nuclear-armed Iran is of great concern to the leaders of Saudi Arabia. Saudi Arabia has never been very cozy with Iran or Russia, although the Saudis did recently purchase some weapons from Russia. In my opinion, the attempt to subvert Israel will continue to be done in a more "civilized" way, by pressuring them to make land-for-peace agreements.

Amir Tsarfati, a popular sought-after Israeli speaker and a very knowledgeable Bible teacher. He lives in Jerusalem and travels throughout the world. During a number of speaking engagements at various churches, he has stated that he believes the battle of Ezekiel 38 and 39 is coming soon. He also stated that he disagrees with the argument by some prophecy teachers regarding Ezekiel 38, teaching that Israel has to be living peacefully before that battle can take place. He believes all the physical conditions for the battle of Ezekiel 38 and 39 are already in place today.

Amir is a strong Hebrew Christian who carefully follows prophetically related events. Living in Jerusalem gives him an advantage when discussing and discerning the meaning of the relevant prophetic passage, Ezekiel 38:11. "Dwelling safely" does not mean the Israelis dwell in peace; they are surrounded by enemies. The Israelis are a *peaceful people* and the conditions that exist are considered *secure* despite the ongoing hatred Israel is subjected to. Some walls to protect the Israeli population from Palestinian missile attacks do exist. However, there are no extensive walls surrounding *all* of Israel. Each village or community in Israel does not have "bars" or "gates." The common situation for cities or villages during the time of Ezekiel was one where rock walls and gates were very prevalent. In my opinion, these are the types of walls, fences and barriers Ezekiel was referring to in verse 11. These rock barriers no longer exist. In general, the people of modern Israel move about freely and have secure borders, and the current "secure" border circumstances qualify for the fulfillment of Ezekiel 38 and 39.

Another point to consider is the fact that Israel as a whole is quite rebellious against God and is not engaged in a genuine spiritual relationship with the Lord.

Generally speaking, Israel is secular to the core, and government leaders have a history of settling for false peace agreements by giving away chunks of land, land that was given to them by God Himself. Therefore, we could say that Israel has no spiritual walls, fences or barriers. Israel at the moment is lacking spiritual walls or hedges of protection from the Lord. In general, they are living carelessly, without a genuine relationship with the Lord, and this is a contributing reason why they are opening themselves up to being pounced on by many enemies.

In order for the battle of Ezekiel 38 and 39 to occur, there will be plenty of enemies who will eagerly march against Israel. To imply that the Israelis will ever be living peacefully before the Gog-Magog battle simply cannot be true. Clearly those who participate in the Gog-Magog war will be great enemies of Israel. I don't believe for a minute that Israel will let down her guard until the son of perdition—the Antichrist—deceives them into thinking he is their savior. This argument is also in keeping with the conditions necessary for the Pre-Tribulation Rapture of the Church.

"You will say, I will go up against a land of unwalled villages; I will go to a peaceful people, who dwell safely, all of them dwelling without walls, and having neither bars nor gates" (Ezekiel 38:11).

The passage says the people of Israel are a "peaceful people"—not that they are living in "peace." The verses from Psalm 83:17 and 18 correlate with what will transpire when the Lord Almighty supernaturally intervenes during the battle of Ezekiel 38 and 39. As a student of Bible prophecy, it is my opinion that a portion of Psalm 83 is speaking of a partially fulfilled prophecy—the Arab League, and their despotic verbal rumblings. I have already addressed the prayer aspect of the psalm. Next, it also speaks of events that will take place as described in Ezekiel 38 and 39 and, when the Lord confounds the enemies of Israel and shows His indignation, halting the onslaught against His nation, Israel. If you carefully read through all the passages in Ezekiel 38 and 39, and Psalm 83, their unmistakable interdependence and similarities cannot be denied.

"O my God, make them like a whirling dust like the chaff before the wind! As the fire burns the woods and as the flame sets the mountains on fire, so pursue them with Your tempest, and frighten them with Your storm.

Fill their faces with shame, that they may seek Your name O LORD. Let them be confounded and dismayed forever; Yes, let them be put to shame and perish. That they may know that You, whose name alone is the LORD, And the most high over all the earth" (Psalm 83: 13-18).

The previous verses are very similar to the verses of Ezekiel 39 and 2, 3, and verse 7. They appear to be speaking about the same event as you can see here:

"And I will turn you around and lead you on, bringing you up from the mountains far north, and bring you against the mountains of Israel. Then I will knock the bow out of your left hand and cause the arrows to fall out of your right hand.

So I will make My holy name known in the midst of My people Israel, and I will not *let them* profane my holy name anymore. Then the nations shall know I am the LORD, the Holy One of Israel" (Ezekiel 39:2, 3, 7).

In both Psalm 83 and Ezekiel 39, the Lord is describing what will happen when the Russian-led, predominately Muslim army descend from the north to decimate Israel. It is the Lord Himself who will give the Russians the idea to invade Israel (Ezekiel 38:4, 11) so He can be glorified, and reveal Himself to the nations. He will not be defending Israel for Israel's sake, but for His Name's sake, so the nations of the world will see He is in control—Almighty God that He is. No dangling carrot is necessary for this invasion to take place. Israel does not have to be bigger or richer for this battle to ensue. It is God's battle to fight, and He intends to make Himself known.

God Almighty has a plan to personally foil the wicked plans of the enemy. He will use the enemy's extreme hatred for Israel to bring His redemptive plans for His chosen nation and the world to fruition. Both Psalm 83 and Ezekiel 39 make it perfectly clear that it is the Lord Himself who will intervene in such a mighty way that no one will be able to deny His awesome power. The nations will realize God defended Israel, and destroyed the enemy. The Israeli Defense Forces—as great as they are—will not be responsible for Israel's victory. To say that they will save Israel from the enemy is an assault upon the promises of God and His Holy Word. Psalm 83 and Ezekiel 39 both state God and God alone will be the One to deliver Israel during this prophesied battle. Psalm 83 and Ezekiel 38 each reveal that God's awesome presence will be undeniable.

The book of Exodus is filled with examples of how God took complete control over the elements when He unleashed plagues and judgments upon Egypt. God has a history of exerting absolute control utilizing matter: "nature" to bring about his judgments and miraculous interventions. When He executed judgment on Sodom and Gomorrah, He rained down fire and brimstone (Genesis 19:24). It makes no sense that the same living God would suddenly rely on human technology to bring about His signature, sovereign judgment. God is the same yesterday, today and forever. When God tells us in Scripture that He is going to showcase His enormous overpowering miracles displaying His authenticity to the world, we should believe Him. He does not need to employ understudies using man-made super weapons to assist Him with the job.

"For I *am* the LORD, I do not change" (Malachi 3:6a).

Brimstone is one of the natural elements that God will use against the invading troops during this prophesied attack against Israel. Notice how Almighty God used natural materials throughout history when delivering judgment onto a people or situation:

Brimstone - gaphrith, related to gopher wood, and so expressing any inflammable substance, as sulphur, which burns with a suffocating smell. It is a mineral found in quantities on the shores of the Dead Sea. It was the instrument used in destroying Sodom and Gomorrah, the adjoining cities of the plain (Genesis 19:24), for divine miracle does not supersede the use of God's existing natural agents, but moves in connection with them. An image of every visitation of God's vengeance on the ungodly, especially of the final one (Deuteronomy 29:23; Job 18:15; Psalm 11:6; Isaiah 34:9; Ezekiel 38:22; Revelation 19:20; Revelation 20:10; Revelation 21:8).

Because of the awe-inspiring miracles performed by the Lord during the battle of Ezekiel 38 and 39, Israel and the Jews as a whole will experience a huge resurgence in their quest for God—for their Messiah. The entire world will have a chance to see God in action, as the true Protector of Israel and many will come to salvation around that time during a brief revival.

Ezekiel 35

Speculation that there will be a separate major Arab-Israeli war where Israel will gain greater borders prior to the Gog-Magog war (battle of Ezekiel 38 and 39) is built upon on a weak foundation. Both Psalm 83 and Ezekiel 35 are cited to support this hypothesis. As already discussed in great length Psalm 83 cannot be a war because it is an imprecatory prayer. Furthermore, Ezekiel 35 is a parallel passage of Isaiah 63:1-6 that firmly states when Jesus the Messiah returns at the Second Coming He will personally slaughter His enemies who are hiding in the ancient territory of Edom. He will then wipe out the wicked—those who have mobilized their armies on the Plain of Megiddo before He touches down on the Mount of Olives. Ezekiel 35 refers to the destruction of Edom (the territory of Southern Jordan east of the Dead Sea) at the Second Coming and cannot be used to support an earlier war.

When Israel Is Living Securely

Some naïvely and illogically propose that an Israeli conquest resulting in larger borders would give Israel more peace and security (by subduing Islam and bringing millions of Allah worshippers under docile control). In fact, the opposite would be true. Expanded borders would ultimately endanger Israel *even more* because her enemies would know full-well that an army the size of the Israeli Defense Forces (IDF) could not handle the massive number of enemies that would need to be controlled within greatly expanded borders. Israelis would be even *more on guard* and *less secure* than they are today. It is during the Gog-Magog invasion that Islam will take a serious hit, by God Himself. This will happen when Israel has a security agreement(s) as she has now. In the future, just prior to the beginning of the seven-year Tribulation period, Scripture tells us that Israel *will* sign a *peace* (shalom) covenant with the Antichrist (Daniel 9:27).

> "After many days you will be summoned; in the latter years you will come into the land that is restored from the sword, whose inhabitants have been gathered from many nations to the mountains of Israel which had been a continual waste; but its people were brought out from the nations, and they are living **securely,** all of them.
>
> And you will say, 'I will go up against the land of unwalled villages. I will go against those who are at rest, that live **securely**, all of them living without walls and having no bars or gates, therefore prophesy, son of man, and say to Gog, 'Thus says the Lord GOD: On that day when My people Israel are living securely, will you not know it?'" (Ezekiel 38: 8, 11, 14).

What does "living securely," mean in reference to Israel and the battle of Ezekiel 38 and 39? We see in the previous passages that the Lord says Israel will be living "securely" when attacked. In verse 14, He states even more specifically, "**My people Israel are living securely**." The word for secure or safe when translated into Hebrew is "batach." The word *batach* does not imply peace or absolute peace, but rather "to trust in," "to be secure," "be careless." The word for safe (as some translations have it) or secure, as used in the three verses above (NASB) is not the Hebrew word "shalom" (peace). Dr. Arnold Fruchtenbaum agrees that Israel *is* dwelling securely, as you will read next and as already cited earlier:

> They dwell securely (38:11, 14). This has often been misconstrued as meaning a state of peace, but this is not the meaning of the Hebrew root *batach*. The nominal form of this root means "security." This is not the security due to a state of peace, but a security due to confidence in their, own strength. This, too, is a good description of Israel today. The Israeli army has fought four major wars since its founding and won them swiftly each time. Today Israel is secure, confident that her army can repel any invasion from the Arab states. Hence, Israel is dwelling securely. Israel is dwelling in unwalled villages (38:11). This is very descriptive of the present-day *kibbutzim* in Israel. (Arnold G. Fruchtenbaum, *Footprints of the Messiah*, pages 121-122.)

Notice that Dr. Fruchtenbaum does not say that the nation of Israel will be more secure or safe because she will conquer the enemy nations that surround her. He makes an excellent point that Israel is *already dwelling securely* because of the confidence in her ability to protect herself.

The Israelis will not be living peacefully when they are attacked. But they will be living under a *sense* of "security" or "securely" with generally secure borders as would be implied by already having a number of security agreements, for example going back to the Camp David Accords.

In 1978 at Camp David a treaty between Israel and Egypt was

negotiated (known as the Camp David Accords), setting the groundwork for a final agreement between Egypt and Israel. On September 17, 1978 Egyptian President Anwar Sadat of Egypt and Israeli Premier Menachem Begin signed the pact at the White House in Washington D.C, and again on March 26, 1979 they signed the final official, document reflective of the Camp David Accords, formally ending the state of war between Egypt and Israel.

Unfortunately, it also included a provision for Israel to withdraw from the Sinai-Peninsula—which she did in stages—in exchange for the promise of more "secure" borders. The news cameras broadcasted and witnessed these historic events to the entire world. And there have been other treaties since. Although the treaties with Israel often contain the word "peace," all the so-called peacemakers seem to really want is for Israel to give up more land for the hollow promise of more peace. Peace is not really part of the equation. Land grabbing is, however. Israel is a tiny nation about the size of New Jersey surrounded by enemies who have large parcels of land. **Israel could fit into the state of Florida 8 times**!

We read in Ezekiel 38:14: "On that day when My people Israel are living securely, **will you not know it**?" In essence this prophetic verse has been fulfilled. Security agreements have been signed and we "know it." The Camp David Accords were not peace (shalom) treaties, but rather *security* agreements. Secure borders were established. Even the security fences that have been constructed throughout parts of Israel over the years denote a feeling of *security*, despite the endless and frequent missile attacks launched by the Palestinians. Having protective fences as Israel has now in some areas does not create an isolated existence, as would be the case when an entire nation or "village" is living behind "bars or gates."

The Israeli Defense Forces (IDF) also provide a sense of confident security. Certainly the Jews in Israel are more secure today than they have been in the past, considering prior to their regathering in 1948 they were dispersed throughout the world seeking a safe-haven. Nowhere were the Jews in more danger than in Europe when they were hunted down, brutally tortured and murdered by Hitler and his bloodthirsty, satanically driven henchmen.

Since that time, the Iranian hierarchy and its proxy nations and allies have been the most vocal enemies in their intention to totally destroy Israel and murder Jews. On July 27, 2012 the U.S. president signed a politically motivated bill to strengthen SECURITY cooperation with Israel: H.R. 4133, the United States Enhanced Security Cooperation Act of 2012. Once again the word "security" is the dominating word.

Lexicons - Old Testament Hebrew Lexicon - New American Standard:

Yashab - To dwell, remain, sit, abide (Qal) to sit, sit down to be set to remain, stay to dwell, have one's abode (Niphal) to be inhabited (Piel) to set, place (Hiphil) to cause to sit to cause to abide, set to cause to dwell to cause (cities) to be inhabited to marry (give an dwelling to) (Hophal) to be inhabited to make to dwell. **Yashib batach -** To dwell securely; **Batach -** See *Strong's Old Testament Hebrew Lexicon* on the following page for a careful analysis of the word Hebrew word batach.

The Old Testament Hebrew Lexicon

Strong's Number: 982	encodedOriginalWord
Original Word	Word Origin
בטח	a primitive root
Transliterated Word	Phonetic Spelling
batach	baw-takh'
Parts of Speech	TWOT
Verb	233

Definition

1. to trust
    a. (Qal)
        1. to trust, trust in
        2. to have confidence, be confident
        3. to be bold
        4. to be secure
    b. (Hiphil)
        1. to cause to trust, make secure
        2. to feel safe, be careless

Translated Words

KJV (120) - bold, 1; careless, 1; confidence, 4; confident, 2; hope, 1; hoped, 1; ones, 1; secure, 4; sure, 1; trust, 103; women, 1;

NAS (120) - bold, 1; careless, 1; complacent, 3; confident, 2; fall down, 1; felt secure, 1; have, 2; have confidence, 1; put my trust, 3; put their trust, 2; put your trust, 1; relied, 1; rely, 8; secure, 5; trust, 51; trusted, 15; trusting, 3; trusts, 19;

Unwalled Villages Defined

Before modern Israel was reestablished nearly everyone in ancient Israel lived in walled villages. Jerusalem was surrounded by walls until 1860 when Sir Moses Montefiore built the first dwellings outside its walls. Throughout Israel today most all of the population lives in unwalled towns and cities. In Ezekiel's time villages were surrounded by walls built from heavy rocks for protection to fend off her enemies.

More recently when the Jews began to return to Israel they established new Jewish settlements. In order to protect against Arab attacks, watchtowers and stockade fences were built, especially used at night. These settlements were essentially small villages based on agriculture but were primarily established for defense and were surrounded by a wall or fence. The first kibbutzim (plural of "kibbutz") were founded some forty years before the establishment of the modern State of Israel (1948). Degania (from the Hebrew "dagan," meaning grain), located south of Lake Kinneret, was established in 1909 by a group of pioneers on land acquired by the Jewish National Fund.

In contrast, modern Israel is a nation consisting of unwalled settlements (villages) and cities. This is true despite the security checkpoints that control entry into some of the settlements, and also true regardless of the wall(s) that Israel has between certain Jewish and Palestinian-controlled areas. Walls, bars and gates still exist, *but they do not* play the same first line of defense position that they did in ancient times or in the recent history of Israel when the Jews began to return to their land.

Additionally, to a great extent modern weapons have made the protection provided by walls, bars and gates of little effect. They do not provide protection from rockets, mortars or missiles. So when Ezekiel wrote that Israel would be living in "unwalled villages" when attacked, it is correct to say they once did live in "walled villages" but they no longer do. Today they live in "unwalled villages," secure borders as Ezekiel described when he said that at the time of the Gog-Magog invasion the nation of Israel would be living "securely" and in "unwalled villages" and "without bars and gates."

The following comments are quoted from the late Grant Jeffrey's book, *Prince of Darkness – Antichrist and the New World Order* (pp.193-194), wherein he gave some intelligent insights relating to the timing of the battle of Ezekiel 38 and 39 (Gog-Magog war) as well as his thoughts regarding Israel's position relating to "dwelling safely" when attacked.

A final question concerns the timing of this future war of Gog and Magog. Some writers conclude that the battle will occur during the seven-year treaty period leading up to the battle of Armageddon. However, there is no mention of the Antichrist or his seven-year treaty to protect Israel. If this battle takes place within the seven-year treaty period leading to Armageddon you would expect the prophet to refer to either (1) the Antichrist defending Israel against this attack or, (2) to his betrayal of Israel by refusing to protect them as agreed in his treaty.

Ezekiel's prophecy about the war of Magog is silent about the Antichrist or the Messiah although they are central figures in the period leading to the battle of Armageddon. This silence convinces me that the war of Gog and Magog will occur at some point in time prior to the Antichrist arising to conclude his fateful seven-year treaty with the Jews.

Some have suggested that the prophet's description found in Ezekiel 38:8 (that Israel will "dwell safely") can only occur after the Antichrist signs his treaty to guarantee their security. Ezekiel declared: "After many days you will be visited. In the latter years you will come into the land of those brought back from the sword and gathered safely" from many people on the mountains of Israel, which had long been desolate; they were brought out of the nations, and now all of them dwell safely."

Does the phrase "dwell safely" mean that Israel has found true lasting peace with her neighbors? In the light of the grim history of the Middle East during the century it is unlikely that Israel will disarm to any degree before the Messiah returns. Israel will remain an armed camp surrounded by enemies committed to her destruction until God changes the hearts of mankind. The phrase "dwell safely" may simply indicate that Israel will be living in an expectation that they will not be attacked at that time, perhaps because of the recent peace agreement with the PLO [Palestine Liberation Organization].

Who Are the Palestinians?

In this chapter, I am including a thorough summation of the so-called Palestinian peoples (counterfeit Arabs). The quote below is extracted from Victor Sharpe's article, which follows. Notice his reference to Psalm 83 in his article, and *not as a war*; but more in keeping with what great scholars have always taught it to be—an imprecatory prayer, which is presently a partially fulfilled prophecy. (Tehillim is the book of Psalms in Hebrew.)

Ancient Romans, as well as so-called Palestinian Arabs, **have fulfilled the Hebrew Scriptural prophecy that declares**: "They lay crafty plans against Your People... they say: "Come, let us wipe them out as a nation; let the name of Israel be remembered no more." – Tehillim 83:3-4 (Psalm 83:3-4)

Counterfeit Arabs
By Victor Sharpe

They are the Arabs who call themselves Palestinians.

They are indistinguishable from those Arabs who live in the surrounding artificial states such as Iraq, Jordan, Saudi Arabia or the other entities throughout the Middle East created by the colonial powers, France and Britain. Both powers were victorious after the Ottoman Turkish Empire lay defeated at the end of World War I.

Both of these European powers carved artificial borders across the corpse of what had been Turkey's empire in the Middle East, and both France and Britain have left a resulting legacy of war and violence ever since. One such territory, previously occupied by Ottoman Turkey for 400 years, was the geographical entity known sometimes as Palestine.

But there is no such thing as a Palestinian people; no such thing as a Palestinian history; and no Palestinian language exists. There has never been any independent, sovereign Palestinian state in all of recorded history, let alone an Arab independent state of Palestine.

You will search in vain for Palestinian Arab coinage or Palestinian Arab archaeological artifacts specifically related to any Palestinian Arab king or ancient leader. But what you will find are coins, pottery, ancient scrolls, all providing conclusive, empirical and millennial evidence of Jewish civilization dotting the land known correctly as Israel – not Palestine.

The present-day so-called "Palestinians" are an Arab people sharing an overwhelmingly Muslim Arab culture, ethnicity and language identical to their fellow Arabs in the Middle East and North Africa, with few if any distinctions.

Yasser Arafat, the arch-terrorist, who imposed himself undemocratically upon the Arabs who call themselves Palestinians, was fond of creating the absurd myth that Palestinian Arabs were descended from the Canaanites and the Philistines. As we know, the bigger the lie the bigger the number of people will believe it. And so Arafat twisted history in order to disinherit the indigenous native people of the land: the Jews.

Canaanites, without doubt, were the first known inhabitants of the Land of Israel before the first Hebrews, Abraham, Isaac, Jacob and their wives— settled there, and before Moses brought their descendants back to the Promised Land during the Exodus from Egypt.

The Canaanites lived both along the coastal plain and in the mountain regions, which run like a spine down the biblical territory of Samaria and Judea. Their language was similar to Hebrew and their territory stretched north into present day Lebanon and included the present day Golan Heights.

The Canaanites were finally subdued during the reign of King David. Most Canaanites were gradually assimilated into the Jewish people and were no longer a distinguishable people. After the 8th century B.C., the Canaanites no longer existed and the only people, therefore, who can trace back an historic link to ancient Canaan are the Jews, not the Palestinian Arabs.

So much for Arafat's nonsense and for the on-going attempts by today's Palestinian Arabs, financed by vast Arab oil wealth, to hoodwink the world. The term "Philistines" provides the source from which the term "Palestinians" is derived.

Like the Arabs who gave themselves the concocted name "Palestinian," the Philistines were alien peoples who entered the land from other lands, mostly from the Mediterranean island of Crete. That is why they were also known as the Sea People.

The modern "Palestinian Arabs" are primarily the descendants of those itinerant Arabs who illegally flooded British Mandatory Palestine from Arab territories as far away as Sudan, Egypt, Syria and what was Mesopotamia (modern Iraq).

They were attracted during the early decades of the 20th century by new employment opportunities provided by the Jewish pioneers, whose heroic efforts were turning the desert green again and restoring centuries of neglect that the land had endured under a succession of alien occupiers.

Britain, during its Mandate over the territory, turned a blind eye to the flood of illegal Arab aliens entering, while at the same time often arbitrarily limiting Jewish immigration into their ancient, biblical and ancestral homeland.

This was a betrayal of the Mandate given to Britain to facilitate a Jewish Homeland in the geographical territory known as Palestine. The Philistines were non-Semitic peoples who had entered the land from their homes throughout the Aegean Islands in general and from Crete in particular.

These ancient Cretans arrived in Southern Canaan and along the Egyptian coastline and were known as "Pelestim and Keretim" by the Hebrew tribes. It appears that their first settlement may have been Gaza. Later they settled in Ashdod, Ashkelon, Gat and Ekron: the Pentapolis. Their territory was primarily along the coastal Mediterranean; interestingly, a territory not dissimilar to the present day Gaza Strip.

They attempted at different times to invade Judah but were turned back by the various Jewish biblical heroes and finally defeated by King David. From that time onwards they were diminished as a threat and as a separate people, finally disappearing from history and any "Palestinian" Arab attempt to claim a lineage with them is as absurd as that of links with the early Canaanites.

Moving fast forward to 73 A.D., the first attempt of the Jews to reclaim their independence from the repressive yoke of Roman occupation ended when Jewish warriors and their families fled to the fortress of Masada from Jerusalem.

The Romans had destroyed the Jewish capital city along with the Second Jewish Temple. Historically documented and universally recognized, Masada, which rises to great height overlooking the Dead Sea, is where the heroic last stand took place and where the surviving warriors and their families took their own lives rather than be sent as slaves throughout the mighty Roman Empire.

The Land where these stirring and epochal events took place was in the province known as Judaea. There is absolutely no mention of any place called "Palestine" before that time. After the suppression of the Second Jewish Revolt in 135 A.D. against the Roman occupation, the Emperor Hadrian replaced the name of Judea (Yehuda in Hebrew from where the name Yehudim, Jews, originates) to Syria-Palaestina after the "Philistines" who were the ancient enemies of the Israelites. Hadrian did so with the explicit purpose of effacing any trace of Jewish history.

Ancient Romans, as well as so-called Palestinian Arabs, have fulfilled the Hebrew Scriptural prophecy that declares: "They lay crafty plans against

Your People… they say: 'come, let us wipe them out as a nation; let the name of Israel be remembered no more." – Tehillim 83:3-4 (Psalm 83:3-4)

They failed, as Israel is reconstituted as a modern Jewish State in its ancestral and biblical homeland. No such name as Palestine occurs in any ancient document. It is not written in the Bible, neither in the Hebrew Scriptures nor in the Christian Testament, not even in Assyrian, Persian, Macedonian, Ptolemaic, Seleucian or other Greek sources.

There are no "Palestinian" people ever mentioned, not even by the Romans that invented the term. If "Palestinians" allegedly are the historic inhabitants of the Holy Land, why did they not fight for independence from Roman occupation as Jews did? How is it possible that not a single "Palestinian" leader revolted against the Roman invaders or is mentioned in any historic record?

Why, is there no Palestinian rebel group mentioned, as for example the Jewish Zealots? Why does every historic document mention the Jews as the native and aboriginal inhabitants, and the Greeks, Romans and others as foreigners dwelling in Judea; but no "Palestinian" people neither as native or as foreigner?

What is more, there is no reference to any "Palestinian" people in the Koran, although Muslims claim that their prophet was once in al-Aksa (meaning the farthest place) which Muslims, for political purposes, chose to be Jerusalem, an event not even mentioned in the Koran.

Saladin, a Kurd, knew the Jews and invited them to resettle in Jerusalem. He had no trouble in recognizing Jerusalem as their eternal capital city and the territory as their rightful Homeland. But he did not know any so-called Palestinians and to claim otherwise that Palestinians are the original people of Eretz Yisrael, the Land of Israel, is not only counter to secular history but also is opposed to Islamic history.

The so-called "Palestinians" who claim Jerusalem -- want it so that they can take it away from the Jews for whom Jerusalem, known also as Zion, is the eternal, 3,000 year old Jewish capital. Perhaps what links the modern day Arabs who call themselves "Palestinians" with the ancient Philistines is that both are invaders.

The Philistines wanted to take from the Israelites the Holy Ark of the Covenant, while today's so-called "Palestinian Arabs" want to take from the Jewish people the Holy City of the Covenant – Jerusalem.

So let me close, beginning with the words of a Christian Arab, Joseph Farah, who has made his home here in America and who knows of what he writes:

> There has never been a land known as Palestine governed by Palestinians. Palestinians are Arabs, indistinguishable from Jordanians (another recent invention), Syrians, Iraqis, etc. Keep in mind that the Arabs control 99.9 per cent of the Middle East lands. Israel represents one-tenth of one per cent of the landmass. But that's too much for the Arabs. They want it all. And that is ultimately what the fighting in Israel is about today... No matter how many land concessions the Israelis make, it will never be enough."
> —Joseph Farah, *Myths of the Middle East*

Let us see what other Arabs have said:

"There is no such country as Palestine. 'Palestine' is a term the Zionists invented. There is no Palestine in the Bible. Our country was for centuries, part of Syria. 'Palestine' is alien to us. It is the Zionists who introduced it."

Auni Bey Abdul-Hadi, Syrian Arab leader to the British Peel Commission, 1937:

"There is no such thing as Palestine in history, absolutely not."

Professor Philip Hitti, Arab historian, 1946:

"It is common knowledge that Palestine is nothing but Southern Syria."

Representative of Saudi Arabia at the United Nations, 1956:

Concerning the Holy Land, the chairman of the Syrian Delegation at the Paris Peace Conference in February 1919 stated: "The only Arab domination since the Conquest in 635 A.D. hardly lasted, as such, 22 years."

The preceding declarations by Arab politicians were issued before, 1967 as they had not the slightest knowledge of the existence of any Palestinian people. How and when did they change their mind and decide that such people existed?

When the State of Israel was reborn in 1948 the Arabs had still not discovered that "ancient" people. They were too busy attempting to annihilate the reconstituted sovereign State of Israel, and did not intend to create any Palestinian entity, but only to distribute the seized Jewish lands among the already existing Arab states.

The Arab armies were miraculously defeated by a tiny handful of Jewish defenders. The Arabs attempted again to destroy Israel in 1967, and were humiliated in only six days, in which they lost the lands that they had previously stolen and usurped in 1948.

Those lands included Judea and Samaria, which comprise the biblical and ancestral Jewish heartland, tracing its history back some 4,000 years.

Now the world forgets such empirical history and prefers to name the ancestral Jewish territory, the West Bank, which was illegally occupied by the Jordanian Arabs for 19 years from 1948 until its liberation in 1967.

In all those years, when Jordan occupied Judea and Samaria and Egypt occupied the Gaza Strip, neither of them created a "Palestinian" state, since the still non-existing Palestinians would have never claimed their alleged right to have their own state.

Paradoxically, during the British Mandate, which lasted from 1920 to 1948, it was not any Arab group but the Jews that were known as Palestinians!

But read what other Arabs declared after the Six-Day War:

"There are no differences between Jordanians, Palestinians, Syrians and Lebanese. We are all part of one nation. It is only for political reasons that we carefully underline our Palestinian identity…yes the existence of a separate Palestinian identity serves only tactical purposes. The founding of a Palestinian state is a new tool in the continuing battle against Israel."

Zuhair Muhsin, military commander of the PLO and member of the PLO Executive Council:

"Never forget this one point: There is no such thing as a Palestinian people, there is no Palestinian entity, there is only Syria. You are an integral part of the Syrian people. Palestine is an integral part of Syria. Therefore it is we, the Syrian authorities, who are the true representatives of the Palestinian people."

Syrian dictator Hafez Assad to the PLO leader Yasser Arafat:

"As I lived in Palestine, everyone I knew could trace their heritage back to the original country their great grandparents came from. Everyone knew their origin was not from the Canaanites, but ironically, this is the kind of stuff our education in the Middle East included. The fact is that today's Palestinians are immigrants from the surrounding nations!

I grew up well knowing the history and origins of today's Palestinians as being from Yemen, Saudi Arabia, Morocco, Christians from Greece, Muslim Sherkas from Russia, Muslims from Bosnia, and the Jordanians next door. My grandfather, who was a dignitary in Bethlehem, almost lost his life by Abdul Qader Al-Husseni (the leader of the Palestinian revolution) after being accused of selling land to Jews.

He used to tell us that his village Beit Sahur (The Shepherds Fields) in Bethlehem County was empty before his father settled in the area with six other families. The town has now grown to 30,000 inhabitants."

Walid Shoebat:

"During the long years of alien occupation of the Land of Israel, though Jews were always living in the Land in whatever numbers they could sustain, visitors were always struck at how the land had become a barren waste with malarial swamps and a remarkably sparse population."

The following reports are from travelers to the desolate landscape that had become a mournful waste are quite telling.

Mark Twain:

"There is not a solitary village throughout its whole extent (valley of Jezreel, Galilee); not for thirty miles in either direction... One may ride ten miles hereabouts and not see ten human beings. For the sort of solitude to make one dreary, come to Galilee...Nazareth is forlorn... Jericho lies a mouldering ruin...

Bethlehem and Bethany, in their poverty and humiliation... untenanted by any living creature...A desolate country whose soil is rich enough, but is given over wholly to weeds... a silent, mournful expanse... a desolation... We never saw a human being on the whole route... hardly a tree or shrub anywhere.

Even the olive tree and the cactus, those fast friends of a worthless soil had almost deserted the country... Palestine sits in sackcloth and ashes... desolate and unlovely..." —Mark Twain, *The Innocents Abroad* (1867)

One wonders, therefore, where were the "Palestinians" hiding so that Mark Twain could not see them? Where was that so-called "ancient" people in the mid nineteenth century? Of course, Arab politicians now attempt to discredit Mark Twain, retreating into that realm of all scoundrels by calling him racist:

In 1590 a "simple English visitor" to Jerusalem wrote:

"Nothing there is to be seen but a little of the old walls, which is yet remaining and all the rest is grass, moss and weeds much like to a piece of rank or moist ground."

Gunner Edward Webbe, Palestine Exploration Fund:

"The land in Palestine is lacking in people to till its fertile soil." British archaeologist Thomas Shaw, mid-1700s: "Palestine is a ruined and desolate land."

Count Constantine Francois Volney, XVIII century French author and historian:

"The Arabs themselves cannot be considered but temporary residents. They pitched their tents in its grazing fields or built their places of refuge in its ruined cities. They created nothing in it. Since they were strangers to the land, they never became its masters. The desert wind that brought them hither could one day carry them away without their leaving behind them any sign of their passage through it."

Comments by Christians concerning the Arabs in Palestine in the 1800s:

"The country is in a considerable degree empty of inhabitants and therefore its greatest need is of a body of population."

James Finn, British Consul in 1857:

"The area was under populated and remained economically stagnant until the arrival of the first Zionist pioneers in the 1880s, who came to rebuild the Jewish land. The country had remained "The Holy Land" in the religious and historic consciousness of mankind, which associated it with the Bible and the history of the Jewish people.

Jewish development of the country also attracted large numbers of other immigrants – both Jewish and Arab. The road leading from Gaza to the north was only a summer track suitable for transport by camels and carts... Houses were all of mud.

No windows were anywhere to be seen... The plows used were of wood... The yields were very poor... Schools did not exist... The rate of infant mortality was very high... The western part, toward the sea, was almost a desert... Many ruins were scattered over the area, as owing to the prevalence of malaria, many villages were deserted by their inhabitants."

The Report of the British Royal Commission (1913):

Far too many otherwise decent people have come to accept Arab oil financed falsehoods masquerading as history about the origins of the so-called Palestinian Arabs. These lies now permeate the mainstream media, schools, colleges, and universities and are perpetrated by the tenured leftist professors and the colleges who all too eagerly accept Saudi blood money.

✡✡✡✡✡

The historical facts given above may be of help to those who have otherwise fallen hook, line and sinker for duplicitous Arab propaganda and what constitutes one of the biggest scams ever perpetrated upon the world.

The following two books are also excellent resources for researching the myth that the Jews stole Arab land:

From Time Immemorial: The Origins of the Arab-Jewish Conflict Over Palestine - John Peters

Myths and Facts: A Guide to the Arab-Israeli Conflict, published by American-Israeli Cooperative Enterprise (AICE).

Additionally, another important book: *Should Israel Exist? A Sovereign Nation under Attack,* written by Dr. Michael Curtis. He exposes the ongoing anti-Israel rhetoric that unjustly condemns Israel and refutes the worldwide propaganda against Israel, dispelling the victim mentality and false claims propagated by the Palestinians and their supporters.

Israel Is the Most Unique Nation in the World
The Weekly Standard, May 11, 1998
Charles Krauthammer

Israel is the very embodiment of Jewish continuity: It is the only nation on earth that inhabits the same land, bears the same name, speaks the same language, and worships the same God that it did 3,000 years ago.

You dig the soil and you find pottery from Davidic times, coins from Bar Kokhba, and 2,000-year-old scrolls written in a script remarkably like the one that today advertises ice cream at the corner candy store.

Israel became a nation about 1300 BCE, two thousand years before the rise of Islam. The people of modern day Israel share the same language and culture shaped by the Jewish heritage and religion passed through generations starting with the founding father Abraham. Since the Jewish conquest in 1272 BCE, the Jews have had dominion over the land for one thousand years with a continuous presence in the land for the past 3,300 years.

After the Romans conquered Jerusalem about 2,000 years ago, Jewish people were expelled and dispersed to the Diaspora, and the Land of Israel was ruled by Rome, by Islamic and Christian crusaders, by the Ottoman Empire, and by the British Empire.

Throughout centuries Jews prayed to return from the Diaspora to Israel. During the first half of the 20th century there were major waves of immigration of Jews back to Israel from the Arab countries and from Europe. In 1948 Jews reestablished their sovereignty over their ancient homeland with the establishment of the modern State of Israel.

It was only after the Jews reinhabited their historic homeland of Judea and Samaria, that the myth of a Palestinian nation was created and marketed worldwide. Jews come from Judea, not Palestinians.

There is no language known as Palestinian, or any Palestinian culture distinct from that of all the Arabs in the area. There has never been a land known as Palestine governed by Palestinians. Palestinians are Arabs indistinguishable from Arabs throughout the Middle East.

Joshua 21:43-45

"So the LORD gave Israel all the land which He had sworn to give to their fathers, and they possessed it and lived in it. And the LORD gave them rest on every side, according to all that He had sworn to their fathers. and no one of all their enemies stood before them; the LORD gave all their enemies into their hand. Not one of the good promises which the LORD had made to the house of Israel failed; all came to pass."

Part Four

Understanding Bible Interpretation

The Word of God Not the Word of Man

The following is extracted from an article titled, "The Stand of Accountability."

The "church" is divided as much on doctrine as it is on who is Jesus Christ. Self indulgence, emotionalism, and extra-biblical, even non-biblical teaching, has replaced sound doctrine in much of the church. Discussions on doctrine and theology often are now argued in terms of who wrote what book that is currently popular, instead of the context of the Word of God.

This is 2 Timothy 4:3-4 playing out: "For the time will come when they will not endure sound doctrine; but after their own lusts shall they heap to themselves teachers, having itching ears; And they shall turn away their ears from the truth, and shall be turned unto fables." This opens the door to great deception.

I cannot urge you enough to study the Word of God on your own. Teachers, preachers, and others who self-proclaim their church offices will not stand in your place before the Lord on Judgment Day. It will be you, and you alone. You won't be able to quote passages from some so-called Bible teacher in your defense. It will be about your relationship with the LORD.

With the exponential increase in events that can be related to prophecy and the desire of the masses to chase after the newest opinion on Scripture, I now have a fuller understanding of what apostle Paul wrote in Philippians 2:12 to "work out your own salvation with fear and trembling." Read the Word in its context. Get close to Jesus. We are living in prophetic times.

—Bill Wilson, *The Daily Jot*

Chapter Fifteen

Interpretation of Scripture
(Biblical Hermeneutics)

"But we will devote ourselves to prayer,
And to the ministry of the word." —Acts 6:4

Considering all the confusion in interpreting Bible prophecy and Scripture in general, this is a guide to understanding the basic laws of Bible interpretation. Studying the Bible should be a priority for all believers every day. A Spirit led-believer does so with great care, and makes it a common practice. We can never assume a popular doctrine or teaching is true, even if it is said to be so by your favorite pastor or Bible teacher. God holds us all individually accountable for what we accept as truth:

"Now these were more noble than those in Thessalonica, in that they received the word with all readiness of the mind, examining the Scriptures daily, whether these things were so" (Acts 17:11).

As I have already pointed out, many churches and some Bible teachers are increasingly becoming apostate, exactly as the Lord forewarned. And if not apostate, then all too often offer deficiently researched Bible interpretations, which contradict the Word of God when closely examined. Too many widely accepted teachings are simply parroting what someone read on a website or in a book without taking the time to carefully study the teaching to see if it correctly lines up with Scripture. This is all the more reason to hold our Bibles closely and study the truths of Scripture every day.

Many excellent books are available but we must always go to Scripture first as our best and final voice of authority. Much of what is passed off today as biblical "truth" is based on the opinions of individuals who gather their information from commentaries, articles, chitchat, and not regular carefully researched Bible study. None of us can correctly interpret or understand what has been written in the Bible without the teaching of the Holy Spirit (1 John 2:27).

We should always keep the Golden Rule of Interpretation in the forefront of our minds as we study the Bible, and all books relating to biblical matters, including this book:

> When the plain sense of Scripture makes common sense, seek no other sense; therefore, take every word at its primary, ordinary, usual, literal meaning unless the facts of the immediate context, studied in the light of related passages and axiomatic and fundamental truths, indicates clearly otherwise.

We know that a physical dragon cannot cast one-third of the stars in space down to earth (Revelation 12:3-4), but the devil who is called the great dragon (Revelation 12:9) can lead one-third of the angels in heaven (Daniel 8:10) to rebel against God and wreck havoc on earth. Good common sense tells us that when Jesus (Yeshua) is called the "Lamb of God" (John 1:29); it does not mean He is a literal lamb. It is symbolic of the fact that He is the Paschal Lamb sacrifice for the sins of the elect.

Those who try to interpret the Scriptures by not using a strict rule of understanding can make any passage say anything they want. For example, as discussed earlier, flawed methods of interpretation have caused some to claim and teach that the two million army of demons spoken of in Revelation 9:16 is the Red Chinese army.

The greatest teacher is the Holy Spirit. As we let Him have more of us, more of our commitment and time, and as we allow Him to renew our minds and grow as believers with pure hearts, He will guide us and teach us. Studying the Bible cannot be a hobby. It is something all believers are commanded to do (2 Timothy 2:15). The more we read the Word of God under the guidance of the Holy Spirit, the more we will understand. Some people who say they read their Bibles do not seem to grasp the meaning of some of the Scriptures. It seems that they are looking at the words but not processing and actually studying what they see.

When something does not line-up with Scripture, we must all be careful not to embrace such teachings. This is an ongoing challenge. I never assume because someone has written a lot of articles, sold a lot of books or has a popular media "following" that everything they are teaching is biblically sound. I find those who are the most trustworthy and knowledgeable teachers simply consider themselves "students of the Bible" and are quite humble and unassuming. They are not striving for great personal attention and adulation.

Many hard working Bible teachers and preachers make tremendous contributions, and they should be applauded for their diligence and devotion to teaching the Word of God. Yet, we do not rely on the teachings of men to know and understand Scripture. We study what others say and write to see if our understanding is correct and when we see that our understanding differs greatly from the majority of commentators and Bible teachers, we must go back and study the Bible even more.

After we have done that and we are thoroughly convinced that our understanding is correct and the majority understanding is wrong—so be it. There are times when the majority is wrong and the minority is right. The perfect example is Martin Luther. As a Roman Catholic priest he concluded that salvation is by grace through faith alone apart from the Catholic Church. He was the minority and the Catholic Church was the majority yet he was right and the Catholic Church was wrong. Let the holy infallible, inherent Word of God be our daily bread, and on occasion, may we take just a few nibbles here and there from the works of men.

If we simply say, "I have a difference of opinion on some biblical topics" without undertaking a very serious in-depth Bible study and carefully revisiting the Scriptures in question, we can hinder our spiritual growth and our understanding of the Word of God. And if we are in positions of leadership many people could be led astray. The truth is in the Word of God. We are to be diligent in studying our Bibles, not material derived from media campaigns that make references to the Bible (2 Timothy 2:15). To simply say, "We can all disagree as long as we all love the Lord" is a weak position. I would say that is just the kind of "lukewarm" attitude that the Lord abhors (Revelation 3:16).

If we really "love the Lord" we should all stop teaching the philosophies of men and wholeheartedly begin to study the Scriptures and teach the truth of the Bible. And that means not supporting multiple teachings (theories) on the same Scriptures, which only cause confusion exposing a person to be of weak character and conviction—lacking spiritual and biblical integrity making him "a double-minded man, unstable in all his ways" (James 1:8).

"If you instruct the brethren in these things, you will be a good minister of Jesus Christ, nourished in the words of faith and good doctrine which you have carefully followed. But reject profane and old wives' fables, and exercise yourself toward godliness" (1 Timothy 4:6-7).

The Word of God does not leave room for speculation and guessing games that contradict its content. Selective analysis derived from passages to create desired interpretations is essentially rewriting the true meaning of the Scriptures. To say, "I believe a particular teaching" is not the same as saying, "This is what Scripture clearly teaches." To simply "believe" or assume something to be true does not make it so. As believers, we must be careful not to become part of the growing apostasy or contribute to the false teachings that are prevalent. When we take our faith seriously and study the Scriptures carefully, the Holy Spirit will teach us:

"These things I have written to you concerning those who are trying to deceive you. As for you, the anointing which you received from Him abides in you, and you have no need for anyone to teach you; but as His anointing teaches you about all things, and is true and is not a lie, and just as it has taught you, you abide in Him" (1 John 2:27).

When we carefully study God's Word and follow the Golden Rule of Interpretation there are no contradictions in interpretation. The application of Scripture can vary, but not the foundational meaning of the God-breathed verses. Contradictions are caused by men and their own ideas; some from a lack of knowledge, "group think" and some out of the need to further personal goals of advancement without true regard for biblical scrutiny. Only a sound doctrinal approach without a pie in the sky blindness can truly edify others and help bring seekers to a deeper and correct understanding of God's Word.

If a believer and even a seminary student tries to learn what the Bible teaches by studying primarily commentaries or books, he or she will be doing just the opposite of what the Bereans and all of the early Christians did. If every Christian would diligently study the Bible every day (Acts 17:11), a false teacher could never gain converts. Instead of being tempted to partake in cults or get caught-up in the mistakes of biblically weak teachers, false teachers and false prophets, a well-versed believer would have strong discernment and would not be deceived.

Much misinformation exists, especially when it comes to Israel and the Middle East. We must carefully study the Scriptures before accepting any proclamations we read or hear. A spirit of deception is in the Church today regarding many of the prophecy teachings. Time will show this to be true. Beware of those who use God's Word as an avenue for self-adulation and personal profit.

Straying from Biblical Truth

"For the time will come when they will not endure the sound doctrine; but, having itching ears, will heap to themselves teachers after their own lusts; and will turn away their ears from the truth, and turn aside unto fables" (2 Timothy 4:3-4).

An important message to carefully ponder is extracted from an article by Daniel B. Wallace titled, "Scripture Twisting." Dr. Wallace is Senior Professor of New Testament Studies at Dallas Theological Seminary:

> One of the curious phenomena of recent times is *how* Christians have been using the Bible. Rather than recognize that it is a book made up of 66 books, each written to a specific people for a specific reason, we tend to wrench verses right out of their contexts because the *words* agree with what we already believe. Sometimes believers say silly things like, "God gave me a verse today." What's wrong with that? Two things: First, this approach to Scripture does not honor the *divine* authorship of Scripture. God gave the verse at least 1900 years ago. You may have discovered it today, but it's been there all along.
>
> To say that God *gave* a verse today is really an existential statement, as though the Bible didn't become alive until we read it a certain way. But revelation has ceased. It's all there in the Book. This manner of speaking almost sounds as if revelation continues. But the work of the Spirit today is decidedly not on the cognitive level: He is not bringing us new revelation. His work in relation to the Bible is primarily in the realm of conviction: He helps to drive home the message of the Bible, once it is properly understood. Second, this approach (i.e., the "God gave me a verse today" approach) to Scripture does not honor the *human* authorship of the Bible.
>
> When Paul wrote to the Galatians, he wrote a coherent, holistic message. He never intended for someone a couple millennia later to rip verses out of their context and wield them any way they so chose! Certainly we have a right to quote verses of Scripture; but we do not have a right to ignore the context or to make them say what

the language cannot say. Otherwise, someone could come along and say "Judas hanged himself;" "Go and do likewise!" Hence, one reason for the abuse of Scripture is due to a lack of respect for the Bible as a divine and human work. In this approach it becomes a magical incantation book—almost a book of unconnected fortune cookie sayings!

Part and parcel of this abuse of Scripture is *laziness*. That is, most people simply don't take the trouble to read the context or to do their homework on the meaning of the Bible. And even when they are confronted with overwhelming evidence that is contrary to their view, they often glibly reply, "That's just your interpretation." This kind of response sounds as if all interpretations are up for grabs, as though all interpretations are equally plausible. Such a view is patently false.

Another reason for Scripture twisting is simple *dishonesty*. Peter reminds his audience that Paul wrote things that are hard to understand, which the unstable and wicked twist to their own destruction (2 Peter 3:15-16). I'm afraid that this approach to Scripture represents the attitude of far too many folks. Not just heretics, either. Too often preachers fall prey to the temptation, "Can it preach?" rather than following the conviction, "Is it true?"

We cannot always divine the reasons why some folks use the Bible in a way it was never intended to be used. But we do have the responsibility to be good stewards of the Word. Should not our attitude be the same as the Bereans? When the Bereans heard the gospel that Paul preached, Luke tells us that they were more noble-minded than the Thessalonians because they received the things that Paul said with joy, but also searched the Scriptures to check him out (Acts 17:11)! We should listen to the Word being taught with a critical ear and a smile on our face.

Dr. Wallace's message may be threatening to some people. An indifferent attitude or more often, stubborn pride is the root cause of unwillingness to look within oneself and actually do as the Lord commands: Receive *the word with all readiness of the mind, examining the Scriptures daily, whether these things were so* (Acts 17:11b). We should never assume because someone is standing in a room delivering a sermon or message that what we are hearing is in keeping with the truths of Scripture. But it seems too many believers elevate people over and above God's inerrant Word (because they are unwilling to do the hard work and study).

These same people won't miss a church service somehow thinking what they hear in church is all truth but they will not take time at home to see if what they are being fed is correct. They do not question their pastor although Scripture commands that we should. Instead, they compromise their walk with their Lord and even become legalistic in their approach to serving Him. Entering a church building dogmatically on a regular basis or reading articles and books does not make for spiritual growth unless what is being taught is diligently examined against the Scriptures.

Although there are some excellent anointed preachers and teachers we are to be obedient to the Word of God, and not place anyone on a pedestal or be captive to one man's ideas without taking self-responsibility by *carefully studying* (not only reading) our Bibles. It is no secret that the Church today is filled with one confusing and contradictory teaching after another.

> "Be diligent to present yourself approved to God as a workman who does not need to be ashamed, accurately handling the word of truth" (2 Timothy 2:15).

A Day of Reckoning

"Beloved, do not believe every spirit, but test the spirits to see whether they are from God, because many false prophets have gone out into the world. We are from God; he who knows God listens to us; he who is not from God does not listen to us. By this we know the spirit of truth and the spirit of error" (1 John 4:1, 6).

I believe a day is coming when some widely-accepted popular doctrines and prognostications taught by various Bible prophecy cliques, Bible teachers, commentators (lecturers) will reach a point of meltdown. The interpretation of certain prophecies and passages in the Bible—which includes their timing in some cases, will prove to have been misunderstood (misinterpreted) and wrongly taught. Many of these teachings are derived by one "expert" echoing another, and by mishandling Scripture using the eisegesis method of interpretation (injecting one's own ideas into the text). Many teachings will be evidenced to be false and millions will be shocked when this happens.

I am not only referring to the time of the Bema Seat judgment when all believers will stand face-to-face with Christ and give an accounting of their lives, but also to the span of time before the seven-year Tribulation actually begins. Lack of sound discernment seems to be a serious problem. A spiritual blindness has taken hold of huge numbers of people in the Church. Too many people accept various teachings without studying the premise from which they are derived; or question if there is a true premise at all. Most will deny it, but the motives of many who teach are for self-advancement and self-adulation. They want to be the next big deal in the world of Bible prophecy or in various Christian groups. Sadly, "Every man for himself" seems to have become a way of life for some, even in the Church.

Trying to awaken these people and those who follow them is sometimes not much different than trying to convince far-left liberals to start reevaluating what they believe to be true, and come to the realization that what they accept as truth is simply wrong. Some well-meaning people in leadership positions don't carefully think things through, but rather accept what they have been taught and repeat it to others. Many people are very genuine but too trusting in what they hear or read, and don't seriously study the Bible for themselves; they depend solely on others to teach them—which is not at all what the Lord expects of His own.

Far too many Christians seem to have replaced studying the Word of God with gleaning information on websites, blogs, articles; television and radio preaching and church attendance. All those mediums can be very beneficial but they should not be used as primary learning tools to replace diligent personal Bible study. Bible study goes hand in hand with strengthening our relationship with Christ. As we hide His Word in our hearts, the inner-transformation of renewing our minds is accelerated. *Thy word have I hid in mine heart, that I might not sin against thee* (Psalm 119:11). The more we delve into His Word, the stronger our bond is with Him.

> "Do not be deceived, God is not mocked; for whatever a man sows, this he will also reap. For the one who sows to his own flesh will from the flesh reap corruption, but the one who sows to the Spirit will from the Spirit reap eternal life" (Galatians 6:7-8).

To avoid being a part of "group think" and spiritual compromise, Luke urged all believers to examine *the Scriptures daily, whether these things were so* (Acts 17:11b). It's all about self-responsibility. James warned that not many should be Bible teachers because they will incur a stricter judgment, a greater condemnation (James 3:1).

Once again, I will mention James' epistle about the danger of being double-minded (James 1:9)—that is, being so weak-willed that one can be tossed to and fro with the wind as many are by either teaching various questionable doctrines and/or not taking a stand against teachings that some know are not really in keeping with the Scriptures. Instead, these sell-out rationalizers make excuses for the problematic teachings of others for two main reasons: To either ride on the coat tails of the individuals they make excuses for because they are famous or popular; or because the "go-along to get-along" person lacks scriptural understanding and/or biblical integrity.

The intent of the heart is the crux of the matter. Are we truly living for the Lord or living to advance ourselves and gain great notoriety under the false projection of "doing the Lord's work?"

"For the word of God is living, and active, and sharper than any two-edged sword, and piercing even to the dividing of soul and spirit, of both joints and marrow, **and quick to discern the thoughts and intents of the heart**" (Hebrews 4:12).

"Examine yourselves, whether ye be in the faith; prove your own selves. Know ye not your own selves, how that Jesus Christ is in you, except ye be reprobates?" (2 Corinthians 13:5).

When Christianity Becomes Big Business

"Beware of false prophets, who come to you in sheep's clothing, but inwardly are ravening wolves" (Matthew 7:15).

Sensationalism sells. Christianity, and more specifically—Bible prophecy has become big business for some, and unless we carefully study and understand our Bibles, the proponents of sensationalized self "discoveries" will continue to mislead and confuse people—while they intensely market themselves as prophetic geniuses (by randomly cherry picking Scripture) and even extracting new "hidden" meanings. This is usurping God's authority by taking His written inherent Word and spinning it into a web of confusion.

It is impossible to deny the fact that some professing believers may get involved in projects that are not for God's benefit, but obviously for selfish-gain. When Christianity becomes big business—compromise becomes a common standard. God is not mocked, and those who think they can manipulate situations to

When prophecy "teachers" take the giant leap from "teacher" to self-ordained "prophet" time will surely prove their prophecies to be wrong, and they will join the class of false prophets who have made a mockery of biblical truth—inevitably resulting in overwhelming public disdain toward Christians and tremendously hindering the ability to effectively share the gospel.

shine a light upon themselves by using God in the process are missing the point of true, absolute surrender to Him. They might fool some people, but they cannot fool God.

People like this probably try to persuade themselves (and really believe) God has given them a special calling above all others, propping themselves up onto "spiritual" pedestals. In reality, some people are merely creating an opportunity for themselves where they can transfer their own worldly lust for power and control into a more docile arena—such as Christian businesses or ministries. It's the same old worldly power trip, the same old song and dance, camouflaged in spiritual sackcloth.

"Pride *goes* before destruction, and a haughty spirit before a fall. When pride comes, then comes dishonor, but with the humble is wisdom" (Proverbs 16:18; 11:12).

Unraveling Bible Translation Confusion

In relation to interpreting and understanding the Word of God, an issue that has caused division in the Body of Christ is the King James Only teaching. I do not wish to get caught up in this divisive issue; I am simply pointing out a real problem that divides the Church. Sadly, this is an unnecessary conflict which could be easily remedied if each believer did a thorough balanced study on the topic. Even soon after I was first saved many decades ago, I saw King James Only dynamics in various churches, which brought about nothing productive and certainly did not glorify God. I refer to the KJV translation sometimes but certainly not exclusively.

The great scholar, Dr. James D. Price, in his excellent book, *King James Onlyism: A New Sect,* documents how in his research he found that the King James Only idea could be traced back to the 1950s but did not have much influence until the early 1970s. The idea became more serious in the 1980s. At the time that he was working on his doctoral studies in the 1960s Dr. Price states:

> There was not the slightest hint that anyone thought that the King James Version was the only acceptable Bible to use. The historical evidence indicates that this doctrine was unknown to the early leaders of Fundamentalism, but originated and developed in the last few decades of this century.

Dr. Price addresses the fallacy of those who fall into the more radical side of King James Onlyism, those who teach that anything but the KJV is the work of Satan and anyone who uses any version except the KJV is a heretic and an instrument of the devil.

He further states:

> The idea that the King James version was the only Bible one should
> use was unheard of. Everyone in conservative Christian circles un-
> derstood that the King James Version was one of the many transla-
> tions of the Hebrew and Greek texts of the Bible and that the final
> authority for doctrine, faith, and practice always has been the origi-
> nal Hebrew words written by Moses and the prophets and the origi-
> nal Greek words written by the apostles.

> It was not unusual for the pastor and visiting speakers to make refer-
> ence to the Greek or Hebrew texts from which they derived a better
> wording or more accurate renderings. They made favorable references
> to the wording of the Revised Version of 1881 (RV), to the American
> Standard Version of 1901 (ASV), and to other modern versions. In those
> early days, it was popular in fundamental circles to own an American
> Standard Version of the Bible. (*King James Onlyism: A New Sect*,
> "Introduction: The King James Only Doctrine Is a New Idea")

In his excellent thoroughly researched book, *The King James Only
Controversy: Can You Trust the Modern Translations?*, James R. White, accomplished author and director of the highly respected Christian apologetics
organization, Alpha and Omega Ministries, makes this heartfelt appeal:

> This book is a plea for understanding. It is my desire that the reader,
> upon completing this work will first and foremost *want* to under-
> stand *why* our English traditions of the Bible read as they do. This is
> what I have found to be lacking in most KJV Only advocates with
> whom I have spoken: A desire to *truly know* why a person might be
> willing to use something other than the KJV, to *really understand*
> why some readings in the modern translations are in fact superior
> to those in the KJV.

You cannot get far with someone who does not wish to travel with you. And I know that many in the KJV Only camp will never set foot upon a path I have attempted to clear in these pages. I have written this book for those who have a godly desire to know the truth.

And I admit to a desire to aid in the vindication of godly men who have labored diligently in the field of textual study and translation, one hardly fraught with riches and glory. The constant denigration of their work, their spirituality, and even their intelligence cries out for solid refutation and even rebuke, and this I hope I have provided.

King James Onlyism is a human tradition. It has no basis in history. It is internally inconsistent, utilizing circular reasoning at its core, and it involves the use of more double standards than almost any system of thought I have ever encountered. Yet it is embraced by fellow believers, and as such must be addressed if I am to follow Christ's command, "Love one another."

Finally, as I said in the beginning, my desire is for the peace of Christ's church. I truly hope this work will help quell restless spirits in congregations who through the zeal for a human tradition are causing dissension and discord. May the facts of the matter, rather than the emotions of the moment convince them to refrain from disturbing the brethren, and may the church focus instead upon the weighty and important issues that face her.

On page 15 of his book, James R. White mentions some of the most divisive KJV Only publications which includes a book by King James Only activist, Barry Burton. In his poorly written and poorly edited book, *Let's Weigh the Evidence: Which Bible Is the Word of God?* Burton unleashes his vitriol against anything and anyone not using the KJV. One of the many problems with his book is on page 22 where he incorrectly cites Romans 14:10b and 12, stating that those verses are in reference to the judgment seat of Christ.

Instead of citing the correct Scripture (2 Corinthians 5:10) Burton misquotes the Scripture all together and even from the wrong book of the Bible. Using incorrectly cited verses he then goes on berating and accusing the New American Standard Bible (NASB) translation of being wrong and he does so in a most unscholarly ridiculous manner. This is a perfect example of an outright lie that gullible folks who do not do their Bible study homework will accept as truth.

On page 22 of his book, this is what Barry Burton states:

MORE...VERSES THAT ATTACK THE DEITY OF CHRIST...

Then he goes on to incorrectly cite Scripture:

Romans 14:10b and verse 12 (King James)

"For we shall all stand before the judgment seat of ***Christ***...
So then every one of us shall give account of himself to ***God.***"

Mr. Burton then states this: (I include his use of multiple punctuation marks):

Do you see the logic of it?????

When we stand before the judgment seat of *Christ*...
we are giving account *to God.*

THEREFORE ... <u>Christ is God!</u>

Romans 14:10b and verse 13 (New American Standard)

"For we shall all stand before the judgment seat of **God**...
So then each one of us shall give account of himself to **God**."

Mr. Burton then wails:

Do you see that? Do you SEE that? Do you see THAT? Just one
small word is CHANGED...YET... There is no proof that Jesus is
God in these verses!!!

If a Jehovah's Witness ever comes to your door and says, "Of course
we don't believe that Christ is really God. He was the first being
God created."

If you don't have the REAL word of God in your home... you may
have a hard time proving that Jesus is really God.

What we *can* see is that Barry Burton is very confused, contentious and
his teaching is false. Not only does he cite the wrong Scripture all together, he is dead wrong on how the NASB translation reads. The word
Christ *is* in the NASB translation but he screams that it is not. And the
verse he uses in his book as cited above, which he calls a KJV translation is not like any KJV translation readily available. See the correct
Scriptures below:

2 Corinthians 5:10 - King James Version (KJV)

"For we must all appear before the judgment seat of Christ; that
every one may receive the things done in his body, according to that
he hath done, whether it be good or bad."

2 Corinthians 5:10 - New American Standard Bible (NASB)

"For we must all appear before the judgment seat of Christ, so that each one may be recompensed for his deeds in the body, according to what he has done, whether good or bad."

Following is a example of a disturbing description from a church's belief statement:

We believe the Holy Bible, as it appears in the English language, is the Authorized 1611 King James Bible. We believe this Bible is the product of God's watchful hand of preservation, is perfect, and should not be criticized or corrected. The Scriptures shall be interpreted according to their normal grammatical—historical meaning, and all issues of interpretation and meaning shall be determined by the pastor. The King James Version of the Bible shall be the official and only translation used by the church.

Whatever happened to 2 Peter 1:20?

"Knowing this first, that no prophecy of scripture is of private interpretation."

And how about Acts 17:11 cited earlier?

"Now these were more noble than those in Thessalonica, in that they received the word with all readiness of the mind, examining the Scriptures daily, whether these things were so."

And what about 2 Timothy 2:15?

> "Be diligent to present yourself approved to God as a workman who does not need to be ashamed, handling accurately the word of truth."

A pastor or Bible teacher does not have the final word on "All issues of Scripture interpretation and meaning." To teach that smacks of pride, arrogance, questionable motives and has the earmarks of a cult leader anointing himself into a papal position, crowning himself as a Protestant pope. When I first read the church's belief statement I was so astonished that I took it to both Dr. James Price and Dr. F. Kenton Beshore, who are both very learned scholars. They each had the *same reaction*, the same as my own. They each stated the pastor sounds like a "Protestant pope" and were quite disturbed by what the pastor states in the church's statement of faith. Both scholars expressed great concern for how this pastor is leading his congregation.

No one has all the answers. When a pastor/teacher states that *he* will determine the interpretation and meaning of Scripture and that only one translation of the Bible is accurate, then a devoted student of the Bible should stop any further involvement with that pastor and church.

Bible study is best when it is not limited to just one translation. Cross-reference study between several translations allows us to better grasp the intended meaning of any passage. We can find some extreme positions that we must stay away from. To say that the "Authorized 1611 KJV" translation is the only acceptable translation shows a lack of scholarship. The King James Only advocates will argue that they had documents that other translations did not, but that is simply false. There is more documentation readily available today than ever before supporting other translations.

Some excellent books to read on this topic are: *King James Onlyism: A New Sect* by Dr. James D. Price, *The King James Version Debate: A*

Plea For Realism, D. A. Carson. *King James Only, The King James Only Controversy: Can You Trust the Modern Translations?* by James R. White.

We must be careful not to elevate particular Bible translations above the Word of God and God Himself. There is a danger of worshipping a false god by making a particular translation the only way. Some fringe KJV preachers go to extremes; they claim a person cannot be saved hearing the gospel preached in a translation other than the KJV; denying the power of the Word of God and the power of the Holy Spirit, therefore elevating the King James translation above the Word of God and above God Himself. To them the KJV is God Almighty. They have made the KJV a false god which they worship. God can speak to anyone through any translation in any language. To claim that God can only save through one translation is placing the Creator of the universe in a box that they control. The KJV Only extremists have literally usurped God and they have become the vicars of their god, the KJV.

How to Identify a Christian Cult

"You therefore, beloved, knowing this beforehand, be on your guard so that you are not carried away by the error of unprincipled men and fall from your own steadfastness" (2 Peter 3:17).

A number of cults exist within what is broadly considered the Christian church. Not all are easily recognizable. They vary in degrees of cohesiveness and legalism. The first thing to look for is exclusiveness; the church/organization and leader are followed regardless of some questionable teachings. Many devoted believers who love the Lord and are seeking genuine fellowship and spiritual growth may find themselves unwittingly involved in a church that actually restricts the Holy Spirit from ministering to them. A sort of slow brainwashing, an indoctrination takes place with some teachings that are not biblically sound. Most of these dear folks are sincere in their quest to serve the Lord, but are sincerely deceived and being misled.

In time, church attendance and group functions and anything related to the church/group become a huge priority. Slowly but surely and sometimes suddenly, close friends, other believers and family members are neglected, choosing the church or group instead. By deliberately avoiding those who do not follow their church's teachings, these people think they are being true to the Lord, but they are actually doing the opposite.

This is especially true if the church came together under seemingly extraordinary events, which the congregants feel were God-directed. We must remember Satan can orchestrate very attractive and amazing situations that can deceive people. The world has many beautiful church buildings that came to be by the dedicated hard work of the congregants, when so many things seemed to just fall into place giving birth to a new church. That is all well and good if it is the God of the Bible who is exalted, and not the pastor and his contrived unbiblical ideas. (Consider the beautiful churches that the Mormons have built, and the Catholics, etc.)

Many fascinating storylines can be heard on how particular groups and churches came to be. Some of them are God-directed and some are not. The test of authenticity is sound doctrine, and not divisive teachings endorsed only by the church leader regardless of how exceptionally nice that person can be and how nice the congregants are. In such cases a genuine personal relationship with Jesus Christ turns into allegiance to the pastor and the church (even when some of the teachings are false and problematic). Church attendance, group activities, reading and "studying" the designated Bible chosen by the pastor takes the place of an authentic relationship and walk with the Lord God Almighty.

What makes it difficult for those who have become entangled in such situations is that some of the teachings they are exposed to are very sound, so they think all is well but they are weak in their understanding of Bible interpretation making it possible for false teachings to seep in, contaminating the truth of God's holy Word. One thing for sure, those who are participating in such an environment with these dynamics will rarely, if ever, recognize and admit that they have become part of cult. And trying to convince them that they have crossed the line from walking with the Lord to walking with indoctrinated teachings of their church leader is a daunting, if not an impossible task.

Cult identification experts, Janja Lalich, Ph.D. and Michael D. Langone, Ph.D. state, "Concerted efforts at influence and control lie at the core of cultic groups, programs, and relationships. Many members, former members, and supporters of cults are not fully aware of the extent to which members may have been manipulated, exploited, even abused." The following is a list of social-structural, social-psychological, and interpersonal behavioral patterns commonly found in cultic environments which may be helpful in assessing a particular group or relationship. Not all of these points apply to each person affected by a cult or a legalistic church but many of them will.

1. Church members think they are the only ones who understand Scripture, as interpreted by the pastor or group leader. They consider those who reject their version of the truth inept, unlearned and/or lost; flawed in their understanding of what they consider to be the "real" Bible.
2. Fellowship outside the church is discouraged.
3. A haughty spirit of superiority may exist toward those who reject the church's teachings.
4. Reading Bible translations that the pastor (leader) does not approve of is discouraged or forbidden.
5. Church members are not allowed to question what is taught or the materials used. The leader's belief system, ideology and practices are considered as the Truth, as law. Questioning, doubt, and dissent are discouraged, even reprimanded.

6. Congregants become isolated from others and are watched over overtly or covertly.

7. Church members are discouraged or not allowed to read works written by those outside of the church's belief system.

8. Church participants may become distant toward friends and family; church attendance and the pastor's directives take first place.

9. Even when errors in Scripture are pointed out, church members will not reject the group leader's flawed analysis. Spiritual blindness and spiritual stagnation take place.

10. The leader (pastor) is not accountable to any authorities (unlike, for example, teachers, military commanders or ministers, priests, monks, and rabbis of mainstream religious denominations).

11. The church leader acts as the sole authority of the group.

12. Church members become overly zealous in attending their church and adhering to its teachings and "rules."

13. The guidance of the Holy Spirit is replaced with the guidance of the pastor/ministry claiming to be the voice of the Lord. Of course the church members are oblivious to this sleight of (spirit) and they mistakenly think they are being led by the Holy Spirit.

14. The group's questionable teachings cause a polarized us-versus-them mentality which may cause conflict with believers who do not accept extra-biblical teachings (concepts and practices claimed to be supported by or taught in the Bible, but are based on incorrect interpretations).

Daily Bible Study

Daily Bible study is very important and necessary in order to grow as a believer (Deuteronomy 17:19; Revelation 3:1). It is a good idea to designate a special place at home for Bible study. Be willing to invest in some good study materials: Bibles, Bible dictionaries. Always go to Scripture to check the validity of information offered in any books or commentaries and focus first and foremost on the Word of God. If you have a computer nearby, you may want to use some of the following resources during your study time:

http://www.blueletterbible.org - An excellent resource for online Bible study.

http://asv1901.com/ - A full online presentation of the excellent and reliable 1901 Standard American Version of the Bible.

http://www.biblegateway.com/ - An exceptional site for looking up Scripture, all popular Bible versions are included as well as passage translations in a number of foreign languages.

http://www.e-sword.net/ - A fast and effective way to study the Bible online.

http://www.bible-history.com/ - Bible Maps, Study Tools, Archeology, Ancient documents and much more.

http://www.bibletools.org/.

http://www.biblestudytools.com/concordances/strongs-exhaustive-concordance/-*Strong's Exhaustive Concordance Online.*

The Strongest Strong's Exhaustive Concordance of the Bible - James Strong LL.D., S.T.D., S.T.D. Fully Revised and Corrected by John R. Kohlenberger III and James A. Swanson.

Thayer's Greek-English Lexicon of the New Testament - Joseph Thayer.

Brown-Driver-Briggs Hebrew and English Lexicon - Francis Brown.

An Intermediate Greek-English Lexicon - Liddell and Scott.

Exegetical Fallacies - D.A. Carson

A Greek Lexicon of the New Testament and Other Early Christian Literature: Bauer, Arndt, Gingrich and Danker.

Greek-English Lexicon of the New Testament Based on Semantic Domains - Louw and Nida.

Holman Illustrated Bible Dictionary, 2003 Edition.

Lexical Semantics of the Greek New Testament, Louw and Nida.

Semantics of New Testament Greek, J.P. Louw.

I especially like the 1901 American Standard Version of the Bible, which is translated from the original tongues. I never do a Bible study without it, and I place that translation at the top of my Bible study list. The 1901 American Standard Version of the Bible (ASV), the King James, New King James, and the New American Standard should be part of a Bible study repertoire; but the Kings James and New King James translations have some problems to be aware of, which I have pointed out earlier in Chapter Nine, Chapter Twelve and also in this chapter.

When doing a Bible study be sure to cross-reference each of these translations by doing careful word studies and you will see, contrary to the *King James Only* advocates there are mistakes in that translation. We must do our own homework and not accept everything some well-meaning Bible teachers offer as fact. Let's take passages from the book of Mark and the book of Ephesians as an example:

Will the World Ever End?

"Heaven and earth will pass away, but My words will not pass away" (Mark 13:31).

Some analysts try to teach that the world will never end, but the Bible does not say that. The word "world" is not found in the original Greek text. For example, the King James translation of the Bible uses the word "world" in Ephesians 3:21:

"Unto him *be* the glory in the church by Christ Jesus throughout all ages, world without end. Amen."

But that is not an accurate translation. The old English version of the King James Bible stating "world without end" carried a meaning in that day of "endless duration." However, the word "world" should never have been inserted into the King James when indeed it is not found in the original Greek text. The 1901 American Standard Version of the Bible, translated out of the original tongues correctly teaches:

"Unto him *be* the glory in the church and in Christ Jesus unto all generations for ever and ever. Amen" (Ephesians 3:21).

The New American Standard Bible translation accurately states:

"To Him be the glory in the church and in Christ Jesus to all generations forever and ever" (Ephesians 3:21).

The New King James Bible has corrected and clarified the passage:

"To Him be the glory in the church by Christ Jesus to all generations, forever and ever. Amen" (Ephesians 3:21).

This type of misinterpretation of Scripture is a good example of how the intended meaning of a verse can be changed. Without careful study and research that goes into interpreting the meaning of a verse, the accurate and true meaning of Scripture is changed to take on the meaning of something else, entirely.

Many good audio Bibles are available today. It is good to read the Scriptures out loud, even speaking along with the narrator saying the verses together. I like to listen to Scripture when I am driving. It is also uplifting to listen to Scripture at home while doing chores or making dinner. Listening to Scripture helps keep our hearts and minds focused on the Lord giving us a strong foundation for knowing and sharing the Word of God. Repeating Scripture out loud as we read our Bibles is very helpful in grasping the meanings of the passages.

We should always pray before studying the Bible that the Holy Spirit will lead us and guide us. Have reference tools available as noted above (Bibles, a good variety of Bible dictionaries, concordances) to look up pertinent information regarding some of the following points:

1. Determine who the message is being given to and why.
2. Determine if the message is to be understood as being literal or symbolic; using the Golden Rule of Interpretation.
3. Determine the context (what is the subject).
4. Determine the dispensation and if the message is for us today.
5. Find as many passages dealing with the subject as you can.
6. Put together the message of all the passages to determine what is being said.
7. Give clear statements far more importance than unclear statements.
8. Base the message of an unclear statement on a clear one.

A basic hermeneutical principle that everyone must adhere to with no variation when studying Scripture is this:

Take everything literally unless the Scriptures say it is symbolic, or unless it is physically impossible for it to be literal or be fulfilled in a literal manner, with the exception of miracles.

An example to show how this principle works can be found in Revelation twelve:

"And there appeared another wonder in heaven; and behold a great red dragon, having seven heads and ten horns, and seven crowns upon his heads. And his tail drew the third part of the stars of heaven, and did cast them to the earth" (Revelation 12:3-4a).

There is not and there will never be a literal dragon with seven heads and ten horns. If there were such a creature it could not sweep a third of the stars in space and cast them down to earth. Therefore, the dragon and the stars are symbolic. In verse 9 it says the devil—who is called a "great dragon," and his angels were cast down to earth. We can determine from this that the devil is the dragon and the angels are the stars.

We also know from Daniel 8:9-11 that the "little horn" (Antichrist) casts some of the stars of heaven down to earth. These stars are fallen angels that followed the devil in his rebellion. We see from Daniel and Revelation that the devil and the Antichrist together cast down angels to earth. We know the "little horn" is the Antichrist because in verse 11 of Daniel 8 he claims to be equal to the "prince of the host" (Jesus Christ).

In 2 Thessalonians 2:4 we see the Antichrist will claim to be "God." In chapter nine of Revelation there are two separate groups of demonic creatures mentioned verses 9:1 and verses 11:16-19. These demonic creatures are real and not symbolic. It is not impossible for there to be creatures as depicted in these passages. They do not do things that are physically impossible for a creature to do.

Hunger and Thirst for the Word of God

Scripture teaches we should have a daily hunger and thirst for God and His Word (not substitutes such as commentaries or articles, etc.): Job 23:12; Deuteronomy 8:3; Psalm 42:1-2; 63:1 and 143:6. Hungering and thirsting for God and His Word means a person desires to know the Lord and have fellowship with Him. The way we do that is by spiritually feeding on and drinking in His Word.

The first way of drinking in His Word is by hearing Scripture; simply read the passages concerning hearing Scripture. Read them out loud. Then move on to reading Scripture, Bible study and memorization. Always pray first for wisdom and guidance from the Holy Spirit. Learning and studying the Word of God and prayer are closely linked together.

Hearing Scripture: Selective listening to: Sermons/teaching in church, radio, television, CDs, DVDs: Proverbs 8:34; Luke 8:15, 21; 11:28; James 1:22; Revelation 1:3.

Reading Scripture: Deuteronomy 17:19; Psalm 42:1-2; 63:1; 143:6; Revelation 1:3.

Bible study: Deuteronomy 8:3; Matthew 4:4; John 5:39; Acts 17:11 and 2 Timothy 2:15.

Memorization of Scripture: Deuteronomy 6:6; Psalm 37:31; 40:8; 119:11; Proverbs 2:1; 3:1; 3: 4:1; 22:17-18.

Meditation on Scripture: Joshua 1:8; Job 23:12; Psalm 1:2.

Holiness and obedience are two reasons we study the Bible: John 15:3; Romans 12:1-2; Ephesians 5:26; 6:14, 17; 2 Timothy 3:16-17; Titus 3:5; Joshua 1:8; 1 John 2:3-4.

Getting closer to and knowing our God and Savior is another reason to study the Bible (Jeremiah 9:24; Hosea 6:3; John 17:3; Philippians 3:10; Colossians 1:10; 2 Timothy 1:12; 1 John 2:3). Most people eat at least three meals a day. Must we be told to eat? Do most believers hear, read, study, memorize and *meditate* on Scripture three times a day? Should we not feed our souls as much or more than we feed our bodies? What about feeding our minds?

Do too many believers spend more time watching secular movies, television shows, participating in social media than seriously studying the Bible? Should not all believers be genuinely eager to read the letters that our God and Savior wrote to us in the Bible? Some believers read the New Testament but many do not read the Old Testament. Events recorded in the Old Testament were written for our benefit (1 Corinthians 10:6). We should carefully study the entire Bible from Genesis to Revelation. "For I shrank not from declaring unto you the whole counsel of God" (Acts 20:27).

The Importance of Discipleship

Every true, born-again believer is a disciple of Jesus the Messiah. We should all strive to live like disciples, but we need to learn and understand what that involves. Jesus commissioned His disciples to be witnesses to His resurrection, and to make "disciples of all nations."

"But ye shall receive power, when the Holy Spirit is come upon you: and ye shall be my witnesses both in Jerusalem, and in all Judaea and Samaria, and unto the uttermost part of the earth" (Acts 18).

"Go ye therefore, and make disciples of all the nations, baptizing them into the name of the Father and of the Son and of the Holy Spirit: teaching them to observe all things whatsoever I commanded you: and lo, I am with you always, even unto the end of the world" (Matthew 28:19-20).

When a person is truly saved, trusting solely in Jesus Christ, the Messiah, as Lord and Savior he or she is then considered one of His disciples. Although every believer is technically considered a disciple, one must attempt to live like a disciple: Pray often each day: Ephesians 6:18; Thessalonians 5:17. Read Scripture daily: Deuteronomy 17:19; Revelation 1:3. Listen to Scripture on a daily basis: Proverbs 4:1; 8:34; Luke 8:15, 21; 11:28; James 1:22; Revelation 1:3.

Engage in regular, careful Bible study: John 5:39; Acts 17:11; 2 Timothy 2:15. Cultivate relationships with other believers: Acts 2:42; 46-47; Hebrews 3:13; 10:24-25. Share your testimony with others when you feel led by the Holy Spirit: Acts 2:47; 1 Peter 3:15. Help others become disciples: Matthew 28:18b-20; Mark 16:15; 2 Timothy 2:2.

If a believer concentrates on the practices listed above he or she will become an effective disciple of Messiah Jesus. This does not happen quickly. It takes many years to grow in the Lord and become a strong disciple. But it starts with the daily discipline of being in prayer, focused study and application of the Word of God and regular fellowship with other believers. Learning and studying the Word of God and having a strong prayer life are closely linked together.

Some Basic Laws of Interpretation

As Taught by the Great Scholar, the Late Dr. David Cooper

The Golden Rule of Interpretation

Since the Scriptures are God-breathed and are very specific, there is only one way for us to arrive at the purpose which the Holy Spirit had in mind in giving. This meant exactly what He said. In order to understand the Scriptures, we must know the use of language: the grammar, the specific meaning of words, and the fundamental laws of speech, especially the principles which are characteristic of the Scriptures. Since the space is limited for this discussion let us look only at the most important and fundamental rules of hermeneutics, the most basic, and in need the all-inclusive one, of which is the *Golden Rule of Interpretation.*

Jesus gave the Golden Rule of conduct which is "All things therefore whatsoever ye would that men should do unto you, even so do ye also unto them: for this is the law and the prophets" (Matthew 7:12). This is a basic criterion in one's relation to his fellow-men. The *Golden Rule of Interpretation* is just as fundamental in the field of the interpretation of language as our Lord's precept is in the realm of old ethics and conduct.

Origen, a great Christian scholar who lived during the latter part of the second and in the first part of the third century of the Christian era, came under the influence of Greek philosophy in the form of Neoplatonism. He adopted some of the so-called principles of this philosophic system and evolved what has become known as the allegorical method of interpretation of the Word but claimed that in addition, there was this hidden, spiritual meaning. Everything to him was therefore allegorical.

He read into the Scriptures this so-called spiritual meaning and built up a mystical system of theology. This method of interpreting the Word wrought havoc in the early church and started what is known as "spiritualizing the Scriptures." Its baneful effects have been felt throughout the centuries. The Christian world has never entirely freed itself from the tentacles of this heathen, subjective approach to God's holy infallible Word.

The only antidote to this vicious method of handling the Bible is the principle called the Golden Rule of Interpretation: When the plain, obvious sense of Scripture makes common-sense, we are to seek no other sense. We are to stop there and are not to read subjectively into the record something that is foreign to the context.

The Word of God is spiritual and does not need our "doctoring" it in order to make it more so. If one man can read into a given contest his own ideas and claim that such is the significance of the passage, another can do the same thing and can read into the record *his* conception of its meaning. Whenever we adopt the spiritualizing method, we open the floodgates to every type of speculation, suggestion, and theorizing. We must not therefore go beyond the plain, literal meaning of the Scriptures unless the facts of the context indicate a deeper, hidden, or symbolic meaning.

When therefore such evidence is lacking, one must positively accept the literal meaning of the text. On the other hand, if there is absolute proof that the language is, for instance, symbolic, then we are to interpret the given passage in the light of the text.

On the other hand if there is absolute proof that the language is, for instance, symbolic, then we are to interpret the given passage in the light of all the evidence, not only of the immediate connection, but in the light of that which is found in parallel case—if there be such.

But suppose the plain, literal meaning does not make common sense. In that event we may be assured that, since the Scriptures do not make nonsense, a figurative or metaphorical sense is intended. Then we are to interpret such a passage in the light of the usage found in parallel cases.

Almost every word in all languages has not only a literal, primary, original meaning but has derived connotations. For instance in English there are listed as high as twenty-six meanings for a single word. This fact may be seen by a glance in an unabridged dictionary. Whenever the literal sense of a given word does not fit in with the facts of the connection, we are to select that definition which is in perfect accord and agreement with them.

But in every instance, let me emphasize, we are to take the primary, ordinary, usual, literal meaning if possible.

An abridged statement of this most important rule is: "When the plain sense of Scripture makes common sense, seek no other sense; therefore, take every word at its primary, ordinary, usual, literal meaning, unless the facts of the context indicate clearly otherwise." This rule assumes that all truth harmonizes that there are no discrepancies between accurate statements of facts.

But for those who wish the maxim stated in its unabridged form, I give it in the following words:

"When the plain sense of Scripture makes common sense, seek no other sense; therefore, take every word at its primary, ordinary, usual, literal meaning, unless the facts of the context indicate clearly otherwise."

If anyone follows this criterion, in the spirit and letter of the principle, he can never go wrong.

On the other hand, if he fails to follow it, he can never be right. (May I suggest that the reader memorize and master this rule in order that he may be governed thereby in all his study of the Word?) This principle is true, not only as it applies to the Bible, but also to any written document or oral conversation regarding any subject.

Law of First Mention

"The law of first mention" is another most important principle involved in the Scriptures. That is meant by it is that the first mention of any fundamental word or institution usually presents the general conception of the subject and its use throughout the Scriptures.

As an illustration of this law, I need only to call attention to the sacrifices that were required by the Lord from Cain and Abel. The very fundamental teaching concerning atonement for sin, with all its implications, in found in these sacrifices, as recorded in Genesis 4.

Once more, the promise and the covenant which God made with Abraham (Genesis 12:1-3) constitute the bold outline of all that is involved in the divine plan which runs through the Scriptures. It becomes therefore of paramount importance that one study words, doctrines, and institutions in their original, initial mention.

Interpretation and Application

As we have just seen in our study of the *Golden Rule of Interpretation,* we must seek diligently, by the application of this standard, to ascertain the exact thought of the speaker or writer whose message is studied. When this is learned, we can determine whether or not there is involved in the discussion some fundamental principle.

If there is such set forth in the given case, we are at liberty to apply it to a similar situation; but, before we must be certain that there is an analogy justifying such an application. It is at this crucial point that many mistakes are made. All too often efforts are made to see a spiritual lesson in a given Scripture and, without due consideration, to apply it to another case which only apparently is analogous.

If we are certain that we have discovered the fundamental, underlying principle in a given case, we are warranted in applying it to a like situation under similar circumstances; for one of the basic tenets of true science is that "like causes under like conditions produce like results."

My caution to everyone is that he be certain to discover the exact thought of the writer and that he be absolutely sure in making an application of the principle discovered to a similar situation. Such a procedure is legitimate and proper.

Law of Double Reference

There is what is known among Bible students as "the law of double reference of manifold fulfillment of prophecy." We find many applications of this principle.

The prophets constantly spoke of a local or current event, and, without giving any intimation of a change of scenery, began to describe a more remote and a greater one, which by far transcended the situation which gave rise to the prediction. This principle might be illustrated by a stereopticon which gives the dissolving effect.

One picture is thrown upon the screen. Presently it begins to fade and at the same time the dim outline of another begins to appear. By the time the first has faded, the second is in full view. The prophets often blended a prediction relating to the first coming of Christ with one foretelling the Second Advent. In such presentations the entire Christian Dispensation is passed over. One must master this rule if one is to understand the messages of the prophets.

The Law of Recurrence

The principle which obtains throughout the prophetic word is that which is known by Bible students as "the law of recurrence." According to the meaning of this phrase, after the prophets made a statement relative to something in the future, they often gave a fuller discussion covering the same ground but laying the emphasis in a different place. The second presentation is but supplemental to the first. It therefore clarifies the picture.

As an illustration of this principle, may I note Genesis 1 and 2? In chapter 1, we have a synopsis of the work of the six days of reconstruction. In chapter 2, however, the Holy Spirit gives a second discussion, especially regarding the creation of man. The first account relative to this miracle is found in 1:26-31.

In Genesis 2:7-25 is a second and a fuller description together with a record of his residence in the Garden of Eden. These two accounts are not to be explained upon the basis advanced by the destructive critics; that they came from two sources and are therefore contradictory; but upon the sound, fundamental principle of the law of recurrence.

Another illustration of this important law is found in the prophecy of Ezekiel 38 and 39, which foretells the invasion of Palestine by the nations constituting the great northeastern confederacy. (For the full discussion of this most important and timely theme, see the volume *When Gog's Armies Meet the Almighty*.) In chapter 38 the prophet gives the full description of this stupendous world-changing event.

In it he presents the general outline of the incidents that will at that time take place. In chapter 39 he simply covers the same ground speaking of the identical affairs but laying emphasis on different things. One must recognize that this duplicate account, given according to the principle of the law of recurrence, is but a second view of the one prediction.

John, in Revelation 17, 18, and 19 follows this same law. In chapter 16 he gives the outline of events as they occur during the second half of the Tribulation. When we reach the end of chapter 16, we are at the very close of that period; but in chapter 17 he goes back to the beginning of this second half of it and speaks of the overthrow of Babylon and harlot.

The facts of this chapter show that this interpretation is correct. Chapter 18 speaks of the literal city of Babylon, which is destroyed at the end of the Tribulation. In chapter 19 we read of the marriage supper of the Lamb, and Christ's coming all the way to earth at the conclusion of the Tribulation. Thus, when John pens these three chapters, after having given the outline of the second half of the Tribulation in chapter 16, he is simply following the law of recurrence.

This is a most important law, which finds many applications throughout the Scriptures. The Bible student should master this principle to the extent that he can recognize an application of it whenever he comes across it.

Comparing Scripture with Scripture

God gave His Word as He wanted us to have it, and as He wanted us to study and teach it. An investigation of the Scriptures shows that He only gave any portion of it as there was a demand for the enunciation of some new principle of the reiteration and the augmentation of one that He had already revealed.

A study of the life of our Lord shows that He often repeated Himself. We are told that circumstances alter cases. After all, people's experiences are more or less of a certain definite type. These and other facts show why it was necessary for God to repeat certain doctrines in sending messages to various people or groups or individuals.

The biblical writers, meeting a local and a similar situation, were forced to repeat many things. For instance, almost all the books of the New Testament either discuss, refer to, or at least hint at, the great fundamental teaching of regeneration of the soul by the Spirit of God. It was necessary for each writer in meeting the situation before him to refer to this fundamental spiritual phenomenon.

To one person or group it was necessary to discuss a certain phase of the doctrine; to another the same writer presented a different aspect of the same teaching. On one occasion, he stated it more fully than he did at another time. What is true regeneration is also correct of the various teachings of the Word of God.

In view of these facts, we can see how it was that the inspired writers discussed the same subject. If a person is wishing to understand thoroughly any one topic of the Scriptures, it becomes necessary for him to study what each writer has said on the subject. He must, as far as it is possible, get all the facts which called forth the explanation.

Moreover he must study it in the light of the facts of its context. When he has thus examined the various passages bearing upon a given question and has gleaned from each reference what is said, he can put all the information together and thus have a complete picture.

It is therefore necessary for everyone to compare scripture with scripture. In following this principle he must be absolutely certain that he views each passage in its proper perspective. When he does so, he will see that one account usually supplements another.

Examining Quotations in the Light of Both Contexts

In the New Testament we see many quotations taken from the Old. Whenever we find in the New such a quotation; if we are not familiar with the passage; we should immediately turn to the chapter from which it was taken. Then we should study the entire connection and be certain that we get the drift of thought of the original writer. Speaking figuratively, we must see the quotation in the original setting. When we have done this, we are to study the context of the New Testament in which this quotation is found. Frequently the application will throw light upon the passage in its original connection and vice versa.

Often we observe that a passage is applied in a certain way to something in the New Testament; and, when we examine all the facts, we see that the thing to which it is referred by the New Testament writer does not fill out the complete picture set forth in the Old Testament connection. In this event we must conclude that the thing to which it is applied in the New Testament is but a partial and an incomplete fulfillment of the original prediction and that God in His own good time will fulfill the passage to the very letter.

As an illustration of this principle, I may call attention to such passages as Isaiah 13 and 14 and Jeremiah 50 and 51. These chapters give five predictions concerning Babylon and it being destroyed. Then we look at the history of that city, we see that it was never overthrown in the manner or to the extent as set in these prophecies.

We do know from ancient history that it gradually declined in power and finally sank beneath the historical horizon. It was never destroyed as was foretold. We who believe the Word of God must conclude that Babylon will yet be rebuilt and demolished just as foretold by these men of God.

This is confirmed by Revelation 18. I could give numerous examples of this principle, but these suffice. Let us therefore be careful in studying quotations that we examine both contexts and arrive at the definite, specific idea of the inspired writer.

Hebrew Poetry

Thought-rhyme was the fundamental idea of Hebrew poetry. No effort was made at meter, verse, and rhyme as we have in modern poetry. What is Hebrew parallelism? The answer is this: Two statements are made relative to a given matter, one of which is made by the selection of certain words. This or a similar idea is repeated by the choice of different terms. The second, therefore, is supplemental to the first and becomes a comment upon it. Sometimes one of the statements is in literal language, whereas the other is more pictorial and graphic; but each supplements the other.

Upon this simple basis all Hebrew poetry was built. Contrasts were expressed as we see in the book of Proverbs, which is pure poetry. Frequently three parallel statements, each supplementing the others, were employed. These fundamental conceptions were worked out by the poets and came to involve an entire composition such as one of the psalms. One must however understand this fundamental conception in order to comprehend the poetical books of the Scriptures.

Symbolic Language

All peoples, both ancient and modern, have symbols. The Hebrews had theirs. Those appearing in the Scriptures however are of divine origin. In fact, the Tabernacle and the Temple, with all of their ceremonial services, were typical or symbolic of the realities which we have in Christ. That they had such a significance if set forth clearly In the New Testament. The book of Hebrews especially interprets the spiritual significance of the ritualism of the Old Testament.

As one examines the types and shadows of the Scriptures, one must be extremely careful not to read into the sacred text something that is not there. A person will do well if he takes as symbolic and typical only those things that are thus recognized by the inspired writers.

Untold damage has been done from time to time by overly-zealous people in their attempts to see a typical or a symbolic meaning in certain persons or things in the Scriptures. The safest rule by which to be guided on this point may be stated thus: Recognize only those things as typical or symbolic which are thus designated in the Scriptures, and never give to any passage a typical meaning unless the Scriptures so indicate.

To illustrate the point, let us look at an example or two. Joseph, we are often told, is a type of Christ. Isaac's taking Rebekah as his bride is also a type of Christ's taking His Bride, the Church. What inspired writer gives any intimation to this effect? I have never seen anything in the Scriptures to warrant these positions. I admit that there are striking similarities in the cases; but analogies are not equivalent to a "thus saith the Lord."

We do well, therefore, to have Scriptural authority for whatever we say. One can, by allowing his imagination to run wild, see that a certain person or thing in the Old Testament is typical of something in the New. Another person, looking at the same thing, will see a different signification. Thus there are untold possibilities of speculation and error, which are dangerous whenever there is not a "thus saith the Lord" for a given position.

God has chosen certain things as symbols. For instance, beasts, as we learn from Daniel 7, are employed as emblems of world kingdoms. Whenever, therefore, a beast is the word used in the Scriptures and the facts of the context show that it has this metaphorical sense, one must understand that it signifies a civil government. God never mixes His symbols.

Again, a pure, chaste virgin is used as a symbol of the true Church. A harlot represents a false ecclesiasticism. God has interpreted these symbols. Man should not attach any signification to them other than that which was given by Him. I might further illustrate this principle by calling attention to the Lord's Supper.

The loaf represents the body of Jesus, whereas the fruit of the vine is symbolic of His blood. Whenever we see these emblems, we know their significance and do not attempt to read into them any idea other than that which the Lord Jesus gave them. Whenever we come to a symbol we must therefore seek the divine interpretation of the same and never deviate from that meaning.

Figurative Language

The language of all peoples seem to have begun largely with figures of speech — at least primitive writing indicates this position. It is by comparison that we appreciate and understand things. Thus figures have remained in our language and adorn it greatly. In fact, it is most difficult for us to speak without using some figures of speech and how they are used in order to understand what the biblical writers meant.

The fact that a figurative expression occurs in a given passage is no warrant for one's taking its meaning and forcing it upon another passage unless the facts of the given context show that the same figure was used in a like manner. To be more specific, let me call attention to the expression found in Ephesians regarding Christ's "having cleansed it [church] by the washing of water with the Word" (Ephesians 5:26).

This statement is figurative language. We must not force this metaphorical sense upon another passage, which might in some way resemble this one passage, unless the facts of the latter context permit such an interpretation.

Let us always bear in mind that figurative language, though ornate and beautiful, stands for definite realities. It is therefore necessary for one to understand the figure and see the reality signified in order to comprehend the message wherever such usage is employed.

Obscure Passages Must Be Interpreted In the Light of Plain Ones

Whenever anyone sees that a passage is capable of more than one interpretation -- viewed in the light of all the facts of the connection—he must select that translation which accords with plain statements found in other portions of the Word when rightly interpreted. As an illustration of this principle, I may call attention to Psalm 45:6: "Thy throne, O God, is for ever and ever . . ."

In the original text of this statement there are only four words. Nevertheless, they can be rendered grammatically to make four or five translations. By supplying different words, the number of renderings can be multiplied. This thing has been done by certain ones who have been unwilling to accept the plain meaning. But our one concern is, "What did the psalmist have in mind when he by the Spirit of God used these words?"

One must study the entire psalm in order to see the proper connection; then he must compare all the facts discovered with statements found in other places which are capable of only one interpretation.

It is of utmost importance that one observes this rule. The assumption lying underneath is that all truth harmonizes. Whenever there are any seeming discrepancies, the trouble lies with our non-comprehension of the data, or lack of the facts.

Studying the Exact Grammar

In the English language there are eight parts of speech. These, taken together, constitute language. Each of them has a definite, specific use and relation to other parts of speech. It becomes absolutely necessary, if one is to arrive at the exact meaning of a word, that he knows grammar, since each part of speech has a definite purpose and since words likewise have accurate definitions. One therefore must, if he is to arrive at the exact idea which the Holy Spirit had in mind, have an adequate knowledge of grammar and the meaning of words.

By conservative scholars, the grammatical-historic principle of interpretation is the only one upon which a person can afford to rely. What is meant by this term? A person must acquire, if possible, the historical data concerning any statement in order to see it in its proper perspective.

He must, therefore, know the writer, the one to whom a document was sent, for what purpose it was written, and under what conditions in order to evaluate properly the message. He must also know the grammar thoroughly and the significance of language. With such definite information in hand, one can, by the aid of the Holy Spirit, understand, as a rule, the message I therefore accept the correctness of this method of exegesis.

The Meanings of Words

The student should have a good English dictionary at hand when he studies the Scriptures - unless he has an adequate idea of the vocabulary that is used in the Bible. If a person will only look in an unabridged dictionary of the English language, he will see that some words have many meanings or shades of ideas. This statement being true, one must know these various definitions in order to comprehend rightly the exact meaning of a given passage.

Though I am speaking simply from the English point of view, all Greek and Hebrew students know that the same principles apply with reference to the original text. Whenever a word does have a number of meanings, we must select that one which will accord with all the facts of a given context, and which will not clash with any other plain statement of truth.

The Difference Between Biblical And Present-Day Terminology

Our English dictionaries give the current meaning of words as they are employed now by the best speakers and writers. They also give colloquial usages. The Bible employs a certain definite usage that was current when the Scriptures were given. Words sometimes now have a meaning entirely different from what they had when our translation was made or when spoken originally.

For instance, a prophet was simply a spokesman from God who delivered a message to the people. Sometimes he discussed things past; on other occasion, matters regarding things present in his day; and often those things lying in the future. At the present time, the word, "prophetic," as we have already noticed, is largely used with reference to future things.

There are many changes that have taken place in our language. This fact demands that we compare Scripture with Scripture in order to see the usage to which a term was applied then. We must not therefore read back into the Scriptures definitions of words as they are being used today; because, as started, practices have been introduced and changes have been made which have definitely determined present-day usage.

We cannot therefore afford to read back into the Scriptures ideas and definitions of words as employed today unless we see from all the facts that the current meaning is in the conformity with the biblical usage.

The Revised Version (American Standard Version) puts the original meaning of the Word of God in our current vernacular. It is a most excellent translation and presents the message of the original text more nearly accurately than former official versions. For this reason I [Dr. Cooper] always prefer using the Revised Version (American Standard Version 1901).

In Conclusion

The Assurance of God's Saving Grace

How Can I Be Saved?

How does all of this history and prophecy surrounding God's chosen nation—Israel, and today's world events affect you? Yeshua Ha Mashiach, Jesus the Christ, made some startling statements when He was on planet Earth. He assured us that we could have eternal life and spend all of eternity in a place so incredible that even John the revelator struggled to describe it; as there are no words to fully convey the breathtaking majesty and magnificence of what he was shown. (So much for those who claim to have been to heaven and back, John 3:13; 1:18).

The apostle Paul was forbidden to speak about what he saw in heaven (2 Corinthians 12:4). Those in the Bible—Ezekiel, Isaiah, and the apostle John each had visions of the very throne room of heaven and wrote about what they saw and heard. Those in the Bible who wrote about seeing heaven were expressly commanded by God to do so and were carried along by the Spirit of God as they wrote (2 Peter 1:21).

> The relatively brief accounts they each gave are part of the God-breathed text. The Almighty Himself had those men record that information for our benefit in the precise words that He chose. No extra biblical account of heaven can legitimately make that claim. Heaven is real, hallucinations are not. Not one biblical person brought back from the dead ever gave a recorded account of his or her postmortem experience in the realm of departed souls. (*The Glory of Heaven*, John MacArthur, pp. 38, 39)

When a believer dies, Scripture teaches: "Absent from the body, present with the Lord" (2 Corinthians 4:8); there is no other place to go if you are a believer. And Scripture makes is abundantly clear that those who are not saved go to a frightening place called hell. (Hell is referenced in the Bible repeatedly—dozens of times, in both Old and New Testaments.) Accounts of those who claim to have been to heaven seem to always denote "experiences" of some sort very much centered on themselves.

But the passage is clear, "We are confident, yes, well pleased rather to be absent from the body and to be *present with the Lord.*" So where do those who claim to have had heaven visions really go? What are these subjective ideas and experiences that go beyond God's inerrant Word?

The mind is certainly capable of hallucinations and imaginary visions similar to being in a dream state, even imagining communicating with the dead (demonic spirits) while in their supposed visionary state, which is strictly forbidden in Scripture (Deuteronomy 18:10-12).

Paul spoke of how he was humbled by God after his experience and did not bring attention to himself (1 Corinthians 4-6), but reluctantly mentioned his experience fourteen years later in a third person narrative and did not boast of his experience or make it a public extravaganza (2 Corinthians 12:2-7). All the glory in the biblical accounts were given to God and not to the visionary. These were not personal random revelations based on a death or near death experience; they were God-breathed, God-directed accounts carried along by the Holy Spirit.

I have recently read the disturbing news about the huge bestseller, *The Boy Who Came Back from Heaven.* Tragically, this fraud will place all of the Christian community in a very negative light.

Tyndale House, a major Christian publisher, has announced that it will stop selling *The Boy Who Came Back from Heaven*, by Alex Malarkey and his father, Kevin Malarkey.

The best-selling book, first published in 2010, describes what Alex experienced while he lay in a coma after a car accident when he was 6 years old. The coma lasted two months, and his injuries left him paralyzed, but the subsequent spiritual memoir with its assuring description of "Miracles, Angels, and Life Beyond This World" became part of a popular genre of "heavenly tourism," which has been controversial among orthodox Christians.

Earlier this week, Alex recanted his testimony about the afterlife. In an open letter to Christian bookstores posted on the Pulpit and Pen Web site, Alex states flatly: "I did not die. I did not go to heaven."

Referring to the injuries that continue to make it difficult for him to express himself, Alex writes, "Please forgive the brevity, but because of my limitations I have to keep this short...I said I went to heaven because I thought it would get me attention. When I made the claims that I did, I had never read the Bible. People have profited from lies, and continue to. They should read the Bible, which is enough. The Bible is the only source of truth. Anything written by man cannot be infallible."

We truly are living in the time Paul described in 2 Timothy 3:2-5:

"For men will be lovers of themselves, lovers of money, boasters, proud, blasphemers, disobedient to parents, unthankful, unholy, unloving, unforgiving, slanderers, without self-control, brutal, despisers of good, traitors, headstrong, haughty, lovers of pleasure rather than lovers of God, having a form of godliness but denying its power. And from such people turn away!"

When Christ came to this earth He came on a rescue mission. After Adam and Eve had fallen into the serpent's trap, God's perfect plan for humanity was thwarted and a curse fell upon mankind. The only solution was to find a way to reconcile mankind to God. Jesus the Christ came to die, to take all the world's sins upon Himself. He also has given every man and woman free will to choose to follow Him or reject Him. By accepting Christ as our Savior and Lord, turning away from our sins and repenting—we are given a new lease on life.

Jesus explained to Nicodemus that in order to enter heaven each person must be born-again spiritually. When we sincerely invite Jesus Christ into our lives and truly repent, we are created anew in Christ (spiritually) and we are born-again by the Spirit of God. The Holy Spirit immediately comes and dwells within each believer and is reconciled to God from his or her lost state.

"Wherefore if any man is in Christ, he is a new creature: the old things are passed away; behold, they are become new" (2 Corinthians 5:17).

Jesus came into the world as a Jew. Israel was where He served and ministered. Israel is where He will rule and reign from after His Second Coming on a new rejuvenated earth. We all have a choice to make. We either believe Him and all the incredible prophecies that have come to pass, and those that are soon to be fulfilled or we go into denial and refuse His free gift of salvation offered by the Creator and King of the universe.

Pride was the root cause of Adam and Eve's sin, and pride is still the root of nearly all sins. Will you choose Jesus the Savior or let pride rule you straight into a path of eternal destruction? If you have never made a serious and lasting commitment to Jesus Christ and received Him as your Lord and Savior you can do so right now. This world is on a collision course with God and He is the One who will be standing when all the evil forces of the world come against Him and are destroyed at the final battle at Armageddon.

Which side do you want to be on? The side that is destroyed and sentenced to an eternity in a frightening destination: Hell and the lake of fire? Or will you come to a realization of the tremendous gift the Lord is offering you – a new glorified body and eternal life with Him and all the blessings that come with being a child of the true and living God?

Tomorrow is promised to no one. Your life could end today. Are you prepared to leave this life and face eternity? Eternity exists for everyone. Where we will spend it is the clincher. Christ made it abundantly clear that only through Him can anyone enter into the kingdom of heaven.

> "Jesus said to him, 'I am the way, and the truth, and the life. No one comes to the Father except through me'" (John 14:6).

> "And there is salvation in no one else; for there is no other name under heaven that has been given among men by which we must be saved" (Acts 4:12).

> "Whoever denies the Son does not have the Father; the one who confesses the Son has the Father also" (1 John 2:23).

> "And this is the testimony: that God has given us eternal life, and this life is in His Son" (1 John 5:11).

> "For God so loved the world that He gave His only begotten Son, that whoever believes in Him should not perish but have everlasting life. For God did not send His Son into the world to condemn the world, but that the world through Him might be saved.

> He who believes in Him is not condemned; but he who does not believe is condemned already, because he has not believed in the name of the only begotten Son of God" (John 3:16-18).

Jesus Christ is the only possible way to enter into the sinless presence of the only and true holy God of the Bible. That is why God the Father sent His

Son so we would all have a chance to be redeemed and reconciled unto Him. Please think carefully. History as we have known it is coming to a fast, sudden halt. Be sure you are on the winning side with Christ. Don't fall for the lie that the Bible is a book of myths and that there is no such place as hell. Once you take your last breath it will be too late to choose Jesus Christ over an eternity without Him.

You can decide to let go of the ways of the world right now and live according to the Scriptures. Choose to receive Christ as your Lord and Savior and begin to have a personal relationship with Him. A relationship with Christ is not about rituals and only going to church; it is about having a regular prayer life with Him, reading the Bible and being led by the Holy Spirit to live our lives.

Nevertheless, it is important to connect with other believers for support and fellowship. If you don't know any believers try to find a church in your area that actually teaches the Bible, preferably verse-by-verse. Many churches today are Christian in name only without a biblical foundation, so we must be very careful where we get involved. We can have a close, personal relationship with the Lord when we are born-again by the Holy Spirit and come to repentance. The spiritual rebirth Jesus spoke of is necessary in order to be saved, in order to have a personal relationship with Him, and to be able to understand the Word of God through the guidance of the Holy Spirit.

"But the natural man [unsaved person] does not receive the things of the Spirit of God, for they are foolishness to him; nor can he know them because they are spiritually discerned" (1 Corinthians 2:14).

"Jesus answered and said to him, 'Truly, truly, I say to you, unless one is born-again he cannot see the kingdom of God.' Nicodemus said to Him, "How can a man be born when he is old? He cannot enter a second time into his mother's womb and be born, can he?'

Jesus answered, 'Truly, truly, I say to you, unless one is born of water and the Spirit, he cannot enter into the kingdom of God. That which is born of the flesh is flesh, and that which is born of the Spirit is spirit. Do not marvel that I said to you, 'You must be born-again'" (John 3:3-7).

"The Lord is not slow about His promise, as some count slowness, but is patient toward you, not wishing for any to perish but for all to come to repentance" (2 Peter 3:9).

When we sincerely accept Christ and receive Him as our Lord and Savior, we are filled with God's Holy Spirit and are spiritually "born-again." Water baptism is a public testimony showing we have placed our faith in Jesus. Being baptized as a child, a ritual performed by some religious groups will not get us into heaven. Neither will church or synagogue attendance.

Each person is personally accountable to God and must make his or her own decision to either accept or reject God's saving grace. God gave us free will. It is up to each of us to choose eternal life with God or eternal torment and separation from God. Choose Jesus Christ and you will be saved forever.

[Jesus said,] "Truly, truly, I say to you, he who hears My word, and believes Him who sent Me, has eternal life, and does not come into judgment, but has passed out of death into life" (John 5:24).

You can come to faith in Christ, and be born-again by praying a personal prayer of repentance and faith. The words you use are not important. Your sincerity and genuine commitment to the Lord is what counts. Saying a prayer then walking away and forgetting about the Lord does not count for salvation. The sincere intent of your heart is what matters to God. There has to be true *repentance*, a true change of heart—a repentant heart that will seek Him first and leave behind habits and lifestyles that are contrary to His will and His teachings. The following Scripture expresses the heart confession necessary in order to be saved:

"That if you confess, with your mouth Jesus as Lord and believe in your heart that God has raised Him from the dead, you will be saved; for with the heart man believes, resulting in righteousness, and with the mouth he confesses, resulting in salvation" (Romans 10:9-10).

If you are not sure what to say, follow this simple heartfelt prayer (but you must mean it with all your heart), truly repent and place God first in your life:

Heavenly Father, I accept Your Son, Jesus Christ, as my Lord and Savior. I believe in His death, burial and resurrection. I realize I have made many mistakes in my life. I have been confused and deceived by the lies, of this world. Please forgive me. I ask you to come into my life, regenerate me and fill me with your Holy Spirit so I can be born-again and saved by your grace.

I want this to be a new beginning and have a close, personal relationship with you. I want to learn more about you through prayer and careful Bible study. Help me to truly repent and live my life in a way that is pleasing to you. Please write my name into the Book of Life. I pray this in the name of Jesus the Christ (Yeshua Ha Mashiach), the Messiah of Israel and of the world. Amen.

If you have made a genuine, new commitment to Messiah Jesus by receiving Him as your Lord and Savior, this is the most important day of your life. It is also the most significant event of your life. You have now become an heir of God. It is through Christ's strength in you that you will be able to move forward and overcome obstacles that may come your way.

Growing in the Lord is a daily surrender of your will for what God's will is for your life. After all, He is now your Heavenly Father (Abba), in Hebrew, which means daddy. He wants what is best for you. Go to Him with all your concerns and pour your heart out to Him. Everything that is important to you matters to God. Nothing is too small or insignificant.

"Behold, now is the accepted time; behold, now is the day of salvation" (2 Corinthians 6:1b).

Appendix A

Who Is Involved in the Gog-Magog Invasion?

Exactly which nations will participate in the Gog- Magog war cannot be firmly established—no one but God Himself knows for sure. But we have some historical facts and Scripture passages which give us strong clues. We know from Genesis 10:2, that *Magog* was the second son of Japheth. Gomer, Tubal, and Meshech were also sons of Japheth. Togarmah was a grandson of Japheth, being the third son of Gomer. Magog's land was located in what is today called "Caucasus" and the adjoining "Steppes." Rosh, Meshech and Tubal were called "Scythians" by the ancients.

They roamed as nomads in the country around and north of the Black and Caspian Seas, and were known as the wildest barbarians. Josephus, the great Jewish historian of the first century said, *Magog* founded those that from him were named Magogites, but who by the *Greeks* were called Scythians." Secular history books trace the fierce Scythian people who lived in the northern regions above the Caucasus Mountains, as the forerunners of modern Russia.

Gesenius, a great Hebrew scholar of the early 19th century identified "Meshech" as Moscow, the capital of modern Russia in Europe. He identifies "Tubal" as Tobolsk, the earliest province of Asiatic Russia to be colonized, and also the name of the city where Peter the Great built the old fortress after the pattern of the Kremlin at Moscow.

The Biblical and Theological Dictionary states: "Magog signifies the country or people, and *Gog,* the king of that country; the general name of the northern nations of Europe and Asia, or the districts north of the Caucasus of Mt. Taurus" (p. 417).

The first in the list of those allied with Russia is **Persia**. Of these, Persia is the easiest to identify. Ezekiel at that time was living in the capital of Persia which was ancient Babylon. It had been overthrown by the Medes and the Persians. The Persians came up from Iran and overran all of what is modern Iraq, and made Babylon their capital. This is seen very clearly through the book of Daniel; thus Persia would be modern day Iraq and Iran.

The second name associated with Russia is **Cush,** who, according to Genesis 10:6, is listed as the first son of Ham. His name is mentioned in Ezekiel 30:4-5 but is there rendered "Ethiopia." Again, Gesenius, who is recognized as one of the great scholars of history, summarized all of the evidence as follows: 1) The Cushites were black men, 2) They migrated first to the Arabian Peninsula and then across the Red Sea to the area south of Egypt, and 3. "Indeed all the nations that have sprung from Cush and enumerated in Genesis 10:7 are to be sought in Africa." So, with little doubt, we can identify Cush as Ethiopia.

Put is the third nation appearing on the list. The first settlement of Put was called Libya by the ancient historians, Josephus and Pliny. The Greek translation of the Hebrew Old Testament, called the *Septuagint,* translates Put as Libya but would probably today include the North African Arab nations such as Algeria, Tunisia and Morocco.

The late Dr. David L. Cooper identified Put as Somaliland east and north of Ethiopia. Thus Cush and Put are identified by the best scholars as those nations including Ethiopia, Somaliland, and the nations of North Africa all of which are Muslim and largely anti-Israeli.

Gomer, the fourth ally, was the eldest son of Japheth and the father of Ashkenaz. Gesenius speaks of Gomer as being Ashkenaz, "The proper name of a region and a nation in Northern Asia, sprang from the Sumerians who are the ancient people of Gomer. The modern Jews understand it to be Germany, and called that country by this Hebrew name." In the Talmud, Gomer is Germani—thus the Germans. It is interesting to note that the term *Ashkenaz* has come to designate Jews from Europe-originally those in the Rhine Valley—as distinguished from the term *Sephardic* used for Jews from Spain and North Africa. That the descendants of Gomer moved northward and established themselves in Germany seems to be an established fact stated leading Bible scholar, Dr. Arno Gaebelein, in his commentaries written in the early 1900s.

The fifth ally of Russia is said to be **Togarmah**, which is generally identified as Turkey or Armenia. Of this people, the late prophecy scholar, Dr. Harry Rimmer stated, "Geographically, Togarmah has always been the land we call Armenia. It is so named in the records of Assyria. Indeed all Armenian literature refers to the land and its people as the House of Togarmah, they hold an unbroken tradition which antedates their literature by centuries, linking them to Togarmah the grandson of Japheth." Gesenius stated, "They are the northern nation and country abounding in horses and mules." He continued by saying, "some of the Sons of Togarmah founded Armenia according to their own claim today."

While Turkey is a member of NATO, and thus presently allied with the West, it is also an Islamic religion country, and more so in 2016—considering the events that have transpired under President Tayyip Erdogan's heavy-handed Islamist domination over that nation. It seems clear that Russia will be allied with the Islamic nations in this invasion.

Identifying the western powers certainly includes England. The *merchants of Tarshish, with the young lions thereof,* would be those nations that have been colonized out of England, such as the United States and Canada. Sheba and Dedan we would identify as being that area in the southern part of Arabia such as Yemen and Oman. Yemen is strategically located at the very tip of the Red Sea and Oman controls the crucial Strait of Hormuz at the mouth of the Persian Gulf.

Where the Scripture says the prince of Rosh, it is referring to the old name for Russia. The prophet identifies two cities in Russia—Meshech and Tubal. The name for the city of Moscow used to be Meshech. Tubal would be the present city of Tobolsk. Although there was a city in Russia named Leningrad, the capital of Russia did not become Leningrad, even though Lenin was one of the founders of the Communist Party. Stalin, a leader of Russia, had a city named after him (Stalingrad), but it also did not become the capital of Russia. In 1918, St. Petersburg, the former capital of Russia, became Leningrad, at which time the capital was moved to present-day Moscow. Thus, it is very interesting to note that this prophecy is exact in all of its minute details.

Gog will be the future ruler of Russia. (Or he may already be in power right now making strong inroads into the Middle East.) We have seen in many instances that the Kremlin changes its leadership suddenly. Things happen so quickly these days. Gog could become the dictator of Russia overnight. As many other countries have done, the capital of Russia has been changed several times in its history. It is curious to note that at various periods of time the capital has been called *Volgograd.* Note that the word "gog" appears in the center of this name.

Appendix B

A.T. Robertson's Notes on 2 Thessalonians 2:1-3

Robertson's Word Pictures in the New Testament

Verse 1

Touching the coming of our Lord Jesus Christ (*υπερ της παρουσιας του Κυριου 'ημων' Ιησου Χριστου — huper tēs parousias tou Kuriou 'hēmōn' Iēsou Christou*). For *ερωτωμεν — erōtōmen* to beseech, see note on 1 Thessalonians 4:1; 1 Thessalonians 5:12. *υπερ — Huper* originally meant over, in behalf of, instead of, but here it is used like *περι — peri* around, concerning as in 2 Thessalonians 1:4; 1 Thessalonians 3:2; 1 Thessalonians 5:10, common in the papyri (Robertson, *Grammar*, p. 632).

For the distinction between *Παρουσια Επιπανεια — ParousiaΑποκαλυπσις — Epiphaneia* (Epiphany), and *Παρουσια — Apokalupsis* (Revelation) as applied to the Second Coming of Christ see Milligan on *Thessalonian Epistles*, pp. 145-151, in the light of the papyri. *επιπανεια — Parousia* lays emphasis on the **presence** of the Lord with his people, *αποκαλυπσις — epiphaneia* on his **manifestation** of the power and love of God, *και ημων επισυναγωγης επ αυτον — apokalupsis* on the **revelation** of God's purpose and plan in the Second Coming of the Lord Jesus.

And our gathering together unto him (*kai hēmōn episunagōgēs ep' auton*). A late word found only in 2 Maccabees. 2:7; 2 Thessalonians 2:1; Hebrews 10:25 till Deissmann (*Light from the Ancient East*, p. 103) found it on a stele in the island of Syme, off Caria, meaning "collection." Paul is referring to the Rapture, mentioned in 1 Thessalonians 4:15-17, and the being forever with the Lord thereafter. Cf. also Matthew 24:31; Mark 13:27.

Verse 2

To the end that (*εις το — eis to*). One of Paul's favorite idioms for purpose, *εις το — eis to* and the infinitive.

Ye be not quickly shaken (*μη ταχεως σαλευτηναι υμας — mē tacheōs saleuthēnai humas*). First aorist passive infinitive of *σαλευω — saleuō* old verb to agitate, to cause to totter like a reed (Matthew 11:7), the earth (Hebrews 12:26). Usual negative *μη — mē* and accusative of general reference *υμας — humas* with the infinitive.

From your mind (*απο του νοος — apo tou noos*). Ablative case of nous, mind, reason, sober sense, "from your witte" (Wycliffe), to "keep their heads."

Nor yet be troubled (*μηδε τροεισται — mēde throeisthai*). Old verb *τροεω — throeō* to cry aloud (from *τροος — throos* clamour, tumult), to be in a state of nervous excitement (present passive infinitive, as if it were going on), "a continued state of agitation following the definite shock received (*σαλευτηναι — saleuthēnai*)" (Milligan).

Either by spirit (*μητε δια πνευματος — mēte dia pneumatos*). By ecstatic utterance (1 Thessalonians 5:10). The nervous fear that the coming was to be at once prohibited by *μηδε — mēde* Paul divides into three sources by *μητε μητε μητε — mēte, μητε δια λογου — mētemēte δι επιστολης ως δι ημων — mēte* No individual claim to divine revelation (the gift of prophecy) can justify the statement.

Or by word (*ως οτι ενεστηκεν η ημερα του κυριου — mēte dia logou*). Oral statement of a conversation with Paul (Lightfoot) to this effect **as from us**. An easy way to set aside Paul's first Epistle by report of a private remark from Paul.

Or by epistle as from us (ενιστημι — *mēte di' epistolēs hōs di' hēmōn*). In 1 Thessalonians 4:13-5:3 Paul had plainly said that Jesus would come as a thief in the night and had shown that the dead would not be left out in the Rapture. But evidently someone claimed to have a private epistle from Paul which supported the view that Jesus was coming at once, **as that the day of the Lord is now present** (τα ενεστωτα — *hōs hoti enestēken hē hēmera tou kuriou*). Perfect active indicative of τα μελλοντα — *enistēmi* old verb, to place in, but intransitive in this tense to stand in or at or near. So "is imminent" (Lightfoot). The verb is common in the papyri. Paul hoped for the return of Christ but did not claim that Christ's return was imminent.

In 1 Corinthians 3:22; Romans 8:38 we have a contrast between ως οτι — *ta enestōta* the things present, and *ta mellonta* the things future (to come). The use of *hōs hoti* may be disparaging here, though that is not true in 2 Corinthians 5:19. In the *Koiné* [28928]š it comes in the vernacular to mean simply "that" (Moulton, *Proleg.*, p. 212), but that hardly seems the case in the N.T. (Robertson, *Grammar*, p. 1033). Here it means "to wit that," though "as that" or "as if" does not miss it much. Certainly it flatly denies that by conversation or by letter he had stated that the Second Coming was immediately "at hand."

It is this misleading assertion that accounts both for the increased discouragement of the faint-hearted to encourage whom Paul writes 1:3-2:17, and for the increased meddlesomeness of the idle brethren to warn whom Paul writes 3:1-18 (Frame). It is enough to give one pause to note Paul's indignation over this use of his name by one of the over-zealous advocates of the view that Christ was coming at once.

It is true that Paul was still alive, but, if such a "pious fraud" was so common and easily condoned as some today argue, it is difficult to explain Paul's evident anger. Moreover, Paul's words should make us hesitate to affirm that Paul definitely proclaimed the early return of Jesus. He hoped for it undoubtedly, but he did not specifically proclaim it as so many today assert and accuse him of misleading the early Christians with a false presentation.

Verse 3

Let no man beguile you in any wise (*μη τις υμας εχαπατησηι κατα μηδενα τροπον — mē tis humas exapatēsēi kata mēdena tropon*). First aorist active subjunctive of *εχαπαταω — exapataō* (old verb to deceive, strengthened form of simple verb *απαταω — apataō*) with double negative (*μη τισ μηδενα — mē tis, mēdena*) in accord with regular Greek idiom as in 1 Corinthians 16:11 rather than the aorist imperative which does occur sometimes in the third person as in Mark 13:15 (*μη καταβατω — mē katabatō*). Paul broadens the warning to go beyond conversation and letter. He includes "tricks" of any kind. It is amazing how gullible some of the saints are when a new deceiver pulls off some stunts in religion.

For it will not be (*οτι — hoti*). There is an ellipse here of *ουκ εσται — ouk estai* (or *γενησεται — genēsetai*) to be supplied after *οτι — hoti* Westcott and Hort make an anacoluthon at the end of 2 Thessalonians 2:4. The meaning is clear. *οτι — Hoti* is causal, because, but the verb is understood. The Second Coming not only is not "imminent," but will not take place before certain important things take place, a definite rebuff to the false enthusiasts of 2 Thessalonians 2:2.

Except the falling away come first (*εαν μη ελτηι η αποστασια πρωτον — ean mē elthēi hē apostasia prōton*). Negative condition of the third class, undetermined with prospect of determination and the aorist subjunctive. *Αποστασια — Apostasia* is the late form of *αποστασις — apostasis* and is our word apostasy. Plutarch uses it of political revolt and it occurs in 1 Maccabees

2:15 about Antiochus Epiphanes who was enforcing the apostasy from Judaism to Hellenism. In Joshua 22:22 it occurs for rebellion against the Lord.

It seems clear that the word here means a religious revolt and the use of the definite article (η — *hē*) seems to mean that Paul had spoken to the Thessalonians about it. The only other New Testament use of the word is in Acts 21:21 where it means apostasy from Moses. It is not clear whether Paul means revolt of the Jews from God, of Gentiles from God, of Christians from God, or of the apostasy that includes all classes within and without the Body of Christians. But it is to be **first** ($\pi\rho\omega\tau o\nu$ — *prōton*) before Christ comes again. Note this adverb when only two events are compared (cf. Acts 1:1).

And the man of sin be revealed, the son of perdition ($\kappa\alpha\iota$ $\alpha\pi o\kappa\alpha\lambda\upsilon\pi\tau\eta\iota$ o $\alpha\nu\tau\rho\omega\pi o\varsigma$ $\tau\eta\varsigma$ $\alpha\nu o\mu\iota\alpha\sigma$ o $\upsilon\iota o\varsigma$ $\tau\eta\varsigma$ $\alpha\pi\omega\lambda\epsilon\iota\alpha\varsigma$ — *kai apokaluphthēi ho anthrōpos tēs anomias, ho huios tēs apōleias*). First aorist passive subjunctive after $\epsilon\alpha\nu$ $\mu\eta$ — *ean mē* and same condition as with $\epsilon\lambda\tau\eta\iota$ — *elthēi* The use of this verb $\alpha\pi o\kappa\alpha\lambda\upsilon\pi\tau\omega$ — *apokaluptō* like $\alpha\pi o\kappa\alpha\lambda\upsilon\pi\sigma\iota\nu$ — *apokalupsin* of the Second Coming in 2 Thessalonians 1:7, seems to note the superhuman character (Milligan) of the event and the same verb is repeated in 2 Thessalonians 2:6, 2 Thessalonians 2:8.

The implication is that **the man of sin** is hidden somewhere who will be suddenly manifested just as false apostles pose as angels of light (2 Corinthians 11:13.), whether the crowning event of the apostasy or another name for the same event. Lightfoot notes the parallel between the man of sin, of whom sin is the special characteristic (genitive case, a Hebraism for the lawless one in 2 Thessalonians 2:8) and Christ.

Both Christ and the adversary of Christ are revealed, there is mystery about each, both make divine claims (2 Thessalonians 2:4). He seems to be the

Antichrist of 1 John 2:18. The terrible phrase, the son of perdition, is applied to Judas in John 17:12 (like Judas doomed to perdition), but here to the lawless one (*o ανομος* — *ho anomos* 2 Thessalonians 2:8), who is not Satan, but some, one definite person who is doing the work of Satan. Note the definite article each time.

⮌ Acknowledgments ⮌

My deepest gratitude and thanks to everyone who has assisted and encouraged me in my work for the cause of Christ. I would especially like to thank the staff at the World Bible Society. You are all so generous and ever-mindful of rightly dividing the Word; not giving into compromise. I would especially like to thank Shelley Thompson, a cherished lady of faith who so thoughtfully reaches out to assist me any way she can The Lord must have a very special place in heaven reserved especially for her. And our Carolyn, another dear dedicated godly woman who gives so much of herself. And of course, Lois "Lolo" Beshore, Dr. Beshore's wonderful wife; a great accomplished woman deeply devoted to the Lord; a lady to emulate and admire.

I also want to thank my beloved son, Chad, who has proven to be a very proficient proofreader and computer whiz—quite advanced for his years. And most of all, all the glory and praise goes to the King of kings and Lord of lords, our precious Savior, Jesus Christ. I can without a doubt attest to God's sovereign grace and blessings, and His patient guidance in my life. We are living in very perilous times as forewarned in Scripture. Each day we are faced with new challenges from those who are enemies of the cross. May the Lord God of Israel have mercy on us and protect us from those who would work to silence our love for, and devotion to our Savior and Messiah, Yeshua Ha Mashiach—our soon coming King.

✑ About the Author ✑

Kit R. Olsen is a Christian author, also specializing in Christian book editing and ghostwriting for international publishers and ministries. She has edited and revised thousands of articles and has written hundreds of articles (FAQs) for Christian ministries. Kit created and maintained a Christian "Dear Abby" type Web-based ministry for five years ("Dear Esther"), providing sound biblical counsel, responding to selected letters submitted by readers. This ministry provided a fresh insightful Christian alternative to secular advice columns, providing wise counsel to those in need of guidance, comfort, encouragement and biblical instruction.

Kit has been involved in evangelism using the written word since 1995. Her magazine—*Southern Nevada Christian Review*—a successful witnessing venture was her first Christian publication. She worked for many years as researcher, writer, editor, and media representative with David and Juneau Chagall when their Hebrew-Christian television ministry was still in production. She is experienced in audiovisual production, media graphics and photography, varied forms of writing including music and accompanying lyrics; copywriting, editing, design and layout of advertising material; media graphics and marketing. Born in Austria, Kit moved to the USA as a young child; English is her third language. She has an accomplished broad classical education which includes studying with legendary acting coaches Stella Adler and Lee Strasberg in New York City during her college years; she is a withdrawn member of the Screen Actors Guild (SAG-AFTRA). Kit has traveled and worked all around the world and has a small evangelical outreach ministry, Friends of Yeshua Ministries. She is also a homeschooling mom.

Prior to working primarily with the Christian community Kit began writing and editing professionally while still a senior in college as an editor for the National Institutes of Health editing medical protocols, and later wrote copy for Meredith Enterprises, then located on Madison Avenue. She also wrote and produced documentary slideshows for the State of New York before moving on to various other media communications work which led to investing in a very successful independent office equipment business in upstate New York before discount computer stores took over the market.

The World Bible Society has published five of Kit's books, including an excellent in-depth commentary on the book of Revelation titled, *Revelation God's Greatest Triumph*, co-authored with the late Dr. F. Kenton Beshore. Also, *King of Kings and Lord of Lords - Heralding His Soon Return*, a heartwarming techno-savvy adventure with an engaging story line which takes place primarily in Jerusalem—highlighting the spiritual battlefield in which we live. Part Two of the book continues to focus on the salvation message and a call to living wholesome godly lifestyles, despite the obvious moral downward spiral with which we are bombarded at every turn; *A Better World Is Coming Soon - Don't Miss It* (First Edition); *A Better World Is Coming Soon - Don't Miss It* (Expanded Edition), an exceptional book on Bible prophecy, an eschatological anthology which also documents her personal testimony.

After much success and a long struggle to find authenticity in a world of deceit, corruption and compromise—Kit ultimately walked away from a blossoming career in the entertainment industry, unable to reconcile the moral depravity that is especially prevalent in the world of Arts and Entertainment—choosing instead to serve Christ (Joshua 24:16; John 12:26).

NOTES

Updated 2017 Presidential Inaugural Introductory Commentary

1. http://www.nationalreview.com/article/439433/iran-ransom-payment-obama-stonewalls-details-17-billion-tehran

Chapter One

1. http://www.hebrew4christians.com/Articles/Israel/israel.htm

Chapter Two

1. http://www.raymondibrahim.com/11325/muslim-apologetic-tawriya
2. Lecture notes compiled from Dr. F. Kenton Beshore; the Upper Room at Mariner's Church.

Chapter Three

1. "The Balfour Declaration" http://en.wikipedia.org/wiki/Balfour_Declaration_of_1917 Levenberg, Haim (1993). *Military Preparations of the Arab Community in Palestine: 1945–1948*. London: Routledge. p.74.
2. Hughes, M. (2009) The banality of brutality: British armed forces and the repression of the Arab Revolt in Palestine, 1936–39, *English Historical Review* Vol. CXXIV No. 507, 314-354.
3. Khalidi, Rashid (2001). The Palestinians and 1948: the underlying causes of failure. In Eugene Rogan and Avi Shlaim (eds.). *The War for Palestine*. Cambridge: Cambridge University Press, pp. 21, 35.
4. Morris, Benny (1999). *Righteous Victims: A History of the Zionist- Arab Conflict, 1881–1999*. John Murray. p. 160.
5. Morris, Benny (2008), *1948: The First Arab-Israeli War*, Yale University Press, New Haven, pp. 66-69.

6. Issa Khalaf, *Politics in Palestine: Arab Factionalism and Social Disintegration, 1939-1948,* SUNY Press, 1991 p.153.
7. Henry Laurens. *La Question de Palestine.* Vol.2, Fayard, 2007 p. 67.
8. Dominique Lapierre et Larry Collins (1971), pp. 131–153.
9. Dominique Lapierre et Larry Collins (1971), p. 163.
10. Gelber, Yoav (2006). *Palestine 1948. War, Escape and the Emergence of the Palestinian Refugee Problem.* Sussex Academic Press. p. 85.
11. Dominique Lapierre and Larry Collins (1971), pp. 369–3
12. Baylis Thomas, *How Israel was Won: A Concise History of the Arab-Israeli Conflict,* Lexington Books 1999 p. 65.
13. John B. Quigley. *Palestine and Israel: A Challenge to Justice,* Duke University Press, 1990, p. 59.
14. Morris, Benny (2004), *The Birth of the Palestinian Refugee Problem Revisited,* Cambridge University Press, Cambridge UK. pp. 242–243.
15. Morris, Benny (2004), *The Birth of the Palestinian Refugee Problem Revisited,* Cambridge University Press, Cambridge UK. p. 242.
16. Baylis Thomas, *How Israel was Won: A Concise History of the Arab-Israeli Conflict,* Lexington Books 1999 p. 69.
17. Morris, Benny (2008). *1948: A History of the First Arab-Israeli War.* Yale University Press. p. 185.
18. Henry Laurens (2005), pp. 85–86.
19. Morris, Benny (2004), *The Birth of the Palestinian Refugee Problem Revisited,* Cambridge University Press, Cambridge UK. pp. 248–252.
20. Morris, Benny (2004), *The Birth of the Palestinian Refugees Problem Revisited,* Cambridge University Press, Cambridge UK. pp. 252–254.
21. Joseph Heller, *The Birth of Israel, 1945-1949: Ben-Gurion and His Critics,* University Press of Florida, 2001, pp. 275-276.

Pages 40-54
1. Schiff, Zeev & Haber, Eitan, editors, *Israel, Army and defense - A dictionary,* Zmora, Bitan, Modan, 1976, Tel-Aviv Hebrew.

2. Rubin, Barry M. (1994). *Revolution Until Victory?: The Politics and History of the PLO*. Harvard University Press, p. 11.

3. Middle East: Incident at Samu, Time, November 25, 1966.

4. Tessler, Mark (1994). *A History of the Israeli-Palestinian Conflict*. John Wiley & Sons. p. 378. "Towards the War of June 1957: Growing tensions in the region were clearly visible long before Israel's November attack on Samu and two other West Bank towns. An escalating spiral of raid and retaliation had already been set in motion..."

5. Shemesh, Moshe (2007). *Arab Politics, Palestinian Nationalism and the Six-Day War: The Crystallization of Arab Strategy and Nasir's Descent to War, 1957-1967*. Sussex Academic Press, p. 118.

6. Maoz, Zeev (2009). *Defending the Holy Land: A Critical Analysis of Israel's Security and Foreign Policy*. The University of Michigan Press. 2009. p. 242.

7. Maoz, Zeev (2009). *Defending the Holy Land: A Critical Analysis of Israel's Security and Foreign Policy*. The University of Michigan Press. p. 84.

8. *The Encyclopedia of the Arab-Israeli Conflict: A Political, Social, and ... - Google ספרים*. Books.google.co.il.

9. Bar-On, Mordechai (2004). *A Never-Ending Conflict: A Guide To Israeli Military History*. Greenwood Publishing Group. p. 181.

10. Shlaim, Avi (2012). *The 1967 Arab-Israeli War: Origins and Consequences*. Cambridge University Press. p. 106. "Nasser responded by taking three successive steps that made war virtually inevitable: he deployed his troops in Sinai near Israel's border on 14 May; expelled the UNEF from the Gaza Strip and Sinai on 19 May; and closed the Straits of Tiran to Israeli shipping on 22 May."

11. Churchill & Churchill, *The Six-Day War*, Houghton Mifflin Company (1967) p. 21.

12. Pollack, Kenneth, *Arabs at war: military effectiveness 1948– 1991*, University of Nebraska Press (2002), p. 290.

13. Segev, 2007, pp. 149–52. *The Arab-Israeli Dilemma*, By Fred John Khouri, p. 234.

14. Segev, 2007, p. 151.

15. UNSC Resolution 228 of 1966.

16. Oren, 2002/2003, p. 312.

17. *Lightning Out of Israel*, Associated Press, p. 50.

18. Oren, p. 129.

19. Douglas J. Murray; Paul R. Viotti (1994). *The Defense Policies of Nations: A Comparative Study.* JHU Press. p. 500.

20. Moshe Shemesh, *Arab Politics, Palestinian Nationalism and the Six-Day War,* Sussex Academic Press 2008, p.172.

21. Moshe Shemesh (2008). *Arab Politics, Palestinian Nationalism and the Six-Day War: The Crystallization of Arab Strategy and Nasir's Descent to War, 1957-1967.* Sussex Academic Press. p. 161.

22. Moshe Shemesh, *Arab Politics, Palestinian Nationalism and the Six-Day War,* Sussex Academic Press, 2008, p. 172.

23. Yearbook of the United Nations 1967 (excerpts), December 31, 1967.

24. Fred Khouri, *The Arab Israeli Dilemma*, pp. 242-43.

25. Parker, Richard B. *The Politics of Miscalculation in the Middle East*, pp. 18-19.

26. Sachar, 2007, pp. 504, 507-508.

27. *First United Nations Emergency Force (Unef I) — Background.* UN.

28. Martin Van Creveld (6 August 2008). "Sword and the Olive: A Critical History of the *Israeli Defense Force.*" Public Affairs. p.153.

29. Chaim Herzog, *The Arab-Israeli Wars*, Random House (1982) p.148.

30. John Pimlott, *The Middle East Conflicts*, Crescent (1983) p. 53.

31. Randolph Churchill, Winston Churchill, *The Six-Day War*, Houghton Mifflin Company (1967) p. 28.

32. Zeev Schiff, *A History of the Israeli Army*, Straight Arrow Books (1974) p. 145.

33. Leslie Stein, *The Making of Modern Israel 1948-1967, Polity*, p. 265.

34. Parker, Richard Bordeaux. *The Six-Day War: A Retrospective*. P. 71 (University Press of Florida, 1996), and *Six Days of War*, by Michael Oren, p. 52.

35. Ami Gluska. *The Israeli Military and the Origins of the 1967 War: Government, Armed Forces and Defence Policy 196367*. Routledge. January 9, 2007. p. 118.

36. Oren, pp. 64-65.

37. Omer-Man, Michael (27 May 2011). "This Week in History: Casus Belli in the Red Sea," *JPost*.

38. Oren, p. 65.

39. Tessler, Mark A. *A History of the Israeli-Palestinian Conflict*, p. 386.

40. Stein, pp. 266-267.

41. Quigley, John. *The Case for Palestine*, (p. 158) (1990).

42. Shemesh, Moshe. *Arab Politics, Palestinian Nationalism and the Six-Day War*, p. 180.

43. Brecher, Michael. *Decisions in Crisis: Israel, 1967 and 1973*.

44. Parker, Richard B. *The Politics of Miscalculation in the Middle East*, p. 16.

45. Oren, Six days of War, p. 65.

46. Shlaim (2007) p. 238.

47. Mutawi (2007) p. 93.

48. Stanley Sandler, *Ground Warfare: An International Encyclopedia*, Volume 1, ABC-CLIO (2002), p. 418.

49. Shemesh, Moshe. *Arab Politics, Palestinian Nationalism and the Six-Day War,* p. 182, 187.

50. Robin Rolf Churchill, Alan Vaughan Lowe, *The Law of The Sea*, St. Martins Press (1988) p. 89.

51. Tessler, Mark A. (1994). *A History of the Israeli-Palestinian Conflict*. Indiana University Press. p. 334.

52. "Legal Status of the Gulf of Aqaba and the Strait of Tiran: From Customary International Law to the 1979 Egyptian-Israeli Peace Treaty" (*Boston College International and Comparative Law Review*, by Ann Ellen Danseyar, 12-1-1982 (Volume 5, Issue 1, Article 5) p. 127.

53. "Legal Status of the Gulf of Aqaba and the Strait of Tiran: From Customary International Law to the 1979 Egyptian-Israeli Peace Treaty" (Boston College *International and Comparative Law Review*, by Ann Ellen Danseyar, 12-1-1982 (Volume 5, Issue 1, Article 5) p. 132.

54. Cohen, Raymond (1988), p. 12.

55. *Statement to the General Assembly by Foreign Minister Meir, 1 March 1957.* Israel Ministry of Foreign Affairs – The State of Israel. "Interference, by armed force, with ships of Israeli flag exercising free and innocent passage in the Gulf of Aqaba and through the Straits of Tiran will be regarded by Israel as an attack entitling it to exercise its inherent right of self-defence under Article 51 of the Charter and to take all such measures as are necessary to ensure the free and innocent passage of its ships in the Gulf and in the Straits."

56. Churchill, p. 38.

57. Thomas, Baylis. *How Israel Was Won: A Concise History of the Arab-Israeli Conflict,* pp. 161-162.

58. Parker, Richard B. *The Politics of Miscalculation in the Middle East*, p. 49.

59. "1967: a war of miscalculation and misjudgment (Le Monde Diplomatique, (English edition)." Mondediplo.com. 2007-06-05.

60. "On This Day 5 June." BBC. June 5, 1967.

61. Churchill, pp. 52, 77.

62. Bailey 1990, p. 225.

63. Oren, p. 198.

64. Oren, p. 196.

65. Quigley, John B. *The Case for Palestine: An International Law Perspective*, p. 163.

66. Robarge, 2007.

67. BBC Panorama.

68. John Pimlott, *The Middle East Conflicts 1945 to Present*, Crescent Books, (New York, 1983), p. 53.

69. Oren, Michael (6/6/2011). "Remembering Six Days in 1967." *Foreign Policy.* "Michael Oren is Israel's ambassador to the United States and author of Six Days of War: June 1967 and the Making of the Modern Middle East."
70. Q&A with Michael Oren, JPost.com, 5 June 2007.
71. "The United States has often walked a fine line between preemption and prevention. In fact there have only been a handful of clear-cut cases of military preemption by any states in the last 200 years (Israeli preemption in the Six-Day War of 1967 is perhaps the most cited example)." U.S. National Security Strategy: a New Era U.S. Department of State (2002).
72. "Classic examples of preemptive wars include the July Crisis of 1914 and the Six-Day War of 1967 in which Israel preemptively attacked Egypt..." Mueller Karl P. (2007). Striking first: preemptive and preventive attack in U.S. national security. (PDF). Rand Corporation.
73. Distein, Yoram, *War, aggression and self-defense,* p.192, Cambridge University Press (2005).
74. NPR, The Mideast: A Century of Conflict.

Chapter Four
1. "Jerusalem1967: Reunification of Jerusalem." *CAMERA committee for Accuracy in Middle East Reporting in America.*
2. http://.sixdaywar.org/content?ReunificationJerusalem.asp.
3. http://en.wikipedia.org/wiki/Six-Day_War.
4. http://www.jewishvirtuallibrary.org/jsource/myths3/MF1967.html.

Chapter Five
1. http://www.biblestudy.org/biblepic/the-garden-tomb-of-jesus.html.
2. http://en.wikipedia.org/wiki/Jerusalem_in_Christianity, *Encyclopedia Judaica.* "The Greatest Lie Ever Told about Jerusalem," Emanuel A. Winston.

3. http://www.eretzyisroel.org/~jkatz/templemount.html.

4. http://www.israeltoday.co.il/NewsItem/tabid/178/nid/24445/Default. aspx?hp.

Chapter Six

1. https://en.wikipedia.org/wiki/Eisegesis

Chapter Seven

1. Finis Jennings Dake, "Summary of Obadiah," The Dake Annotated Reference Bible (Lawrenceville, GA: Dake Bible Sales, 1963, p. 899).

Chapter Nine

1. https://news.yahoo.com/israel-pm-admits-forces-operating-war-hit-syria-Yahoo News.

2. http://nationalinterest.org/blog/the-buzz/russias-big-guns-reach-syrias-front-lines-14513

3. http://www.pre-trib.org/data/pdf/Ice-ConsistentBiblicalFu24.pdf.

4. http://www.pre-trib.org/articles.

5. http://www.studylight.org/con/ntb/view.cgi?n=3937.

6. Churchyard, Gordon, "Enemies All Round Us," *Easy English Bible,* http://www.easyenglish.info/.

7. "Charles H. Spurgeon's Bible Sermons," *Classic Bible Commentaries.*

8. McGee, J. Vernon, *Thru the Bible: Joshua through Psalms*, p.806.

9. Ice, Thomas, http://www.pre-trib.org/data/pdf/Ice-ConsistentBiblical Fu24.pdfhttp://www.pre-trib.org/articles.

10. *The Criswell Study Bible*. Nashville, Tennessee. Thomas Nelson Publishers. 1979. p. 686).

11. Dr. David Jeremiah, The *Jeremiah Study Bible*, Dr. David Jeremiah, Worthy Publishing 2013, p. 761).

12. Heslop G., William, Sermon Seeds on the Psalms, the Higley Press, Indiana, 1956.

13. http://www.studylight.org/con/ntb/view.cgi?n=3937. 12. *Wikipedia the Free Encyclopedia*, http://en.wikipedia.org/wiki/Materiel.
14. http://www.gatestoneinstitute.org/4660/gaza-war-over.
15. http://ukrainianweek.com/History/51842.
16. http://www.ezekielsfire.com/chapter-two/ezekiel-38-and-39-tetrad-three-and-four/.
17. Bible Tools, Obadiah 1:11-15, Richard T. Ritenbaugh.

Chapter Ten
1. Fruchtenbaum, Arnold, *Footsteps of the Messiah*, page 121, ("The Pre-Tribulation View").
2. http://www.omegashock.com/2014/01/23/at-war-with-gog-and-magog/.
3. http://www.cnn.com/2014/07/09/world/meast/israel-palestinians-iron-dome/index.html

Chapter Eleven
1. http://www.israelnationalnews.com/News/News.aspx/191966#. VPOYLZs5Dwqunnamed Israeli minister with good ties with the US administration "revealed the attack plan to John Kerry."
2. http://legalinsurrection.com/2013/11/john-kerry-pretty-much-threatens-israel-to-concede-key-issues-to-palestinians/. http://www.thestar.com/news/world/2014/06/22/teen_killed_during_targeted_attack_on_vehicle_in_golan_heights_area_by_syrian_forces.html.
3. http://palwatch.org/main.aspx?fi=157&doc_id=896.
4. http://www.gatestoneinstitute.org/5862/united-church-of-christ, "United Church of Christ and The "Big Lie" Susan Warner.
5. http://thefederalist.com/2015/05/14/the-popes-misguided-recognition-of-a-palestinian-state- wont-help-anyone/, David Harsanyi.
6. http://beholdisrael.com/app/index.php/c_main/entry/98.
7. http://beholdisraelblog.wordpress.
8. http://www.defeatobama.us/israel.shtm.1.

9. http://www.wnd.com/2012/02/ayatollah-kill-all-jews-annihilate-israel/. *Breaking Israel News,* http://www.breakingisraelnews.com/46278/israels-trouble-with-iran-intensifies-before-the-coming-of-messiah-jewish-world/#zCAOcjPzvtE5BtXw.97.

10. http://english.farsnews.com/newstext.php?nn=9102112759.

11. http://www.wildolive.co.uk/christians_against_israel.htm. https://www.kickstarter.com/.

12. http://www.haaretz.com/jewish-world/jewish-world- news/1.575067.

13. http://www.breakingisraelnews.com/44426/heeding-his-call-united-church-christ-divests-israel-biblical-zionism/?utm_source=Breaking+Israel+News&utm_campaign=fcc8511438

14. http://www.jewishjournal.com/rabbijohnrosovesblog/item/the_presby-terian_church_usa_is_at_it_again_in_its_unfair_criticism_of_israel.

15. http://www.icjs.org/featured-articles/open-letter-presbyterian-church-0.

16. http://www.israelnationalnews.com/Articles/Article.aspx/11922#. V2x6DU36t9C Op-Ed: The Global Counterterrorism Forum: No Room for Israel

17. The Jewish Telegraphic Agency's report in *Ha-aretz,* February 20, 2014.

18. http://palwatch.org/main.aspx?fi=157&doc_id=896.

19. *CBN News Inside Israel*, June 23, 2014.

20. "Gaza in Arizona: The secret militarization of the U.S.-Mexico border," Todd Miller and Gabriel M. Schivone, www.tomdispatch.com.

Chapter Twelve

1. *The Coming Financial Crisis*, John Truman Wolfe, Lisa Hagen Books

2. "Chris Putnam Discusses Bible Prophecy." https://www.youtube.com/watch?v=7RMaINohzz4.

3. Robertson, A.T. Commentary on 2 Thessalonians 2:1. "*Robertson's Word Pictures of the New Testament.*" http://www.studylight.org/commentar-ies/rwp/view.cgi?bk=52&ch=2. Broadman Press 1932, 33. Renewal 1960.

Chapter Thirteen

1. Olsen., Kit R., *A Better World Is Coming Soon - Don't Miss It* - Updated Expanded 2013 Edition, select pages, World Bible Society.
2. *World Net Daily -WND,* http://www.wnd.com/2013/03/white-house-map-of-israel-erases-jerusalem-biblical-territories/.
3. http://en.wikipedia.org/wiki/Tactical_nuclear_weapon 3.Fruchtenbaum, Arnold, *Footprints of the Messiah*, pages 121- 122).
4. http://brianmclaren.net/archives/2014/07/.

Chapter Fourteen

1. Olsen, Kit R., *A Better World Is Coming Soon - Don't Miss It*, Updated Expanded Edition. select pages, World Bible Society, 2013.
2. http://www.cais-soas.com/CAIS/Languages/aryan/inscription_of_dari-ush_grt_rstm.htm.

Chapter Fifteen

1. Olsen, Kit R., *A Better World Is Coming Soon - Don't Miss It*, Updated Expanded Edition, select pages, World Bible Society, 2013.
2. Evangelical Outreach; http://www.evangelicaloutreach.org/kjvo.htm.
3. Langone, Micheal, PhD., "Definitional Ambiguity," Langone, Michael, Ph. D.; "On Using the Term "Cult.""

Chapter Sixteen

1. http://www.biblicalresearch.info/.

In Conclusion

1. *The Washington Post,* http://www.washingtonpost.com/blogs/style-blog/wp/2015/01/15/boy-who-came-back-from-heaven-going-back-to-publisher/.

Appendix A

1. *The Rapture, the Apocalypse, Armageddon, the Millennium*, Dr. F. Kenton Beshore, pp.40-41, World Bible Society, 2012.

Appendix B

1. *Robertson's Word Pictures in the New Testament*, Thessalonians 2:1-3. Robertson, A.T. Commentary on 2 Thessalonians 2:1-3, pages 519-520, Holman Bible Publishers, 2000. http://www.studylight.org/commentaries/rwp/view.cgi?bk=52&ch=2. Broadman Press 1932, 33. Renewal 1960.

KING OF KINGS
AND LORD OF LORDS
Heralding His Soon Return

KIT R. OLSEN

Publisher's Note

Sample Book Reviews of Our Author's Previously Published Book

We were very successful with Kit's previously published book, *King of Kings and Lord of Lords - Heralding His Soon Return*. If you have not read it, we urge you to do so. You will be delightfully entertained by our author's versatile skillful delivery and you will want to share the book with others. Kit not only appeals to the lost millennial youth with a unique up-to-date *techno-savvy* approach, she writes in a manner so charming that her subject matter resonates with people of all ages. The story line is portrayed through the lives of endearing characters living in Jerusalem. She meticulously interweaves fantasy with biblical truth emphasizing the soon coming Pre-Tribulation Rapture, Christ's Second Coming, the salvation message and important godly precepts—very much needed in today's youth culture. This intriguing adventure is an educational fun-to-read book; one that also appeals to non-Christians when used as a witnessing tool, especially with the millennial generation.

5 out of 5 stars **Far Beyond *Left Behind,* in one book ...**
By Mike Don August 29, 2014
Far beyond *Left Behind,* in one book...it deals with the truth of the spiritual battles occurring today, through a relatable story. It's later chapters are filled with a glossary and applications of each of the terms identified.

5 out of 5 stars **By Vera M Payne on August 13, 2014**
King of Kings and Lord of Lords is a real page turner and an eye opener.
The author masterfully weaves the truth of the battle between mortal flesh and spiritual wickedness in a very special story that younger generations will understand and enjoy. The reader will rightfully find that the strength needed to defeat the enemies of Christ can only come from faith in Christ Himself.

> "For we wrestle not against flesh and blood, but against principalities, against powers, against the rulers of the darkness of this world, against spiritual wickedness in high places" (Ephesians 6:12).

The book wraps up with an excellent presentation of God's blueprint, especially for young adults, effortlessly explaining how they can become born-again and grow in their faith and walk with the Lord. The reader will be left with an authoritative explanation of the return of Christ and His future plans for His people, all in the light of last days Bible prophecy.

I highly recommend this fun and educational book for young and old readers alike, no matter their gender! "So it is up to us now, to be Defenders of the Faith." (pg. 90)

5.0 *out of 5 stars* I really enjoyed this book
By Adrienne Payne on August 8, 2014
I really enjoyed this book, and I would recommend it to anyone who is first learning or teaching Bible prophecy. It is excellent for educating children and teens because of its clear, simple, and tactful delivery of key principles of the Rapture and the end times. Regardless, the story in itself is engaging, and that alone will allow anyone to enjoy it.

I personally admire how the writing has traditional aspects (hints of John Bunyan and C.S. Lewis), yet reads like a modern story with an exciting technical angle that will interest all ages. Every character has something to offer, and I loved Yossi's adorable maturity.

The Scripture references throughout truly tie the book together and carried a lot of wisdom through the story. This is very well written and speaks to everyone, but it especially targets today's young adults. I see this really helping to grow young adults in the faith. It will provide them with valuable truth and a better understanding of Bible prophecy and how it applies to them.

And personal feedback from author, Donald Duck:

Good Morning Kit: 12/13/15 5:57 AM
My next article is attached. I have now read three chapters of *King of Kings and Lord of Lords - Heralding His Soon Return.* It is great. It makes me want to read all day, but I can't. Anyway, I love it. I have some friends that want to read it. Also, I think my wife Rachel would enjoy reading it. Thank you. I probably haven't seen more than half a dozen books for youth, but yours is the best. Yours in Christ, Daymond.

Hello Kit, 12/23/15 at 11:01 AM
I finished your book. You don't know what a compliment that is. I can't remember the last time I read a whole book. Blessings to you, Daymond.

5.0 out of 5 stars You realize how much you've missed good, wholesome writing...
By Patrick Wyett on August 28, 2014
While reading *Kings and Lord of Lords Heralding His Soon Return*, you realize how much you've missed good, wholesome writing. This is a great book both for kids and those of us who haven't been a kid for a while. The first part is an uplifting tale that's a fresh change from the world's usual gray to dark themes. There's an innocence that harkens back to another time, yet set in the here and now with the promise, for Christians, of a forever future beyond comprehension. Need some calm and reassurance in your day? Read this story.

The second part of the book is practical, scriptural guidance on a variety of topics, with the Lord's leading, addressing attitudes and behaviors that many pastors refuse to address from the pulpit. You'll find yourself nodding in agreement, or perhaps, getting a spiritual adjustment that's been sorely needed. Kit misses nothing in her particularly relevant advice for today's sensual and self-centered culture. There is a better way. Read all about it in *King of Kings and Lord of Lords Heralding His Soon Return*.

5.0 out of 5 stars Captivating
By happyhappyday73, Tim Cameron on August 13, 2014
Having just finished reading this book, I know it will capture kids interest and it creates/lays such a good foundation of the big picture of the global conflict being played out BUT having already been won.

I love that this was written for outreach with the youth in mind. Very much a "prepare the way" type of work. As we see this world descending into chaos, its vitally important to offer HOPE and the answer to "What in the world is going on?" And I think this book does just that. In a word this book is "captivating."